T0134519

Human–Computer Interaction Series

Editor-in-Chief

Jean Vanderdonckt
Louvain School of Management, Université catholique de Louvain,
Louvain-La-Neuve, Belgium

The Human–Computer Interaction Series, launched in 2004, publishes books that advance the science and technology of developing systems which are effective and satisfying for people in a wide variety of contexts. Titles focus on theoretical perspectives (such as formal approaches drawn from a variety of behavioural sciences), practical approaches (such as techniques for effectively integrating user needs in system development), and social issues (such as the determinants of utility, usability and acceptability).

HCI is a multidisciplinary field and focuses on the human aspects in the development of computer technology. As technology becomes increasingly more pervasive the need to take a human-centred approach in the design and development of computer-based systems becomes ever more important.

Titles published within the Human–Computer Interaction Series are included in Thomson Reuters' Book Citation Index, The DBLP Computer Science Bibliography and The HCI Bibliography.

More information about this series at http://www.springer.com/series/6033

Torkil Clemmensen

Human Work Interaction Design

A Platform for Theory and Action

 Springer

Torkil Clemmensen 🄳
Department of Digitalization
Copenhagen Business School
Frederiksberg, Denmark

ISSN 1571-5035   ISSN 2524-4477   (electronic)
Human–Computer Interaction Series
ISBN 978-3-030-71798-8   ISBN 978-3-030-71796-4   (eBook)
https://doi.org/10.1007/978-3-030-71796-4

This Springer imprint is published by the registered company Springer Nature Switzerland AG
The registered company address is: Gewerbestrasse 11, 6330 Cham, Switzerland

Foreword

Human Work Interaction Design (HWID) focuses on the integration of work analysis and interaction design methods for pervasive and smart workplaces. HWID was founded in 2005–2006, as the Working Group #6, part of the International Federation for Information Processing (UNESCO), specifically of its Technical Committee 13 on Human-Computer Interaction (HCI). HWID had its first conference edition in February 2006, in my hometown (Funchal, Portugal). One year before that, I had the pleasure and fortune of meeting Professors Annelise Mark Pejtersen, Torkil Clemmensen, and Rikke Ørngreen during the INTERACT workshop that gave birth to this research field. I then involved myself further as the working group's secretary officer, from 2011 until 2014, and afterward became the groups' chair, from 2014 until 2017. I still support the group as vice-chair up to the present day. Back then, the essential idea was to adapt the well-known framework of Cognitive Work Analysis into a more practical, modern format, an objective that was quite clearly attained if one judges the number of case studies, projects, papers, students, and scholars who were influenced—in one way or another—by this working group's ideas.

The many different revolutions brought about by computer systems, interfaces, and interactive techniques, have meant that HWID is a rapidly evolving discipline, like most HCI areas. Since 2005, HWID has evolved throughout the years, both as a theoretical discipline and as a practical design approach, strongly rooted in the psychology-grounded thoughts of Torkil Clemmensen. Torkil's influence on my HCI practice and theory is subtle, yet extremely valuable. Therefore, it is with great enthusiasm that I write this Foreword, in the expectation that the book will influence the reader in the same way that it has influenced me, profoundly.

Some of the original goals of this research field included the following:

- To encourage empirical studies and conceptualizations of the interaction among humans, their variegated social contexts, and the technology they use both within and across these contexts.
- To promote the use of knowledge, concepts, methods, and techniques that enable user studies to procure a better apprehension of the complex interplay between

individual, social, and organizational contexts and thereby a better understanding of how and why people work in the ways they do.

- To promote a better understanding of the relationship between work domain-based empirical studies and iterative design of prototypes and new technologies.

This new book goes well beyond covering these important topics. One of the interesting aspects I noted is that this book presents HWID as a new platform designing sociomaterial solutions that are valued by local needs and practices.

In the future, very much as in humankind's recent past, interactive technologies and systems will continue to be central to almost every human activity. Novel ways of designing and evaluating them from a socio-technical perspective will never be enough. Further research will have to be conducted to ensure that society and societal-positive impact will always be the top priority of any interactive system or technology. Fortunately, this book provides us with comprehensive coverage of how HWID can be used for both 'theory and action', starting with its roots in cognitive work analysis, all the way until the most recent and exciting HWID applications to the so-called 'smart workplace'. The focus on effectively combining theory with practice is particularly appealing to me. The book excels in presenting the reader with a usable platform, a common vocabulary for large design and development teams, practical ways to overcome 'wicked problems' (Chap. 3), and many more. But it is equally enlightening in the way it handles and explains the more theoretical aspects of HWID. In the era of design thinking as a popular management approach, we now have HWID, which "deems meeting business goals as the top priority but acknowledges that employees and other stakeholders might have other needs that require fulfilment".

Perhaps more importantly, this new book provides a solid shape to an area that was in good need of a solid reference. This reference will most surely appeal to a wide range of readers, from beginner-level students who need practical solutions and case studies to improve their solutions, all the way to theoretical scholars searching for socio-technical approaches that can be effectively adopted by design teams. I believe that readers will find good inspiration from the chapters of this book and that it will become a capstone reference in HCI and its related fields.

Funchal, Madeira Island, Portugal   Pedro F. Campos
June 2021

About IFIP TC Working Group 13.6

This section is from the HWID website:

- https://barbara-barricelli.unibs.it/HWID/mission.html.

See also the IFIP TC13 Human-Computer Interaction Technical Committee:

- http://ifip-tc13.org/working-groups/working-group-13-6/.

Mission

The Working Group 6 on Human Work Interaction Design (HWID) is part of the International Federation for Information Processing (IFIP) and specifically of its Technical Committee 13 on Human-Computer Interaction (HCI). It focuses on the integration of work analysis and interaction design methods for pervasive and smart workplaces. The group was founded by Annelise Mark Pejtersen, Torkil Clemmensen and Rikke Ørngreen in 2005. HWID has its roots and inspiration from the 70's Cognitive Work Analysis (CWA) methods. Today, HWID is a lightweight version of CWA, addressing the concept of Work in HCI. The mission of the group is to empower users by designing smarter workplaces, in many different work domains. In 2021, the group counted more than 60 members.

Aims

The aims of the HWID working group are:

- To encourage empirical studies and conceptualizations of the interaction among humans, their variegated social contexts and the technology they use both within and across these contexts.

- Promote the use of knowledge, concepts, methods, and techniques that enable user studies to procure a better apprehension of the complex interplay between individual, social, and organizational contexts and thereby a better understanding of how and why people work in the ways they do.
- Promote a better understanding of the relationship between work domain-based empirical studies and iterative design of prototypes and new technologies.
- Establish a network of researchers, practitioners, and domain/subject matter experts working within this field.

Scope

The group provides the basis for an improved cross-disciplinary cooperation and mutual inspiration among researchers, but also leads to a number of new research initiatives and developments, as well as to an increased awareness of HWID in existing HCI educations. Complexity is a key notion in the working group, it is not a priori defined or limited to any particular domains. A main target of the work group is the analysis of and the design for the variety of complex work and life contexts found in different businesses. It studies how technology is changing human life and work contexts in numerous, multifaceted ways:

- Interfaces between collaborating individuals; advanced communication networks.
- Small and large-scale distributed systems.
- Multimedia and embedded technologies.
- Mobile technologies and advanced 'intelligent' robots.
- Communication, collaboration, and problem solving.
- Large information spaces, variability, discretion, learning, and information seeking.
- Methods, theories, tools, techniques, and prototype design on an experimental basis.

Preface

This book exists because Human Work Interaction Design (HWID) offers solutions to the integration of work analysis and interaction design methods. It fosters new strategies aimed at designing systems that may psychologically improve the way people work. This book presents a novel human work interaction design platform for designing sociomaterial solutions that are valorized by local needs and practices. The character of these solutions cannot be determined in detail from the outset, but they are thought as tools for job crafting, organizing, and community building. The human work interaction design approach entails that the solutions we pursue are anchored in existing technical solutions and social arrangements (e.g., excel sheets, meeting calendars) and that they are objectified, that is, made fact-like, by developing socio-technical relation artefacts. These include problem definitions, need identifications, personas, workplace interaction patterns, collaborative sketches, converged workflows, and more. This results in solutions that are felt as matters-of-the-fact and natural parts of stakeholders' everyday life, and thus deeply embedded and implemented in their workday. Moreover, and importantly, HWID is applied as a social-relativistic type of participatory design, which involves a variety of innovative evaluation methods. For example, 'innovation contests' can be used to decide between the expected multitude of ideas for solutions, and 'design-in-use' will be applied to test out tools in everyday life conditions involving project partners and other relevant stakeholders.

I am uniquely qualified to write about HWID because I am a human factors psychologist turned business school IS and HCI professor, and therefore have a keen interest in and some knowledge about crossing the borders between computer technology, human psychology, organization, and design. I was also the first chair of IFIP TC 13.6 HWID working group from 2006–2012, and since then a vice-chair of the group. Before cofounding HWID in 2005, I collaborated with Risø national laboratory's system group that included Annelise Mark Pejtersen, who was a HWID cofounder. From Risø's cognitive work analysis I learned among other things the value of supporting discussions among stakeholders in design by casting psychological insights in an engineering language, and by using multiple different social science and engineering approaches within one framework. However, I also learned that such socio-technical design frameworks need to be as simple and easy to understand and remember, because their value lies in the discussions and learning, not in the receipe. So, if HWID is a continuation of cognitive work analysis from Risø, then I should be one of those who can offer ideas about that. I believe that the HWID in this book is simple and easy to understand (though the writing and line or argument may be poor and filled with errors, apologies for that).

What I hope the reader will get out of reading it is to understand, appreciate, and practice that the core of socio-technical HCI design is so to speak in the hyphen between the social and the technical. While it is important to study and practice organizational and work design and equally important to study and practice interaction design, the most important and core applicable knowledge lies in the gap, the hyphen, in this focal point of genuinely thinking about the social and the technical at the same time. While this notion of the socio-technical eventually may be replaced by notions of sociomateriality or ecosystems, currently it is having a revival because social science and humanities are fighting a survival struggle against data science in the multidisciplinary IT research and practice communities. After reading this book, the reader should be willing and able to fight for and to spread the message that the social science and humanities perspectives are integral to technology development, even in cases when the technology is on its lowest technology readiness levels.

Frederiksberg, Denmark   Torkil Clemmensen

Acknowledgments

Thanks to the chairs and vicechairs and founders of IFIP TC13 WG 13.6 HWID, who are all long-term discussion partners and contributors to the ideas in this book. This list includes Pedro Filipe P. Campos, Frederica Conçalves, Jose Abdelnour-Nocera, Arminda G. Lopes, Dinesh Katre, Rikke Ørngreen, Annelise Mark Pejtersen, Janni Nielsen, Xiangang Qin, Ganesh Bhutkar, and Judith Molka-Danielsen.

Thanks to my colleagues in IFIP TC 13 for a steady support to HWID over the years.

Further acknowledgement of the contribution by the organizers of the HWID working conferences and workshops and the keynote speakers and participants. They should also be on the list of main contributors. This list includes Lene Nielsen, Morten Hertzum, Virpi Roto, Philippe Phalangue, Pradeep Yammiyavar, Åsa Cajander, Marta Kristín Lárusdóttir, Paolo Amaldi, Xianghong Sun, Masaaki Kurosu, Verena Fuchsberger, Weina Qu, and many more. Actually, academic research is fun, and you meet a lot of nice people.

Thanks to my co-teacher Mads Bødker and to my master level students who had to endure me using HWID as an organizing framework in the instantiations of the course on 'UX in Organizations' and before that 'Social Informatics'. Their ideas and applications of HWID on real-life cases were serious tests of the approach and provided input to its further development.

This book was supported by grant no 8142-00005A to the 2019 project "A Human Work Interaction Design theorizing platform" from the Danish government's independent research foundation (DFF).

Contents

Chapter 1
A Platform for Theorizing about Socio-Technical HCI Design

Abstract Human Work Interaction Design (HWID) is a socio-technical HCI design approach. This introductory chapter presents HWID as a platform with five parts: context, human work, interaction design, relations between human work and inter-action design, and theory and methodology. The platform is to be used for building locally valorized theory and action in the form of IT artefacts. The contexts for a HWID project can, for example, be a small- and medium-sized manufacturing company that suffers from problems with productivity and worker satisfaction related to the use of algorithms. Current knowledge about socio-technical HCI design approaches offers solutions to such design cases. This book focus on what HWID can offer to socio-technical HCI design researchers, practitioners, and policymakers.

Keywords Human work interaction design · Socio-technical · HCI design

Sharing with CSCW theoretical roots in cognitive engineering (Rasmussen et al., 1994) and ecological design (Rasmussen & Vicente, 1990) research at the Risø National laboratory in Denmark, an alternative approach to socio-technical HCI design called Human Work Interaction Design (HWID) emerged around 2005 (Clemmensen et al., 2005). It has since grown steadily, and now is the time for sharing this approach with a wider audience. In this book, the HWID approach will be used to discuss socio-technical HCI design theory, cases, methods, and reflections about impact. The main benefits of the HWID approach include that it meets the requirement of taking both the social and the technical into account, while focusing strongly on the relations between the social and the technical, and that it, in its most recent instances rather than being a defined theory, is merely an open multi-sided platform for its' users' theorizing efforts. Furthermore, HWID as a theorizing platform is sitting in a social-relativistic paradigm, and as such it can contribute both to the design of systems supporting work satisfaction, and to increasing the company's capacity (Hirschheim & Klein, 1989). Below we outline the HWID platform, Fig. 1.1. Note that we use the notion of 'worker' to cover 'employees' and 'users' though sometimes we also use other labels for the human in HWID if there is a need to be specific in the discussion at that point.

T. Clemmensen, *Human Work Interaction Design*,
Human–Computer Interaction Series,
https://doi.org/10.1007/978-3-030-71796-4_1

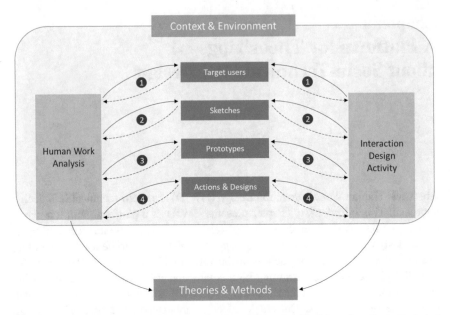

Fig. 1.1 A generic Human Work Interaction Design platform for theorizing about Socio-Technical HCI. (Italian version, drawing by courtesy of the chair of IFIP TC 13.6 WG, Barbara Rita Barricelli, (2019))

- The context bar indicates that all studies take place in national, political, cultural, technological, and other contexts, which are parts of both content and methods for work analysis and interaction design.
- The social is any organizational and work analysis of relevance for the worker's experience of and actions toward task, procedures, workspace/place, and work domains. This includes society level analysis.
- The technical focusses on interaction designs activities such as persona and scenario writing, sketching, prototyping, think aloud usability evaluation, and more. Also interaction in a wider sense such a collaboration with technology can be in focus.
- The relations between the social and the technical, that is, 'facilitating between users and designers', are the main questions that guide the theory building and valorization of the generic HWID platform for a specific project. This is supported by designing 'relation artefacts', which are IT artefacts that relate the social and the technical. These include for example target user representations, sketches and prototypes of solutions, and organizational action and interaction design interventions.
- Any local HWID theory should be confronted with existing general theory and methods from for example HCI, CSCW, IS, and Design communities. In addition, work domain-specific theory, for example, theory about an industrial process, in a project should be held up against established knowledge.

Any specific HWID project produces a *holistic design gestalt that includes several relation-theories* and related data. It is these 'design gestalts' that can be shared, annotated, compared, and contrasted to create more general socio-technical HCI insights and knowledge.

1.1   On the Use of the HWID Platform

Socio-technical HCI theory is not simply there to be *used,* but rather adapted and further developed in each new project for specific purposes (Clemmensen et al., 2016). A tentative taxonomy for theorizing may suggest five different ways of theorizing with five different researcher *personas:* (1) *Meta-theoreticians* consider *theory itself as an object of analysis.* They identify unique features and principles, as well as problematic aspects, of the theory and compares it to other similar theories in HCI, (2) *Theory-tool-makers* use the *theory as a theoretical influence in the development of a new analytical tool, and* identify needs and requirements for new theoretical tools and employ the *theory*, sometimes in combination with other theories, to inform and guide the development of such tools, (3) *Construct-developers* employ *theory as a tool for conceptual analysis and development.* They apply the theory to address central issues and challenges in HCI, often in response to the emergence of new technologies. By doing so they also develop new sub-concepts of existing concepts, or expand the application scope of existing concepts, (4) *Data interpreters* used the *theory as a tool for empirical analysis.* They use key theoretical constructs of the theory to identify and categorize specific empirical phenomena, (5) *Design-oriented researchers* use *theory as a framework for design.* The theory guides the iterative design process and helps developing claims about the nature of the design process. These researchers provide new design illustrations, claims, and guidelines (Clemmensen et al., 2016). Thus, instead of inviting to theory use as passive consumption of a theory 'product', the HWID platform should be used to support possibilities for theory development and support its users in becoming 'theory-makers'.

The HWID platform presented in this book is not a precise predictive theory, model, or framework, but rather, metaphorically speaking, a multi-sided platform. This is a metaphor from economy: multi-sided platforms get two or more sides on board and enable interactions between them (e.g., Airbnb, eBay, Uber, and XBox). The HWID platform gets various sides, such as researchers, consultants, policy-makers, companies, workers, employer and employee organizations, on board, and enables co-design and interactions between them. This also means that the HWID platform reminds its project managers to treat 'multi-sidedness' as a given characteristic of any socio-technical HCI design project. It helps recognizing that each project makes choices that determine how close or how far it is from a multi-sided theorizing platform, and that these choices carry significant trade-offs in terms of stakeholder participations.

The openness of the platform implies that there will be various interpretations of what socio-technical HCI theory is (Clemmensen et al., 2016). When developed on a HWID platform, the meaning of theory itself will vary from project to project and from paper to paper; it is not fixed and immutable. In this respect, the HWID platform approach goes against the view that a given theory always has a particular form (Gregor, 2006; Newman, 1994). The diversity of interpretations of a theory in different contexts will be shaped by several factors. These include that several forms of theory may be developed, ranging from theory as a gestalt or framework for understanding context, to specific emphasis on a few suggested concept-relations from the HWID platform such as 'persona development is associated with identifying target user groups'. Second, depending on the purpose of developing theory on the HWID platform different concepts and principles may be used. For example, for empirical analysis, identifying work analysis instances and interaction design activities may be important, while for more design-oriented projects the artefact-relations will be central. Third, HWID platform can also help develop theory in combination with existing other theory for different purposes and in different ways, such as comparing, adapting theory to new work domains or to new technologies, or formulating design guidelines. Fourth, the various HCI communities, AIS HCI, ACM HCI, IFIP HCI, and more, have for cultural and historical reasons each different classic HCI texts that function as authoritative theory texts, introductions to the theory, or source of definitions, frameworks for empirical analysis, or loose guidelines; theory developed on the HWID platform could be linked back to an HCI community's relevant classic HCI texts, and thus grounding in an existing body of knowledge the newly HWID-developed local theory. The platform itself should not be driven by fixed definitions but be flexible and open to new interpretations and change.

The HWID platform is intended to support accessible and easy to understand socio-technical HCI theorizing. A focus of it is to generate and valorize local theory in a local community on a generalizable multi-sided platform. In this sense, HWID-generated knowledge is community-based knowledge. Thus, international theory development happens through use of the platform to generate local theory in countries and regions around the world. The already existing body of knowledge indicates that the platform makes socio-technical theorizing available to a large variety of HCI researchers, consultants, and policymakers, across various communities and geographical regions (Abdelnour-Nocera et al., 2015; Barricelli et al., 2019; Campos et al., 2012; Clemmensen et al., 2006; Katre et al., 2010).

1.2   The Context(s) of HWID

Work design today is more than designing for motivation, and includes also designing for workers' psychological health, their abilities to simultaneously exploit capabilities and explore new possibilities, and in general their development as humans (Parker, 2014). Specifically, work design for digitalized workplaces is about designing user experiences (UX) at work and collaboration with technology such as AI, robots, IoT, and in general automation and algorithms. Developing knowledge about designing such human-computer interactions (HCI) and collaborations for the workplace requires research linking the often-opposing streams of human work and interaction design research together, while keeping the user psychology in mind. This book is about exploratory research on the relations between empirical work analysis and interaction design activities, that is, about theorizing for socio-technical HCI design with a distinct psychological flavor.

Work designs that do not connect the social and the technical components of organizations are historically known to decrease both productivity and worker satisfaction, de-power workers in decision-making, focus on individual operations of machines (instead of whole tasks beyond any spatial-temporal boundaries), and lead to enlargement (do more) rather than job enrichment (do interesting things that you like) (Cherns, 1987; Mumford, 2006). Despite this, even in today's digitalized world, technological skills in a company often dictate the design space, making it difficult for technology-driven industry to accommodate human-computer interaction (HCI) design approaches, such as experience design (Roto et al., 2017). Emerging working conditions such as organizations' abilities to track workers performance digitally evokes additional discussions about how system design and the institutional context become important elements influencing meaningful work experiences (Stein et al., 2019). Most recently, socio-technical areas of conflict turn out to be crucial for implementing Industry 4.0 within small- and medium-sized enterprises (SMEs) in Europe, that is, digitalization within an integrated organizational and technological development that includes employees, departments, and the entire value-added chain need further socio-technical research focused on SMEs (Ludwig et al., 2018).

HWID can, for example, be helpful when designing the beginning or advanced use of assistive technologies in work practices on the factory floor, which can be a step in a digitalization process (Mucha et al., 2016). It could for example be a case of an SME that specializes in glass processing and produces individual pieces with special specifications for the offshore oil and gas industry in the North Sea. This SME installed a 100,000€ collaborative robot in order to explore if and how it could be used in their production, Fig. 1.2 left side. The idea was that a robot can work alongside human workers and interact in collaboration with the human worker (Kragic et al., 2017), as it were itself a human worker with agency and intentionality (Görür et al., 2018), specialized in pick-and-place and grabbing (Sanchez-Tamayo & Wachs, 2018), and perhaps in need of training (Schulz, 2017) and programming (Materna et al., 2017) from the human worker.

The situation in the company was that the 100,000 Euro collaborative robot was not used enough, and it remained idle much of the time. It had the potential to transform the company from an SME with specialized small batch products to one with large batch manufacturing as well. For example, the collaborative robot had the potential to do serial processing during the night. However, the robot was purchased only with the intent to discover if and how such technology could be useful in the company. No deliberate plans or analyses of production flow(s) or human-robot interactions preceded the acquisition, and subsequent attempts to train the human workers on the factory floor, Fig. 1.2 right side, failed to show increase in use. This illustrates how current technology-driven decisions do not realize the potential for transformation of work and company capacities in SMEs. The creation of robust new

Fig. 1.2 The technical and the social in a European glass processing SME

knowledge through exploratory research into socio-technical HCI design is needed to realize UX-at-work and enable human collaboration with technology such as robots, automation, and in general, algorithms.

Current knowledge about socio-technical HCI design includes 'Practice-Based Computing' that aims to provide CSCW and HCI with a novel founding assumption that computer applications are socially embedded (Volker Wulf et al., 2018), and 'Experience-Driven design' that aims to define the intended human experience before functionality and computer technology (Hassenzahl, 2010; Roto et al., 2017). 'Practice-based computing' studies how digital technologies are appropriated over (long) time (Volker Wulf et al., 2018), by using 'Grounded Design' to understand the transformation and fitting between designed artefacts, social practices, and the context of use (Stevens et al., 2018). Thus, where Practice-Based Computing emphasizes the conceptualization of notions of social changes across empirical cases, HWID is a platform that supports the development of domain-specific theoretical gestalts. 'Experience-driven design' uses psychological 'need cards' to provide orientation and inspiration for the design of interactive products, and 'interaction vocabulary' that supports the designer in aligning her or his choice with the intended experience (Diefenbach et al., 2013). This approach is also used for designing for work contexts (Harbich & Hassenzahl, 2017). While 'Experience-driven design' always focusses on psychological needs, HWID acknowledges the importance of workgroup and organizational level work analysis. Many other approaches may fall under the term socio-technical HCI design; interestingly CSCW 'Design Tensions' (Gross, 2013) conceptualizes design not as problem solving, but as goal balancing, i.e., conflicts solved through compromise. Socio-technical HCI may also be studied as 'organizational design and engineering' that departs from concepts of organizations and work rather than technology (Alter, 2010), 'participatory design' which is a wide and diverse field (Simonsen & Robertson, 2012), 'Agile UX development' that takes up the tradition of merging HCI and software engineering (Cajander et al., 2013), as cross-cultural design for IT products and services (Rau et al., 2012), and more approaches which are outside this book. The field of socio-technical system design is rich and varied with many approaches that each have variants and own discussions.

Note that this book does not contain many descriptions where the work domain and its challenges become explicit in the text, nor does the book explicitly deal with cultural backgrounds. As introduced above, HWID's notion of work is primarily understood as work analysis in the form of task analysis or work practice studies in the ethnographic field study tradition. HWID does not have a sociological concept of work where work is something that takes place in society, it rather tends to have a psychological concept of work, that is, work as targeted activity (play is without goals, learning is the goal of learning, work has external goals). Therefore, there are not so much work domain-specific description or explanation of interaction design activities. Chapter 8 does have descriptions of the robot manufacturing projects with the collaborative robots, and there are also in other chapters case studies with examples from several work domains. However, the book does not provide 'facts' about work domains, something like when people work, how they talk to each other, what they do when they sit down at the computer, etc., to be translated into technological designs (Dourish, 2006). Similarly, this book does not unfold the concept of interaction design as such. The book focuses on the connections between work analysis and interaction design, between the social and the technical.

1.3 Content

In the remainder of this book, the HWID approach in Fig. 1.1 will be used to discuss socio-technical HCI theory, cases, methods, and reflections about impact. Chapter 2 gives the theory, and Chaps. 3, 4, 5, 6 present and illustrate four types of HWID relations. Specific advice for researchers, consultants, and policymakers is given in Chaps. 7, 8, 9. Chapters 10 and 11 are reflective chapters that ponder some of the many open issues related to theorizing about socio-technical HCI and summarize and conclude the book.

References

Abdelnour-Nocera, J., Oussena, S., & Burns, C. (2015). *Human Work Interaction Design of the Smart University*. https://doi.org/10.1007/978-3-319-27048-7_9.

Alter, S. (2010). Designing and engineering for emergence: A challenge for HCI practice and research. *AIS Transactions on Human-Computer Interaction, 2*(4), 127–140.

Barricelli, B. R., Roto, V., Clemmensen, T., Campos, P., Lopes, A., Gonçalves, F., & Abdelnour-Nocera, J. (2019). *Human Work Interaction Design. Designing Engaging Automation: 5th IFIP WG 13.6 Working Conference, HWID 2018, Espoo, Finland, August 20–21, 2018, Revised Selected Papers* (Vol. 544). Springer.

Cajander, Å., Larusdottir, M., & Gulliksen, J. (2013). Existing but not explicit-the user perspective in scrum projects in practice. *INTERACT*, 762–779. Springer.

Campos, P., Clemmensen, T., Abdelnour Nocera, J., Katre, D., Lopes, A., & Ørngreen, R. (2012). *Human Work Interaction Design. Work Analysis and HCI Third IFIP 13.6 Working Conference, HWID 2012, Copenhagen, Denmark, December 5–6, 2012, Revised Selected Papers*. Springer, Berlin, Heidelberg.

Cherns, A. (1987). Principles of Sociotechnical Design Revisted. *Human Relations, 40*(3), 153–161. https://doi.org/10.1177/001872678704000303.

Clemmensen, T., Campos, P., Orngreen, R., Mark-Pejtersen, A., & Wong, W. (2006). *Human work interaction design: Designing for human work*. Springer Science + Business Media.

Clemmensen, T., Kaptelinin, V., & Nardi, B. (2016). Making HCI theory work: An analysis of the use of activity theory in HCI research. *Behaviour & Information Technology, 35*(8), 608–627. https://doi.org/10.1080/0144929X.2016.1175507.

Clemmensen, T., Orngreen, R., & Pejtersen, A. M. (2005). Describing users in contexts: perspectives on human-work interaction design. *Workshop Proceedings of Workshop 4, Held in Conjunction with the 10th IFIP TC13 International Conference on Human-Computer Interaction. INTERACT 2005, Rom, Italy., 5*, 60. Retrieved from http://citeseerx.ist.psu.edu/viewdoc/download?doi=10.1.1.123.7265&rep=rep1&type=pdf.

Diefenbach, S., Lenz, E., & Hassenzahl, M. (2013). An Interaction vocabulary. Describing the How of Interaction. *CHI '13 Extended Abstracts on Human Factors in Computing Systems*, 607–612. https://doi.org/10.1145/2468356.2468463.

Dourish, P. (2006). Implications for design. *Proceedings of the SIGCHI Conference on Human Factors in Computing Systems*, 541–550.

Görür, O., Rosman, B., Sivrikaya, F., & Albayrak, S. (2018). Social cobots: anticipatory decision-making for collaborative robots incorporating unexpected human behaviors. *Proceedings of the 2018 ACM/IEEE International Conference on Human-Robot Interaction*, pp. 398–406. ACM.

Gregor, S. (2006). The nature of theory in information systems. *MIS Quarterly*, 611–642.

Gross, T. (2013). Supporting Effortless Coordination: 25 Years of Awareness Research. *Computer Supported Cooperative Work (CSCW), 22*(4), 425–474. https://doi.org/10.1007/s10606-013-9190-x.

Harbich, S., & Hassenzahl, M. (2017). User experience in the work domain: A longitudinal field study. *Interacting with Computers, 29*(3), 306–324.

Hassenzahl, M. (2010). Experience design: Technology for all the right reasons. *Synthesis Lectures on Human-Centered Informatics, 3*(1), 1–95.

Hirschheim, R., & Klein, H. K. (1989). Four paradigms of information systems development. *Communications of the ACM, 32*(10), 1199–1216.

Katre, D., Orngreen, R., Yammiyavar, P., & Clemmensen, T. (2010). Human Work Interaction Design: Usability in Social, Cultural and Organizational Contexts: Second IFIP WG 13.6 Conference, HWID 2009, Pune, India, October 7-8, 2009, Revised Selected Papers: Preface. In *IFIP Advances in Information and Communication Technology* (Vol. 316). Springer.

Kragic, D., Gustafson, J., Karaoguz, H., Jensfelt, P., & Krug, R. (2017). *Interactive, Collaborative Robots: Challenges and Opportunities*. Retrieved from https://www.ijcai.org/proceedings/2018/0003.pdf.

Ludwig, T., Kotthaus, C., Stein, M., Pipek, V., & Wulf, V. (2018). Revive old discussions! socio-technical challenges for small and medium enterprises within industry 4.0. *Proceedings of 16th European Conference on Computer-Supported Cooperative Work*. https://doi.org/10.18420/ecscw2018_15.

Materna, Z., Kapinus, M., Beran, V., SmrĚ, P., Giuliani, M., Mirnig, N., ... & Tscheligi, M. (2017). Using persona, scenario, and use case to develop a human-robot augmented reality collaborative workspace. *Proceedings of the Companion of the 2017 ACM/IEEE International Conference on Human-Robot Interaction,* 201–202. ACM.

Mucha, H., Büttner, S., & Röcker, C. (2016). Application areas for human-centered assistive systems. *Human-Computer Interaction–Perspectives on Industry 4.0. Workshop at i-KNOW 2016 Graz, Austria, Oct 2016.*

Mumford, E. (2006). The story of socio-technical design: Reflections on its successes, failures and potential. *Information Systems Journal, 16*(4), 317–342. https://doi.org/10.1111/j.1365-2575.2006.00221.x.

Newman, W. (1994). Preliminary analysis of the products of HCI research, using pro forma abstracts. *Conference on Human Factors in Computing Systems—Proceedings.*

Parker, S. K. (2014). Beyond motivation: Job and work design for development, health, ambidexterity, and more. *Annual Review of Psychology, 65,* 661–691.

Rasmussen, J., Pejtersen, A. M., & Goodstein, L. P. (1994). *Cognitive systems engineering.*

Rasmussen, J., & Vicente, K. J. (1990). Ecological interfaces: A technological imperative in high-tech systems? *International Journal of Human-Computer Interaction, 2*(2), 93–110.

Rau, P.-L., Plocher, T., & Choong, Y.-Y. (2012). *Cross-cultural design for IT products and services.* CRC Press.

Roto, V., Kaasinen, E., Heimonen, T., Karvonen, H., Jokinen, J. P. P., Mannonen, P., ... & Koskinen, H. M. K. (2017). Utilizing Experience Goals in Design of Industrial Systems. *Proceedings of ACM SIGCHI Conference on Human Factors in Computing Systems (CHI'17),* 6993–7004. https://doi.org/10.1145/3025453.3025620.

Sanchez-Tamayo, N., & Wachs, J. P. (2018). Collaborative robots in surgical research: A low-cost adaptation. *Companion of the 2018 ACM/IEEE International Conference on Human-Robot Interaction,* 231–232. ACM.

Schulz, R. (2017). Collaborative robots learning spatial language for picking and placing objects on a table. *Proceedings of the 5th International Conference on Human Agent Interaction,* 329–333. ACM.

Simonsen, J., & Robertson, T. (2012). *Routledge international handbook of participatory design.* Routledge.

Stein, M. K., Wagner, E. L., Tierney, P., Newell, S., & Galliers, R. D. (2019). Datification and the Pursuit of Meaningfulness in Work. *Journal of Management Studies.* https://doi.org/10.1111/joms.12409.

Stevens, G., Rohde, M., Korn, M., Wulf, V., Pipek, V., Randall, D., & Schmidt, K. (2018). Grounded design. A research paradigm in practice-based computing. *V. Wulf; V. Pipek; D. Randall; M. Rohde,* 139–176.

Volker Wulf, Pipek, V., Randall, D., Rohde, M., Schmidt, K., & Stevens, G. (Eds.). (2018). *Socio-Informatics—A practice-based perspective on the design and use of IT artifacts.* Oxford: Oxford University Press.

Chapter 2
Human Work Interaction Design
for Socio-Technical Theory and Action

Abstract This chapter introduces and compares systematically HWID to current research knowledge about socio-technical HCI. It introduces to the existing body of HWID research, and to traditional and more recent approaches to work analysis and interaction design. Then it compares systematically HWID and Experience Design (Hassenzahl et al in Synth Lect Human-Cent Inform 3(1):1–95, 2010), HWID and Practice-Based Design (Volker Wulf et al in Socio-informatics—a practice-based perspective on the design and use of IT artifacts. Oxford University Press, Oxford, 2018), and HWID and 'Design Tensions' for group work (Gross in Comput Supp Cooperat Work (CSCW) 22(4):425–474, 2013). This is followed up with a summary overview and outline of what is unique and what HWID as a platform for socio-technical HCI theorizing shares with other socio-technical HCI design approaches. The chapter ends with an introduction to four types of HWID relation artefacts.

Keywords Human work interaction design · Practice-Based design · Design tensions · Experience design · HCI theory

In HWID, the 'view of the human' is as distributed over organization, work, individual, and interaction designs. In contrast, in HCI the dominant view of the human user is cognitive psychology's Mr. Bubblehead as an individual user of interactive devices and systems (Card et al., 1983). Going further to socio-technical HCI design, there are both organization and interaction designs. HWID is socio-technical HCI design but has a focus on the individual human worker. HWID thus overlaps with other socio-technical and HCI design approaches, but it is unique in its distributed focus across organization, work, individual, and interaction. In addition, design in HWID consists of movements from the social to the technical and back again. A design movement from the social to the technical is, for example, when you as a participant or stakeholder (user, worker, designer, client, manager, researcher, etc.) start out designing as a social science or humanities (SSH) designer and gradually then moves to designing as a natural or technical science designer. A design movement can also begin the other way around, with designing like a natural or technical science designer and then gradually move toward designing like a social science or humanities (SSH) designer. Such movements across disciplinary borders are characteristic for HWID. Thus, actions in HWID include both solving organizational problems and creating interaction designs that fulfill workers' needs.

HWID should be relevant to both researchers, consultants, and policymakers. While each of these groups has a chapter dedicated to them (Chaps. 7–9), this chapter presents the theoretical background for HWID and ends with an opening to the presentation in the following Chaps. 3–6 of the most important parts of HWID, that is, the relation artefacts that links the social and the technical in HWID.

2.1 The Aim with the HWID for Theory and Action

A brief history of Socio-technical HCI: Why and how HWID is socio-technical

A key defining feature of the original Tavistock institute's socio-technical approach was that the researchers and practitioners there were interested in social change for groups of people. Many of the staff had experiences from the institute's war time services of personnel selection, resettlement, and psychological warfare during WWII. Furthermore, many staff were interested in individual psychological issues because many of the staff were psychiatrists and believed in the power of psychoanalysis and the value of understanding themselves when helping others. These experiences were the backdrop on which the 'action research' of socio-technical approaches developed and why empirical analysis and theory development became embedded in organizational and individual change (Mumford, 2006).

Socio-technical HCI design today builds directly on the original Tavistock institute's socio-technical approach with its focus on innovative and balanced relations between technology, organization, tasks, and IT users. It is thus more relaxed and less 'system theory' than approaches that view technology and technology development as purely technical issues (Bjørn-Andersen & Clemmensen, 2017). On the other hand, socio-technical HCI design is less 'participatory' in its ambitions, compared to the critical-theory approaches often associated with Scandinavian versions of participatory design (Bannon et al., 2018). It aims to design for organizational capacity enhancement and managements' interest, while at the same time fighting for employees' interests in what (Bannon et al., 2018) names a "…form of user-centered design, concentrating on more local issues of usability and user satisfaction".

Socio-technicality in IS and HCI/CSCW is not fully identical with traditional socio-technical approaches, and on top of that socio-technical HWID may be only partly overlapping, and in various and changing ways, with the other approaches. Generally speaking, IS accepts the technology as it is and focus their studies on how the social, the people, can be made to change, while HCI accepts the social, the people, as they are, and focus their studies on how the technology can be redesigned (Lanamäki & Väyrynen, 2016). Historically, CSCW started out being close to the IS perspective with a focus on people and wanted to introduce a sociology instead of the then dominating psychological perspective (Bannon, 1991), while more recently

CSCW has become more like a subfield of HCI (Lanamäki & Väyrynen, 2016). However, as Wynne and Hult (2019) argue, reviews of HCI (Grudin, 2012) and CSCW (Blomberg & Karasti, 2013) indicate that the two fields are not well aligned. Grudin (2012) pins the HCI field as of engineering origins, with mainstream HCI striving for value neutrality and with only accessibility, sustainability, and fitness as the social, while Blomberg and Karasti (2013) present CSCW as a clearly social science and nearly anthropological field much closer to the IS socio-technicality. Other related fields or sub-fields, such as cognitive engineering, have turned out related but different socio-technical approaches, such work interaction design (Hemmecke & Stary, 2018) and also HWID. Since HCI is not mentioned explicitly by Mumford in her review of socio-technical design approaches (Mumford, 2006), we may argue that socio-technical HCI design approaches (such as HWID) constitutes a change and perhaps a much needed renewal of traditional socio-technical design approaches.

The roots in cognitive work analysis

The HWID IFIP 13.6 working group was founded among others by Annelise Mark-Pejtersen, who before that was one of the inventors of cognitive work analysis (Rasmussen et al., 1990). Cognitive Work Analysis (CWA) was developed to design for complex socio-technical work systems. Inspired by ecological psychology with its valuable invariants (affordances) in the environment (Gibson, 1977; Gibson & Carmichael, 1966), CWA models different types of constraints. The aim is to model how work could proceed within a given work system, rather than how work is actually done (work practices) or how it should be done (normative). CWA consists of four phases. The first phase is a work domain analysis that identifies system constraints on operators' behavior. The second phase on operator control tasks identifies which tasks/decision activities need to be performed in the operation of the system being analyses (e.g., for a power plant start-up, normal operation, fault detection and compensation, and shutdown). The third phase of mental strategy analysis is a discussion of the different methods by which an operator can perform the previously identified tasks and decision activities. The fourth phase is worker competencies analysis, that is, a description of the levels of cognitive control used in controlling the system, indicating which types of knowledge, skills, and mental competencies are involved in performing system tasks (Vicente & Pawlak, 1994). Other phases may be added such as social organization and cooperation analysis, and team work analysis (Burns, 2013). CWA is usually applied to analyse complex work domain such as control rooms in large organizations to help design training and interaction designs.

HWID as a working group under IFIP TC 13 was created to take up the legacy of CWA, but to aim at a broader set of domains, including less complex work domains such as office work, and with a liberal interpretation of the constraining 'environment' as any context for design and use. In its first workshop entitled "Describing Users in Context—Perspectives on Human-Work Interaction" (Clemmensen et al., 2005) and a first summary of the early research production (Orngreen et al., 2008) it was clear that focus of HWID was on the interaction between humans and work. For example, there was research by Pedro Campos on 'work styles' (Campos & Nunes, 2005) and by Jose Abdelnour-Nocera on 'users' (Abdelnour-Nocera et al., 2005). A workshop at Nordichi 2008 conference interpreted the focus of HWID to be more narrowly on the relations between work analysis and design of interactions, that is, focus on creativity and creative techniques that connect human work and interaction design (Clemmensen, 2008). Clemmensen later formulated this in a model of relations between human work analysis and interaction designs (Clemmensen, 2011a, b). The root in CWA became explicit with the HWID 2012 keynote of Burns on new dimensions of CWA (Burns, 2013), the 2015 CWA paper on smart universities (Abdelnour-Nocera et al., 2015), and the HWID2021 keynote by Philippe Palanque on task modeling and work analysis.

HWID aims at productivity and well-being in the age of AI, robotics, and IoT

HWID for theory and action aims to support organizations' problem solving and individual workers' UX-based job design for productivity and well-being in the age of digitalization with AI, robotics, and IoT. Digitalization enables extensive automation and machine agencies, which calls for a (renewed) and more multidisciplinary focus on human work design (Parker & Grote, 2020; Wang et al., 2020) including HCI (Clemmensen et al., 2021). An important mission of HWID is to encourage and support individual workers' use of human work interaction design to craft the digitalization of their own jobs. This should be done in a way that involves their user experiences and employee experiences to provide general well-being and productivity in their digital workplace. In this sense, HWID supports 'job crafting'. Job crafting, understood as individual employees proactively change their tasks and roles, has for the last 20 years been hotly debated as a way to support diversity of the workforce (Zhang & Parker, 2019). However, the burgeoning research in job crafting does as much psychological work research before that not take technology seriously, and the major approaches to job crafting such as 'job role crafting' and 'work design' (Zhang & Parker, 2019) does not even mention technology. The 'job role crafting' approach wants to improve meaning and work identity. It defines job crafting as 'the physical and cognitive changes individuals make in the task or relational boundaries of their work' (Wrzesniewski & Dutton, 2001), that is the idea that people (workers) can revise their work identities and increase and improve the meaning of their work through crafting either their job tasks, the way they think about their job (cognitive crafting), or crafting the relations that they have to colleagues and subordinates and superiors. Compared to socio-technical models such as Leavitt's diamond model with tasks, structure, actors, and technology, Wrzesniewskui and Duttons' approach to job crafting does not explicitly focus on technology. Due to the lack of appreciation of the technology design aspect of job crafting in existing job crafting theory as explained above, we offer a HWID interpretation of job crafting as "the designs that employees create to relate their organization's digital work and workers and the interaction designs in their job with their personal abilities and needs". It should be clear that we with this HWID interpretation of job crafting put digitalized work and the human-computer interactions and human-technology collaborations and their relations at the center of the HWID for theory and action.

The aim with the HWID for theory and action is an expansive one. The aim is to support workers in enriching and expanding their jobs rather than preventing risks by limiting and reducing their jobs, though this may also be a fully legitimate aim. Furthermore, the distinction between cognitive (re-frame your thinking about your job) and behavioral (change your job behavior) crafting (Zhang & Parker, 2019) is blurred in HWID, as human-computer interaction often merges these categories of human action into design of interactive cognitive behaviors, and in addition support meta-cognitive action and theory by allowing participants to reflect on their proto-types. HWID interpretation of job crafting builds on the assumption that individual job crafting is done in front of colleagues and with a willingness and intent to share and reflect on the crafting together with colleagues (Clemmensen & Nørbjerg, 2019a, b).

HWID for theory and action is not about sociological approaches to design such as ethnomethodology that says that we should focus on peoples everyday life as given (Button & Sharrock, 2009), though this is partly covered by the HW of HWID. It rather aims to show how psychological approaches to design can illuminate indi-viduals' constructions of their 'work-worlds'. The book is also not about innovation with 'minimal viable products' for commercial markets (Eisenmann et al., 2012), though this is partly covered by the ID of HWID. It rather aims to show how proto-typing can be part of workers' crafting of their technology use in their own jobs. Thus, the aim is not (only) about product design that aims to create novel products, but about design as psychological 'UX crafting' for productivity and well-being in the age of AI and robotics. It is thus about psychology as a science of design. Finally, it is not about end-user development for smart environments, but it is about workers' design-in-use for their everyday work situations and jobs.

HWID aims at socio-technical solutions

The assumption in this book is that digital artefacts are part of the solutions, but not the whole of solutions, to improved user experiences, employee experiences, and in general well-being and productivity in the digital workplace. Care should, however, be taken not to indulge in 'solutionism' (Blythe et al., 2016). Other possible inter-ventions in organizations may relate to digital artefacts in a richness of ways to create and valorize the local socio-technical solutions. No reason to hide, however, that the reader should feel at home in this book if they want to try out digital solutions and experiences. These include Chatbots, VR, AR, HoloLens, user experience, employee experience, customer experience, brand experience, etc., and Big data, data analytics, IoT, sensors, AI, machine learning, and not the least, novel interaction designs, and perspectives on UX & usability. Thus, the assumption here is that all digital solutions from their onset should be considered socio-technical solutions.

HWID aims at producing a specific kind of knowledge

HWID is about an important and specific type of knowledge and knowledge produc-tion that may be characterized as design research that is 'grounded how to knowl-edge'. It is about the empirical or theoretical knowledge behind design choices, the design choices themselves (form and function), and also about design methods. In different IT-related fields this is called by different names. HCI and the design communities call this design research or research through design and make a distinction toward doing research for design purposes versus using design approaches as a research method (Fallman, 2003; Zimmerman et al., 2007). More recently the notion of design fiction help to focus on the use of very early prototypes to design and evaluation imagined futures (Blythe, 2014; Wu et al., 2019). Furthermore, HCI has conceptualized this type of knowledge production as a psychological science of design that seeks to understand and support human beings interacting with and through technology development (Carroll, 1997a, b), mostly by focus on designing for usability and UX, analyzing and designing specific user interfaces and interaction designs, and studying and improving the processes of technology. Within information systems (IS) research this type of knowledge is called theory for design and action, where the IT artifact itself is considered a contribution of design science and where the contribution also includes foundational constructs, models, and methods for the design (Gregor, 2006). IS research of this kind includes design science that focuses on the IT artefact (Von Alan et al., 2004), grounded design cases that build knowledge across design cases (Rohde et al., 2017), and action design science (Sein et al., 2011) that allows the user (the researcher) to choose to focus mostly on the organization or mostly on the IT artefact when producing and arguing for the novel how to knowledge produced by the research.

The validity of HWID knowledge understood as a kind of design research hence relates to evaluation, reflection, and theory building (Blythe, 2014; Carroll, 1997b; Fallman, 2003; Gregor, 2006; Rohde et al., 2017; Sein et al., 2011). Thus it should have utility to a community of users and not at least to individual workers, the artefact should have both novelty and support the workers' perception of novelty of the artifact, the claims that it is effective and easy to use should be persuasive, the models and methods should demonstrably be easy to use and give high quality results, and finally, the knowledge produced and the artefact should be interesting and inspiring and provide (documented) quality experiences for the workers.

2.2   The Body of HWID Research

HWID as presented in this book is not a theory or a method but a platform from which to launch a richness and multitude of targeted and locally valorized sociomaterial designs. Thus, HWID studies published so far should reflect and illustrate the richness of local HWID designs created. In this section we discuss the body of HWID research, and we reflect on the heritage and future of HWID as a platform.

What we know and don't know about HWID

HWID research has until now largely been published at workshops and conferences, in line with the format and aim of HWID being an IFIP TC 13 working group and could thus be expected to be mainly work-in-progress papers. Indeed, Gonçalves et al. (Gonçalves et al., 2015a) reviewed 54 HWID-related papers from workshops, conferences, and journals from the period 2009–2014, and found that 80% of the papers were about the early phases in system development. They grouped the papers into six topical groups and mapped these groups to the HWID platform to find research gaps for future research. It appeared that the groups of papers covered all areas of the platform well for a variety of work and leisure domains, for example, public communication in India, elderly care in Japan, creative writing business in Portugal, and industrial manufacturing in Austria (Gonçalves et al., 2015). The area in the strongest need for more research papers was the development of the HWID platform itself. Furthermore, many papers had been on studying design sketching, early prototypes, and some on implemented systems-in-use, while very few (3) papers were about mature design (mature prototypes) or early implementation (content templates). They recommend an update of the HWID platform and the approach to using it so that it can be also useful for research in mature prototyping and organizational implementation.

Evolving the heritage and future of HWID as a platform

Scientific conferences and other meetings are indeed an opportunity for researchers to discuss an early stage of their research, and to coordinate, exchange, and disseminate knowledge. They are thus of key importance to produce scientific knowledge, and perhaps even more so in fast developing areas driven by technology developments such as HCI. This is also true for the HWID research areas.

HWID Working conferences. A working conference (like the HWID 2006, 2009, 2012, 2015, 2018, 2021, etc.) is defined as a smallish conference, with selection of papers done based on full paper submissions, at least three reviews per paper, conference proceedings to be distributed at the event, usually only one stream/track, and expected attendance below 100 participants (Hammond, 2003). While larger conferences that aim to function as an outlet for finished research do usually have an acceptance rate of between 15 and 40%, a working conference aim to accept a majority of submissions as full papers or posters. There will be some flexibility for the organizers of a working conference, so small deviations from the indicated characteristics might occur (Hammond, 2003).

The knowledge production from a working conference may be shaped by the one-track (thematic) and inductive (bottom-up) shared theorizing that is happening before, during, and after the event. Before it happens in the revision of papers before (pre-conference review), during the event within and between papers discussion (which can be structured in various ways) and note-taking takes place, and after revision by post-conference review and copyediting of the proceedings from the working conference. This whole collective process that involves everyone taking part in the working conference leads to a body of knowledge (mostly the proceedings book) that is fragmented and with little consistent use of theory or sharp focus but is thematic in a sense that a larger multitrack conference is not. The thematic character of the produced body of knowledge from the HWID working conferences thus covers:

- *Context*: Usability in Social, Cultural, and Organizational Contexts, HWID2009 (Katre et al., 2010). Artificial Intelligence and Low Desire Society (HWID2021, in preparation).

- **Technical->Social**: Designing for Human Work, HWID2006 (Clemmensen et al., 2006).
- **Social->Technical**: Work Analysis and HCI, HWID2012 (Campos et al., 2013).
- **IT artefacts**: Work Analysis and Interaction Design Methods for Pervasive and Smart Workplaces, HWID2015 (Abdelnour Nocera et al., 2015); Designing Engaging Automation, HWID2018 (Barricelli et al., 2018).

The first three themes provide empirical studies from social, technical, and contextual perspectives. The last theme presents local solutions, and theoretical and methodological reflections about HWID's relation to the larger bodies of HCI, IS, and Design literatures.

HWID Workshops and SIGs at conferences. A scientific workshop is an event taking place at a conference. Participation will be by invitation or open call for position papers. Participations will only be accepted if the participant has a position paper accepted by the workshop chairs. There are no special requirements for publication, and the expected attendance is below 50 people. A workshop will have a specialized topic which all participants contribute to in their submitted position papers. Workshop proceedings are usually not published but will often be available to the public anyway by archiving in universities working paper series or in international repositories. Similarly, SIGs are special interest group meetings at conferences that enable conference attendees sharing a common interest to meet informally for 80 min of facilitated discussion during a scheduled session at the conference. SIGs offer excellent opportunities for dialog and deliberation on a specific topic. The conference provides the SIG with meeting space and advertises SIG meetings to the rest of the conference in the extended abstracts and conference program.

HWID workshops are usually held at IFIP INTERACT HCI conferences,[1] because HWID is a working group under IFIP TC 13 HCI. HWID workshops and SIGs can also be held at other academic conferences if accepted. For example, there was a CHI 2013 SIG on HWID (Clemmensen et al., 2013). Since INTERACT is biannual, and the first HWID workshop was held at INTERACT 2005, a long series of HWID workshops has been held. The topics have generally reflected what was going on in the working conferences. For HWID workshops, some proceedings are available on the HWID website.[2] The outcome of HWID workshops has however also been published in adjunct proceedings,[3] in books presenting selected and revised papers from IFIP TC13 workshops (e.g., (Clemmensen et a., 2018)), and in practitioners outlets such as ACM Interactions (e.g., (Hertzum et al., 2018)).

Valuable knowledge may lay dormant in HWID workshop papers. The knowledge production from workshops and SIGs is easily forgotten since most publications are hardly accessible, and since presentations usually represent emergent work by the involved researchers which later is published in more acknowledged outlets such as major conferences and journals. However, there are several papers presented at

---

[1] http://ifip-tc13.org/interact/.

[2] Currently at https://hwid.unibs.it/.

[3] See for example https://fis.uni-bamberg.de/handle/uniba/21159, http://ifip-tc13.org/wp-content/uploads/2018/03/INTERACT_2017_Adjunct_v4_final_24jan.pdf.

workshops that never are developed any further, but could have been, and hence valuable knowledge lay dormant in those papers. For example, a workshop from a Nordichi 2008 conference resulted in a panel discussion about how to combining usability with empirical studies of human work with Masaaki Kurosu, Kerstin Roese, Dinesh Katre, Rikke Ørngreen, Annelise Mark-Pejtersen (Clemmensen, 2008). This panel discussion was influential in establishing the notion of usability in context to link human work and interaction design.

HWID seminars (independents workshops) and tutorials. Notwithstanding the HWID events related to key HWID research (working conferences) and general HCI research (workshops and SIGs associated with major HCI conferences including INTERACT), there are also HWID events that are mainly about dissemination and teaching HWID and thus aims to engage audiences outside core interested researchers. Seminars are such events organized for educational purposes and not intended for publication. Fruitful discussions and collaboration initiatives are targets of seminars. Furthermore, seminars aim at a high scientific quality of the presentations and discussions, which can be achieved in many different ways: Traditional topics, new and upcoming topics, urgent or novel research approaches, advancement in academic disciplines and methods, scientific and theoretical challenges, challenges with design and applications, and so on (Pejtersen and Noirhomme, 2012).

Tutorials are methods of transferring knowledge and will mostly be used by participants seeking to learn about, rather than discuss or challenge, novel research knowledge. Tutorials are more interactive and specific than a book or a lecture, as often a tutorial seeks to teach by example and supply the information for participants to complete specific tasks. A tutorial thus can range from providing a set of instructions to complete a task, for example, a specific way of collecting and analyzing data, to an interactive problem solving session. A number of HWID presentations have been given at yearly IFIP TC 13 HCI seminars around the world. They have mostly been about introducing the HWID platform and presenting updates to the platform for the local and international audiences. Not many HWID tutorials have been held. AT HCII2021 there was a tutorial that introduced the audience to HWID as a kind of socio-technical HCI. The knowledge production of seminars and tutorials is thus characterized by participants seeking to learn about, rather than discuss or challenge, novel research knowledge.

Theorizing opportunities: Out of the working conferences and the workshops at conferences came gradually the practice of using workshops at research tools to theorize across design cases. From the end-discussion at the first HWID workshop at INTERACT in 2005, to the HWID 2018 working conference that for the first time used the term 'theorizing' in the program, the theorizing workshop idea gradually emerged. For example, at the INTERACT 2017 workshop one day of theorizing was coupled with a preceding day of field studies, which turned out to be very fruitful (Hertzum et al., 2018). The HWID workshops and other events became social events that used the HWID platform to generate learning and (some) insights. A considerable number of papers have been published from the HWID events. HWID as a platform for knowledge production has shown potential in the past and may well be used in the future. The theorizing workshops to which we return to in Chap. 7 may be a preferred tool for producing more mature, deep, and useful HWID knowledge.

HWID research may provide some help to bridge the gap between published academic papers on one hand and on the other hand useful knowledge for UX professionals, companies, governments, etc. It may never be entirely fixed what relation there is between theory (understood as a statement of relations among concepts within a set of boundary assumptions and constraints) and useful knowledge (understood as knowledge that have an impact on HCI practice now and in the future). However, within HCI and wider applied IT fields, two issues are at play. First, instead of doing a research cycle of problem → research → theory → *knowledge* → *practice* → new problems, etc., many researchers may tend to operate in a cycle of problem → research → theory, and not care for knowledge and practice. To remedy this situation, researchers should instead of focusing on theory, focus on *understanding*. Understanding means investigating how and why something came about, how we can make sense of what happened, how such an understanding might help develop policy, strategies, new artefacts, etc. that support and develop *practices* (Hirschheim, 2019). Another, but related, way to saying this is that we need other types of theory than only those that focus on explanation and prediction, we also need, for example, design theories and design patterns in order for the research being able to grasp and shape new phenomena early (Dennis, 2019). Second, the question of whether academic research should be useful for practice here and now and/or 30 years ahead is unresolved within the field. Some researchers argue for immediate relevance through action design research with theory-ingrained artefacts in organizations (Sein et al., 2011), while others argue that HCI research including social science and humanities HCI research should not only document knowledge from what can be observed in the current practice of information systems. Instead, HCI research should (also) create knowledge that is disconnected from current practice and which focus on changing the future (and not merely on documenting the present or the past) (Dennis et al., 2018). With these two issues in mind, HWID theory evolves around broad understanding of HCI and IS phenomena and practices both here and now and in future fictitious scenarios.

The level, form, and type of HWID-generated theory

HWID is a platform that serves to develop locally valorized sociomaterial action designs. When compared to established distinctions between macro, meso, and micro levels, HWID in the form of a platform for theory and action is in the midrange—meso level—as it is about organizations and designs. HWID could even be about the macro level in the sense of being a grand theory about society(ies) and the world, like-, for example, when discussing human's future abilities to create their own workplace, or when studying global re-design of the cultures that we live in to increase sustainability. However, the solutions delivered by HWID are micro levels in the form of locally valorized sociomaterial theory-ingrained solutions related to events, artefacts, etc. In addition, HWID deals not with empirical or conceptual research problems but is focused on 'constructive' research problems, where there are no known solutions, or partial solutions, or issues with deployment and implementations of solutions (Oulasvirta & Hornbæk, 2016). HWID is thus a type of design-based research (Zimmerman et al., 2007).

HWID as a type of design-based and constructive research is first and foremost concerned with the design phenomenology, that is, the study of form and configuration of IT artefacts (Cross, 2001). Sometimes HWID is about other kinds of design knowledge. This can be knowledge about design practices and processes (for example the method of 'Contextual persona' (Cajander et al., 2015)) or about designers' epistemology, that is, designers' ways of knowing about organizations, work, interaction design, UX and usability (for example, how designers and researchers can study UX in factories (Wurhofer et al., 2015)). However, the idea that both organizational and interaction design knowledge is linked into the IT artefact is a defining feature of HWID research. Each HWID artefact reflects a specific, local, framing of the problem, and contributes to a body of HWID research IT artefacts with similar framings or with very different framings to address the same problem. In design-based research, such artefacts can be used in the research community's discussion, new artefacts can contribute to ongoing discussions, and can become patterns for future design (Zimmerman et al., 2007). We return to HWID artefacts at the end of this chapter and in the following chapters.

In the family of socio-technical research design approaches, HWID is a unique approach in terms of theory type, form, and levels, Table 2.1. We have already touched on how Design Thinking for managers (Gruber et al., 2015; Kolko, 2015) and Action Design Research (ADR) (Sein, Henfridsson, Purao, Rossi, & Lindgren, 2011) compares to HWID. Compared to ADR, HWID can potentially include macro level analysis as part of the empirical analysis of human work while ADR does not, and theory in HWID comes in the form of holistic socio-technical patterns, while in ADR theory is a theory-ingrained IT artefact. ADR and Design Thinking for managers take a management perspective. In the following sections we will compare HWID to three socio-technical research design approaches that focus on employees' experiences and perspectives. These approaches are Practice-Based Design (Ludwig et al., 2018; Rohde et al., 2017), Experience Design (Harbich & Hassenzahl, 2017; Hassenzahl et al., 2015; Klapperich et al., 2018), and CSCW Design Tensions (Gross, 2013; Gross et al., 2005), (Table 2.1).

Other related approaches include the notion of 'ordinary user experiences' from University of Salzburg (Meneweger et al., 2018), and the perspective of user-centered design in organizations from Uppsala University (Cajander, 2010).

2.3   HWID and Practice-Based Design (PBD)

In somewhat contrast to HWID's 'relational' approach, Practice-Based Design (Volker Wulf et al., 2018; Wulf et al., 2015) argues that even a strong work domain analysis paired with good user-centered design with real user participation is not enough to account for the changes in social practices resulting from new technological artefacts. Rather, Practice-Based Design aims to build a repository of design

Table 2.1 The type, form, and levels of theory in socio-technical research design approaches

Approach (socio-technical design-based research approaches)	Type (difference between theory and method)	Form (how is theory ingrained)	Level (what level and relations between levels)
HWID Human Work Interaction Design (Abdelnour-Nocera & Clemmensen, 2019)	Theory is 'sociomaterial locally valorized solutions' (local theories and actions)	'Holistic pattern of HWID' (with asymmetrical socio-technical relations)	Macro, Meso, and Micro (it can vary what theory is, depending on the context bar)
PBD Practice-Based Design (Ludwig et al., 2018)	No theory, but some knowledge production	'Design cases' and insights across design cases	Micro (always about local appropriation of a prototype design)
ED Experience Design (Harbich & Hassenzahl, 2017; Hassenzahl et al., 2015; Klapperich et al., 2018)	Theory is theory-driven design	'Needs theory', from psychology + novel design artefacts	Macro and micro (not meso, because no concept of organization)
DTs Design Tensions in CSCW (Gross, 2013; Gross et al., 2005)	Theory is design principles	'Design Tensions', embedded in philosophical and sociological assumptions	Meso (always about the organization and small group)
ADR Action design research (Sein et al., 2011)	Theory is an 'ensemble artefact' (IT artefact instantiation + arguments)	'Theory-ingrained artefact'	Meso and Micro (not Macro because the social is limited to organizations)
DTM Design thinking for managers (Gruber et al., 2015)	Theory is a method	Design thinking process with a number of steps	Meso (always about management)

case studies and generalize by doing comparative analysis with concept building. The focus of concept and theory building should be on features of social practice (e.g., awareness), IT design principles (e.g., tailorability), and social changes stemming directly from appropriation of IT artefacts (e.g., over the shoulder learning). Where HWID is a platform that supports the development of domain-specific theoretical gestalts with a hint of psychology, Practice-Based Design emphasizes the conceptualization of notions of social changes across empirical cases. The question is if HWID can be compared to or even combined with a Practice-Based Design approach to conceptualize notions of socio-technical changes across empirical cases.

Comparing and combining HWID and PBD

To appreciate the strength and weakness of socio-technical HCI design approaches, and to help selecting one to apply in concrete projects, a comparison of HWID and PBD may be helpful, **Error! Reference source not found.**

The two approaches to socio-technical HCI Design, HWID and PBD, share a notion of context as wider organizational, regional, national, cultural, social, technological, political contexts. For example, HWID has used in studies of government websites in 28 Indian states (Katre & Gupta, 2011), and PBD has applied in research reports on FARCs appropriation of their enemy's new technology (de Castro Leal et al., 2019). The two approaches both would admit inspiration from critical theory and its researcher situatedness and contextualized research.

However, HWID and PBD differ in other aspects. The socio-technical problem definition and psychological need-finding are in HWID a movement through multiple interrelated artefacts that show what the needs and problems are, while PBD pays more attention to how to involve participants. The socio-technical sketching of alternative solutions in HWID happens through multiple interrelated artefacts with focus on ideations, brainstorming, and thinking divergent, while in PBD sketching may happen as part of the participatory design, but it is not important in itself to ideate. The socio-technical hypothesis prototyping in HWID is about testing individual and collective (group) hypotheses about UX, while in PDB mature prototypes are not tested but instead put to work in organizations and studied for how they are appropriated by stakeholders. The socio-technical interventions in HWID have a sociomaterial focus on the unnoticeable and ordinary integration of solutions into the larger work ecosystems, while PBD focus on the social changes that the new designs spur. The differences may also be seen in the closely related contrasting theory that for HWID would be network theories such as activity theory and actor network theory, while PBD would be closer to object theories such as affordance theory and appropriation theory.

2.4 HWID and Experience Design (ED)

HWID and Experience Design (ED) theory (Buchenau & Suri, 2000; Hassenzahl, 2010) have clear overlaps. HWID can be used for knowledge production in the form of theory-based design fictions that allow us to explore and visualize future work experiences with technology. A question is, however, if the experiences designed with the HWID platform are of the subjective, holistic, situated, and dynamic kind that has come to be known as 'user experiences'? A comparison of HWID with Experience Design (ED) theory (Buchenau & Suri, 2000; Hassenzahl, 2010) shows that they overlap and can be combined.

ED assumes that experiences are subjective, holistic, situated, dynamic, and positive. Subjective because experiences depend on the individual's psychology, holistic since it takes design for including not only the product but the wider experience, situated in the sense that experiences are both unique and common patterns at the same time, and finally, dynamic as IT artefacts often change over time in the distribution of their pragmatic and hedonic qualities and overall experiences. That focus is on positive experiences in ED stems from the design wish not so much to remedy negative frustration like usability design do, but rather to contribute to a positive psychology of human growth.

With origins in Soviet-Russian activity theory (Clemmensen et al. 2016; Leontiev, 1980) and German work psychology (Hacker, 2003), ED may be associated with motivation theory, action theory, and practice theory. In ED, these different psychological phenomena form a hierarchy. BE goals are about who you want to be (motive), DO goals about what you should do (action) to become what you want to be, and MOTOR goals (practice) how you do the action. However, in contrast to its origins, ED focuses on the positive emotions that come from aligning yourself with the values that you endorse and from the fulfillment of various basic psychological needs. Performing practices is then what enable the need fulfillment and value-alignment in ED. Despite its psychological origins, ED is a design approach, as it focusses on design of practices to enable experience.

The idea of ED is to put the experience before the design. Designers and design approaches should aim at designing user experiences. In ED, User experiences are experiences mediated by technology. Technology is made with material and tools. Designers work with materials and tools. Hence, in ED the IT artefact (product, system) is seen as having qualities. These qualities are pragmatic (related to DO goals) and hedonic (related to BE goals) qualities. In ED, the value or the why of a design is seen as hedonic (identity and stimulation)-related psychological need fulfillment, while the 'what' and 'how' of design are the pragmatic-related task performance goals. There is thus a difference between what are qualities of an IT artefact (pragmatic and hedonic) and what are the subjective, holistic, situated, and dynamic character of an experience (Hassenzahl et al., 2015).

Most recently, a sociological concept of practice has been introduced in ED to make the link between materials and tools toward psychological needs (Klapperich et al., 2018). The notion of social practices indicates that intervening in people's behavior depends on understanding how sets of practices co-evolve (Blue et al., 2016) and looking beyond single human-computer interactions to instead focus on socially shared practices (Kuijer et al., 2013). This fits nicely with the activity theory roots of ED where activity is a societal practice.

Comparing and combining HWID and ED

HWID does not necessarily put the experience before the design like ED does, Table 2.2. As a socio-technical approach, HWID can begin with the experience but can also start elsewhere.

Despite HWID and ED shares heritage and inspiration from activity theory with their focus on artefact mediation of human experiences, the two approaches are slightly different in all aspects. HWID, though being an action theory in the sense of being a platform for action, does not have levels like activity theory or ED do. Who you are—which is the BE goal level in ED—is relational in HWID in the sense of actor network theory, see, for example, (Frauenberger, 2019) and not distinguishable from what you do (DO goals in ED) or how you do it (also relational). Furthermore, HWID is contextual in a widest possible sense even more than Engeström' expanded activity theory (Engeström, 1999), while ED is situated in a context of the use of positive practices (Klapperich et al., 2018).

Socio-technical problem definition and psychological need-finding in HWID are done through multiple interrelated artefacts that capture needs and problems, while ED takes point of departure in basic innate psychological needs and with little or no consideration of other problems (but see, for example, (Schrepp et al., 2006)). Socio-technical sketching of alternatives in HWID is much about brainstorming visually with patterns, collaborations, and flows, while in ED sketching aims to empathize with individual experiences phenomenologically. Socio-technical hypothesis proto-typing in HWID not only designs hypotheses about workers' experiences, but also about organizational business goals, while ED prototypes design for individual experi-ences. Finally, In HWID socio-technical intervention (evaluation) is mostly about how the prototype fits with the organizational environment, while ED evaluation focuses on assessing need fulfillment. In sum, HWID does not assume that UX is dynamic (or static), it is holistic (in a broader sense than ED's single human expe-riences), contextual (rather than ED's situated), and collective (rather than ED's subjective or objective dimension).

Hybrid HWID-ED model for UX in organizations

Based on the above, this section proposes a possible model of the relationships between HWID, wider context, and Experience Design (ED) with the aim of providing a holistic understanding of the factors that impact UX in organizations.

Figure 2.1 is a visual representation of the relation between HW and ID explicitly expressed and articulated through the prototype design artefact in a chosen case. The HW-ID relations are placed at the base of the triangle because they provide ground-work information: information on users' characteristics, problems, and needs, the technology they work with, and how they interact with it. HWID as a whole then provides the base that leads up to Experience Design to provide positive and authentic experiences, that is, Positive Design (Desmet & Pohlmeyer, 2013). Positive Design visually sits atop HWID, showing how with a socio-technical understanding of a case through HWID designers can go further and elevate an experience so that it not only succinctly addresses pain points but creates a positive experience with the potential of increasing job satisfaction. This may be achieved using ED by analyzing what makes for meaningful work for the individual users, and then building on the HWID solution to address these emotional desires. In addition, the wider context (or envi-ronment) is analyzed through, for example, theorizing about paradigms for design (Gardien et al., 2014) and/or the use of empirical data. As shown in Fig. 2.1, the wider context permeates the whole structure, as the surroundings wherein an organization is embedded inevitably impact all aspects of it and is reciprocally impacted by the users' experiences.

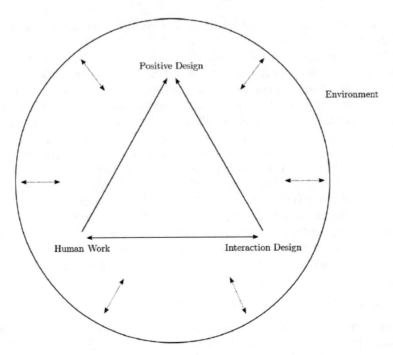

Fig. 2.1 A proposal for a hybrid HWID-ED model. Saigot, M., Bogdzeviciute, G., & Kim, Y. (2020). Improving system efficiency and job satisfaction at CBS MBA Admission Office (unpublished work, personal communication)

2.5   HWID and Design Tensions (DTs)

Since HWID is a multi-sided platform, knowledge production as the design will entail compromises between stakeholders. In CSCW research, design can be understood as designing compromises toward a set of basic tensions: availability, privacy, conventions, and tailoring (Gross, 2013). Gross's four design tensions are explained and compared to HWID in the following.

First, the design tension of availability stems from conflicting user needs: users want to interact with computers and with other users, but they also want not to be disrupted too often. Mediated by IT artefacts, today users have access to information and means for communication (nearly) anytime and anyplace. At the same time, frequent uncontrollable interruptions lead to stress, and under specific conditions systems can successfully predict users' interruptibility (Akbar et al., 2019). However, personal availability is based on an constant negotiation between actors who apply subtle tactics to communicate their availability (Hancock et al., 2009). In HWID, to design availability in a system, an ongoing relation-weaving between the capture of users' expectations of other users' availability is important (from HW->ID) and the creation of new concepts for mediating users' availability across time and space (from ID->HW). The resulting mediating relation artefacts should not only allow users to specify availability but also to facilitate an ongoing adaptation of their availability over time and between their tasks.

Second, the design tension of privacy like that of availability stems from conflicting user needs. Users may have unbalanced expectations to the information they want to get about other users, compared to the information that is being shared. From a rational, utilitarian perspective, data must be captured and shared because it is important for productive group work that the group members know about all team members' situations, activities, and results. On the other hand, from a privacy perspective, users have the right to have their data protected. That means that users need to know, to get feedback on, when important data about them is captured (e.g., by telling them to accept 'cookies' on websites). They also need to be able to configure their important privacy settings in their applications (think social media privacy settings). In HWID, for the design of privacy in applications the move from the HW gives the designer information about users' need for feedback on their applications' data sharing, and the move from ID gives the designer information about the configurations of type and recipients of data that different interaction designs offer.

Third, the design tension of conventions originates from a conflict between the individual users and their roles in the group. Conventions are informal rules in a group on how members should behave and what to expect from others. From the perspective of a group member there is a conflict between having few conventions which allow for great personal freedom, and having many conventions, which on the other hand mediates mutual expectations and a common ground to stand on in the group. Like availability and privacy, convention is a dynamic concept—mutual arrangements in teams could emerge or disappear over time. Conventions are strongly related to awareness—team members do not only need to establish conventions, but also need to be clear that everybody involved knows and follows these conventions. This interplay of conventions and awareness about them provides an important basis for the establishment of common ground in teams (Convertino et al., 2011). Conventions are in general symmetrical in teams where everybody follows the same rules and principles; yet it is basically also possible to agree on asymmetrical conventions (e.g., different deadlines for some users in some circumstances). Since conventions in teams in general have a long lifetime and evolve over time, it is very important for long-term team members to follow this evolution, and for newcomers to be inaugurated. So, for the design of cross-cultural conventions in systems it is essential to understand the cultural compatibility of conventions and to design for the management and adaptation and propagation of conventions in the system.

Fourth, the design tension for tailoring refers to the need to make domain-specific adaptations in the system. So, while it is desirable to have a preconfigured system with well thought-out defaults for individual functionality and team functionality, individual user needs and the team requirements could be highly domain specific (Luff et al., 2008). Tailoring also refers to the previous three tensions—availability, privacy, and conventions—but also goes beyond them and refers to any aspect of the system where the trade-off is between a convenient pre-configuration and an inadequate one-size-fits-all. A simple yet powerful principle from classical interactive systems is 'details on demand' where the system provides the users with a modest number of options that they can easily deal with but where the system also allows more advanced users to dig deeper and make advanced selections and configurations. Furthermore, decisions on regulations for tailoring and user rights of who can tailor awareness information capturing and presentation might be culture dependent. So, for the design of cross-cultural tailoring in systems it is important to understand users' desires and needs for personal tailoring.

Comparing and combining HWID and DTs

The notion of design-as-compromises is shared by HWID (with its relations) and CSCW design tensions (DTs), but besides this, the two approaches are more complementary than comparable, Table 2.4.

As approaches to socio-technical HCI design, HWID and DTs do not negate each other, and they can very well be combined. For example, HWID can be used first for theory production, followed by the use of CSCW design tensions for conceptually enhancing theory. The two approaches are thus perhaps less comparable and more complementary. Regarding the notion of context, HWID has a 'context bar' that allows the design-as-compromises to be seen in a wider perspective. For example, national cultural differences as expressed in differences in users' groupwork and interaction with IT artefacts may potentially have decisive impact on the compromises made. Complementing HWID's empirical and deliberately vague notion of context, DTs notion of context is theory-driven. For example, DTs context can be existing conventions for human-robot interaction or existing tailoring of awareness to situations at hand. Regarding socio-technical problem definition and psychological need-finding, HWID has multiple interrelated notions of needs and problems that capture empirically work and interaction, while DTs complements this by consulting theory early in the design process to defined problems and aims. Socio-technical sketching alternatives in HWID are about multiple sketching: interaction patterns, collaborative sketches, workflows, where the purpose is to ideate alternative solutions to a problem/need, while in DTs due to its theory-driven approach it is less important to visually brainstorm solutions with sketching. Socio-technical hypothesis prototyping in HWID focus on individual and collective UX prototyping of hypotheses usually developed from the sketching process, and DTs complements this approach with low, mid, and hi-fi prototypes that are design-concept-driven. Similarly, the socio-technical intervention (evaluation) in HWID has a sociomaterial focus on how the prototypes emerge in the organization, while in DTs theory comes before testing by doing an evaluation with respect to specific design tensions.

2.6 Socio-Technical Approaches to HCI Compared

HWID consists of the social, the technical, and their relations in context in ways that overlap with but also is unique when compared to related socio-technical HCI design approaches. For overview purposes, Table 2.2 HWID-PBD, Table 2.3 HWID-ED, and Table 2.4 HWID-DTs are combined in Table 2.5. PBD tends to focus on the

Table 2.2 HWID and PBD compared on HWID dimensions

Approach	Notion of context(s)	Socio-technical problem definition and psychological need-finding	Socio-technical sketching alternatives	Socio-technical hypothesis prototyping	Socio-technical intervention (evaluation)	Contrasting theories (beyond the approaches in this table)	Example literature
HWID	Wider organizational, regional, national, cultural, social, technological, political contexts	Multiple interrelated notions of needs and problems: Organizational problem definitions, Workers' need findings, Persona creations	Multiple sketching: Interaction patterns, Collaborative sketches, Workflows; purpose to ideate alternative solutions	Individual and collective UX prototypes: Organizational action hypotheses, Prototyped worker experiences, Field evaluations, and UX tests	Sociomaterial focus with Interaction interoperability checks, Digital legacy interventions, & Organizational strategy alignment	Activity theory, actor network theory, critical theory	Abdelnour-Nocera and Clemmensen (2019) Clemmensen (2011a, b)
PBD	Wider organizational, regional, national, cultural, social, technological, political contexts	Participatory design approach to requirement specification	Sketching not important	Mature, industry-level prototypes, accepted by companies into daily operation	Ethnographic studies of companies and workers appropriation of prototypes	Affordance theory, appropriation theory, participatory design	Volker Wulf et al. (2018) Ludwig et al. (2018)

Table 2.3 HWID and ED compared on HWID dimensions

Approach	Notion of context(s)	Socio-technical problem definition and psychological need-finding	Socio-technical sketching alternatives	Socio-technical hypothesis prototyping	Socio-technical intervention (evaluation)	Contrasting theories (beyond the approaches in this table)	Example literature
HWID	Wider organizational, regional, national, cultural, social, technological, political contexts	Multiple interrelated notions of needs and problems: Organizational problem definitions, Workers' need findings, Persona creations	Multiple sketching: Interaction patterns, Collaborative sketches, Workflows; purpose to ideate alternative solutions	Individual and collective UX prototypes: Organizational action hypotheses, Prototyped worker experiences, Field evaluations, and UX tests	Sociomaterial focus with Interaction interoperability checks, Digital legacy interventions, & Organizational strategy alignment	Activity theory, actor network theory, critical theory	Abdelnour-Nocera and Clemmensen (2019) Clemmensen (2011a, b,)
ED	No explicit context, some captured in notion of positive practices	Basic psychological needs are defined apriori, specific needs found from sampling positive experiences. No organizational problem definition	Experimental and embodied sketching is a central activity; purpose to empathize and speculate	UX prototypes, focus on the individual experiences	UX evaluation, focus on assessing need fulfillment	Design for meaning, Research through design, Activity theory, practice theory, Behavioral economics	Harbich and Hassenzahl (2017) Hassenzahl et al. (2015) Klapperich et al. (2018)

Table 2.4 HWID and DTs compared on HWID dimensions

Approach	Notion of context(s)	Socio-technical problem definition and psychological need-finding	Socio-technical sketching alternatives	Socio-technical hypothesis prototyping	Socio-technical intervention (evaluation)	Contrasting theories (beyond the approaches in this table)	Example literature
HWID Human Work Interaction Design	Wider organizational, regional, national, cultural, social, technological, political contexts	Multiple interrelated notions of needs and problems: Organizational problem definitions, Workers' need findings, Persona creations	Multiple sketching: Interaction patterns, Collaborative sketches, Workflows; purpose to ideate alternative solutions	Individual and collective UX prototypes: Organizational action hypotheses, Prototyped worker experiences, Field evaluations, and UX tests	Sociomaterial focus with Interaction interoperability checks, Digital legacy interventions, & Organizational strategy alignment	Activity theory, actor network theory, critical theory	Abdelnour-Nocera and Clemmensen (2019) Clemmensen (2011a, b)
DTs Design tensions	Theory as context, for example, existing conventions, for human-robot interaction, or existing tailoring of awareness to situations at hand	Considered early in the design process by consulting theory	Not important to visually brainstorm solutions (due theory-driven approach)	Design concept-driven low, mid, hi-fi prototypes	Theory before testing, evaluation with respect to specific design tensions	Phenomenological philosophy	Kusunoki et al. (2014) Gross (2013) Dimitriadis et al. (2007)

Table 2.5 Comparison of HWID and PBD, ED, and DTs

Approach	Notion of context(s)	Socio-technical problem definition and psychological need-finding	Socio-technical sketching alternatives	Socio-technical hypothesis prototyping	Socio-technical intervention (evaluation)	Contrasting theories (beyond the approaches in this table)	Example literature
HWID Human work interaction Design	Wider organizational, regional, national, cultural, social, technological, political contexts	Multiple interrelated notions of needs and problems: Organizational problem definitions, Workers' need findings, Persona creations	Multiple sketching on different organizational levels: Interaction patterns, Collaborative (team) sketches, Workflows	Individual and collective UX prototypes: Organizational action hypotheses, Prototyped worker experiences, Field evaluations, and UX tests	Sociomaterial focus with Interaction interoperability checks, Digital legacy interventions, & Organizational strategy alignment	Activity theory, actor network theory, critical theory	Abdelnour-Nocera and Clemmensen (2019) Clemmensen (2011a, b)
PBD Practice-Based Design	Wider organizational, regional, national, cultural, social, technological, political contexts	Participatory design approach to requirement specification	Sketching not important	Mature, industry-level prototypes, accepted by companies into daily operation	Ethnographic studies of companies and workers appropriation of prototypes	Affordance theory, appropriation theory, participatory design	Volker Wulf et al. (2018) Ludwig et al. (2018)
ED Experience Design	No explicit context, some captured in notion of positive practices	Basic psychological needs defined apriori, specific needs found from sampling positive experiences. No organizational problem definition	Experimental and embodied sketching is a central activity; purpose to empathize and speculate	UX prototypes, focus on the individual experiences	UX evaluation, focus on assessing need fulfillment	Design for meaning, Research through design, Activity theory, practice theory, Behavioral economics	Harbich and Hassenzahl (2017) Hassenzahl et al. (2015) Klapperich et al. (2018)

Table 2.5 (continued)

Approach	Notion of context(s)	Socio-technical problem definition and psychological need-finding	Socio-technical sketching alternatives	Socio-technical hypothesis prototyping	Socio-technical intervention (evaluation)	Contrasting theories (beyond the approaches in this table)	Example literature
DT Design tensions	Theory as context, for example, existing conventions, for human-robot interaction, or existing tailoring of awareness to situations at hand	Considered early in the design process by consulting theory	Not important to visually brainstorm solutions (due theory-driven approach)	Design concept-driven low, mid, hi-fi prototypes	Theory before testing, evaluation with respect to specific design tensions	Phenomenological philosophy	Kusunoki et al. (2014) Gross (2013) Dimitriadis et al. (2007)

human work, ED on the interaction design, and DTs on the tension between the two.

However, there are also other HWID-related approaches that tackle the socio-technical design in each their way. Most notably, action design research (ADR) offers a choice between focusing on the organization or focusing on the technical in its four-stage design model (organizational problem formulation, build-intervene-evaluate, reflect and learn, formalize learning) (Sein et al., 2011). Compared to HWID that is a vague, loose, and open platform with multiple problems and needs, ADR is strictly step and stage oriented and with a starting point in the formulation of a committing organizational problem (Sein & Rossi, 2019). Another example with a focus on the organization is the design thinking management (DTM) approach that offers a version of user-centered design to be used by managers to do management (Kolko, 2015). Compared to HWIDs platform approach, DTM is a top-down hierarchical approach to co-design. HWID is compared to DTM and ADR in Table 2.6. More socio-technical design approaches such as Activity Theory (Clemmensen et al., 2016), user-centered design for organizations (Cajander, 2010), HCI-oriented actor network theory (Fuchsberger et al., 2014), sociomaterial design (Bjørn & Østerlund, 2014), and more are perhaps related and can be added to the comparison.

Furthermore, in socio-technical HCI design approaches sketches and prototypes may be understood and used in multiple ways. Table 2.7 provides more details on these two types of relation artefacts across the HWID-related socio-technical HCI design approaches from Tables 2.5 and 2.6.

From Table 2.7 it should be noticed that in HWID sketches and prototypes are not just terminology-establishing devices or first examples of finished systems, means to speculate about the future and explore experiences in situ, means to do co-design and dig out novel concepts, novel examples of theory applied, or visions for stakeholder reviews; rather in HWID sketches and prototypes are connectors, linkers, relation builders, mergers, etc. This also goes for relation artefacts that represent user needs and organizational problems, and evaluations and interventions. This 'relational' perspective on socio-technical HCI design is what characterizes HWID.

Directions of determinism in socio-technical approaches to HCI

A final comparative note is needed to point out that the socio-technical HCI design approaches differ in the directions of the socio-technical interventions. Sometimes technology is assumed to lead to social changes, sometimes social changes are assumed to change technology, for example (Seaver, 2018). The HWID platform, like the other approaches, can support any of the directions for socio-technical interventions, as shown by the series of HWID working conferences HWID2006, 2009, 2012, 2015, 2018 (Abdelnour Nocera et al., 2015; Barricelli et al., 2018; Campos et al., 2013; Clemmensen et al., 2006; Katre et al., 2010) and HWID2021 (in preparation). For example, it went in the direction of technological determinism in 2006, from *Technical->Social:* Designing for Human Work, HWID2006, and social determinism, from *Social->Technical:* Work Analysis and HCI, HWID2012. In fact, HWID is agnostic about the direction. In contrast, the other socio-technical HCI design approaches tend to favor one direction over the other. PBD is mostly interested in the effects of new technology on the users in the sense of how they appropriate the

Table 2.6 Comparison of HWID and ADR and DTM

Approach	Notion of context(s)	Socio-technical problem definition and psychological need-finding	Socio-technical sketching alternatives	Socio-technical hypothesis prototyping	Socio-technical intervention (evaluation)	Contrasting theories (beyond the approaches in this table)	Example literature
HWID Human work interaction Design	Wider organizational, regional, national, cultural, social, technological, political contexts	Multiple interrelated notions of needs and problems: Organizational problem definitions, Workers' need findings, Persona creations	Multiple sketching on different organizational levels: Interaction patterns, Collaborative (team) sketches, Workflows	Individual and collective UX prototypes: Organizational action hypotheses, Prototyped worker experiences, Field evaluations, and UX tests	Sociomaterial focus with Interaction interoperability checks, Digital legacy interventions, & Organizational strategy alignment	Activity theory, actor network theory, critical theory	Abdelnour-Nocera and Clemmensen (2019) Clemmensen (2011a, b)
ADR Action design research	Organizational and system development context	Organizational problem definition, no explicitly employee or customer need-finding	Sketching not important	Build and evaluate prototypes, focus can be on organization or on IT system	Evaluation depends on IT artefact, focus on generating design theory	Design Science, Action Research	Sein et al. (2011), Sein and Rossi (2019)
DTM Design thinking management	Organizational and management context	Organizational problem definition and employee and customer needs are the same	Expert sketching for and with users; purpose to ideate a novel solution	Organizational prototypes, prototypes are the primary driver for change and vessel for management	UX evaluation, focus is on management goals for change	Resistance towards change, Waterfall system development, interaction design	Gruber et al. (2015) Kolko (2015)

Table 2.7 Examples and use of sketches and prototypes in socio-technical HCI design approaches

	Sketches, examples	Typical use of sketches	Prototypes, examples	Typical use of prototypes
HWID Human Work Interaction Design	Freehand drawings or low-fidelity prototypes that connect work analysis and interaction design	Creates alternative version of 'relation artefacts' to explore alternative solutions	Sociomaterial local solutions, with holistic patterns of relations to human work and interaction design	Work place simulations to test 'relation artefacts' and relation-patterns' validity
PBD Practice-Based Design	Working on the artefact-exploring design ideas that could work in the problematic present situation	Create artefact's functional language 'vocabulary'	Working with the artefact—Mature, industry-level prototypes, accepted by companies into daily operation	Ethnographic studies of companies and workers appropriation of mature functional prototypes
ED Experience Design	Early prototypes/concepts of experience supporting designs (e.g., experimental vignettes with scenarios)	Explore non-existent future technology scenarios and contexts	Functional prototypes	In situ explorations and other design fictions role-plays to explore and test experience designs
DT Design tensions	Not important to visually brainstorm solutions (due theory-driven approach)	Rapid prototyping with toolkits recommended, sketching as part of co-design	Design concept-driven low, mid, hi-fi prototypes	Focus is not on the prototypes, but on insightful concepts underlying the prototypes
ADR Action Design Research	Design ideas (alpha prototypes) for existing or new systems, based on domain theory	Create theory ingrained artefacts	Build and evaluate medium mature (beta) prototypes	Create ensemble IT artefact
DTM Design Thinking Management	What if we do this? – visualizations/Post it notes	Synthesize and frame-Gallery/showroom discussions	How can we achieve this? – paper prototypes	Vision and opportunity reviewing with stakeholders

technology, which is a weak version of technological determinism. ED starts 100% with the human needs and thus is a good example of social determinism. DTs appear to use a two-directedness exactly to point out design tensions and requirement for design compromises or rather, for work interaction design ambidexterity.

2.7 About the Core of HWID

The dangerous animal that we study

The white rat in the laboratory studies of the HCI in 1980ties was word processing (Card et al., 1983), while the current much more wild animal (a white tiger?) of HCI is human collaborations with algorithms. These can be found in American and Chinese surveillance capitalism (Landwehr et al., 2019; Zuboff, 2015), in the German-European object-relation-AI-society (Denner, 2019), and more places. The terminology varies with geographical parts of the world and with stakeholder groups involved. In Europe, Industry 4.0 and smart manufacturing including use of robots and AI is a preferred terminology in management and politics, while the term cyber-physical systems are used in engineering and computer science to refer to autonomous systems involving AI and robotics. In this book, we refer to human collaboration with automation with examples of algorithms, AI, robots, cyber-physical systems, and other 'smart' artefacts for human work. This is the white rat, or since HCI has (mostly) left the lab and do studies in the field rather, the wild animal that we study in this book.

Our main example of human-automation collaboration is factory workers' collaboration with collaborative robots (smaller industrial robots), as HWID here can contribute with worker-centric theory and actions in the tradition of HCI's end-user focus. The example given in the introduction of was situated in the context of a regional development project that aimed to improve the digital capabilities of SMEs in the Capital Region of Denmark through training activities in individual companies. The training activities were tailored to fit the needs and digital capabilities of the individual companies and their employees. The participants in the project included 18 of the Capital Region's companies, trade unions, employer associations, and educational institutions. The companies came from sectors such as construction, finance, product development, and small-scale production. The training programs included AI-based financial advice, data mining, collaborative robots, and other forms of manufacturing automation.

Factory workers' collaboration with collaborative robots are themselves socio-technical phenomena reaching out to technological tools (human-machine interfaces, machine learning algorithms, control logics, etc.) and to social groups (designers, vendors, suppliers, regulators, politicians, etc.), which includes collaboration with various enterprises and government entities, and in a yet wider sense collaboration with other design entities on a global scale (Light et al., 2017). The responsibilities of these many 'design' entities go far beyond just the designer's responsibility for the end-user experience. Companies with established networks of suppliers often take responsibilities for job creation and development of local and global economies with introduction of new kind of automations, for example, autonomous cars. Business studies of for example supply chain management and social studies of technology shed light on positive and negative aspects of design enterprises and governments' contribution to socio-technical automation. These perspectives are not outside the scope of this book; however, we treat them by discussing them when relevant and from the perspective of socio-technical HCI design psychology.

Examples of workers' collaboration with collaborative robots should be associated with ideas of co-constructing technology and users and of designing your significant other (Wärnestål et al., 2014; Woolgar, 1990). This implies that what workers mean by collaborative robots are evolving and what collaborative robots threat as workers are also evolving. In addition, the idea of designing (or re-creating) your significant others based on past interactions with your mother, father, partner, etc., in your current collaborators (which could be collaborative robots and co-workers) stems from social psychology (Andersen & Baum, 1994). Though less well known in HCI, the idea of designing your significant other points to how the individual workers' psychology actively shapes the collaborative robot and the co-workers. Most radical in this regard is perhaps the idea of a psychological contract—implicit and subjective beliefs regarding a reciprocal exchange agreement—with AI, robots, and IoT environments (Bankins & Formosa, 2020). Thus, HWID may be thought of as designing artefacts that concern reciprocal exchange agreements between workers and interaction designs.

Courageous designers

"I was really afraid of coming here today, of participating in this..." Ph.D. student participant in a workshop about socio-technical HCI design, Germany 2019.

In socio-technical HCI design there is an obligation to be aware of inner life. HCI researchers are happy to talk about the emotions of users using interactive systems, as evident by their widespread use of the UX concept. They are perhaps less open when it comes to talking about the emotions of researchers and designers designing interactive systems (Moncur, 2013). However, being aware of your inner life and emotions as a designer and researcher was originally required by the Tavistock socio-technical approach to design. Because many of the original members were psychiatrists, all early members of Tavistock Institute's staff were required to undergo psychoanalysis (Mumford, 2000). Their idea was that they had to understand themselves before they could assist with the problems of others. They were also concerned with practical use of their work, hence action research. A good example of the Tavistock approach is John Bowlby's attachment theory about children's attachment to parents. When in Tavistock around 1950 Bowlby created this theory by combining psychoanalytic thinking about need fulfillment (psychoanalysts and learning theorists argued that babies become attached to their mothers (parents) because they feed them and fulfill the babies' other basic needs (Bretherton, 2003) and (control) systems psychology of cybernetically controlled behavioral systems organized as plan hierarchies; he thus replaced psychoanalytic concepts of drive and instincts with the contemporary

TOTE (test-execute-test-exit) models of human psychology (Miller et al., 1960).[4,5] Adding to that, his colleague Margaret Ainsworth innovated methods and instruments for doing empirical work such as ethnography, field surveys, and projective testing, and in this showed great personal courage in focusing on sensitive personal experiences in face of public resistance (Bretherton, 2003). She is also to be credited for the idea of the importance of secure attachments in the family for the ability to muster the courage to explore the unfamiliar, which she brought in from her earlier work on security (Bretherton, 1992). Together they pushed the enlargement of child psychology to become child-parent psychology and later family psychology, obviously pointing out that the whole of the family is larger than the individual child's and parent's mental imageries and impacting societies' view of human development.[6] Bowlby and Ainsworth's attachment theory is today used in HCI to explain peoples attachment to their mobile phones (Meschtscherjakov et al., 2014), and it is of key importance to future research into human workplace collaboration with AI (Bankins & Formosa, 2019).

Furthermore, at Tavistock at the same time of Bowlby and Ainsworth were Eric Trist and Bamforth (1951), who first publicly talked about socio-technical design (Emery, 1959). Thus the combination of psychoanalytic ideas with systems psychology's ideas of system equilibrium to focus on psychological health and workers' well-being helped created socio-technical design (Trist & Bamforth, 1951). It appears that the requirement to self-reflect merge with systems psychology in many ways in the past and the future of the socio-technical design approach, from the idea of psychoanalytic self-reflection in practical action research, the whole (psychological system) is greater than its parts (individual psychologies), the wish to think about changes in society, and to how design may be the key to humanity's future. Hence, in the new millennium, we have entered a new need for planetary system equilibrium—most clearly expressed in the climate change—and as designers we should reflect on how psychological processes are part of a future view of culture as a tool that humans use to design their world(s) in the emerging anthropocenic age (Kashima, 2016).

Few in HCI appear to be aware that they need to courageous understand themselves to do design for others, or even acknowledge that they may have 'blind spots' in their design. The need for self-reflection is however acknowledged by humanistic HCI (Bardzell & Bardzell, 2016), intersectionality HCI (Schlesinger, Edwards, & Grinter, 2017), research on HCI and sex (Kannabiran et al., 2018), and potentially by HCI's dealing with other topics that people often look away from such as racism and politics (Hong & Williams, 2019). Most extreme is perhaps the views of the proponents for a humanistic HCI (Bardzell & Bardzell, 2016), who argue that it takes an 'expert' in

---

[4] Attachment theory is today used in HCI to explain people's attachment to their mobile phones.

[5] Miller wrote the famous paper about 7+-2 items in short term memory that has been used so much in HCI for menu design.

[6] HCI today is often criticized for being too much focused on the technical parts and missing the greater picture of for example sustainable design (Abdelnour-Nocera, Clemmensen, Hertzum, Singh, & Singh, 2019; Eriksson et al., 2016).

self knowing to be a designer. In addition, the call for self-reflection is also found in information systems where the notion of self-reflection and know-thy-self has a long tradition in the humanity-oriented IS research (Kroeze, 2019), such as the IS software development paradigm of 'neohumanism'/emancipatory system development (Hirschheim & Klein, 1989). All of these authors complain that not everyone sees the need for self-reflections, and they define the(ir) need for self-reflection in contrast to a larger segment of less self-interested, mainstream design approaches (Bardzell & Bardzell, 2016; Hirschheim & Klein, 1989; Hong & Williams, 2019; Kannabiran et al., 2018; Kroeze, 2019; Schlesinger et al., 2017). HWID is no exception to this, and it also calls for self-reflection as a designer.

An exception is a research on ethics of HCI design that suggests that self-reflection is a must for everyone doing HCI design (Steen, 2013), and that courage, in the form of risk taking and battling in the face of seemingly impossible conditions, is important to 'moral creativity' in science and engineering (Martin, 2006). Virtue ethics, which emphasizes each individual person's character and dispositions, thoughts and feelings, and each individual's specific choices and actions in specific situations, might be important to participatory aspects of socio-technical HCI design. Virtue ethics focuses on people's positive dispositions and on ways to improve one's practices (Steen, 2013). Such dispositions as cooperation, curiosity, creativity, empowerment, and reflexivity have been shown to be important to participatory design (Steen, 2013). The point is that everyone who participate in socio-technical (participatory) design needs to exhibit and exercise such positive dispositions. Perhaps for people in leadership roles who creates conditions for others, self-reflection is in particular important. In a way, the disposition to share power with other designers and with current and future users and in general seek to empower other people and let go of control in the design process is what is meant by courageous design.

In socio-technical HCI design, a disposition towards courage may be critical when trying to support non-expert designers' empowerment, as practitioners sometimes need to challenge people (e.g., management) who are more powerful and senior than themselves (Kelly, 2018). Designers know this from practice but it is perhaps only recently that it has been put into words and scientific papers. At least some design students are courageous enough to admit that doing socio-technical HCI design requires courage in various forms; Stam and Boon, (2018) report that in a design student participatory design project with physiotherapists courage in two forms were required by the designer. The first was bravery of overcoming of fear of not being perceived as being professional enough, and the second was vitality or the courage to engage with participants in activities full of energy and excitement. Coming back to the citation of the Ph.D. student who at the beginning of this chapter expressed her fears of participating in a workshop that required her to participate in design activities, perhaps she would agree with Stam and Boon who argue that *'The first and main thing that a participatory design approach takes is courage'* (Stam & Boon, 2018).

Socio-technical HCI design draws on various concepts of academic research and science ranging from technical sciences to social science and the humanities. It takes the humanistic aspect serious and acknowledges that a full understanding of the social includes contributions from humanities, such as argued to IS by (Kroeze, 2019) and before by (Hirschheim & Klein, 1989) and to HCI by the Bardzells (2016) and others. HWID is a Socio-technical HCI design that takes the H in HCI to require courageous design.

2.8 Summary

The particular take on HWID presented in this book can be summarized as a 'relations' perspective that focuses on the relations between HW and ID, Table 2.8. Fuchsberger et al. (2016) writing about the relations between humans and interactive artefacts argue that it is important how we talk about technology, and we agree with that. Thus note that the HWID 'relation artefacts' are different from the famous notion of 'relational artefact', that is, social robots, that Sherry Turkle studies, e.g., (Turkle et al., 2006). Most obviously, HWID relation artefacts relate the HW with the ID, while Turkle's (2006) relational artefacts are things that people relate to. HWID relation artefacts are simply IT artefacts that relate empirical work analysis and interaction design. The taxonomy of relation artefacts presented in Table 2.8 imposes a certain order in time and space of the design. It has inspiration from aspects of empirical work analysis with focus on people (managers, workers), technical solutions, work tasks, and organizational structures. At the same time, it is inspired by the timing in classic interaction design thinking with phases of requirement analysis, sketching, prototyping, and implementation. However, HWID relation artefacts are more than orders of socio-technical HCI design activities, they are themselves psychological-experience solutions.

From a social science and humanities perspective, human-automation collaboration are socio-technical phenomena that require fundamental research into human work interaction design. This requires further integration of computer engineering and social science and humanities topics in research communities of:

- User Interface (UI) engineering, including design principles (e.g., feedback to give status information such as the Boing MAX case)
- Human-Computer Interaction (HCI), including usability and user experience (e.g., experience of trustworthiness of bodily automation, experiences of living in smart homes), co-design methods with automation as actors (e.g., the next generation of human-drone partnerships), ethical design (e.g., fairness and accountability of data-driven public service systems, gendering, anthropomorphism such as when treating self-driving cars as human-like or designing robot politeness strategies for soliciting help from humans)

Table 2.8 Four types of HWID relation artefacts

Type	Four types of HWID relation artefacts	Explanation
	Key points and directions	
Relation Artefacts Type I: Needs and Problems templates	Organisational problem definitions Workers' needs Persona creations	A movement from the social towards the technical
Relation Artefacts Type II: Socio-Technical Ideation Sketches	Interaction design patterns Collaborative sketches Work flow convergences	A movement from the technical towards the social
Relation Artefacts Type III: Socio-Technical Hypothesis Prototypes	Organizational action hypotheses Prototyped worker experiences UX-at-work field evaluations	A movement from the social towards the technical

(continued)

Table 2.8 (continued)

Type	Four types of HWID relation artefacts	Explanation
	Key points and directions	
Relation Artefacts Type IV: Socio-Technical interventions	Interaction interoperability checks Digital legacy interventions Organisational strategy alignments	A movement from the technical towards the social

- Computer-Supported Cooperative Work (CSCW)—prototyping (e.g., methods for design fiction and electronic prototyping of highly complex systems), appropriation (e.g., design tools for employees' design-in-use of industrial robots), infrastructuring (e.g., integration of autonomous vehicles into public space), awareness (e.g., communicating awareness and intent in autonomous vehicle-pedestrian interaction)
- Information Systems (IS)—organizational adoption and employee acceptance of highly complex, data driven, networked, systems (e.g., mechanisms to protect citizen, customer, and employee privacy and their digital legacy (traces) left in automation, certification of safety critical-medical automation use, and more).

A socio-technical approach to human-automation collaboration would take participatory and co-design approaches seriously in all the above areas and all the way through the lifecycle of an artefact, but it is still unknown how to do that. A way to begin doing that is to have an open mind about how to link the social and the technical. To this purpose, we will dig out four types of 'relation artefacts' in the next four chapters, Table 2.8. The relation artefacts are building blocks in HWID research, practice, and policy projects. The sequence of relation artefacts is common to design process stages and as is also common, it can in principle begin with any of the relation artefacts. Each relation artefact can even be treated as a single design project.

The relation artefacts Type I-IV are presented in the following Chaps. 3–6 with one relation artefact Type per chapter. The sequence suggested in Table 2.8 makes sense in many projects, which suggests that the four chapters should be read in same sequence. The chapters may however also be read individually, as some project will focus on one of the types of relation artefacts, for example, focus on organizational problems and worker needs (Chap. 3), sketching for work (Chap. 4), prototyping action hypotheses (Chap. 5), or intervention/evaluation (Chap. 6).

References

Abdelnour-Nocera, J., & Clemmensen, T. (2019). Theorizing about socio-technical approaches to HCI. In B. R. Barricelli, V. Roto, T. Clemmensen, P. Campos, A. Lopes, F. Gonçalves, & J. Abdelnour-Nocera (Eds.), *Human Work Interaction Design. Designing Engaging Automation* (pp. 242–262). Cham: Springer International Publishing.

Abdelnour-Nocera, J., Clemmensen, T., Hertzum, M., Singh, D., & Singh, V. V. (2019). Socio-technical HCI for ethical value exchange: Lessons from India. *International Conference on Social Implications of Computers in Developing Countries*, pp. 229–240. Springer.

Abdelnour-Nocera, J., Dunckley, L., & Hall, P. (2005). Reconfiguring producers and users through human-work interaction. In *Proceedings of the workshop: Describing Users in Context—Perspectives on Human-Work Interaction, at the INTERACT 2005, Rome, Italy,* pp. 27–33.

Abdelnour-Nocera, J., Oussena, S., & Burns, C. (2015). *Human work interaction design of the smart university.* https://doi.org/10.1007/978-3-319-27048-7_9.

Abdelnour Nocera, J., Barricelli, B. R., Lopes, A., Campos, P., & Clemmensen, T. (Eds.). (2015). *Human work interaction design. Work Analysis and Interaction Design Methods for Pervasive and Smart Workplaces.* https://doi.org/10.1007/978-3-319-27048-7.

Akbar, F., Bayraktaroglu, A. E., Buddharaju, P., Da Cunha Silva, D. R., Gao, G., Grover, T., ... & Pavlidis, I. (2019). Email makes you sweat: Examining email interruptions and stress using thermal imaging. *Proceedings of the 2019 CHI Conference on Human Factors in Computing Systems*, 1–14.

Andersen, S. M., & Baum, A. (1994). Transference in Interpersonal Relations: Inferences and Affect Based on Significant-Other Representations. *Journal of Personality, 62*(4), 459–497. Retrieved from https://doi.org/10.0.4.87/j.1467-6494.1994.tb00306.x.

Bankins, S., & Formosa, P. (2020). When AI meets PC: exploring the implications of workplace social robots and a human-robot psychological contract. *European Journal of Work and Organizational Psychology, 29*(2), 215–229.

Bannon, L., Bardzell, J., & Bodker, S. (2018). Reimagining participatory design. *Interactions, 26*(1), 26–32. https://doi.org/10.1145/3292015.

Bannon, L. J. (1991). *From human factors to human actors. book chapter in Greenbaum, J. & Kyng, M.(Eds.) Design at Work: Cooperative Design of Computer Systems (pp. 25–44).* Hillsdale: Lawrence Erlbaum Associates.

Bardzell, J., & Bardzell, S. (2016). Humanistic HCI. *Interactions, 23*(2), 20–29.

Barricelli, B. R., Roto, V., Campos, P., Clemmensen, T., Karvonen, H., Gonçalves, F., ... & Lopes, A. G. (Eds.). (2018). *Proceedings of Human-Work Interaction Design (HWID'18)—Designing Engaging Automation. IFIP working conference in Espoo, Finland, 20.-21.8.2018. [forthcoming].* Springer Berlin Heidelberg.

Bjørn-Andersen, N., & Clemmensen, T. (2017). The shaping of the Scandinavian Socio-Technical IS research tradition: Confessions of an accomplice. *Scandinavian Journal of Information Systems, 29*(1).

Bjørn, P., & Østerlund, C. (2014). *Sociomaterial-Design: Bounding technologies in practice.* Springer.

Blomberg, J., & Karasti, H. (2013). Reflections on 25 years of ethnography in CSCW. *Computer Supported Cooperative Work: CSCW: An International Journal, 22,* 373–423. https://doi.org/10.1007/s10606-012-9183-1.

Blue, S., Shove, E., Carmona, C., & Kelly, M. P. (2016). Theories of practice and public health: understanding (un) healthy practices. *Critical Public Health, 26*(1), 36–50.

Blythe, M. (2014). Research through design fiction: Narrative in real and imaginary abstracts. *Proceedings of the SIGCHI Conference on Human Factors in Computing Systems,* pp. 703–712.

Blythe, M., Andersen, K., Clarke, R., & Wright, P. (2016). Anti-solutionist strategies: Seriously silly design fiction. *Proceedings of the 2016 CHI Conference on Human Factors in Computing Systems,* pp. 4968–4978.

Bretherton, I. (1992). The origins of attachment theory: John Bowlby and Mary Ainsworth. *Developmental Psychology, 28*(5), 759.

Bretherton, I. (2003). Mary Ainsworth: Insightful observer and courageous theoretician. *Portraits of Pioneers in Psychology, 5*, 317–331.

Buchenau, M., & Suri, J. F. (2000). Experience prototyping. *Proceedings of the Conference on Designing Interactive Systems Processes, Practices, Methods, and Techniques—DIS '00*, 424–433. https://doi.org/10.1145/347642.347802.

Burns, C. (2013). *Cognitive work analysis: New dimensions.* https://doi.org/10.1007/978-3-642-41145-8_1.

Button, G., & Sharrock, W. (2009). Studies of Work and the Workplace in HCI: Concepts and Techniques. *Synthesis Lectures on Human-Centered Informatics, 2*(1), 1–96. Retrieved from http://esc-web.lib.cbs.dk/login? url = https://ebookcentral.proquest.com/lib/kbhnhh-ebooks/det ail.action?docID=881122.

Cajander, Å. (2010). *Usability–Who cares?: The introduction of user-centred systems design in organisations* (The Faculty of Science and Technology, Uppsala.). Retrieved from http://www.diva-portal.org/smash/get/diva2:310201/FULLTEXT01.pdf.

Cajander, Å., Larusdottir, M., Eriksson, E., & Nauwerck, G. (2015). Contextual personas as a method for understanding digital work environments. *IFIP Advances in Information and Communication Technology, 468*, 141–152. https://doi.org/10.1007/978-3-319-27048-7_10.

Campos, P., Clemmensen, T., Nocera, J. A., Katre, D., Lopes, A., & Ørngreen, R. (Eds.). (2013). *Human work interaction design. Work Analysis and HCI.* https://doi.org/10.1007/978-3-642-411 45-8.

Campos, P., & Nunes, N. J. (2005). A human-work interaction design approach by modeling the user's work styles. *Describing Users in Context Perspectives on Human-Work Interaction Design*, 44. In [40]

Card, S. K., Moran, T. P., & Newell, A. (1983). *The psychology of human-computer interaction. 1983.* Hillsdale, NJ: Lawrence Erlbaum Associates.

Carroll, J. M. (1997a). Human-computer interaction: Psychology as a science of design. *Annual Review of Psychology, 48*(1), 61. Retrieved from https://doi.org/10.0.4.122/annurev.psych.48.1.61.

Carroll, J. M. (1997b). Human–computer interaction: psychology as a science of design. *International Journal of Human-Computer Studies, 46*(4), 501–522. https://doi.org/10.1006/IJHC.1996.0101.

Clemmensen, T. (2008). *Cultural Usability and Human work Interaction design-techniques that connects: Proceedings from NordiCHI 2008 Workshop Sunday October 19, 2008.*

Clemmensen, T. (2011a). A Human Work Interaction Design (HWID) case study in e-government and public information systems. *International Journal of Public Information Systems, 7*(3).

Clemmensen, T. (2011b). Designing a simple folder structure for a complex domain. *Human Technology: An Interdisciplinary Journal on Humans in ICT Environments.*

Clemmensen, T., Campos, P. F., Katre, D. S., Abdelnour-Nocera, J., Lopes, A., Orngreen, R., & Minocha, S. (2013). CHI 2013 Human Work Interaction Design (HWID) SIG: Past History and Future Challenges. *Conference on Human Factors in Computing Systems—Proceedings, 2013-April*, 537–2540. https://doi.org/10.1145/2468356.2468824.

Clemmensen, T., Campos, P., Orngreen, R., Mark-Pejtersen, A., & Wong, W. (2006). *Human work interaction design: Designing for human work.* Springer Science+Business Media.

Clemmensen, T., Iivari, N., Rajanen, D., & Sivaji, A. (2021). Organized UX professionals. *HWID2021 Unpublished Proceedings*, 1–25. Retrieved from https://www.hwid2021.com/.

Clemmensen, T., Kaptelinin, V., & Nardi, B. (2016). Making HCI theory work: An analysis of the use of activity theory in HCI research. *Behaviour & Information Technology, 35*(8), 608–627. https://doi.org/10.1080/0144929X.2016.1175507.

Clemmensen, T., & Nørbjerg, J. (2019a). (not) Working (with) Collaborative robots in a glass processing factory. *Worst Case Practices Teaching Us the Bright Side.*

Clemmensen, T., & Nørbjerg, J. (2019b). 'Digital Peer-Tutoring'. Early results from a field eval-uation of a 'UX at work'enhancing learning format. In P. Abdelnour Nocera, J., Parmaxi, A., Winckler, M., Loizides, F., Ardito, C., Bhutkar, G., Dannenmann (Ed.), *Beyond Interactions INTERACT 2019 IFIP TC 13 Workshops, Paphos, Cyprus, September 2–6, 2019, Revised Selected Papers.*

Clemmensen, T., Orngreen, R., & Pejtersen, A. M. (2005). Describing Users in Contexts: Perspec-tives on Human-Work Interaction Design. *Workshop Proceedings of Workshop 4, Held in Conjunction with the 10th IFIP TC13 International Conference on Human-Computer Interac-tion. INTERACT 2005, Rom, Italy.*, *5*, 60. Retrieved from http://citeseerx.ist.psu.edu/viewdoc/download?, doi = https://doi.org/10.1.1.123.7265&rep=rep1&type=pdf.

Clemmensen, T., Rajamanickam, V., Dannenmann, P., Petrie, H., & Winckler, M. (2018). *Global thoughts, local designs.* Springer.

Convertino, G., Mentis, H. M., Slavkovic, A., Rosson, M. B., & Carroll, J. M. (2011). Supporting common ground and awareness in emergency management planning: A design research project. *ACM Transactions on Computer-Human Interaction, 18*(4), 22:1–34.

Cross, N. (2001). Designerly ways of knowing: design discipline versus design science. *Design Issues.* https://doi.org/10.1162/074793601750357196.

de Castro Leal, D., Krüger, M., Misaki, K., Randall, D., & Wulf, V. (2019). Guerilla warfare and the use of new (and Some Old) technology: Lessons from FARC's armed struggle in Colombia. *Proceedings of the 2019 CHI Conference on Human Factors in Computing Systems*, 1–12.

Denner, V. (2019). Denner's view Artificial Intelligence in Europe. Retrieved from https://www.bosch.com/stories/denners-view-artificial-intelligence-in-europe/.

Dennis, A. R. (2019). An unhealthy obsession with theory. *Journal of the Association for Information Systems, 20*(9), 13.

Dennis, A. R., Valacich, J. S., & Brown, S. A. (2018). A comment on "is information systems a science?" *Communications of the Association for Information Systems, 43*(1), 14.

Desmet, P., & Pohlmeyer, A. (2013). Positive design: An introduction to design for subjective well-being. *International Journal of Design, 7*(3).

Dimitriadis, Y., Asensio-Pérez, J. I., Hernández-Leo, D., Roschelle, J., Brecha, J., Tatar, D., … & DiGiano, C. (2007). *From socially-mediated to technology-mediated coordination: A study of design tensions using Group Scribbles.*

Eisenmann, T. R., Ries, E., & Dillard, S. (2012). Hypothesis-driven entrepreneurship: The lean startup. *Harvard Business School Entrepreneurial Management Case*, pp. 812–095.

Emery, F. E. (1959). Characteristics of socio-technical systems: The emergence of a new paradigm of work. *ANU/CCE: Canberra.*

Engeström, Y. (1999). Expansive visibilization of work: An activity-theoretical perspective. *Computer Supported Cooperative Work (CSCW), 8*(1), 63–93.

Eriksson, E., Pargman, D., Bates, O., Normark, M., Gulliksen, J., Anneroth, M., & Berndtsson, J. (2016). HCI and UN's Sustainable Development Goals: Responsibilities, barriers and oppor-tunities. *Proceedings of the 9th Nordic Conference on Human-Computer Interaction*, 140. ACM.

Fallman, D. (2003). Design-oriented human-computer interaction. *CHI '03 Proceedings of the SIGCHI Conference on Human Factors in Computing Systems*, 225–232. Ft. Lauderdale, Florida, USA — April 05–10, 2003: ACM.

Frauenberger, C. (2019). Entanglement HCI the next wave? *ACM Transactions on Computer-Human Interaction (TOCHI), 27*(1), 1–27.

Fuchsberger, V., Murer, M., Krischkowsky, A., & Tscheligi, M. (2016). Interaction design labels: concepts, inscriptions, and concealed intentions. *Proceedings of the 2016 ACM Conference on Designing Interactive Systems*, 108–120.

Fuchsberger, V., Murer, M., & Tscheligi, M. (2014). Human-computer non-interaction: the activity of non-use. In *Proceedings of the 2014 companion publication on Designing interactive systems* (pp. 57–60).

Gardien, P., Djajadiningrat, T., Hummels, C., & Brombacher, A. (2014). Changing your hammer: The implications of paradigmatic innovation for design practice. *International Journal of Design, 8*(2). Retrieved from http://www.ijdesign.org/index.php/IJDesign/article/view/1315.

Gibson, J. J. (1977). The theory of affordances. *Hilldale, USA, 1*(2), 67–82.

Gibson, J. J., & Carmichael, L. (1966). *The senses considered as perceptual systems* (Vol. 2). Houghton Mifflin Boston.

Gonçalves, F., Campos, P., & Clemmensen, T. (2015). Human work interaction design: An overview. *IFIP Advances in Information and Communication Technology, 468*, 3–19. https://doi.org/10.1007/978-3-319-27048-7_1.

Gregor, S. (2006). The nature of theory in information systems. *MIS Quarterly*, 611–642.

Gross, T. (2013). Supporting Effortless Coordination: 25 Years of Awareness Research. *Computer Supported Cooperative Work (CSCW), 22*(4), 425–474. https://doi.org/10.1007/s10606-013-9190-x.

Gross, T., Stary, C., & Totter, A. (2005). User-centered awareness in computer-supported cooperative work-systems: Structured embedding of findings from social sciences. *International Journal of Human-Computer Interaction*. https://doi.org/10.1207/s15327590ijhc1803_5.

Gruber, M., De Leon, N., George, G., & Thompson, P. (2015). *Managing by design*. https://doi.org/10.5465/amj.2015.4001.

Grudin, J. (2012). Introduction: A moving target—the evolution of human-computer interaction. *Human-Computer Interaction Handbook: Fundamentals, Evolving Technologies and Emerging Applications*. https://doi.org/10.1201/b11963-1.

Hacker, W. (2003). Action regulation theory: A practical tool for the design of modern work processes? *European Journal of Work and Organizational Psychology, 12*(2), 105–130.

Hammond, J. (2003). *IFIP TC.13 Handbook—Version 3*.

Hancock, J. T., Birnholtz, J. P., Bazarova, N., Guillory, J., Perlin, J., & Amos, B. (2009). Butler Lies: Awareness, deception, and design. *Proceedings of the Conference on Human Factors in Computing Systems—CHI 2009*, 517–526. Boston, MA: ACM.

Harbich, S., & Hassenzahl, M. (2017). User experience in the work domain: A longitudinal field study. *Interacting with Computers*. https://doi.org/10.1093/iwc/iww022.

Hassenzahl, M. (2010). Experience design: Technology for all the right reasons. *Synthesis Lectures on Human-Centered Informatics, 3*(1), 1–95.

Hassenzahl, M., Wiklund-Engblom, A., Bengs, A., Hägglund, S., & Diefenbach, S. (2015). Experience-oriented and product-oriented evaluation: Psychological need fulfillment, positive affect, and product perception. *International Journal of Human-Computer Interaction, 31*(8), 530–544.

Hemmecke, J., & Stary, C. (2018). Informing work interaction design by 3rd generation activity theory. *Interaction Design and Architectures*, (37), 100–129.

Hertzum, M., Singh, V. V., Clemmensen, T., Singh, D., Valtolina, S., Abdelnour-Nocera, J., & Qin, X. (2018). A mobile APP for supporting sustainable fishing practices in alibaug. *Interactions, 25*(3). https://doi.org/10.1145/3194324.

Hirschheim, R. (2019). Against theory: With apologies to Feyerabend. *Journal of the Association for Information Systems, 20*(9), 8.

Hirschheim, R., & Klein, H. K. (1989). Four paradigms of information systems development. *Communications of the ACM, 32*(10), 1199–1216.

Hong, J.-W., & Williams, D. (2019). Racism, Responsibility and autonomy in HCI: Testing perceptions of an AI agent. *Computers in Human Behavior*.

Kannabiran, G., Ahmed, A. A., Wood, M., Balaam, M., Tanenbaum, J. G., Bardzell, S., & Bardzell, J. (2018). Design for sexual wellbeing in HCI. *Extended Abstracts of the 2018 CHI Conference on Human Factors in Computing Systems*, W09. ACM.

Kashima, Y. (2016). Culture and psychology in the 21st century: Conceptions of culture and person for psychology revisited. *Journal of Cross-Cultural Psychology, 47*(1), 4–20.

Katre, D., & Gupta, M. (2011). Expert usability evaluation of 28 state government web portals of India. *International Journal of Public Information Systems, 7*(3).

Katre, D., Orngreen, R., Yammiyavar, P., Clemmensen, T. (Eds.) (2010). Human work interaction design: usability in social, cultural and organizational contexts *Second IFIP WG 13.6 Conference*, *HWID* 2009, Pune, India, October 7–8, 2009, Revised Selected Papers. https://www.springer.com/gp/book/9783642117619.

Kelly, J. (2018). Towards ethical principles for participatory design practice. *CoDesign*, 1–16.

Klapperich, H., Laschke, M., & Hassenzahl, M. (2018). The Positive Practice Canvas: Gathering Inspiration for Wellbeing-Driven Design. *NordiCHI*, 74–81. https://doi.org/10.1145/3240167.3240209.

Kolko, J. (2015). Design thinking comes of age. *Harvard Business Review*, *93*(9), 66–71. Retrieved from https://hbr.org/2015/09/design-thinking-comes-of-age.

Kroeze, J. H. (2019). Is the Philosophy of the information systems discipline informed by the arts and humanities? *Phronimon, 20*, 30 p.

Kuijer, L., Jong, A. de, & Eijk, D. van. (2013). Practices as a unit of design: An exploration of theoretical guidelines in a study on bathing. *ACM Transactions on Computer-Human Interaction (TOCHI)*, *20*(4), 1–22.

Kusunoki, D. S., Sarcevic, A., Weibel, N., Marsic, I., Zhang, Z., Tuveson, G., & Burd, R. S. (2014). Balancing design tensions: Iterative display design to support ad hoc and multidisciplinary medical teamwork. *Proceedings of the SIGCHI Conference on Human Factors in Computing Systems*, 3777–3786.

Lanamäki, A., & Väyrynen, K. (2016). Six issues in which IS and CSCW research communities differ. *COOP 2016: Proceedings of the 12th International Conference on the Design of Cooperative Systems, 23–27 May 2016, Trento, Italy*, 3–19. Springer.

Landwehr, M., Borning, A., & Wulf, V. (2019). The high cost of free services: problems with surveillance capitalism and possible alternatives for IT infrastructure. *Proceedings of the Fifth Workshop on Computing within Limits*, 1–10.

Leontiev, A. N. (1980). *The Development of Mind, including Activity and consciousness*. Marxists Internet Archive Publications.

Light, A., Powell, A., & Shklovski, I. (2017). Design for existential crisis in the anthropocene age. *Proceedings of the 8th International Conference on Communities and Technologies*, 270–279. ACM.

Ludwig, T., Kotthaus, C., Stein, M., Pipek, V., & Wulf, V. (2018). Revive Old discussions! socio-technical challenges for small and medium enterprises within industry 4.0. *Proceedings of 16th European Conference on Computer-Supported Cooperative Work*. https://doi.org/10.18420/ecscw2018_15.

Luff, P., Heath, C., & Sanchez Svensson, M. (2008). Discriminating conduct: Deploying systems to support awareness in organisations. *International Journal of Human-Computer Interaction (IJHCI)*, *24*(4), 410–436.

Martin, M. W. (2006). Moral creativity in science and engineering. *Science and Engineering Ethics*, *12*(3), 421–433.

Meneweger, T., Wurhofer, D., Fuchsberger, V., & Tscheligi, M. (2018). Factory Workers' ordinary user experiences: An overlooked perspective. *Human Technology*, *14*(2), 209–232. https://doi.org/10.17011/ht/urn.201808103817.

Meschtscherjakov, A., Wilfinger, D., & Tscheligi, M. (2014). Mobile attachment causes and consequences for emotional bonding with mobile phones. *Proceedings of the SIGCHI Conference on Human Factors in Computing Systems*, 2317–2326. https://doi.org/10.1145/2556288.2557295.

Miller, G. A., Galanter, E., & Pribram, K. H. (1960). *Plans and the structure of behavior*.

Moncur, W. (2013). The emotional wellbeing of researchers: Considerations for practice. *Proceedings of the SIGCHI Conference on Human Factors in Computing Systems*, 1883–1890. ACM.

Mumford, E. (2000). Socio-technical design: An unfulfilled promise or a future opportunity? In *Organizational and social perspectives on information technology*, pp. 33–46. Springer.

Mumford, E. (2006). The story of socio-technical design: reflections on its successes, failures and potential. *Information Systems Journal, 16*(4), 317–342. https://doi.org/10.1111/j.1365-2575. 2006.00221.x.

Orngreen, R., Pejtersen, A. M., & Clemmensen, T. (2008). Themes in human work interaction design. In *IFIP International Federation for Information Processing* (Vol. 272). https://doi.org/ 10.1007/978-0-387-09678-0_4.

Oulasvirta, A., & Hornbæk, K. (2016). HCI research as problem-solving. *Proceedings of the 2016 CHI Conference on Human Factors in Computing Systems—CHI '16.* https://doi.org/10.1145/ 2858036.2858283.

Parker, S. K., & Grote, G. (2020). Automation, algorithms, and beyond: Why work design matters more than ever in a digital world. *Applied Psychology.*

Pejtersen, A. M., & Noirhomme, M. (2012). *Guidelines for the TC13 on HCI Meeting and TC13 HCI Workshop.*

Rasmussen, J., Pejtersen, A. M., & Schmidt, K. (1990). *Taxonomy for cognitive work analysis.* Citeseer.

Rohde, M., Brödner, P., Stevens, G., Betz, M., & Wulf, V. (2017). Grounded Design—A Praxeological IS Research Perspective. *Journal of Information Technology,* Vol. 32, pp. 163–179. https:// doi.org/10.1057/jit.2016.5.

Schlesinger, A., Edwards, W. K., & Grinter, R. E. (2017). Intersectional HCI: Engaging identity through gender, race, and class. *Proceedings of the 2017 CHI Conference on Human Factors in Computing Systems,* 5412–5427. ACM.

Schrepp, M., Held, T., & Laugwitz, B. (2006). The Influence of Hedonic Quality on the Attractiveness of User Interfaces of Business Management Software. *Interacting with Computers, 18*(5), 1055–1069. https://doi.org/10.1016/j.intcom.2006.01.002.

Seaver, N. (2018). What should an anthropology of algorithms do? *Cultural Anthropology, 33*(3), 375–385.

Sein, Henfridsson, Purao, Rossi, & Lindgren. (2011). Action Design Research. *MIS Quarterly.* https://doi.org/10.2307/23043488.

Sein, M. K., & Rossi, M. (2019). Elaborating ADR while drifting away from its essence: A commentary on Mullarkey and Hevner. *European Journal of Information Systems, 28*(1), 21–25.

Stam, D., & Boon, B. (2018). What you gain and what it takes: a student's reflection on a participatory design project. *Proceedings of the 15th Participatory Design Conference: Short Papers, Situated Actions, Workshops and Tutorial-Volume 2,* 9. ACM.

Steen, M. (2013). Virtues in participatory design: Cooperation, curiosity, creativity, empowerment and reflexivity. *Science and Engineering Ethics, 19*(3), 945–962.

Trist, E. L., & Bamforth, K. (1951). Defences of a work group in relation to the social structure and of coal-getting: An examination of the psychological situation and some social and psychological consequences of the Longwall method technological content of the work system. *Human Relations, 4,* 3–38.

Turkle, S., Taggart, W., Kidd, C. D., & Dasté, O. (2006). Relational artifacts with children and elders: The complexities of cybercompanionship. *Connection Science, 18*(4), 347–361.

Vicente, K., & Pawlak, W. (1994). Cognitive work analysis for the DURESS II system. *Cognitive Engineering Laboratory, Department of Industrial Engineering, University of Toronto, Toronto, Canada CEL,* 3–94.

Volker Wulf, Pipek, V., Randall, D., Rohde, M., Schmidt, K., & Stevens, G. (Eds.). (2018). *Socio-Informatics—A practice-based perspective on the design and use of IT artifacts.* Oxford: Oxford University Press.

Von Alan, R. H., March, S. T., Park, J., & Ram, S. (2004). Design science in information systems research. *MIS Quarterly, 28*(1), 75–105.

Wang, B., Liu, Y., & Parker, S. K. (2020). How does the use of information communication technology affect individuals? A work design perspective. *Academy of Management Annals, 14*(2), 695–725.

Wärnestål, P., Svedberg, P., & Nygren, J. (2014). Co-constructing child personas for health-promoting services with vulnerable children. *Proceedings of the SIGCHI Conference on Human Factors in Computing Systems*, 3767–3776.

Woolgar, S. (1990). Configuring the user: the case of usability trials. *The Sociological Review*, *38*(1_suppl), 58–99.

Wrzesniewski, A., & Dutton, J. E. (2001). Crafting a job: Revisioning employees as active crafters of their work. *Academy of Management Review*, *26*(2), 179–201. https://doi.org/10.5465/AMR.2001.4378011.

Wu, Y., Lyckvi, S., & Roto, V. (2019). What is Fair Shipping, Anyway: Using Design Fiction to Raise Ethical Awareness in an Industrial Context. *CHI 2019*, 436:1–436:13. New York, NY, USA: ACM.

Wulf, V., Müller, C., Volkmar, P., Randall, D., Rohde, M., & Stevens, G. (2015). Practice-Based Computing: Empirically Grounded Conceptualizations Derived from Design Case Studies. In V. Wulf, K. Schmidt, & D. Randall (Eds.), *Designing Socially Embedded Technologies in the Real-World* (pp. 111–150). https://doi.org/10.1007/978-1-4471-6720-4_7.

Wurhofer, D., Fuchsberger, V., Meneweger, T., Moser, C., & Tscheligi, M. (2015). Insights from user experience research in the factory: What to consider in interaction design. In J. A. Nocera, B. Barricelli, A. Lopes, P. Campos, & T. Clemmensen (Eds.), *HWID2015 -Human Work Interaction Design. Work Analysis and Interaction Design Methods for Pervasive and Smart Workplaces. IFIP Advances in Information and Communication Technology* (Vol. 468, pp. 39–56). https://doi.org/10.1007/978-3-319-27048-7_3.

Wynn, E., & Hult, H. V. (2019). Qualitative and Critical Research in Information Systems and Human-Computer Interaction: Divergent and Convergent Paths. *Foundations and Trends® in Information Systems*, *3*(1–2), 1–233. https://doi.org/10.1561/2900000014.

Zhang, F., & Parker, S. K. (2019). Reorienting job crafting research: A hierarchical structure of job crafting concepts and integrative review. *Journal of Organizational Behavior*. https://doi.org/10.1002/job.2332.

Zimmerman, J., Forlizzi, J., & Evenson, S. (2007). Research through design as a method for interaction design research in HCI. *Conference on Human Factors in Computing Systems—Proceedings*, 493–502. https://doi.org/10.1145/1240624.1240704.

Zuboff, S. (2015). Big other: surveillance capitalism and the prospects of an information civilization. *Journal of Information Technology*, *30*(1), 75–89.

Chapter 3
Relation Artefacts Type I

Abstract This chapter touches on the perhaps most crucial and difficult part of HWID, of finding psychological needs from both an interaction design and a work analysis point of view. The chapter presents three sub-types of relation artefacts Type I: organizational problems, worker needs, and contextual personas. It further develops a terminology that acknowledges that computer algorithms (e.g., robots, work automation) are themselves socio-technical systems that embed designers, vendors, suppliers, and managers, even when their primary users and collaborators are workers. Finding human and non-human actors' psychological needs is not a well-defined procedure, but an interpretative act that requires courage and will, and the chapter ends with a summary of how this is done.

Keywords Human work interaction design · Relation artefacts · Psychological needs · Organizational problems · Contextual personas

Finding user needs is central for HCI (Carroll & Campbell, 1989). In socio-technical HCI design, finding users' needs involves both social and technical design. In HWID, this is done by designing relation artefacts Type I. This may begin with designing the social and organizational problem, proceed with the designing the psychological worker (user) needs, and end up with the technical design of the user persona, Fig. 3.1.

This chapter illustrates the design movements from the social to the technical with these three sub-types of relation artefacts Type I.

To help to understand the sub-types and to follow the structure of the chapter Table 3.1 presents the key characteristics of each of the three sub-types.

Below we unfold and discuss the relation artefact Type I sub-types.

Fig. 3.1 Relation artefacts
Type I

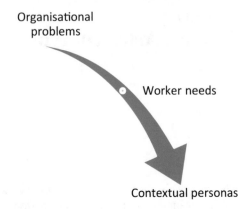

Table 3.1 Overview of key characteristics of relation artefact Type 1 sub-types

Relation artefact Type I sub-types	Key characteristics
1. Organizational problem definitions	An IS organizational (management) problem definition, but one that prepares for a HCI individual (worker) problem definition. It can be applied to mundane everyday organizational problems, not only wicked problems. It includes acknowledging that the capabilities of (some) IT artefacts are coequal with the people and the organizational and social contexts in meeting business needs
2. Workers' needs	User needs translate into worker needs in work contexts. Workers are co-responsible for identifying their own and their colleagues' user needs, including non-human actors. Workers' customization of their work systems (algorithms, devices, etc.) is a central way to actively identify their own and their colleagues' user needs
3. Persona creations	Personas embed the organizational design problems and the employee needs identifications in interaction design activities. Contextual personas are created by analyzing collected, interpreted, and focused data with a theoretical model of work. HWID opts for psychological need- and social metaphor-based contextual personas

3.1   Organizational Problem Definitions

Relevance of HWID for Organizations

While human–computer interaction (HCI) design expands individual human problem solving (Oulasvirta & Hornbæk, 2016), and Information System (IS) design extends the boundaries of organizational capabilities (Von Alan et al., 2004), the relevance of HWID design for organizations is that it points out that organizational capabilities include expanding the individual worker's problem solving. Thus, the HWID organizational problem definition focus on worker-experienced issues with current intellectual and computational tools for work and organizational activities that service the research and practitioner communities and their clients. The organizational problem definition should help constructing novel worker (employee, customer, user, etc.) interactions for organizational IT in a two-way process. HWID is slightly different from mainstream HCI and IS in that it begins with the IS organizational problem definition but with an eye to the HCI individual problem definition.

The relevance of HWID varies over time. HWID's socio-technical interventions emerge from the designers' temporary engagement of stakeholders in relations between human work and interaction design. It sees the notion of design itself and design practices as in flux, since new design contexts and practices challenge old ideas about what design is, and since digital information technologies and the globalization indicates a general shift from design of the material to the immaterial (McKay, Marshall, & Hirschheim, 2016). In contrast to HCI design that provides IT constructions as solutions to specific interaction research problems at a point in time (Oulasvirta & Hornbæk, 2016) and from ADR/design science that provides types of justified IT artefacts in response to organizational management problems (Sein, Henfridsson, Purao, Rossi, & Lindgren, 2011; Von Alan et al., 2004), HWID stems from designers' somewhat loose and wavering engagement with stakeholders in relations between human work and interaction design.[1] It can begin at any time in an organization, self-initiated by any worker at any level in the organization. It may never end but its relevance may vary as various relation artefacts are produced. Thus, HWID can be about both local initiatives optimizing (the use of) existing systems and about developing and introducing new systems. For new systems, relation artefacts Type I will be seen by stakeholders as very relevant, as finding the users' needs is paramount for new systems. The general rule here is that relevance is highest for relation artefacts Type I and is gradually less with Type IV as being just part of the work (Type IV becoming so sociomaterial, so embedded in everyday activities, that it makes no sense to argue that it is more or less relevant). Furthermore, the movement from the social to the technical in relation to artefacts Type I and III would by organizational oriented employees mostly be seen as ensuring relevance, while the movement from the technical to the social in Type II and IV would be seen by technical specialists as ensuring relevance.

The relevance of HWID is local. It sees design as localized, though still universal. The ambition is to take the high ground between on one hand producing universal knowledge across projects and on the other hand producing local contextual knowledge. Studies of engineering knowledge and other professional knowledge have indicated both differences and overlap between academic and practical knowledge of a topic; for example, for a process control problem a professor in process control theory may explain the problem by referring to causal chains that identify causes

---

[1] The looseness towards what is the object of the project is the most similar attribute of the socio-technical HWID approach with so-called 'sociomaterial' design approaches, see for example (Bjørn & Østerlund, 2014).

to problems, while an industrial process control engineer may spend 90% of their explanation to describe contextual factors for the problem (in Danish: (Clemmensen, 1998), for similar examples from the medical domain that explains how naturalistic decision-making approaches focuses on real-world settings and places a premium on the descriptive adequacy of models, see (Patel, Kaufman, & Arocha, 2002)). It matters being local (both as researcher and as other stakeholders) when it comes to contextual understanding. This is not unique to HWID but shared with other socio-technical HCI design approaches. For example, Action Design Research (ADR) also creates tools as IT artefacts for solving specific organizational information problems, based on relevant (socio-technical psychological) behavioral science theory, by aligning action design research with real-world production experience. HWID like ADR and other socio-technical HCI design approaches is action design that becomes relevant by producing answers to specific organizations' concrete local problems.

The rigor, then, if wanted, is in the socio-technical HCI design theorizing. The intellectual tools that are produced are local theories regarding relation artefacts and their place in concrete projects. These project 'gestalts' can be published in research papers that explain the tools development and use. Furthermore, as a platform for socio-technical theorizing, HWID produces locally valorized relation artefacts Type I that should be important to national and regional research funding agencies, organizational IT consultants, and policymakers.

Beyond Wicked Problems

The understanding of socio-technical HCI design as the solving of organizational problems (Von Alan et al., 2004) needs translation and redefinition to be valid for HWID that rather sees design as socio-technical interventions in the organization. HWID is like organizational design science research focused on the creation of innovations that define the ideas, technical capabilities, practices, and products through which the analysis, design, implementation, management, and use of information systems can be effectively and efficiently accomplished; it will, however, add a focus on humans and their psychology. For example, action design research (ADR) (Sein, Purao, & Lindgren, 2011) has four stages, of which the first is problem definition. Problem definition in ADR is focused not only on organizational intervention but on creating academic knowledge ingrained in IT artefacts. This strong focus on academic knowledge about organizational problems is appropriate if the project focus on contributing to academic IS research. In contrast, the first of HWIDs four types of relation artefacts, relation artefact Type I, is characterized by being psychologically (obvious-to-all-involved) relevant to the organization and less concerned with the long-term academic knowledge contribution to understanding organizations.

Hence, HWID can be applied to solve mundane everyday organizational problems. Some would argue that a design approach is only necessary for wicked problems, because for 'tame' problems the problem-solver has all the necessary information to solve the problem (Von Alan et al., 2004). This is never so for wicked problems— "the formulation of the problem is the problem" (Rittel & Webber, 1973). However, unless the problem definition is seen as identifying a research gap, it is not necessary to classify problems into tame or wicked. Instead, if an organizational problem definition is merely an opening position in a project, it is important that it support stakeholders negotiating about what they see as a problem. Obviously, researchers and their previous literature may be stakeholders in this process too.

Negotiating the Problem Using a Family Metaphor

Participation of human and non-human stakeholders is central for the organizational problem definition. A key question in creating relation artefacts Type I is therefore what is the organizational problem and why is this problem worth solving? Finding the answer to this can be supported by design guidelines, such as those proposed by Von Alan et al. (2004): you should design an IT artifact, it should be relevant to a business problem, it should be rigorously evaluated, you should identify your research contribution, tell clearly which version of action design research that you use, think of design as a search process in a problem environment, and be ready to communicate your findings to both technical people and business people. HWID uses and contributes to these guidelines by pointing out that the design guidelines are for all project stakeholders (participants) to follow, not only for researchers or project owners. Furthermore, in HWID the platform approach means that for each project the distribution of participants may have to be negotiated. Hence which guidelines are important will vary across projects depending on which 'family' of stakeholders that emerges for the specific project.

Negotiating why this problem is worth solving from a socio-technical HCI design research perspective includes acknowledging that the capabilities of (some) IT artefacts are coequal with and interdependent of the people and the organizational and social contexts in meeting business needs. That is, acknowledging the non-human actor argument that both human and non-human actors have programs of action, and that the non-human actors' program (IT artefacts) program for action is to be used in a certain way (Fuchsberger, Murer, & Tscheligi, 2014). Socio-technical HCI design research fosters novel IT artefacts, which then must be respected as actors. HWID is perhaps IT artefact-centric (not technology deterministic) in the same sense that the child is at the center of a family collective, or a family network. It is social relativist, facilitating, open for the accidental enrollment of novel members, for the unexpected qualitative jump in developments coming from the IT artefact.

Pushing the family metaphor for negotiating the organizational problem a bit further, and perhaps too far, HWID may be somewhat unique among socio-technical HCI design approaches in promoting an open version of confidentiality for stakeholders in the design project that supports a conflict-tolerant negotiation of the design problem. Remembering Mumford's chapter in Coal and Conflict with the negotiation machinery (Scott, Mumford, McGivering, & Kirby, 1963), conflict is unavoidable in problem negotiation. While not aiming to being nasty to each other, the usual idea about confidentiality—understood as caring and protecting—is in HWID supplemented with an awareness of negotiations about power, courage, and agency, see also (Baez, 2002) for a discussion of power perspectives on confidentiality that may also apply to design projects.

3.2 Workers' Needs

The requirement for a design-psychological understanding of the organizational problem is illustrated in the notion of design thinking as a management approach that focuses on the individual user experience (Kolko, 2015). Design thinking as a management approach unabashedly defines and solves organizational problems in terms of individual employees' goal alignment with organizational business goals (Kolko, 2015). Slightly in contrast to design thinking management, HWID agrees on meeting business goals as a priority but acknowledges that employees and other stakeholders might have conflicting other needs that also require fulfillment.[2] HWID extends and transforms the negotiated organizational design issue into the identification of hedonic (pleasure), eudaimonic (meaning), and pragmatic (e.g., effectiveness, easy to use) needs of consumers, citizens, and employees of the organization.[3]

Transformation of Organizational Issues into Workers' Psychological Needs

User needs are an age-old key notion of HCI that for work contexts translate into worker needs. In UX research, user needs have been conceptualized as basic psychological needs. Basic psychological needs are, for example, needs for Relatedness (feeling in contact with significant others), Security (feeling safe), Competence (feeling capable and effective), Popularity (feeling liked and respected), Stimulation (feeling pleasure and enjoyment), Autonomy (feeling that you cause your own actions), Meaning (feeling that what you do is meaningful) (Hassenzahl et al., 2010), see also https://hassenzahl.wordpress.com/experience-design-tools/. The extension and transformation of the negotiated organizational design issue (in the previous section) into the identification of employees' basic psychological needs involves contextual and conceptual work. For example, the quality criteria of 'novelty' of an IT artifact is important in organizational design research; often the IT artefact is used and justified as a change agent that brings novelty (Hevner & Chatterjee, 2010). Novelty has here been seen as a distinguishing feature of design and as typical of creativity in the organizational context, where novelty is global novelty in the organization (versus only to the person designing at that instant) (Glanville, 1999). In contrast, in the individual need context, the experience of novelty is always the fulfillment of an individual user's (worker, employee) need for stimulation beyond the expected (Hassenzahl et al., 2010).

---

[2] As illustrated by the focus on facilitating relations, HWID is somewhat similar to the social relativism paradigm of Hirschheim and Klein (1989) that focus on facilitating management-workers collaboration, while design thinking management may fall into their functionalistic paradigm, since design thinking management sees managers as experts (in UX) and focus on workers needs as instruments for managements goals.

[3] Some would argue for a distinction in non-pragmatic parts of UX between hedonic (pleasure) and eudemonic (meaning) user needs. See for example (Mekler & Hornbæk, 2016, 2019).

How to Find the Workers' Psychological Needs?

To find workers' psychological needs, traditional user studies approaches are to do ethnographic observation and iterative formative evaluations of prototypes with only around five users, combined with surveys with need scales. The purpose is to sample rich qualitative data that informs the design process and to compare evaluations across IT artefacts. However, among HCI researchers, there is no consensus about the choice of method for user studies (Pettersson, Lachner, Frison, Riener, & Butz, 2018), or even what user needs can be. Clearly, more work is needed to develop the merger of organizational action design research and individual user experience research; for example, organizational design science research guidelines in regard to novelty could be refined for user-centered IS studies to include user perception of novelty (Djamasbi et al., 2018; Djamasbi, Strong, Wilson, & Ruiz, 2016).

Workers should, however, be co-responsible for identifying their own and their colleagues' user needs (Clemmensen & Nørbjerg, 2019a, 2019b). For example, in a study of job crafting in low usability environments (various stamping machines and industrial robots) (Clemmensen, Hertzum, & Nørbjerg, 2021), manufacturing factory floor workers did not put a lot of effort into seeing their tasks as important and meaningful (which was a surprise to the participating researchers). Instead, they focused on their enjoyable tasks and invested in their relationships with their favorite colleagues. The qualitative data showed that the workers identified needs specific to concrete other workers and that they had constructive ideas about how to solve many of the identified needs (Clemmensen et al., 2021).

Interestingly, workers' ability to find their own and their colleagues' basic psychological needs may also cover non-human colleagues such as robots. It appears that humans' need for a sense of agency towards humanoid others covers also non-human actors, and this tendency is stronger if the human self-initiate engagement with the non-human actor (IT artefact); assembling one's robot enhances the quality of our interaction with it (Sun & Sundar, 2016). Workers may thus tend to have more positive evaluations of both the (industrial) robot and the interaction process if they have themselves been involved in configuring and customizing the robot.

Workers' job crafting of IT artefacts and their use may involve their psychological crafting of IT artefacts that are intended for collaborating with the workers. Sun and Sundar (2016)'s study with university students and a humanoid desktop robot indicated that not only does the robot-user assembling their robot enhance the quality of their interaction with it, they also tend to evaluate the robot and the interaction more positively when they expect the robot to be task-oriented rather than interaction-oriented. However, Sun and Sundar (2016) found that setting expectations of the robot's role as task-oriented generated more positive feelings of the robot so that robot-users better liked the robot and enjoyed their experience with the robot more when they expected the robot to perform a task rather than entertain them. They conclude that individuals may have different expectations of robots with different purposes of use, and that this may imply different attitudes and behaviors towards robots, no matter the robots' actual performance.

Customization for User Needs

Workers' customization of their work systems (algorithms, devices, etc.) is in HWID
a key way to not only meet user needs, but also to actively identify workers' user
needs. As a worker it is a way to learn about yourself, your colleagues, and your
significant other IT artefacts (e.g., robots, word processers, cars). Customization
has the potential to fulfill needs you did not know that you have and to move the
fulfillment of your needs just a bit up a UX-at-work scale.

The idea behind designing for customization is that it improves the user experience (UX) of the system. Wang et al. (2016) proposed that the effects of customization on UX of a smartphone can be theoretically modeled as users' beliefs about the
system object (customization) that influences their attitudes towards the system object
(perceived system usability), which in turn shapes their beliefs (flow) and attitudes
(engagement) towards using the system. They tested this proposition via an experimental study with 50 university students who were asked to perform customization
tasks on a (windows) smartphone, and then instructed to complete a comparison
task aimed at contrasting customized user interface with a standard one. The results
from the comparison indicated that customization positively influenced users' UX
in terms of usability, flow, and engagement, and that the feeling of engagement was
mediated through (perceived) usability and flow. Hence, the study demonstrated that
the impact of system customization on UX can be viewed as a process beginning
with users' beliefs about the system object (customization) to their attitudes towards
the system (perceived system usability) and then concluding with their beliefs (flow)
and attitudes (engagement) towards using the system object.

This kind of cognitive-behavioral models presents an alternative to the basic
psychological needs approach to understanding users' needs, and an alternative that
emphasizes that finding worker needs is not necessarily about measuring innate
universal psychological needs, but can be a user driven, voluntary, self-initiated, and
IT artefact-oriented activity.

3.3   Persona Creations

Finding worker (user) needs is not finished without communicating the outcome with
personas. Personas is an interaction design sub-type of Type 1 relation artefacts, as
they embed the organizational design problems and the employee needs identifications in interaction design activities. A persona is a description of a fictional user
designed with the purpose of letting developers empathize with target users and
grounded in empirical data from user research. It is to be used systematically in the
design process by designers to explore the use of an IT system from the persona's
point of view. The persona method may help both identifying target users and their
needs in usage scenarios and communicate these in interaction design activities
(Madsen & Nielsen, 2009).

The idea of 'contextual personas' is to present a modified version of personas developed to better address the new working life where IT is divergent, embedded, and pervasive (Cajander et al., 2015). Contextual personas are created in three steps: (1) inquiry into the organizational context, (2) analysis with a model of employees at work (e.g., UX-at-work/employee well-being/work stress), and (3) evaluation of persona (with focus group with users from persona's target group). The result is a graphical illustration, often created by a professional graphics designer, of a contextual persona, with specific work-relevant information added, Fig. 3.2., ready for imagining novel interaction designs.

Three Steps of Creating Contextual Personas

The first step of creating contextual personas is to study work in its organizational context. This is sometimes called 'contextual inquiry' (Beyer & Holtzblatt, 1999), and the following activities are usually done: (a) field studies with researchers go and study users who do their tasks and discuss the systems used to solve them; (b) cooperation, the user and researcher work together to understand the user's work, the researcher alternate between observing the user when they work and discuss what the user was doing and why, (c) interpretation, the researcher share their interpretations and insights with the user during the interview, and the user can expand or correct the researcher's understanding, and (d) focus, the researcher focus the conversation on topics that are relevant to the survey.

The second step in creating contextual personas is to analyze the collected, interpreted, and focused data with a theoretical model of work. This is the unique step of contextual personas compared to traditional persona methods. Cajander et al. (2015) proposed to use a work-psychological model of job demands and job resources, Karasek and Theorell's demand-control model of stress at work (Karasek & Theorell, 1990), and they also on the basis of the field study data added more categories about working environment problems. Other models of work and workers' needs relevant to contextual persona creation may be the models behind job crafting and employee well-being, which use the categories of demands and resources (Bakker & Demerouti, 2014; Demerouti, Derks, Lieke, & Bakker, 2014) or focus on the self-initiate aspect of job crafting (Niessen, Weseler, & Kostova, 2016).

The third step in creating contextual personas is to do focus groups with users from the target group that the persona is supposed to stand for, and let these users discuss and reflect upon the presentations made in the personas. After the focus groups, the contextual personas should then be revised according to the reflections made by the target users. Finally, the contextual persona should be refined with text and photos/drawings of the faces of each persona (headshot). Each description will, for example, have one page of text describing the personal life, one day at work, and the goals of the persona. Additionally, work specific information coming from the analysis with the work models should be added. Cajander et al. (2015), for example, created contextual personals with information from Karasek's (1990) work model about the need for control, support, and the demands of the persona that were described. Figure 3.2 shows a similar person but based on job crafting theory.

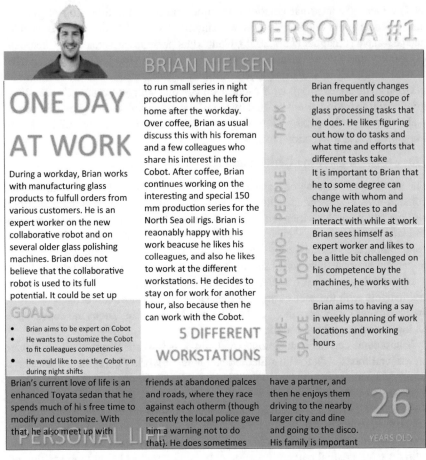

ONE DAY AT WORK

During a workday, Brian works with manufacturing glass products to fulfull orders from various customers. He is an expert worker on the new collaborative robot and on several older glass polishing machines. Brian does not believe that the collaborative robot is used to its full potential. It could be set up

to run small series in night production when he left for home after the workday. Over coffee, Brian as usual discuss this with his foreman and a few colleagues who share his interest in the Cobot. After coffee, Brian continues working on the interesting and special 150 mm production series for the North Sea oil rigs. Brian is reaonably happy with his work beacuse he likes his colleagues, and also he likes to work at the different workstations. He decides to stay on for work for another hour, also because then he can work with the Cobot.

5 DIFFERENT WORKSTATIONS

PERSONA #1

BRIAN NIELSEN

TASK

Brian frequently changes the number and scope of glass processing tasks that he does. He likes figuring out how to do tasks and what time and efforts that different tasks take

PEOPLE

It is important to Brian that he to some degree can change with whom and how he relates to and interact with while at work

TECHNO-LOGY

Brian sees himself as expert worker and likes to be a little bit challenged on his competence by the machines, he works with

TIME-SPACE

Brian aims to having a say in weekly planning of work locations and working hours

GOALS

- Brian aims to be expert on Cobot
- He wants to customize the Cobot to fit colleagues competencies
- He would like to see the Cobot run during night shifts

PERSONAL LIFE

Brian's current love of life is an enhanced Toyata sedan that he spends much of hi s free time to modify and customize. With that, he also meet up with

friends at abandoned palces and roads, where they race against each otherm (though recently the local police gave him a warning not to do that). He does sometimes

have a partner, and then he enjoys them driving to the nearby larger city and dine and going to the disco. His family is important

26

YEARS OLD

Fig. 3.2 An example of a contextual persona. Note the theoretical work model categories on the right side that contextualize the persona into the work situation. Adapted from Cajander et al. (2015), and modified with inspiration from work psychology job crafting theory (Niessen et al., 2016)

Organization- and Worker-Based Contextual Personas

While persona have traditionally been used for improving one particular software system, Cajander et al.'s (2015) contextual personas focus on the worker in the organizational context. The descriptions of these personas are aimed to describe their way of working solving the goals that the software system being developed will support in solving. Contextual personas are not focused on the usage of one system, they are focused on describing the whole context of work, so contextual personas could typically be using 20 software systems for solving various tasks at work. The usage of personas in work contexts may help workers more readily talk about their work situation by being confronted with personas that depict themselves.

Thus Cajander et al. (2015) suggest that contextual personas can be used as trigger material when talking with users about their diverse and multifaceted work and their needs related to that.

Cajander et al.'s (2015) contextual personas, similar to Cooper's personas (Cooper, 2004), Lene Nielsen's story-personas (Madsen & Nielsen, 2009), and Hackos and Redish's (1998) scenarios, all describe the user in the current work situation, though they do it in slightly different ways (for a study of how HCI professionals with different educational backgrounds but similar job positions model the user, see (Clemmensen, 2004)). Cajander et al. point at how Hackos and Redish (1998) describe two types of scenarios, 'task scenarios' that describe the current situation for a persona and 'use scenarios' that describe 'the future use of a computer system' and suggest that contextual personas could also be used to give insights into future work environments. In that case, these 'speculative' personas should be based on data from brainstorming sessions with users, so the descriptions will not be too hypothetical and superficial. Cooper (2004) and more recently Nielsen, Hansen, Stage, and Billestrup (2015), Salminen, Guan, Nielsen, Jung, and Jansen, (2020) have emphasized that personas are grounded in interview data from users and are not based on designers imagination. The contextual personas would need to be complemented with a vision work concerning the future needs and visions of the users as well as other user-centered activities (Cajander et al., 2015).

While drawing on the ideas of Cajander et al.'s (2015) contextual persona of a stepwise approach, focusing on work context, and not being limited to the current work situation, HWID opts for slightly more psychological need and social metaphor-based contextual personas. First, the holistic focus on the work situation is in HWID colored by courageously sensing the individual workers' psychological needs. Second, in contrast to Cajander et al.'s (2015) contextual personas that describe either the current or the future work situation, HWID uses contextual personas in a social relativist organizational approach (family metaphor) with facilitating designers who stay open for the accidental and unexpected coming from the IT artefacts developments.

3.4 Summary

This chapter presented relation artefacts Type I that were defined by having the purpose of socio-technical problem definition and need-finding. Three possible subcategories of relation artefacts type I were introduced: organizational problem definitions, finding workers' needs, and persona creations. These are all IT artefacts that bind the social and the technical together, and thus HWID relation artefacts. Together they present a move from the social to the technical centered around finding user/worker needs. Importantly, they underscore the respect for non-human actors (e.g., robots), the active role of the workers/users, and the importance of considering context for interaction design users in work situations.

Reflecting on the HWID relation artefacts Type I by comparing them to entities in other socio-technical HCI design approaches, Experience Design (ED) seems central. ED is very clear that experience comes before product design. ED puts basic psychological needs as user needs that must be fulfilled by interaction designs to achieve good UX. Overlapping but still a bit different, HWID interprets ED's experience as socio-technical experiences, that is, as not only as fulfillment of universal basic psychological needs but also as organization and workplace problem solving and creation of work identities/work personas. Another important socio-technical HCI design approach for relation artefact Type I is Design Tensions (DTs). DTs research (Gross, 2013) sees design not as problem solving but as ongoing compromises. Similarly, relation artefacts Type I in HWID treats worker/user needs finding, including those of non-human actors, as a continuous active struggle and search that may entail conflicts.

References

Baez, B. (2002). Confidentiality in qualitative research: Reflections on secrets, power and agency. *Qualitative Research, 2*(1), 35–58.

Bakker, A. B., & Demerouti, E. (2014). Job Demands–Resources Theory. In *Wellbeing* (pp. 1–28). https://doi.org/10.1002/9781118539415.wbwell019.

Beyer, H., & Holtzblatt, K. (1999). Contextual design. *Interactions, 6*(1), 32–42.

Bjørn, P., & Østerlund, C. (2014). *Sociomaterial-design: Bounding technologies in practice.* Springer.

Cajander, Å., Larusdottir, M., Eriksson, E., & Nauwerck, G. (2015). Contextual personas as a method for understanding digital work environments. *IFIP Advances in Information and Communication Technology, 468*, 141–152. https://doi.org/10.1007/978-3-319-27048-7_10.

Carroll, J. M., & Campbell, R. L. (1989). Artifacts as psychological theories: The case of human-computer interaction. *Behaviour & Information Technology, 8*(4), 247–256.

Clemmensen, T. (1998). Viden og kompetence i akademisk arbejde: En undersøgelse af ingeniøreres brug af faglig basal viden ved løsning af industrielle problemer. *Psyke & Logos, 19*(2), 559–574.

Clemmensen, T. (2004). Four approaches to user modelling—A qualitative research interview study of HCI professionals' practice. *Interacting with Computers, 16*(4), 799–829. https://doi.org/10.1016/j.intcom.2004.04.009.

Clemmensen, T., & Nørbjerg, J. (2019a). (not) Working (with) collaborative robots in a glass processing factory. *Worst Case Practices Teaching Us the Bright Side.*

Clemmensen, T., & Nørbjerg, J. (2019b). 'Digital Peer-Tutoring'. Early results from a field evaluation of a 'UX at work'enhancing learning format. In P. Abdelnour Nocera, J., Parmaxi, A., Winckler, M., Loizides, F., Ardito, C., Bhutkar, & G., Dannenmann (Eds.), *Beyond interactions INTERACT 2019 IFIP TC 13 workshops*, Paphos, Cyprus, September 2–6, 2019, Revised Selected Papers.

Clemmensen, T., Hertzum, M., & Nørbjerg, J. (2021). *Job crafting in low-usability automation situations: a design case in manufacturing.* Unpublished, in Preparation.

Cooper, A. (2004). *The inmates are running the asylum: Why high-tech products drive us crazy and how to restore the sanity* (Vol. 2). Sams Indianapolis.

Demerouti, E., Derks, D., Lieke, L., & Bakker, A. B. (2014). New ways of working: Impact on working conditions, work–family balance, and well-being. In *The impact of ICT on quality of working life* (pp. 123–141). https://doi.org/10.1007/978-94-017-8854-0_8.

Djamasbi, S., Strong, D., Wilson, E. V., & Ruiz, C. (2016). *Designing and testing user-centric systems with both user experience and design science research principles.*

Djamasbi, S., Galletta, D. F., Nah, F. F.-H., Page, X., Robert Jr., L. P., & Wisniewski, P. J. (2018). Bridging a bridge: Bringing two HCI communities together. *Extended Abstracts of the 2018 CHI Conference on Human Factors in Computing Systems,* W23:1–W23:8. https://doi.org/10.1145/3170427.3170612.

Fuchsberger, V., Murer, M., & Tscheligi, M. (2014). Human-computer non-interaction: the activity of non-use. In *Proceedings of the 2014 companion publication on Designing interactive systems* (pp. 57–60).

Glanville, R. (1999). Researching design and designing research. *Design Issues, 15*(2), 80–91.

Gross, T. (2013). Supporting effortless coordination: 25 years of awareness research. *Computer Supported Cooperative Work (CSCW), 22*(4), 425–474. https://doi.org/10.1007/s10606-013-9190-x.

Hackos, J. T., & Redish, J. (1998). *User and task analysis for interface design* (Vol. 1). New York: Wiley.

Hassenzahl, M., Diefenbach, S., & Göritz, A. (2010). Needs, affect, and interactive products—Facets of user experience. *Interacting with Computers, 22*(5), 353–362. https://doi.org/10.1016/j.intcom.2010.04.002.

Hevner, A., & Chatterjee, S. (2010). Design science research in information systems. In *Design research in information systems: theory and practice* (pp. 9–22). https://doi.org/10.1007/978-1-4419-5653-8_2.

Hirschheim, R., & Klein, H. K. (1989). Four paradigms of information systems development. *Communications of the ACM, 32*(10), 1199–1216.

Karasek, R., & Theorell, T. (1990). *Healthy work: Stress, productivity, and the reconstruction of working life.* New York: Basicbooks.

Kolko, J. (2015). Design thinking comes of age. *Harvard Business Review.*

Madsen, S., & Nielsen, L. (2009). Exploring persona-scenarios-using storytelling to create design ideas. In *IFIP working conference on human work interaction design* (pp. 57–66). Springer.

McKay, J., Marshall, P., & Hirschheim, R. (2016). The design construct in information systems design science. In L. P. Willcocks, C. Sauer, & M. C. Lacity (Eds.), *Enacting research methods in information systems* (Vol. 3, pp. 11–42). https://doi.org/10.1007/978-3-319-29272-4_2.

Mekler, E. D., & Hornbæk, K. (2016). Momentary pleasure or lasting meaning?: Distinguishing eudaimonic and hedonic user experiences. In *Proceedings of the 2016 CHI conference on human factors in computing systems,* 4509–4520. ACM.

Mekler, E. D., & Hornbæk, K. (2019). A framework for the experience of meaning in human-computer interaction. In *CHI conference on human factors in computing systems proceedings (CHI 2019),* May 4–9, 2019, Glasgow, Scotland UK. New York, NY: ACM, Paper no 225. https://doi.org/10.1145/3290605.3300455.

Nielsen, L., Hansen, K. S., Stage, J., & Billestrup, J. (2015). A template for design personas: Analysis of 47 persona descriptions from danish industries and organizations. *International Journal of Sociotechnology and Knowledge Development (IJSKD), 7*(1), 45–61.

Niessen, C., Weseler, D., & Kostova, P. (2016). When and why do individuals craft their jobs? The role of individual motivation and work characteristics for job crafting. *Human Relations, 69*(6), 1287–1313. https://doi.org/10.1177/0018726715610642.

Oulasvirta, A., & Hornbæk, K. (2016). HCI Research as Problem-Solving. In *Proceedings of the 2016 CHI conference on human factors in computing systems—CHI'16.* https://doi.org/10.1145/2858036.2858283.

Patel, V. L., Kaufman, D. R., & Arocha, J. F. (2002). Emerging paradigms of cognition in medical decision-making. *Journal of Biomedical Informatics, 35*(1), 52–75. https://doi.org/10.1016/S1532-0464(02)00009-6.

Pettersson, I., Lachner, F., Frison, A.-K., Riener, A., & Butz, A. (2018). A Bermuda Triangle?: A review of method application and triangulation in user experience evaluation. In: *Proceedings of the 2018 CHI conference on human factors in computing systems* (pp. 461:1–461:16). https://doi.org/10.1145/3173574.3174035.

Rittel, H. W. J., & Webber, M. M. (1973). Dilemmas in a general theory of planning. *Policy Sciences, 4*(2), 155–169.

Salminen, J., Guan, K., Nielsen, L., Jung, S., & Jansen, B. J. (2020). A template for data-driven personas: Analyzing 31 quantitatively oriented persona profiles. In *International conference on human-computer interaction* (pp. 125–144). Springer.

Scott, W. H., Mumford, E., McGivering, 'I. C., & Kirby, J. M. (1963). *Coal and conflict: A study of industrial relations at collieries.* Liverpool University Press.

Sein, H., Purao, R., & Lindgren. (2011). Action design research. *MIS Quarterly.* https://doi.org/10.2307/23043488.

Sun, Y., & Sundar, S. S. (2016). Psychological importance of human agency: how self-assembly affects user experience of robots. In *The eleventh ACM/IEEE international conference on human robot interaction* (pp. 189–196). IEEE Press.

Von Alan, R. H., March, S. T., Park, J., & Ram, S. (2004). Design science in information systems research. *MIS Quarterly, 28*(1), 75–105.

Wang, Y., Tan, C. W., & Clemmensen, T. (2016). Do you get better user experiences when you customize your smartphone?: An experiment with object and behavior-based beliefs and attitudes. In *24th European conference on information systems, ECIS 2016.*

Chapter 4
Relation Artefacts Type II

Abstract This chapter is about relation artefacts type II, which are socio-technical ideation sketches. These are presented as a design movement with three sub-types of Type II from the technical to the social. This begins with interaction design patterns, then do collaborative sketching, and finally converge on new workflows. They are explained with reference to the HWID platform and illustrated with examples of how to sketch interaction and collaboration concepts for workplaces. Novel approaches for supporting designers in sketching algorithms, such as alternative machine learning approaches to the same problem, are discussed. Ways of evaluating sketches from a work analysis and organization perspective are introduced. The chapter ends with a summary of how to sketch alternative solutions for interaction design in a complex work domain. A design case with a simple folder design for a complex work environment that illustrates the relation artefact Type II is presented.

Keywords Human work interaction design · Relational artefacts · Interaction design patterns · Collaborative sketches · Converged workflows

Sketching early and alternative versions of possible solutions to a problem plays a central role in all kinds of design (Buxton, 2010), and is central also in socio-technical ideation sketching, Fig. 4.1. The notion of sketches points to early designs that is more of an idea than a solution and have many rough and undeveloped aspects to it. Importantly, the sketch format is pen and paper to signal to designers and programmers that this is something to be worked on and developed further (Greenberg & Buxton, 2008). Thus, interactive sketches are artefacts that help designers make vague ideas concrete, reflect on possible problems and uses, discover alternate new ideas and refine current ones (Greenberg & Buxton, 2008). The benefits of sketching are not limited to proficient designers but may come to all stakeholders, including users (Tohidi, Buxton, Baecker, & Sellen, 2006).

More generally, design reasoning focus on the parallel creation of a thing (object, service, system) and its way of working (function, aesthetics) to create value (need fulfillments, problem solving) (Dorst, 2011). Thus, designers come up with proposals for both 'what' and 'how' and 'value', and test these together (Dorst, 2011). To

Fig. 4.1 Relation artefacts
type II

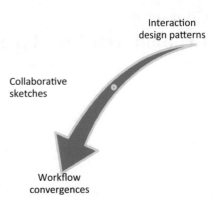

Table 4.1 Overview of key characteristics of relation artefact Type II sub-types

Relation artefact Type II sub-types	Key characteristics
1. Interaction design patterns	Socio-technical idea sketching supported by interaction design patterns deal with open, complex problems in organizations by fulfilling workers needs with novel interaction designs. They add considerations about social arrangements to the standard HCI idea sketching repertoire. In the form of workplace interaction patterns, they may be thought of as 'design frames' for how to organize the social arrangement/organizational structure related to the use of interaction designs
2. Collaborative sketches	Collaborative sketches are the outcome of stakeholder groups' ideation such as brain-storming and commenting on each other's ideas, so the produced sketches are often less valuable than the conversations around them. They may go across levels of scale to be organizational, visual, geographical, cultural, technical solutions. Collaborative sketches are co-designed by workers
3. Workflow convergences	These are organizational evaluations of the collaborative sketches produced with inspiration from workplace interaction patterns. However, stakeholders acting as evaluators may have troubles accurately distinguishing good from bad ideas, so the idea convergence may be supported using organizational devices for hosting and choosing among multiple design ideas for the organizational workflows

be able to do this from seemingly scratch, designers ideate, which is generating, developing, and communicating new ideas (Bellamy et al., 2011). Sketching helps in design reasoning, and it has been an important part of HWID since its inception (Clemmensen, Campos, Orngreen, Mark-Pejtersen, & Wong, 2006).

To help to understand the sub-types and to follow the structure of the chapter, Table 4.1 presents the key characteristics of each of the three sub-types.

Below we unfold and discuss the relation artefact Type II sub-types: interaction design patterns, collaborative sketches, and workflow convergences.

4.1 Interaction Design Patterns

The first sub-type of relation artefacts Type II is interaction design patterns. These support socio-technical idea sketching such as HWID sketching. Proficient designers focus on exploring alternatives, discovering possibilities, and realizing constraints (Bellamy et al., 2011). An idea sketching sequence can be: 1. Gather info, 2. Create triggers (questions designed to help stimulate the flow of new ideas), 3. Sketch ideas, and 4. Present & share (Gallagher, 2017). Designers may use interaction design patterns, for example, 'attract visitor' or 'engage visitor' interaction design patterns for designing interactive exhibits (Borchers, 2008). Such an interaction design pattern may include the context (that is, a sketch of the design situations in which it can be used), problem, solution (for example, in a storyboard sketch), and references to similar designs (Borchers, 2008).

Socio-technical idea sketching is done to deal with open, complex problems in organizations by fulfilling workers needs with novel interaction designs. In addition to the general design reasoning behind sketching, socio-technical idea sketching entails exploring various design tension patterns, CSCW style (Gross, 2013), and similar high level interaction design patterns for work and organizations (Auernhammer & Leifer, 2019; Erickson, 2000; Larner & Walldius, 2019; Walldius & Andersson, 2016). These organizational and workplace interaction design patterns are developed and used as a language for discussing alternative interaction designs and reflecting on their possible impacts. Below we expand on what socio-technical idea sketching is.

Is there anything special about socio-technical ideation sketching?

In large-scale, long-term, socio-technical design projects, the informal freehand sketching may not be easy applicable and may seem like a hassle, but it is crucial for ideation. Seen from a work analysis perspective, sketching methods appears to have mostly been developed for simple work, consumer, or learning domains, and may require adaptation to work equally well for large-scale complex work domains. For example, interaction designs for work domains require making relations between multiple interactions and work tasks visible and explicit and provide dynamic contextual linking for each interaction (Upton & Doherty, 2006). Furthermore, due to the longer duration of large scale projects, 'traceability' of informal freehand sketches present many difficulties, which should be overcome (Kleffmann, Röhl, Book, & Gruhn, 2018). However, informal freehand sketching for work may reveal much about the work itself (Clemmensen, 2006; Erickson, 2000).

In interaction design, both traditional idea sketching, and socio-technical idea sketching have the fourfold purpose to create ideas for new actions and designs, record ideas to trigger creativity, reflect to generate more images in the mind, and present, share, critique, decide on ideas, but they approach the purpose in slightly different ways. In traditional idea sketching, the designer focus on the novel interaction design product or system, and the designers' own contribution to this. Ideas are recorded to trigger the designers' creativity, and reflected upon to generate more images in the designers minds, and shared within the design team, broadly speaking (Bellamy et al., 2011). Participants in the traditional idea sketching are or become designers. On the other hand, socio-technical idea sketching covers also the larger social arrangements that makes the novel interaction design product or system work in the organization. The recording of ideas for interaction design may seem void of technology products and systems as the ideas may pay more attention to who are present (workers, managers), what are they doing (tasks, leisure), and in which location (e.g., office, industry floor) the novel interactions take place, all with the purpose of triggering social or organizational creativity. The reflection of ideas is done by and in the organization to create shared representations and images. The evaluation of the ideas is the organization's evaluation, not like the individual communication of ideas in traditional idea sketching, but systematic collective evaluations.

When would a designer or an organization not need to do socio-technical idea sketching? Firstly, the individual designer designing a product for the mass consumer market may not see the need for an extended study of the social arrangements. However, social arrangements may be related to the use of the novel interactions because the designers' organization, through its' other departments (e.g., marketing, manufacturing), broadly influence the design of the social arrangement for the customer and end-user of the novel interaction (Lachner, Naegelein, Kowalski, Spann, & Butz, 2016). Secondly, an organization may not see the need to do idea sketching when the fit between the novel interaction design and the interaction designs in the existing systems and the organizational flows appear good on the surface. In terms of design reasoning, organizations often takes the road that requires the least effort and fewest resources by attempting conventional problem solving to "create a new 'something' that will save the day while keeping the 'how', 'frame' and 'value' constant" (Dorst, 2011). Thus, the request for socio-technical idea sketching mostly comes when there is both individual designer and organizational awareness about that the novel interactions design requires novel social arrangements.

Attributes of HWID sketching

The attributes of socio-technical idea sketching are not surprisingly overlapping with those for traditional idea sketching (Greenberg, Carpendale, Marquardt, & Buxton, 2011) and user-oriented idea sketching (Tohidi et al., 2006), but include a little more explicit focus on organizational issues, Fig. 4.2. The choice of granularity may reflect both the design product state and/or the state of the social arrangement (e.g., organizational structure) for the use of the product. The sketches should be quick and timely for all stakeholders, which may be challenging as expert designers obviously can sketch what other people cannot, and beyond end-users, managers may lack work domain knowledge relevant to understand the sketch. Sketches should be disposable in the sense that they should be throwaway ready and not necessarily beautiful as architects' drawings, which in organizational settings should link to low cost. Sketches should be plentiful in the sense of presenting at least two alternative ideas for same problem definition, need, and persona (not just ideas for different problems, etc.). They should have a clear vocabulary which goes beyond a sketching

Traditional user idea sketches (Greenberg et al., 2011; Tohidi et al., 2006)	Socio-technical idea sketches (focus on social arrangement and organizational issues)
Sketching for individual use; sometimes also design team collaborative sketches	Multiple sketching on different organizational levels: Interaction patterns, Collaborative (worker) sketches, Workflows
Granularity, consistent with design state. Sketching use no higher resolution than necessary, avoid wasting your time and effort in preparation, and make the sketch granularity fit the granularity in the thinking of the designers at a given design step	Granularity, consistent with product/system design state, but also consistent with the state of social arrangements. No reason to make sketches in higher resolution than target social groups see as relevant.
Quick and Timely. Quick to make, timely in terms of being there when the design team needs it	Quick and timely in organizational cost terms of, and accessible by all stakeholders (employees, managers, etc.)
Disposable, plentiful, clear vocabulary to design team	Disposable, plentiful, clear vocabulary, easy to access and easy to understand by all stakeholders (employees, managers, etc.)

Fig. 4.2 Attributes of socio-technical idea sketches

language of unfinished lines, match-box figures, etc. (Lin, Thomsen, & Landay, 2002) and are accessible (Tran Luciani & Vistisen, 2017) within, across, and beyond participants in the design activities.

An objective of HWID sketching is to balance the micro level of the individual user experience with the macro level that includes the systemic overview of a complex service design in a temporal perspective (Vistisen, Jensen, & poulsen, 2016). A time-sequenced idea sketching implies sketching storyboards with an image for each key state in event sequences. That can be sketching storyboards showing the changing states in the workers-system interaction across one or more usage scenarios. It may also include or simply focus on sketching to explore and show the changing states expected as computation progresses in algorithms or data structure transformations within the organization (Roberts, Jackson, Headleand, & Ritsos, 2016), or aiming at supporting workers in entering and editing pseudocode-like descriptions to support the design of algorithms (Li, Miller, Zeleznik, & LaViola Jr, 2008). For example, a question has been raised about how does one empathize with a smart algorithm in a workplace? And the answer appears to be the standard HCI repertoire, including storyboarding key scenes with the algorithm as an imagined observer that collects data, make conclusions, and communicate insights back to the human worker (Gajendar, 2016). HWID sketching would add considerations about social arrangements to the standard HCI idea sketching repertoire.

The objective of HWID sketching is to reconfigure not only interaction design sequences, but also the social arrangements. To do that, sketches such as storyboards might be broken up into new images, annotating, adding, deleting, or replacing story parts. It may require sketching complex designs illustrating abstract elements including actors, power structures, tasks, and their interactions and relationships.

The creativity involved are the usual creativity thought processes—just with the caveat that often multiple people in the organization are involved in the creativity—of divergent and convergent thinking. Divergent thinking is a thought process or method used to generate creative ideas by exploring many possible solutions. It occurs in a spontaneous, free-flowing, 'non-linear' manner, such that many ideas are generated in an emergent cognitive fashion. Many possible solutions are explored in a short amount of time, and unexpected connections are drawn. In socio-technical idea sketching, divergent thinking might be most obvious in collaborative sketching. On the other hand, convergent thinking is what emerges when the organization tries to make sense of interaction design patterns and the outcomes of collaborative divergent thinking exercises. Convergent thinking is the type of thinking that focuses on coming up with the single, well-established answer to a problem. Knowledge, logic, probabilities, and other decision-making strategies are taken into consideration as the solutions are evaluated individually in a search for a single best answer. It is oriented toward deriving the single best, or most often correct answer to a question.

Workplace interaction patterns

Workplace interaction patterns are results of workplace studies to be reused by designers in new and different situations (Erickson, 2000). Workplace patterns can be understood as representing work practices, including those surrounding work IT systems (Horton & Dewar, 2005). A simple example is that of open versus closed office designs. Everyone who have tried it would know the difference in workplace interaction. When represented as design patterns these could be useful, not to reject or approve changes in the workplace, but rather that as a language for discussing changes and reflecting on their possible impacts in the workplace. That is, as socio-technical idea sketching such as HWID sketching.

Having a workplace interaction pattern language provide a starting point for socio-technical idea sketching of sociomaterial alternatives. Workplace interaction patterns as a form of knowledge representation can help with generalization, reuse of design knowledge, and increased quality of design (Erickson, 2000). For example, with the example of a "Sketch of a Consulting firm Pattern Language" (Erickson, 2000) build on some of the work that Alexander and his colleagues. He uses for example Alexander's patterns of 'The Flow Through Rooms' and 'Office Connections' to discuss the way in which the interconnection of rooms and the traffic through them can facilitate or inhibit spontaneous interaction. The example of a pattern for a Consulting Firm describe the various forces which shape it: the firm's need to act quickly and flexibly to get, keep, and complete projects, balanced with its need to do this with a relatively fixed set of human resources, and limited amounts of time and materials, and the multiple clients, simultaneous projects, loose teams, and informal collaborations that occur in the firm (Erickson, 2000). Furthermore, patterns are abstractions and would link to higher and lower abstractions; for example, the consulting firm pattern could link to higher level patterns such as patterns for service providers in general, and to lower level patters such as specific work interaction patterns. These may be patterns of "maintaining mutual awareness" to help the company to bring a wide range of expertise to bear on problems. This pattern would be supported by a number of smaller scale activity patterns, ranging from 'blanket email' (the custom of addressing email messages with questions or answers to large groups) to 'doing a walkabout' (i.e., wandering through the work areas just to see what others were up to). It could also be supported by spatial patterns such as and 'Open Offices', 'Model Shop' and 'Central Scanning Station'. Erickson (2000) discuss other sub-patterns of the consulting firm example, but points out that they should be used for dialogue.

Idea sketching may further benefit from organizational design patterns that focus on how to organize the social arrangement/organizational structure related to the use of interaction designs. "The platform review board" by Larner and Walldius (2019) is an example of organizational design patterns for workplace interactions that suggest a novel social arrangement (organizational structure) of workers' unions, managers, software producers, and researchers, as an improvement of the ways that gig workers interact with their platforms. The general idea with such organizational design patters is to contribute to the development and use of workplace software through the involvement of relevant social actors, who can provide feedback how the software is used and applied. Organizational design patterns supports the emerging design of work place interactions within work flows and are part of socio-technical and human-centered design practices (Auernhammer & Leifer, 2019). The can be used to sketch and prototype situations including interactions, activities and routines of learning within organizations, and allows to discover design requirements for alternative organizational design solutions (Auernhammer & Leifer, 2019).

HWID workplace interaction patterns for idea sketching could be thought of as 'design frames' in the sense of Dorst (2011). They are in a way 'double inductions' or abduction-2, as they induce both the HOW of interaction principles, the WHAT of the workplace system interfaces, and the VALUE of the proposed interaction pattern, and inspire—by analogical reasoning—to sketching out alternative ideas for workplace interactions. An attempt to illustrate HWID workplace interaction patterns for idea sketching is given in Fig. 4.3. These are supposed to be used in collaborative sketching.

4.2 Collaborative Sketches

The second and central sub-type of relation artefacts type II is collaborative sketches. They are the outcome of collaborative sketching supported by (workplace) interaction design patterns (that were discussed in the previous section). Collaborative sketches are the outcome of stakeholder groups' ideation such as brainstorming and commenting on each other's ideas, so the produced sketches may be less valuable than the conversations around them (Greenberg, Carpendale, Marquardt, & Buxton, 2012). Depending on their use, collaborative sketches are outputs of participatory design, collective creation, co-creation, co-design, team design, or whatever term captures that the value lie in in the contribution of more than one individual person (or AI (Lin, Guo, Chen, Yao, & Ying, 2020) to the design. Collaborative sketching facilitates three categories of activity: Communication, Creation and Collaboration (Craft & Cairns, 2006). Collaborative sketches are nearly per definition socio-technical sketches.

Design principles for workplaces		
Simple HOWS		**Complex HOWS**
Feedback, Consistency, Blockings, and more	Mixed reality, AU, VR	Platform review boards, chatbots, collaborative robots, etc.

			Design principles for workplaces		
	Simple WHATs	Mobile computing	Swipe, press, tick, touch, etc.	Location based map services	OS chatbots, etc.
Branches, job types, etc. (anything that is a good example of a work system interface)		Transportation	Track, monitor, steer, etc.	Heads-up displays, etc.	Cross-company /country Journey planners, etc.
	Complex WHATs	Manufacturing services and production systems	Admin formulars to fill in, standard automation interfaces, etc.	Virtual meetings, etc.	Collaborative robots, automation ecologies, etc.

Fig. 4.3 Examples of HWID workplace interaction patterns for idea sketching

What makes collaborative sketches socio-technical idea sketches is however more than HOW they are produced (collaborative or individual) but also WHAT they sketch and WHO are doing the sketching. That is, they are socio-technical when they sketch both interaction designs and the social arrangements around those. Collaborative sketching can apply multi-scale strategies to meet local and situated needs and sketch across levels of scale that may include organizational, visual, geographical, cultural, technical, and others (Lupfer et al., 2018). An example of collaborative sketching on organizational scale is business model canvas sketching (Osterwalder & Pigneur, 2010). An example of collaborative sketching for interaction design is team-based user experience sketching (Greenberg et al., 2011).

HWID collaborative sketches are co-designed by workers. However, it should not be taken for granted that workers easily can be involved in doing the collaborative sketching. Collaborative design workshops may not only benefit from approaching workers as vulnerable users but also as co-designers and participants that have an equal say in the shaping of the collaborative sketching activities such as brainstorming (Harrington, Erete, & Piper, 2019). Collaborative design workshop techniques for vulnerable users can be adapted and used to inspire the development of techniques for involving low-paid workers in HWID activities on a more global scale. Ideas of considering history and context of a design site as a method of trust building, encourage rich and full accounts rather than stressing frank disclosure, and to value existing assets or environments of underserved communities (Harrington et al., 2019) may add value to well-known techniques of socio-technical design methods from business research (Koutsikouri, Lindgren, Henfridsson, & Rudmark, 2018), social computer science (Pipek & Wulf, 2009), and design psychology (Clemmensen, 2011b). The aim for further development of HWID collaborative sketching could be find ways to ensure appropriate equity between stakeholders participating in collaborative sketching.

In summary, socio-technical idea sketching are not expressions of the creative genius, who reflects in solitude, and who performs individual presentations like in classic idea sketching, but rather social activities with both technical and social purposes and aims. Socio-technical idea sketching shows how the ideas come about as artefact relations between the social and the technical.

4.3 Workflow Convergences

The third kind of relation artefacts type II are workflow convergences. These are organizational evaluations of the collaborative sketches produced with inspiration from workplace interaction patterns. They can be designed in different ways including traditional townhall meetings, focus groups, interviews, etc., and more recent innovative participative designs such as pilot implementation, technochange, and design in use (Hertzum, 2018). In addition, and what we will describe in some detail here, there may be relevant considerations about accuracy of organizational evaluations in choice scenarios (Santiago Walser, Seeber, & Maier, 2019).

For example, a relevant scenario is that an organization has done collaborative sketching and now have several and perhaps plenty of innovative ideas to change the organizational workflows to choose between. However, stakeholders acting as evaluators may be challenged and feel overwhelmed by the complexity and the number of ideas generated and have troubles accurately distinguishing good from bad ideas. In such 'innovation contest' scenarios, digital nudging (using design elements to reduce cognitive load in choice situations) on a convergence platform (organizational device for hosting multiple design ideas) may counteract the convergence challenge (choosing the best among the sketched solutions) (Santiago Walser et al., 2019). Santiago Walser et al. proposed that designing such a convergence platform requires knowing about decision-making processes involved in the idea convergence task. They did an online experiment with 190 participants, who were asked to delete not-promising ideas in presentation modes that had varying levels of information load decomposition from high (few) to low (many) ideas per choice situation. They found that convergence platforms with a high decomposition of information load (few ideas per choice situation) helped evaluators to make accurate choices. Thus, designing organization-specific convergence platforms with a high decomposition of information could help employees and other stakeholders to make more accurate choices among multiple sketched out solutions for changing organizational workflows. This would be particularly relevant for those of the employees (and other stakeholders) who may tend to follow the opinion of the crowd (Santiago Walser et al., 2019). The outcome of such design would contribute to the academic knowledge base on idea-selection processes and how to design organization-specific and local IT platforms to ensure a successful convergence process in organizational choice scenarios.

Workflow convergence is also an issue for a wider set of stakeholders in what may be named 'micro-collaborations' between digital freelancers, trade unions, guilds/professions, employer/workplaces, and universities. For example, the 'platform review board' by Walldius et al. (2009) may act as an evaluator of socio-technical collaborative sketches by both reviewing and facilitating review of interaction designs, and by doing satisfaction surveys of the design of social arrangements around such designs.

4.4 Summary

This chapter presented relation artefacts Type II that were defined by having the purpose of socio-technical ideation sketching, that is, linking the social and the technical of ideas for solutions. Three possible subcategories of relation artefact Type II were introduced: interaction design patterns, collaborative sketches, and workflow convergences. Together they presented a move from the technical to the social centered on collaborative sketches of alternative solutions. Noteworthy, the objective of designing relation artefacts Type II is to reconfigure both interaction design sequences and social arrangements, empower vulnerable users as co-designers and participants in the collaborative design workshops, and subsume to organizational and collective idea-selection processes.

Reflecting on the HWID relation artefacts Type II by comparing them to entities in other socio-technical HCI design approaches, Design Tensions (DTs) (Gross, 2013) sees design not as problem-solving but as ongoing compromises, which sketching alternative solutions may actually support by outlining different and maybe even contradicting positions. However, since DTs is theory-driven, while relation artefacts Type II is mostly empirically driven, they may complement each other in thinking divergent in design.

4.5 Appendix

Design case with HWID sketching

In a study of a simple design for complex work domains, Clemmensen (2011a) did a case of designing a simple folder structure for a new learning management system (LMS) system for a university study program. The aim was to design help the transition from an old LMS to a new LMS by collaborative sketching design for the work and learning activities of teachers, administrators, and students (Clemmensen, 2006). The action research method was used, with the author in a double role as university researcher and project manager of a developer group consisting of students, administrators, and teachers within the university. During the project, various sketches

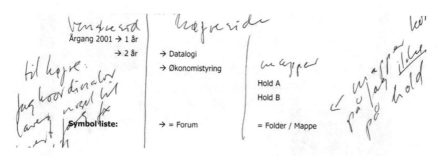

Fig. 4.4 The students' sketch. The typed text is the students' suggestions for a hierarchy in the folder structure, with the top level at the left side and bottom level at the right. The handwritten comments (the author's) are from the discussion when the students explained their sketch to the developer group

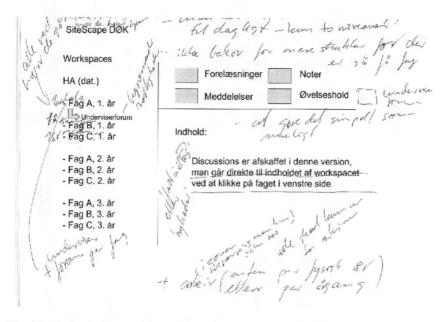

Fig. 4.5 The teachers' sketch. The typed text is the teachers' suggestions for a hierarchy in the folder structure, with the top level at the left side and bottom level at the right. The handwritten comments (the author's) are from the discussion when the teachers explained their sketch to the developer group

of the folder design solution, Figs. 4.4, 4.5 and 4.6, were discussed and evaluated within and across stakeholder groups, which resulted in the convergence on a simple folder design with simple workflows (teachers upload, students download, admin only use the platform in special situations). From the scientific standpoint, analysis

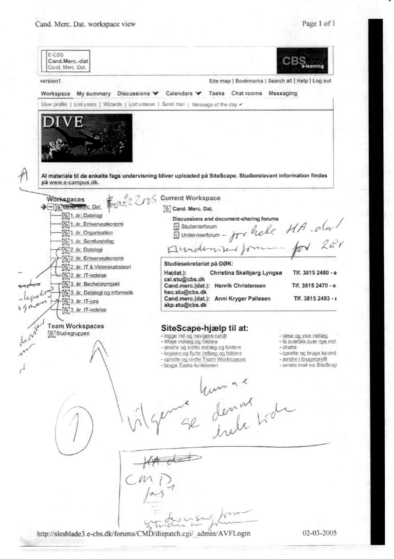

Fig. 4.6 The administrators' sketch, annotated with participant comments

was conducted through grounded theory, inspired by the HWID framework. The findings supported the use of a holistic framework with asymmetrical relations between in and work analysis and interaction design.

In this case, the interaction patterns were possible folder structures that were considered by the multi-stakeholder developer group as workplace interaction patterns. The socio-technical collaborative idea sketching took the form of annotated sketches emerging within each sub-stakeholder group. The group discussion of sketches focused on plusses and minuses of each sketch; each participant in the

Fig. 4.7 The converged simple design for a complex work domain: The folder structure of a Bachelor study program's e-learning site. The figure is in Danish; each entry in the folder structure represents a student class

developer group was required to access the collaborative sketches and test them for three bad things and three good things and be ready to report these at the meeting. In the end, the group converged on a folder design with simple workflows (a year and class structure in which teachers upload, students download, and admin only use the platform in special situations). The converged design is shown in Fig. 4.7. See the full HWID design case in (Clemmensen, 2006, 2011a).

References

Auernhammer, J. M. K., & Leifer, L. (2019). Is organizational design a human-centered design practice? In *Proceedings of the Design Society: International Conference on Engineering Design* (Vol. 1, no. 1, pp. 1205–1214). Cambridge University Press.

Bellamy, R., Desmond, M., Martino, J., Matchen, P., Ossher, H., Richards, J., & Swart, C. (2011). Sketching tools for ideation. In *Proceeding of the 33rd International Conference on Software Engineering-ICSE'11* (pp. 808). https://doi.org/10.1145/1985793.1985909.

Borchers, J. O. (2008). A pattern approach to interaction design. In *Cognition, Communication and Interaction* (pp. 114–131). Springer.

Buxton, B. (2010). *Sketching user experiences: Getting the design right and the right design.* Morgan kaufmann.

Clemmensen, T. (2006). A simple design for a complex work domain-the role of sketches in the design of a Bachelor study's new folder structure for use by teachers, students and administrators. In *Human Work Interaction Design: Designing for Human Work* (Vol. 221, pp. 221–240). https://doi.org/10.1007/978-0-387-36792-7_13.

Clemmensen, T. (2011a). Designing a simple folder structure for a complex domain. *Human Technology: An Interdisciplinary Journal on Humans in ICT Environments.*

Clemmensen, T. (2011b). Templates for cross-cultural and culturally specific usability testing: Results from field studies and ethnographic interviewing in three countries. *International Journal of Human-Computer Interaction, 27*(7), 634–669. https://doi.org/10.1080/10447318.2011.555303.

Clemmensen, T., Campos, P., Orngreen, R., Mark-Pejtersen, A., & Wong, W. (2006). *Human work interaction design: Designing for human work.* Springer Science+Business Media.

Craft, B., & Cairns, P. (2006). Using sketching to aid the collaborative design of information visualisation software-A case study. In *IFIP International Federation for Information Processing* (Vol. 221, pp. 103–122). https://doi.org/10.1007/978-0-387-36792-7_6.

Dorst, K. (2011). The core of "design thinking" and its application. *Design Studies.* https://doi.org/
10.1016/j.destud.2011.07.006.

Erickson, T. (2000). 13 Supporting interdisciplinary design: Towards pattern languages for
workplaces. In *Workplace studies: Recovering work practice and informing system design*
(pp. 252).

Gajendar, U. (2016). Empathizing with the smart and invisible: Algorithms! *Interactions, 23*(4),
24–25.

Gallagher, C. L. (2017). Sketching for ideation: A structured approach for increasing divergent
thinking. In *Proceedings of the 2017 CHI Conference Extended Abstracts on Human Factors in
Computing Systems* (pp. 106–111).

Greenberg, S., & Buxton, B. (2008). Usability evaluation considered harmful (some of the time). In
Proceedings of the SIGCHI Conference on Human Factors in Computing Systems (pp. 111–120).

Greenberg, S., Carpendale, S., Marquardt, N., & Buxton, B. (2011). *Sketching user experiences:
The workbook.* Elsevier.

Greenberg, S., Carpendale, S., Marquardt, N., & Buxton, B. (2012). *3.5-The Collaborative Sketch:
Sketching to brainstorm, express ideas and mediate interaction* (S. Greenberg, S. Carpendale, N.
Marquardt, & B. B. T.-S. U. E. T. W. Buxton, Eds.). https://doi.org/10.1016/B978-0-12-381959-
8.50014-6.

Gross, T. (2013). Supporting effortless coordination: 25 years of awareness research. *Computer
Supported Cooperative Work (CSCW), 22*(4), 425–474. https://doi.org/10.1007/s10606-013-
9190-x.

Harrington, C., Erete, S., & Piper, A. M. (2019). Deconstructing community-based collaborative
design: Towards more equitable participatory design engagements. *Proceedings of the ACM on
Human-Computer Interaction, 3*(CSCW), 1–25.

Hertzum, M. (2018). Three contexts for evaluating organizational usability. *Journal of Usability
Studies, 11*(1).

Horton, K. S., & Dewar, R. G. (2005). Learning from patterns during information technology
configuration. *Journal of Organizational and End User Computing (JOEUC), 17*(2), 26–42.

Kleffmann, M., Röhl, S., Book, M., & Gruhn, V. (2018). Evaluation of a traceability approach for
informal freehand sketches. *Automated Software Engineering, 25*(1), 1–43. https://doi.org/10.
1007/s10515-017-0221-6.

Koutsikouri, D., Lindgren, R., Henfridsson, O., & Rudmark, D. (2018). Extending digital infrastruc-
tures: a typology of growth tactics. *Journal of the Association for Information Systems, 19*(10),
2.

Lachner, F., Naegelein, P., Kowalski, R., Spann, M., & Butz, A. (2016). Quantified UX: Towards
a common organizational understanding of user experience. In *Proceedings of the 9th Nordic
Conference on Human-Computer Interaction-NordiCH '16* (pp. 56:1–56:10). https://doi.org/10.
1145/2971485.2971501.

Larner, J., & Walldius, Å. (2019). The Platform Review Alliance Board: Designing an organizational
model to bring together producers and consumers in the review and commissioning of platform
software. *Journal of Organization Design, 8*(1), 14. https://doi.org/10.1186/s41469-019-0055-8.

Li, C., Miller, T. S., Zeleznik, R. C., & LaViola Jr, J. J. (2008). AlgoSketch: Algorithm sketching
and interactive computation. *SBM*, 175–182.

Lin, J., Thomsen, M., & Landay, J. A. (2002). A visual language for sketching large and complex
interactive designs. In *Proceedings of the SIGCHI Conference on Human Factors in Computing
Systems* (pp. 307–314).

Lin, Y., Guo, J., Chen, Y., Yao, C., & Ying, F. (2020). It is your turn: Collaborative ideation with a
co-creative robot through sketch. In *Proceedings of the 2020 CHI Conference on Human Factors
in Computing Systems* (pp. 1–14). https://doi.org/10.1145/3313831.3376258.

Lupfer, N., Fowler, H., Valdez, A., Webb, A., Merrill, J., Newman, G., & Kerne, A. (2018).
Multiscale design strategies in a landscape architecture classroom. In *Proceedings of the 2018
Designing Interactive Systems Conference* (pp. 1081–1093).

Osterwalder, A., & Pigneur, Y. (2010). *Business model generation: a handbook for visionaries, game changers, and challengers.* Wiley.

Pipek, V., & Wulf, V. (2009). Infrastructuring: Toward an integrated perspective on the design and use of information technology. *Journal of the Association for Information Systems, 10*(5), 1.

Roberts, J. C., Jackson, J. R., Headleand, C., & Ritsos, P. D. (2016). *Creating explanatory visualizations of algorithms for active learning.*

Santiago Walser, R., Seeber, I., & Maier, R. (2019). Designing a digital nudge for convergence: The role of decomposition of information load for decision making and choice accuracy. *AIS Transactions on Human-Computer Interaction, 11*(3), 179–207.

Tohidi, M., Buxton, W., Baecker, R., & Sellen, A. (2006). Getting the right design and the design right. In *Proceedings of the SIGCHI Conference on Human Factors in Computing Systems* (pp. 1243–1252). ACM.

Tran Luciani, D., & Vistisen, P. (2017). Empowering non-designers through animation-based sketching. In *7th Nordic Design Research Conference Nordic Design Research Conference* (pp. 1–8). Nordes, Nordic Design Research.

Upton, C., & Doherty, G. (2006). Visual representation of complex information structures in high volume manufacturing. In T. Clemmensen (Ed.), *IFIP International Federation for Information Processing* (Vol. 221, pp. 27–45). https://doi.org/10.1007/978-0-387-36792-7_2.

Vistisen, P., Jensen, T., & poulsen, S. B. (2016). Animating the ethical demand: Exploring user dispositions in industry innovation cases through animation-based sketching. *ACM SIGCAS Computers and Society, 45*(3), 318–325.

Walldius, Å., & Andersson, A. (2016). Design patterns for user-driven workplace software labeling. In *CHI 2016 Conference CHI4GOOD, San Jose, California, USA* (7–12 May 2016).

Walldius, Å., Sundblad, Y., Bengtsson, L., Sandblad, B., & Gulliksen, J. (2009). User certification of workplace software: Assessing both artefact and usage. *Behaviour & Information Technology, 28*(2), 101–120.

Chapter 5
Relation Artefacts Type III

Abstract This chapter takes the thread with sketching HWID solutions from Chap. 4 further and presents socio-technical hypothesis prototyping as relation artefacts type III. Three sub-types move the design from the social to the technical: Organizational action hypotheses, prototyped worker experiences, and UX-at-work field evaluations and tests. Prototyping hypotheses on a HWID platform means that specific organizational work design hypotheses and interaction design hypotheses should be presented as prototypes, and that these should be UX tested, and field evaluated. The chapter draws on notions about 'justificatory knowledge' for prototypes, and 'appropriating' prototypes. The chapter ends with summary of relation artefacts Type III as expressions of workers actively prototyping specific hypotheses about interaction designs and social arrangements at work.

Keywords Human work interaction design · Relational artefacts · Organizational action hypotheses · Prototyped worker experiences · UX-at-work field evaluations

Although prototyping is a technique widely used in work and organizational settings during the design of a new or updated product, the technique is rarely used to test out hypothetical options during the design of the organization and work itself. However, an example using prototyped hypotheses in work situations is the 'work organization action simulation' by Kember and Murray (1988), which was developed in response to a need identified in the training of engineers, but which ended up being more broadly useful to prototype socio-technical systems and explore technical options in association with the organizational structure. This kind of socio-technical hypothesis prototyping may, furthermore, involve a movement from participatory, organizational designs, towards differentiated re-designs that participants can claim 'applies to us' (Townsend, 2015), down to the level of the individual worker's UX. This movement is what relation artefacts type III are about, as they express a move from organizational action hypothesis over prototyped worker experiences, and to field and UX evaluations of those, Fig. 5.1.

To help to understand the sub-types and to follow the structure of the chapter, Table 5.1 presents the key characteristics of each of the three sub-types.

Fig. 5.1 Relation artefacts
Type III

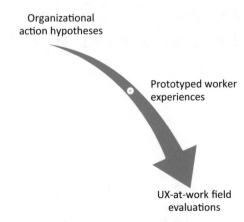

Table 5.1 Overview of key characteristics of relation artefact Type III sub-types

Relation artefact Type III sub-types	Key characteristics
1. Organizational action hypotheses	HWID supports organization strategy making through prototyping organizational action hypotheses by a broader group of stakeholders including workers. This adds social structures, roles, educational backgrounds, etc. to the list of material and methods for prototyping. The possible use of social science and humanities knowledge to qualify what exactly is being tried out is a major advantage of organizational action prototypes
2. Prototyped worker experiences	Organizational action prototypes and prototyped worker experiences overlap, but also differ due to inherent conflict areas between management and workers. Four types of worker-technology relations can be prototyped as hypothetical worker experiences. In addition, job crafting may prototype important subjective, symbolic, and imaginary aspects of working in the age of AI, robots, and automation
3. UX-at-work field evaluations	A good quality UX-at-work is an acceptable level of both pragmatic qualities (effectiveness and efficiency) and hedonic qualities (e.g., feeling of interest stimulation and professional identity confirmation). The interactions among task, structure, technology, and actors determine how UX-at-work is experienced. UX-at-work may be quite ordinary most of the time

Below we unfold and discuss the relation artefact Type III sub-types.

5.1 Organizational Action Hypotheses

Why prototype organizational action hypotheses?

Prototyping is about getting the design right, rather than getting the right design (Tohidi, Buxton, Baecker, & Sellen, 2006). Prototypes are didactic, descriptive, refined, answer questions, test, resolve, make things specific, and depict stuff; they are about incremental iterative refinement (Tohidi et al., 2006). In socio-technical HCI design, an organizational action hypothesis prototype is a specific attempt to solve an organizational problem, Fig. 5.2. Thus, prototyping socio-technical HCI design hypotheses on basis of foregoing sketching is closely linked to management and employees together developing strategies for organizations. Design and strategy making both deal with ill-defined, wicked problems to the benefit of the organization and its stakeholders (Camillus, 2008; Garbuio et al., 2015). However, classical organization strategy making is a deductive reasoning exercise done by the senior management (Calori, 1998; Garbuio et al., 2015). In contrast, HWID supports organization strategy making through prototyping organizational action hypotheses by a broader group of stakeholders including workers, and with a readiness to disengage with any specific prototype or understanding thereof and embrace input from tests of the prototypes with users and other stakeholders. Compared to traditional organizational strategy making that aims to design one specific evolutionary strategy—based on analysis of the past and with some inputs from surveying stakeholders—and then roll-out this, the prototyping approach is much more about multiple throw-away prototypes of specific organizational action hypotheses and how their users appropriate these.

Rather than aiming for control and power by applying strategy analysis deductively or UX design prototyping as a management method, the reason for prototyping

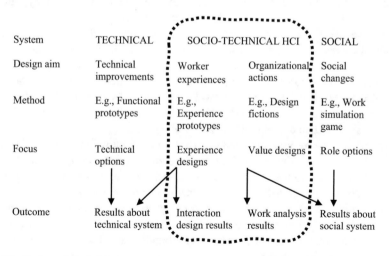

Fig. 5.2 Socio-technical HCI design prototypes. Adapted from Kember and Murray (1988)

organizational action hypotheses is to support a broader group of relevant stakeholders, for example, employees, managers, and external stakeholders, together in thinking strategically with specific organizational action hypotheses about the so far identified organizational problems and workers' needs. It may be seen as prototyping 'strategic hypotheses' (Garbuio et al., 2015). Additionally, prototyping organizational action hypotheses can be done by researchers as part of the iterative generator-test cycle path to develop design theory, and to contribute further development of related justificatory knowledge (Mandviwalla, 2015).

In sum, the aim with prototyping organizational action hypotheses is to set specific goals for organizational problem solving and individual needs fulfillment. It should lead to further use and development of existing and new IT artefacts and associated justificatory knowledge (sometimes called kernel theory). It is done by iteration among design, evaluation, and appropriation/generation of prototypes of varying maturity. It may sometimes include appropriation of the prototype for new uses in the organization, or the generation of new knowledge in the process as a separate activity that is different from design and evaluation.

Organizational action prototypes materials and methods

Prototyping hypotheses involves materials—what the prototype is made of, and methods—how to make the prototype. Classic HCI prototyping can be done in many different materials (paper, tree, foam, HTML, LEGO, program code, dedicated software, etc.), with different scope (a small part of the IT artefact, or broader/deeper part of the IT artefact). Horizontal prototyping includes techniques such as paper prototypes (e.g., animated post-it note sequences) and printouts (wireframes or mockup), storyboards and video-prototypes, Wizard of Oz, clickable/tappable prototypes, and look and feel (experience) prototypes. Vertical prototyping includes functional program code, demo applications, and conceptual running prototypes.

Socio-technical HCI design prototypes such as organizational action hypotheses add to the list of material and methods for prototyping, Fig. 5.2.

First, socio-technical HCI design prototyping aims to design organizational actions. Methods such as design fictions (Sterling, 2009) and design thinking for management prototyping (Kolko, 2015) maximize strategic thinking and discussion and involve just enough engineering to enable concrete discussions about the organizational actions and their impact on work and the social structure. The methods for prototyping organizational actions hypotheses can be varied and may take inspiration from social science and humanities research and practice.

Second, which prototyping granularity (resolution) to aim for depend on the given technical and social design states. Prototyping should be done in the resolution sufficient and necessary to test the hypothesis. Classic HCI low-fidelity prototypes are useful, such as paper prototypes and physical mockups, storyboards, Wizard of Oz, clickable prototypes, high fidelity, experience prototypes, and demo applications. Additionally, when prototyping organizational actions hypotheses, the granularity in social structures, roles, educational backgrounds, etc., should be sufficient and necessary to test the hypothesis.

Third, considerations about choosing prototyping methods include the purpose of the prototyping. Will the method allows the researcher to pursue the chosen purpose (e.g., innovate, apply existing ideas, or both invent and explain) in a way that is credible and useful to the relevant target audience? In addition, considerations for choosing prototyping methods include participant characteristics, such as what is the most suitable method in light of how participants can best be involved as co-designers and help create and evaluate the use of the to-be-designed future solution? Finally, they involve resource constraints, such as what is the optimal prototyping method to apply, given a choice of the balance between emphasizing design theory or emphasizing the IT artifact in the organizational context of interest, towards prototyping hypotheses.

Advantages and disadvantages of organizational action prototypes

The advantages and disadvantages of organizational action prototypes are closely linked to the justificatory knowledge that they embed. In design, justificatory knowledge is a term that can be used to denote the 'external' knowledge including existing IT systems and relevant academic knowledge that provide a basis and explanation for the design (Jones & Gregor, 2007). A good historical example of justificatory knowledge is the use of psychological theory in HCI to develop engineering models of human performance that could be applied by computer scientists and HCI practitioners to develop user interfaces (Card, Moran, & Newell, 1983). Justificatory knowledge for prototyping can for example be existing design theories, practical theories-in-use, and eclectic use of existing research (Iivari, 2020). The possible use of social science and humanities knowledge to qualify what exactly is being tried out is arguable a major advantage of organizational action prototypes.

However, the eclectic use of existing research is an example that shows the major disadvantages of prototypes, which is that these may inadvertently cover up misuse and lack of understanding of the justificatory knowledge, both as it supports the design and as it is changed by the design. Iivari (2020) gives an example of a project that put forward four design principles that each had a distinct source in terms of references as justificatory knowledge; unfortunately this just reduced justificatory knowledge for prototypes from being a coherent design theory to merely unconnected references to existing research. Overall, however, the use of organizational action prototypes appears to be a way to do design theorizing to the benefit of researchers and practitioners. The following paragraphs list advantages and disadvantages of various prototypes and discuss these for prototyping organizational action hypotheses.

Paper prototypes and mockups have the advantages that they are easy and cheap to make, and answers 'what if' questions. They can be extremely precise and give only the context necessary to test the hypothesis. They support co-design with stakeholders by appearing as informal and naïve, letting stakeholders design and be critical. They can be thrown away, and hence researchers and other stakeholders will not be 'married' to a specific solution but will have a mindset of being ready to try out alternatives. They provide specific socio-technical HCI design knowledge in familiar materials that can be translated later to other media and can be helpful to test many variants of hypotheses. For example, they allow parts or whole of proto-type to be replaced, redesigned, remade across a series of tests, can be adapted to different target user groups as they emerge in a given organizational, cultural, social, or technological context, and in general be used in many contexts (e.g., the office, the factory, the street). Hence, they can also be used to try out work and organizational designs such as quickly drawing a new organizational structure.

Paper prototypes and physical mockups do have disadvantages, among which are their low reliability (hard to store, hard to recreate) and low predictive validity (hard to predict if further testing will give accurately the same result), though creating testable manifestations of design action ideas is the objective of paper prototyping. However, disengagement of important stakeholders in co-design may arise when for example ethical issues in sharing free-flowing ideas have received less consideration of important contextual details. Furthermore, the hypotheses tested with the paper prototyping may not appear realistic, paper prototypes may not appear professional, and they are a bit troublesome and difficult to carry out. Finally, the physicality of prototyping with paper, wood, foam, etc. may stand in the way of large scale and anywhere testing, and more advanced paper prototyping and physical mockup prototyping require a specific kind of skills from researchers. All of this apply to organizational action prototyping too, and in addition there are problems of account-ability and power (e.g., if asked to quickly, without time to reflect and think through, prototype social structures in front of superiors).

Storyboards have the advantages of helping to tell a story about how prototypes such as prototyped organizational action hypotheses will play out. It is just like a comic strip with a clear intro, build-up, conflict, solution. It embeds context into socio-technical HCI design hypothesis testing. By allowing researcher to add place, people, and IT artefacts, it gives unexpected insights. It situates the socio-technical HCI design IT artefact in a test setup, which allows role play-type of testing. It helps the researcher focus on the flow of the socio-technical HCI design and test changes in the storyline that hypothetically evoke stronger overall impact. Finally, it helps considering confounding contextual factors for the hypothesis testing, for example, interfaces to other IT artefacts, organizational procedures, physical barriers, etc., and it is in general a great communication tool for communicating the proto-typed hypothesis. Storyboards have disadvantages including that the quality of using storyboard hypothesis testing depends on the facilitator of the participants, evalu-ating storyboards tend to require experts, and that it is difficult to be predictive with storyboarding. The latter is because the knowledge produced is mostly about giving designers insight into people who are not exactly like the designers themselves and about persuading others of the value of the design.

The Wizard of Oz is a technique with the advantage that it can be used to simu-late socio-technical HCI designs such as organizational action prototypes for testing complex interactions. The participant thinks they are interacting with the IT artefact, but a developer is responding to output rather than the IT artefact. For organizational action prototypes, the IT artefact can also be non-human actors like collaborative robots and human colleagues. This can be done early in design to understand partic-ipants' expectations, interactions, etc. The disadvantages include that the technique is expensive, not always necessary, difficult setup, and that is has little predictive validity. Most importantly, the test quality depends on having a well prepared 'wizard' which is not always available. The wizard may further need different (more organizational and social) knowledge and skills when the prototype is an organizational action prototype.

Clickable prototypes such as wireframing tools are often compared to paper prototypes but are strong in other areas. The advantages include that they appear professional, can be used to test in realistic interactions, can be used to test anywhere, it is quite easy to do the test, and it as a degree of reliability and predictive validity since interactions are to a degree codified in the software. For organizational action prototypes, they can help specify organizational hypotheses about for example access to experts and resources, communication sequences, and more. The disadvantages include that clickable prototypes tend to become too formal because their designers spend too much time on irrelevant details. Second, they tend to achieve exaggerated face validity that seduces researchers and participants alike to think the IT artefact really works. Third they stop the designers from testing multiple hypotheses and make in unclear and vague what is being tested, as researchers tend to forget themselves and build advanced and large show-it-all clickable prototypes. Fourth, they may be expensive as they require licensing, training, and maintenance. Finally, they do not support hypothesis testing of co-design and collaboration, as clickable prototypes are tools for individual use; this is a major disadvantage for organizational action prototyping.

Experience prototypes help understand users', employees', workers', and customers' user experiences. The advantages are that they answer "What would it feel like if …?" questions. Using high fidelity experience prototypes enables participants of many kinds to consider contextual, physical, temporal, sensory, social, and cognitive aspects of the socio-technical HCI design IT artefact. They support the design of 'experience before IT artefact' and make the designer think about the experience (e.g., tactile, shared, full-body experiences), rather than the instantiation. They support designers' empathy with participants and their situations, by testing hypotheses about their own experiences and those of their colleagues, users, clients, etc., allows testing hypotheses about the intangible experience, and, not at least, help persuade others that this experience is valuable. For organizational action prototypes, they can help try out for example how changes in power distribution in social structures would feel.

The disadvantages of experience prototypes are that they increase the risk of promoting fake empathy, since no matter how good experience prototyping is at promoting empathy, we cannot be other people. Second, testing experience hypotheses, and in particular organizational action hypotheses, requires that the designer have hybrid and overlapping skillsets, including computer science skills to be able to prototype high fidelity prototypes, psychology skills to understand basic needs, affects, emotions, organizational skills to understand strategy, structure, power, etc., and design skills to create novel experiences. Third, the use of for example video prototyping requires the designer's personal willingness to test hypotheses with active and self-indulging prototyping methods, and for organizational action proto-typing to reveal potential vulnerabilities to other people with some kind of power and influence on the designer.

Demo applications have the advantages that they can illustrate a concept in a way that allows decision makers to say 'yes we want this'. Second, they allow for ecological and external validity by enabling comparisons to other contexts and allow for justifying socio-technical HCI design theory through demonstrating mature prototypes based on the theory. The disadvantages include that they are costly and time consuming and will require other forms for prototyping before the demo can be created, and they require teams of specialist designers to do so. In addition, the theory/framework should be understood and focused at the time of prototyping demo application, but it may be difficult to link the theory/framework sufficiently directly to a demo application. For organizational action prototypes, these are valid advantages and disadvantages too. In addition, compared to traditional interaction-focused HCI prototypes, the potential for non-ethical behavior or direct conflict may be larger for mature organizational action prototypes due to the prototyping of social structures and arrangements.

5.2 Prototyped Worker Experiences

There will be an overlap between organizational action prototypes and worker expe-rience prototypes, however, the two different sub-types of relation artefacts Type III may also help reveal possible conflict areas between management and workers. Proto-typed worker experiences cover specific hypotheses both about interaction design and about the small group, team-oriented, social arrangement around the interaction designs. A very simplified version is to say that the user experiences that workers have at work are what here is called worker experiences. Obviously, what it means to have or to own an experience when at work is controversial and conflictual, which is a discussion that fits well into socio-technical traditions.

Prototypes of emerging changes in social practices

Prototyping may express emerging changes in workers' social practices. These changes can be about basic social phenomena like social inertia, that is, the contin-uation of an old process that slows down the social restructuring (Kon, 1989), resis-tance to change, overcoming which consists of action points arranged in a practical sequence (Appelbaum, Habashy, Malo, & Shafiq, 2012), and others. Other rele-vant input to changes in social practices may come from prototyped organizational action hypotheses (see the previous section), additional ideas for improving specific technological performance, participatory and co-design approaches, evolutionary management, and more. The point is that prototyping can express emerging changes in social practices (Liu et al., 2018).

Prototyping emerging social changes is a design intervention into workers' expe-riences. Emerging changes in social practices can be understood as collective patterns of interaction that consists of a practice of common perception of the world, common language usage, and common identities, all of which are reproduced in specific contexts (Rohde, Brödner, Stevens, Betz, & Wulf, 2017). However, while such a static notion of social practices as common perceptions, language, and identity may be useful and understandable, a different notion of social practices associated with IT use the dynamic modeling of the iterative aspects of the continuously production of social group-technology relations found in 'cultural models' of IT usage (Clemmensen, 2009; Kling & Elliott, 1994). Both understandings do however share the idea that prototyping IT systems for effective use in organizations is a multilayered intervention into social practices. Prototyping emerging social changes may thus include prototyping novel tasks, ways to collaborate around and deal with new technical artefacts, new worker competencies and qualifications, and changes in power structures as expressed in the selection of workplaces, work locations, and working hours.

Prototypes of emerging changes in worker-technology relations

Prototyping worker experiences not only include prototyping changes in worker-social structure relations, but also changes in worker-technology relations. Human-technology-world relations have in HCI been conceptualized as embodied, hermeneutic, alterity, and background human-technology relations (Fallman, 2011; Hogan & Hornecker, 2011; Ihde, 1990). Embodied relations are those where technology is close to or part of the human body and supports our current focus on the world. This can, for example, be glasses that mediates our reading of a screen but also recent AI-driven technologies, such as smartwatches that strongly mediates our fitness exercises over time. Hermeneutic relations are those where technology is used to represent, or go instead of, the world, such as the use of a thermometer to interpret whether a person is sick or not. It can also be those relations where technology are intentional objects that directly interact with their users in attempts to represent everyday things through "familiar uses, anticipated contexts of use, and known ways of interaction" (Rozendaal et al., 2019). Alterity relations are those where technology takes the place of the 'other' human in dialogues, collaborations, and other social arrangements. This can be chatbots/conversational agents, or collaborative or humanoid/social robots, with which humans interact more or less as they would with another human (Reeves & Nass, 1996). Finally, background relations are relations to technologies that run not only in the surrounding environment, such as heating, water, and Internet installations, but also various kinds of ambient agents, such as those found in 'smart homes' and 'smart workplaces' with intelligent lightning, self-adjusting curtains, and autonomous furniture. Some scenarios of factory automation may also become background relations. These four types of worker-technology relations can possibly be prototyped as hypothetical worker experiences.

For example, the hermeneutic human-technology-world relations that intentional objects may mediate can be prototyped as explanatory objects that help the human worker to interpret how the everyday objects should be used. A collaborative robotic arm may thus help the worker to interpret how an industrial robot (the collaborative robot) can be used in a manufacturing process; or an automated CNC bench for steel item production may nudge the worker towards its own re-configuration to a new production series. What is being prototyped is then collaboration with things, things that can intentionality take on tasks and initiate communications, they can negotiate (provide options, etc.) task distribution, and motivate (e.g., nudge) towards improving skills and qualifications (Rozendaal et al., 2019). While such objects may not have or be allocated human-like needs, they do deliver requests for certain actions from others, and it is thus sometimes questionable if people have ultimate control. This lack of full human control may well be acceptable and normal in a business and work context when business goals supersede personal goals. However, it is important to be explicit that the designers of intentional objects prototype human-technology-world relations that may in some scenarios imply the technology autonomously, rather than the human, participate in the activity and mediate the relation.

Job crafting and prototyping in the age of AI, robots, and automation

The notion of 'job crafting' has been taken up by the European commission as a strategy to overcome the challenges of the labor market (Scoppetta, Davern, & Geyer, 2019). As pointed previously, this notion is very much in line with HWID. Arguably, HWID is job crafting with digital tools for digital environments or 'smart workplaces' (Abdelnour-Nocera, Barricelli, Lopes, Campos, & Clemmensen, 2015) in ecologies of automation, machine learning, and software and hardware robots.

The notion of job crafting may help outline what it means to prototype workers' experiences. The operationalization of the concept suggests that workers may do four kinds of job crafting: "1. Task Crafting: changing the number and scope of tasks that a worker does, how they are performed, and what time and efforts goes into each task; 2. Relational Crafting: Changing how, when, or with whom employees relate to and interact with while at work; 3. Cognitive Crafting: Changing workers competencies and qualifications and thereby their perception of their tasks and their work relationships; and 4. Time-spatial Crafting: workers' designing their own workplaces, work locations and working hours" (Scoppetta et al., 2019). Prototyping hypothetical changes in social and technical practices can be a strategy to empower the individual worker within the organizational contexts.

Job crafting is then a design strategy for prototyping hypothetical worker experiences that implies a broad perspective on experiences, while still maintaining that the prototypes should be evaluated. This may go beyond individual user experiences and includes employee experiences such as alignment with business goals and organizational brand, joint experience of agency with automation etc., and experiences of social arrangements. To make such experiences evaluable, a design case approach might be useful (for a discussion of design cases, see Rohde et al. (2017)). This means that prototypes should include enough situated content to make the hypothetical worker experience transferable to evaluation contexts, where findings can be compared, contrasted, and added to existing knowledge about the hypothetical prototyped worker experience.

Job crafting as prototyping hypothetical worker experiences in the age of AI, robots, and automation is a good example of the broad approach needed to prototype worker experiences. Algorithmic experiences is a name for the outcome of human-algorithm interaction (Shin et al., 2020). Prototyping hypotheses about algorithmic experiences can be done in non-work domains, such as transportation (Okamoto & Sano, 2017), recommender systems (Shin et al., 2020), and social media (Alvarado & Waern, 2018), but it is perhaps more difficult for work domains since collaboration is much more complex when workplaces are involved (Wolf & Blomberg, 2019). Design guidelines have been proposed for various AI products, such as recommender systems for ecommerce and music listening; route planning, autocompletion, feed filtering, and photo organizers for mobile phones; task reminders with voice assistants/chatbots, and importance filtering for email systems (Amershi et al., 2019), but the guidelines have not been validated in work domains. However, a work practice lens can help reveal workers experiences with AI support (Wolf & Blomberg, 2019), and their experience of work as supporters (maintenance, etc.) of AI systems (Wolf, 2020). Looking at the workers' practices, both social and human-technology relation practices, with the agentic perspective of job crafting appears a suitable worker-centered and broad approach to prototyping experiences.

Furthermore, a worker-centered approach to prototyping worker experiences may not be enough to support job crafting in all scenarios, since workers and automation/AI/robots may together experience hybrid awareness (Qin, Tan, & Clemmensen, 2019) and symbiotic agency (Neff & Nagy, 2018). That such relationships between human and technological agency in contexts exist, where people work with flexible routines and flexible technologies change the agencies themselves (Leonardi, 2011), is a classic socio-technical insight. However, the understanding of human and technological agency is an unfinished business that needs to be unfolded in more concrete descriptions of what users, actors, and tools, do when interacting with complex technological systems (Neff & Nagy, 2018). Therefore, human work interaction design suggest that job crafting should support a hybrid form of agency that mixes the technical interaction and the social organization of AI into concrete and local sociomaterial relation artefacts.

Finally, job crafting with a focus on worker experiences may include important subjective, symbolic, and imaginary aspects of working in the age of AI, robots, and automation. Anthropomorphic and animistic aspects of organizational actions and experiences can be considered topics for job crafting; no reason why workers should not be supported in anthropomorphizing their work systems and no reason why work systems should not be animated (with spirits) by design. This has already happened to a degree with the Japanese 'cute' design robotics that embeds a manga-like cuteness in human–robot interaction (Berque, Chiba, Ohkura, Sripian, & Sugaya, 2020) and with ideas of 'religious robots' that perform different religious duties and responsibilities in the different religious institutions (Ahmed & La, 2020). Animating a work system might even be one way to ensure a decent UX-at-work.

5.3   UX-at-Work Field Evaluations

The end point of relation artefacts type III is UX-at-work field evaluations and UX testing to embed the prototyping in the interaction design activities in a HWID project. User research using focus groups, field studies, and usability and UX testing at user locations, that is, in the field, are activities frequently done by UX professionals to evaluate prototypes (Inal et al., 2020). Furthermore, heuristic or expert review, analyzing metrics, card sorting, and competitive studies also add to the repertoire of evaluation of prototypes (Inal et al., 2020).

A notion of UX-at-work

UX can be defined as related to the use of systems and other technological artefacts (Law et al., 2009). Though the ISO definition of UX (The International Organization for Standardization, 2019) says that it is "user's perceptions and responses that result from the use and/or anticipated use of a system, product or service", there is no consensus about a UX definition. What originally was new in UX research was—inspired by the positive psychology movement—a focus on positive emotional outcomes such as joy, fun, and pride (Hassenzahl & Tractinsky, 2006); therefore in the following UX is mostly treated as positive design goals.

In work contexts, UX is ideally associated with meaningful, pleasurable, and need-fulfilling activities (Harbich & Hassenzahl, 2017). UX-at-work may involve both pragmatic qualities and positive features such as hedonic qualities (Diefenbach, Kolb, & Hassenzahl, 2014; Väätäjä et al., 2014). While pragmatic qualities have always been associated with use of work systems, recent studies of UX in industry contexts have found indicators and examples of the hedonic qualities of technology use in workers' UX (Harbich & Hassenzahl, 2017; Heikkilä, Honka, & Kaasinen, 2018; Lu & Roto, 2015; Meneweger, Wurhofer, Fuchsberger, & Tscheligi, 2018; Obrist, Reitberger, Wurhofer, Förster, & Tscheligi, 2011; Palviainen & Väänänen-Vainio-Mattila, 2009; Roto et al., 2017; Savioja et al., 2014; Schrepp et al., 2006; Väätäjä et al., 2014; Wurhofer, Fuchsberger, Meneweger, Moser, & Tscheligi, 2015a, 2015b; Wurhofer, Meneweger, Fuchsberger, & Tscheligi, 2018, 2015a, 2015b). Hence a good quality UX-at-work includes an acceptable level of both pragmatic qualities (effectiveness and efficiency) and hedonic qualities (e.g., feeling of interest stimulation and professional identity confirmation).

Evaluation of organizational action hypotheses and prototyped worker experiences requires that UX-at-work evaluations are linked to organizational work analysis. The 'heart model of UX-at-work' (Clemmensen, Hertzum, & Abdelnour-Nocera, 2020) suggests that the interactions among task, structure, technology, and actors determine how UX-at-work is experienced, Fig. 5.3. Evaluation of UX-at-work may focus on evaluating the worker's preferred experiences of the pragmatic and hedonic qualities of these interactions.

Fig. 5.3 A model for
UX-at-work sub-types of
relation artefacts Type III.
Adapted from Clemmensen
et al. (2020)

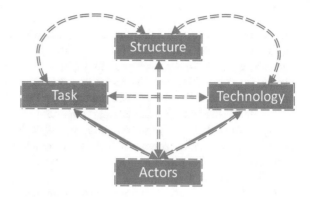

Evaluation of interactions departing in technology

The worker using a technological system may experience pragmatic product qualities, in the sense that the system supports particular 'do-goals' (e.g., to check the status of glass items produced by the collaborative robot). The worker may also experience hedonic product qualities, in the sense that the system supports 'be-goals' such as pleasure in use and professional identity (e.g., to be seen as competent by colleagues for mastering the robot) (Hassenzahl et al., 2010, 2015). Furthermore, the UX of complex systems may be more than the sum of the UX of individual subsystems, because of high levels of interaction and multiple feedback paths between elements in the system (Albers & Still, 2010), see also Fig. 5.3. Thus workers may experience both subsystem-specific hedonic qualities and broader positive experiences during work (Hassenzahl et al., 2015).

The hedonic aspects of interactions departing in technology may not be obvious. Obrist et al. (2011), in a study of UX in a factory, found that the absence of stress constituted 'a perfect workday', which was one of the emotion cue cards that they asked clean-room operators to fill out. Negative emotions like fear and anger were mentioned by the operators, while positive emotions were not. There is however a lack of taxonomy or framework for specifying the types of hedonic experiences that fit workplace contexts (Lu & Roto, 2015). Among possible candidates for such a framework is Schaufeli et al. (2002)'s indicators of work engagement in work psychology, such as vigor, dedication, and absorption. Thus, an example of goals for positive UX-at-work may be that employees are engaged in their work, measured as high levels of vigor, dedication, and absorption (Roto, Clemmensen, Häätäjä, & Law, 2018).

Evaluation of interactions departing in technology may thus be about the employees' use of technology to do temporal and spatial crafting of the job so that the employees become more engaged in their work. First, a classic UX finding is that UX change over time, as users' experience with a novel product over weeks and months goes from the initial 'wow'-moments to familiarity, functional dependency, and finally emotional attachment and identification with the product (Karapanos, Zimmerman, Forlizzi, & Martens, 2009). In a UX-at-work context, a factory worker may experience a wow-feeling of a new machine, soon move to learnability and then usability issues, and finally come to identify with the machine in personal (e.g., "it is my machine") and social (e.g., "we always take turns using our machine") and task (e.g., "this machine is good for my tasks") terms. Furthermore, technology itself in the age of information intensive work may well be considered as, rather than single devices, the everyday computing practices of workers of scheduling time (Franssila & Okkonen, 2012), making it important to evaluate employees' emotions springing from their everyday computing practices. Such developments of engagements and attachments over time to favorite machines and workstations and preferred everyday computing practices may well be worth evaluating with classic UX over time frameworks.

Second, mobile and communication technologies have for long enabled employees to experience their favorite work locations. Working in specific rooms or buildings, from home or in company sites or in public transportation, working indoor or outdoor, all of these are possible with technology. For example, 'digital twins' of pot plants may in the future allow growers sitting at home to experience direct interaction with pot plants located in remote greenhouses, and thereby support the hedonic UX-at-work of employees working in the agricultural sector. Potentially any technology may be evaluated in terms of its support to the employees crafting or organization of their work. Employees using technology to work from their favorite work location may have positive experiences of less time pressures and emotional pressures, but also negative experiences in terms of a loss of job control and feedback from colleagues working in other locations, and being blocked by organization power structures from choosing their own work locations (Cajander et al., 2020). Furthermore, the favorite location's physical environment may not support the favorite computing practices. For example, employees working in a shared work space may complain that even if the work location is fine, the company-offered setup of machinery is not the kind of machine that they are familiar with and identify with Cajander et al. (2020).

Third, automation, AI, robots, allow employees to actively choose their working hours. This may be as simple as a worker on a day shift allocating a serial production task to a collaborative robot to do overnight. A UX principle here may be to only automate the task sequences that the individual does not like to do, and not automate the part of the task that the particular individual worker actually likes to do (Klapperich & Hassenzahl, 2016). It should be about making everyday activities experientially richer rather than designing them away (Hassenzahl & Klapperich, 2014). Furthermore, digital technology may be used to reduce experiences of work fragmentation and negative mental workload, by supporting employees in proactively managing their task load, and organizing and planning their task execution (Franssila, 2019).

Evaluation of interactions departing in actors

Evaluations of interactions departing in actors are based on what is known about users of interactive technologies in work contexts. Being an actor in a workplace can include being a non-human actor (Leavitt, 1965), or a blue or white collar worker, or a gig worker, and more. In addition, employees work in firms that shape the knowledge, norms, qualifications, roles, skills, and values that enter into performing the work. Applying Nielsen's (1993) dimensions of differences among users, socio-technical HCI may have a particular interest in those workers who are domain experts, but who also are high on the dimensions of specific system skills and general computer skills. Hedonic experiences may involve both deep work domain knowledge and much system and computer proficiency, thereby leading to questions such as: Are the decisions made by the system understandable to me? What possibilities do these new controllers afford me and my colleagues? Can the systems really be trusted? However, actors can also be novices (e.g., apprentices, guests, students) or even non-human actors such a robots, AI, and other high-level automation.

Plaskoff (2017) defines the total employee experience as the employees' holistic perception of their relations with the employing organization derived from all their encounters with digital and non-digital touchpoints in their organization. However, actors' total employee experience, including well-being at work, are not clearly brought out in the HCI literature. Klapperich et al. (2018) have suggested that the link between technology use and well-being could be social practices and, in particular, the individual actor's fulfillment of basic psychological needs during these practices. They developed and tested a way for designers to collect data on people's social practices and basic psychological needs. In the context of increasing office workers' physical activity, they collected anecdotes of positive practices and linked them to design ideas for employees' health and well-being at work. However, they acknowledge that "practices may be too wild to be tamed in a way we suggest" (Klapperich et al., 2018). How to make the link from the practical use of technology to the employee's experience of well-being at work is yet a somewhat open question.

One possible way to make the link from the practical use of technology to the employee's experience of well-being at work is to ask the employees themselves to evaluate to what degree that organizational action hypotheses and prototyped worker experiences help the employees to experience that the job psychologically suits them (Niessen et al., 2016). First, the employees may consider if their tasks and responsibilities they have at work do have a deeper meaning; such meaning may come from considering the work domain content, but it may also stem from a well-designed interaction design in a work system that makes the job fit the employee (Franssila et al., 2016). Second, the employees may try to find personal meaning in their tasks and responsibilities at work, a cognitive reflection that is supported by their computer self-efficacy. Third, the employees may cast their tasks and responsibilities as being more than just part of their job, which again is supported by the technology-enabled global network of colleagues and customers that many employees develop as part of their job.

Evaluation of interactions departing in tasks

In relation to usability and UX, work tasks are often conceptualized as goal-driven combinations of low-level operations. Conceptualized in this way, work tasks are important to the quantitative assessment of the usability of work systems (Lindgaard & Chattratichart, 2007). From a practice-based perspective, work tasks are however more than low-level operations because they are embedded in social practices and must be interpreted by workers (Rohde et al., 2017). For example, Norros and Savioja (2008) suggest that work tasks have experience dimensions such as the instrumental experience of appropriate functioning, the communicative experience of a joint culture, and the psychological experience of competence and trust. Thus, work tasks have experience dimensions beyond pragmatic goal fulfillment.

While the outcome of work tasks matter to UX-at-work, so does the way the tasks are performed (e.g., the employee spending time exploring visualizations because this is enjoyable and interesting to do). Liu et al. (2019) argue that a radical focus on instrumentality, such as task efficiency, is very different from approaching work tasks as sustainable and collective work activities from which actors derive immediate pleasure and meaning. Although a task may have produced the desired outcome, there might still be problems with the way in which this outcome was reached, such as expending resources excessively or involving tedious interaction sequences (Norros & Savioja, 2008). Hassenzahl and Klapperich (2014) provide examples of how to design joyful use experiences by meeting the users' psychological needs and automating the boring parts. UX-at-work may also be supported by designs that support non-work needs, such as doing physical activity during work (Klapperich et al., 2018) and keeping in contact with family during the workday (Hassenzahl, Buzzo, & Neuhaus, 2016). Gamification research has explored how to design for both productivity and worker engagement (Neeli, 2012; Vegt, Visch, Vermeeren, & de Ridder, 2018). Gamified job elements have led to improvements in motivation, job satisfaction, and performance (Liu et al., 2018; Vegt et al., 2018). Furthermore, specific training of employees in task management has been shown to decrease negative experiences of work fragmentation (Franssila, 2019), leading to increased well-being at work.

In terms of what UX-at-work evaluations evaluate, the employees' own task management practices may well be worth focusing on (Franssila 2019; Niessen et al. 2016). Employees can experience technology-related changes in task management practices that allow them to concentrate on specific tasks, undertake or seek for additional tasks, and work more intensively on tasks that they enjoy (Niessen et al., 2016).

Evaluation of interactions departing in structure

The use of many business applications is mandated. Workers will only have positive user experiences with such applications if business goals and user goals overlap (Nass, Adam, Doerr, & Trapp, 2012). Business goals are related to the work tasks and to the high-level expectations and wishes for how a system supports a business in fulfilling its mission. Hornbæk and Frøkjær (2008) had students evaluate a website after half of them had been provided with a list of business goals for the website. Compared to the students who had evaluated the website without access to business goals, the students who had been provided with the business goals reported usability problems that were rated higher in utility by the company owning the website. This difference shows that though business goals and user goals may overlap, they emphasize different parts of a system and its use. User goals—the standard focus in usability evaluation—are related to the employees' personal needs (Nass et al., 2012).

In much work, the structure element includes the workers' job descriptions, the instructions about how to use the work system, the procedures for how employee and other actors communicate with each other about their tasks, and so forth. Much of this is captured by the notion of organizational usability, defined as "the match between a computer system and the structure and practices of an organization, such that the system can be effectively integrated into the work practices of the organization's members" (Elliott & Kling, 1997). For example, Gutiérrez et al. (2019) found that an important reason for the modest use of agricultural decision support systems was that their terminology and logic were designed by agricultural scientists and IT developers and failed to consider the work domain expertise and practical needs of farmers. These systems met neither business goals, nor user goals, and were far from providing good UX-at-work.

Structure also includes temporal contexts of use. Shaw et al. (2018) proposed that a technology will stay in use for a long period of time if it repeatedly satisfies the user's motivation and continually extends the user's capabilities and identity, and the technology becomes on object of attachment for its users. That said, it appears that the UX at the time of introducing a novel system differs from that of long-term use (Kujala et al., 2019). Over time, situational contexts (e.g., different work groups) become more predictive of technology use (Shaw et al., 2018).

Even when departing in organizational structure issues, doing HWID UX-at-work field evaluations is user-centric and asks what the employees (workers) as users of technology themselves can do, perhaps with the support of designers etc., to make their job suit them. Concretely, the employees may merge personal goals with business goals by attempting to limit the amount of time they spend with people that they do not get along well with, and only contact them for things that are necessary, and by use of lean media such as formal emails. They can also invest in relationships with people whom they get along with the best (often the other employees around them)—which may be visible in the people at the top of contact lists in the employees' communication systems. Finally, they can actively look for opportunities to work together with people whom they get along well with at work and evaluate their work systems for the degree that these allow them to interact with interesting other people.

Evaluations in the field

Learning from other socio-technical approaches, e.g., 'grounded design' (Rohde et al., 2017), field evaluations, and other qualitative methods are necessary to understand how artefacts mediate social and technical changes in practice, that is, in UX-at-work situations. The use of an artifact needs to be understood by workers as contextual and creative actions that may mediate changes in social practices. 'Justificatory knowledge' (Mandviwalla, 2015) comes from among other evaluations and reflective analysis by stakeholders. This includes workers, who can help create design-relevant explanatory and predictive knowledge about why the artefact has the effects it does (Rohde et al., 2017).

The designers have a responsibility to facilitate evaluations in the field as collective and individual learnings and to help formulate and make explicit such insights for all stakeholders, in words that most can agree to. Workers may have to make meaning out of the artefacts, including both new interactions with the device and new social arrangement around those, and in that process, they may generate new practical design knowledge. This may again later be input to designers' next version of the artefact.

The emergent changes in both interactions with the artefacts and social arrangements around those need to be evaluated. To do this, formative evaluations not only of usability and UX, but also more broadly the usefulness of the artefact in the workers social practices, can be done—and compared to the initially (usually quite vague) UX goals and social goals set historically earlier. The outcome may be a design case, that is, a holistic gestalt that includes both organizational action hypothesis, and prototyped worker's UX-at-work, and the links between those.

UX-at-work testing

UX-at-work may be quite ordinary most of the time. Ordinary UX-at-work can be measured with AttrakDiff and domain-specific survey tools (Clemmensen et al., 2020) and studied in-depth qualitatively (Meneweger et al., 2018). UX-at-work is a term that both covers usability and user experience. While there may be consensus in the HCI community about a usability definition—everybody uses the ISO definition of usability as effectiveness, efficiency, and satisfaction,[1] there is less consensus about UX definitions (Rajanen et al., 2017). However, UX-at-work can be conceptualized as the hedonic and pragmatic qualities of the relations between actors (workers, AI systems), work systems, work tasks, and organizational structure (Clemmensen et al., 2020). What is tested when we test UX-at-work is thus perhaps more contextual than the common UX testing of consumer product, and less prone to dynamic changes over time.

For testing purposes, it is important the UX measurement instrument is valid. Among the many UX questionnaires that lack validation (Bargas-Avila & Hornbæk, 2011), a psychometric tool, AttrakDiff (Hassenzahl, Burmester, & Koller, 2003), stands out as well accepted as valid for capturing the pragmatic and hedonic qualities of interactive products. AttrakDiff has been used to assess the hedonic aspects of UX and how they interact with pragmatic aspects such as perceived usability and goodness (Hassenzahl, 2004; Tuch, Bargas-Avila, & Opwis, 2010). When compared to other UX questionnaires such as VisAWI (Moshagen & Thielsch, 2013) and several aesthetics scales, AttrakDiff is a reliable tools to measure the hedonic aspects of UX (Papachristos, 2018).

In a work context, Schrepp et al. (2006) applied AttrakDiff to do a UX test of a work system. They demonstrated that pragmatic and hedonic qualities impact the attractiveness of user interfaces and that attractiveness ratings correlate with user preferences, thereby validating the AttrakDiff ratings. AttrakDiff has been used to study how UX was influenced by user attributes (playfulness, computer expertise) and product attributes (pragmatic quality, hedonic quality) over a 13-week period

---

[1] But see for example (Hertzum, 2010) for a variety of usability concepts, and (Clemmensen, 2009) for alternative cultural theories of usability.

(Harbich & Hassenzahl, 2017). UX changed over time and these changes were influenced considerably by product attributes and, as time passed, increasingly by user attributes. Morales et al. (2012) contend that it takes little time to complete the AttrakDiff instrument, that completing it does not interfere with the work, and that the results appear to be reliable for complex equipment. They and others conclude that AttrakDiff can be applied in work settings (Clemmensen et al., 2020; Harbich & Hassenzahl, 2017; Morales et al., 2012). However, to elicit explanations about workers' user experiences, AttrakDiff results must be supplemented with richer data such as interviews. Furthermore, AttrakDiff probably must be supplemented by questions about the characteristics of the work situations. These questions can be derived from fieldwork and concern where the workers are, what tasks they are working on, which parts of which systems they are using, what else they are doing, and whom they are together with when interacting at work (Clemmensen et al., 2020).

5.4 Summary

Relation artefacts Type III are defined as having the purpose of socio-technical hypothesis prototyping of the best solution chosen among sketches (see Chap. 4 for socio-technical HCI design sketching). Three possible subcategories of relation artefacts Type III were introduced: organizational action hypotheses prototypes, worker experience prototypes, and prototypes for UX-at-work field testing. Together they presented a move from the social to the technical, centered around workers actively prototyping specific hypotheses about interaction designs and social arrangements at work. Noteworthy, the prototyping drew on theoretical notions of 'justificatory knowledge' for organizational action designs, worker's 'job crafting' of their preferred solutions, and evaluation with a heart (UX-at-work model).

Reflecting on the HWID relation artefacts Type III by comparing them to entities in other socio-technical HCI design approaches, Practice-Based Design (PBD) (Wulf et al., 2018) seems very similar to and useful for HWID. PBD develops mature prototypes of new designs that workers can use in their daily work and PBD studies the local appropriation of these and particularly the social changes stemming therefrom. However, there are possible differences between how prototyping is done in PBD and the design of HWID relation artefacts Type III:

- Similar to PBD, empirical bottom-up field studies are involved in HWID relation artefacts Type III prototyping since workers co-design the prototype and evaluate, but, importantly, they embed formulated hypotheses about interaction designs in the work and organizational setting.
- HWID prototypes as relation artefacts Type III are social-deterministic in the sense that they move from the social to the technical. In contrast, PBD prototyping moves mostly from the technical to social.
- Relation artefacts Type III are prototypes for sociomaterial solutions. Why call it sociomaterial solutions, instead of, for example, PBD's appropriation?

An importance nuance in prototyping of changes in workers' social practices concerns what is prototyped: 1. Social arrangements requiring novel interactions with computers (relation artefact Type III socio-determinism), or 2. Novel social arrangements because of novel interactions with computers (PBD prototyping's techno-determinism). Relation artefacts type III are mostly within a social-deterministic approach where organizational prescriptions take priority over IT system functions in the organizations and the workers appropriation of the prototyped social changes. This is slightly different from technical-deterministic approaches to social change, such as grounded design (Rohde et al., 2017), where novel IT functions are what is primarily appropriated in order to structure novel social practices in the socio-technical system. In technical-deterministic approaches appropriating an IT artifact for use changes the very social practices for which the artifact had originally been designed, that is, the artefacts ' mold' the organizational context (Rohde et al., 2017), while in social-deterministic approaches such as with relation artefacts type III the emerging social changes are directly, explicitly and knowingly what is prototyped.

- Both in HWID and PBD the initial ideas about the prototypes in HWID emerges from objectified conceptual knowledge about 'irritated' social practices (Rohde et al., 2017), but in PBD focus is on the functionality of mature prototypes, while in HWID the sub-types of relation artefacts Type III have slightly different foci.
- Finally, sociomaterial design—sociomateriality as empirical phenomena (and not philosophical stance)—has recently been discussed in depth and has benefits of among other less fixed boundaries around what is being designed (Bjørn & Østerlund, 2014), something that is for future research into HWID.

References

Abdelnour-Nocera, J., Barricelli, B. R., Lopes, A., Campos, P., & Clemmensen, T. (2015). *Human work interaction design: Work analysis and interaction design methods for pervasive and smart workplaces: 4th IFIP 13.6 Working Conference, HWID 2015, London, UK, June 25–26, 2015, Revised selected papers* (Vol. 468).

Ahmed, H., & La, H. M. (2020). Evaluating the Co-dependence and Co-existence between Religion and Robots: Past, Present and Insights on the Future. *International Journal of Social Robotics*, 1–17.

Albers, M., & Still, B. (2010). Usability of complex information systems. In M. Albers & B. Still (Eds.), *Usability of complex information systems: Evaluation of user interaction* (1st ed., pp. 3–16). https://doi.org/10.1201/EBK1439828946.

Alvarado, O., & Waern, A. (2018). Towards algorithmic experience: Initial efforts for social media contexts. In *Proceedings of the 2018 CHI Conference on Human Factors in Computing Systems* (pp. 1–12).

Amershi, S., Weld, D., Vorvoreanu, M., Fourney, A., Nushi, B., Collisson, P., ... Horvitz, E. (2019). Guidelines for human-AI interaction. In *Proceedings of the 2019 CHI Conference on Human Factors in Computing Systems* (pp. 1–13). https://doi.org/10.1145/3290605.3300233.

Appelbaum, S. H., Habashy, S., Malo, J., & Shafiq, H. (2012). Back to the future: Revisiting Kotter's 1996 change model. *Journal of Management Development*.

Bargas-Avila, J. A., & Hornbæk, K. (2011). Old wine in new bottles or novel challenges: A critical analysis of empirical studies of user experience. In *Proceedings of the SIGCHI Conference on Human Factors in Computing Systems* (pp. 2689–2698). https://doi.org/10.1145/1978942.197 9336.

Berque, D., Chiba, H., Ohkura, M., Sripian, P., & Sugaya, M. (2020). Fostering cross-cultural research by cross-cultural student teams: A case study related to kawaii (Cute) robot design. In P.-L. P. Rau (Ed.), *Cross-cultural design. User experience of products, services, and intelligent environments* (pp. 553–563). Cham: Springer International Publishing.

Bjørn, P., & Østerlund, C. (2014). *Sociomaterial-design: Bounding technologies in practice.* Springer.

Cajander, Å., Larusdottir, M., & Hedström, G. (2020). The effects of automation of a patient-centric service in primary care on the work engagement and exhaustion of nurses. *Quality and User Experience, 5*(1), 9. https://doi.org/10.1007/s41233-020-00038-x.

Calori, R. (1998). Essai: Philosophizing on strategic management models. *Organization Studies, 19*(2), 281–306.

Camillus, J. C. (2008). Strategy as a wicked problem. *Harvard Business Review, 86*(5), 98.

Card, S. K., Moran, T. P., & Newell, A. (1983). *The psychology of human-computer interaction.* Hillsdale, NJ: Lawrence Erlbaum Associates.

Clemmensen, T. (2009). Towards a theory of cultural usability: A comparison of ADA and CM-U theory (awarded best paper of the conference) (M. Kurosu, Ed.). In *First international conference on human-centered design, HCD 2009, Held as part of HCI international 2009* (pp. 416–425). San Diego, CA, USA: Springer.

Clemmensen, T., Hertzum, M., & Abdelnour-Nocera, J. (2020). Ordinary user experiences at work: A study of greenhouse growers. *ACM Transactions on Computer-Human Interaction (TOCHI), June*(Article no 16), 1–31. https://doi.org/10.1145/3386089.

Diefenbach, S., Kolb, N., & Hassenzahl, M. (2014). The 'Hedonic' in human-computer interaction: History, contributions, and future research directions. In *Proceedings of the 2014 Conference on Designing Interactive Systems* (pp. 305–314). http://dl.acm.org/citation.cfm?doid=2598510.259 8549.

Elliott, M., & Kling, R. (1997). Organizational usability of digital libraries: Case study of legal research in civil and criminal courts. *Journal of the American Society for Information Science, 48*(11), 1023–1035. https://doi.org/10.1002/(SICI)1097-4571(199711)48:11%3c1023:: AID-ASI5%3e3.0.CO;2-Y.

Fallman, D. (2011). The new good: Exploring the potential of philosophy of technology to contribute to human-computer interaction. In *Proceedings of the SIGCHI Conference on Human Factors in Computing Systems* (pp. 1051–1060).

Franssila, H. (2019). Work fragmentation, task management practices and productivity in individual knowledge work. In *International conference on human-computer interaction* (pp. 29–38). Springer.

Franssila, H., & Okkonen, J. (2012). Adjusting the design target of life-cycle aware HCI in knowledge work: Focus on computing practices. In *IFIP working conference on human work interaction design* (pp. 150–160). Springer.

Franssila, H., Okkonen, J., & Savolainen, R. (2016). Developing measures for information ergonomics in knowledge work. *Ergonomics, 59*(3), 435–448. https://doi.org/10.1080/00140139. 2015.1073795.

Garbuio, M., Lovallo, D., Porac, J., & Dong, A. (2015). A design cognition perspective on strategic option generation. In *Cognition and strategy.* Emerald Group Publishing Limited.

Jones, D., & Gregor, S. (2007). The anatomy of a design theory. *Journal of the Association for Information Systems, 8*(5), 1.

Gutiérrez, F., Htun, N. N., Schlenz, F., Kasimati, A., & Verbert, K. (2019). A review of visualisations in agricultural decision support systems: An HCI perspective. *Computers and Electronics in Agriculture, 163*, 104844. https://doi.org/10.1016/j.compag.2019.05.053.

Harbich, S., & Hassenzahl, M. (2017). User experience in the work domain: A longitudinal field study. *Interacting with Computers, 29*(3), 306–324.

Hassenzahl, M. (2004). The interplay of beauty, goodness, and usability in interactive products. *Human-Computer Interaction, 19*(4), 319–349. https://doi.org/10.1207/s15327051hci1904_2.

Hassenzahl, M., Burmester, M., & Koller, F. (2003). AttrakDiff: ein fragebogen zur messung wahrgenommener hedonischer und pragmatischer qualität. In G. Szwillus & J. Ziegler (Eds.), *Mensch & computer 2003: Interaktion in bewegung* (pp. 187–196). https://doi.org/10.1007/978-3-322-80058-9_19.

Hassenzahl, M., Buzzo, D., & Neuhaus, R. (2016). Perfect days: A benevolent calendar to take back your time. In *Celebration & contemplation, 10th international conference on design & emotion 27–30 September 2016, Amsterdam* (pp. 52–58).

Hassenzahl, M., Diefenbach, S., & Göritz, A. (2010). Needs, affect, and interactive products–facets of user experience. *Interacting with Computers, 22*(5), 353–362. https://doi.org/10.1016/j.intcom.2010.04.002.

Hassenzahl, M., & Klapperich, H. (2014). Convenient, clean, and efficient?: The experiential costs of everyday automation. In *Proceedings of the 8th Nordic Conference on Human-Computer Interaction: Fun, Fast, Foundational* (pp. 21–30). ACM.

Hassenzahl, M., & Tractinsky, N. (2006). User experience-a research agenda. *Behaviour & Information Technology, 25*(2), 91–97.

Hassenzahl, M., Wiklund-Engblom, A., Bengs, A., Hägglund, S., & Diefenbach, S. (2015). Experience-oriented and product-oriented evaluation: psychological need fulfillment, positive affect, and product perception. *International Journal of Human-Computer Interaction, 31*(8), 530–544.

Heikkilä, P., Honka, A., & Kaasinen, E. (2018). Quantified factory worker: Designing a worker feedback dashboard. In *Proceedings of the 10th Nordic Conference on Human-Computer Interaction* (pp. 515–523). https://doi.org/10.1145/3240167.3240187.

Hertzum, M. (2010). Images of usability. *International Journal of Human-Computer Interaction, 26*(6), 567–600. https://doi.org/10.1080/10447311003781300.

Hogan, T., & Hornecker, E. (2011). Human-data relations and the lifeworld. In *Proceedings of IHCI*.

Hornbæk, K., & Frøkjær, E. (2008). Making use of business goals in usability evaluation: An experiment with novice evaluators. In *Proceedings of the SIGCHI Conference on Human Factors in Computing Systems* (pp. 903–912). https://doi.org/10.1145/1357054.1357197.

Ihde, D. (1990). *Technology and the lifeworld: From garden to earth*, Bloomington: Indiana University.

Iivari, J. (2020). A critical look at theories in design science research. *Journal of the Association for Information Systems, 21*(3), 10.

Inal, Y., Clemmensen, T., Rajanen, D., Iivari, N., Rizvanoglu, K., & Sivaji, A. (2020). Positive developments but challenges still ahead: A survey study on UX professionals' work practices. *Journal of Usability Studies, 15*(4).

Karapanos, E., Zimmerman, J., Forlizzi, J., & Martens, J.-B. (2009). User experience over time: An initial framework. In *Proceedings of the SIGCHI Conference on Human Factors in Computing Systems* (pp. 729–738). https://doi.org/10.1080/15710880412331289917.

Kember, P., & Murray, H. (1988). Towards socio-technical prototyping of work systems. *The International Journal of Production Research, 26*(1), 133–142.

Klapperich, H., & Hassenzahl, M. (2016). Hotzenplotz: Reconciling automation with experience. In *Proceedings of the 9th Nordic Conference on Human-Computer Interaction* (pp. 1–10).

Klapperich, H., Laschke, M., & Hassenzahl, M. (2018). The positive practice canvas: Gathering inspiration for wellbeing-driven design. In *NordiCHI* (pp. 74–81). https://doi.org/10.1145/3240167.3240209.

Kling, R., & Elliott, M. (1994). Digital library design for organizational usability. *ACM SIGOIS Bulletin, 15*(2), 59–70. https://doi.org/10.1145/192611.192746.

Kolko, J. (2015). Design thinking comes of age. *Harvard Business Review*.

Kon, I. (1989). The psychology of social inertia. *Soviet Sociology, 28*(1), 7–27. https://doi.org/10.2753/SOR1061-015428017.

Kujala, S., Miron-Shatz, T., & Jokinen, J. J. (2019). The cross-sequential approach: a short-term method for studying long-term user experience. *Journal of Usability Studies, 14*(2), 105–116.

Law, E. L.-C., Roto, V., Hassenzahl, M., Vermeeren, A. P. O. S., & Kort, J. (2009). Understanding, scoping and defining user experience: A survey approach. In *Proceedings of the ACM SIGCHI Conference on Human Factors in Computing Systems* (pp. 719–728). https://doi.org/10.1145/1518701.1518813.

Leavitt, H. J. (1965). Applied organizational change in industry, structural, technological and humanistic approaches. In J. March (Ed.), *Handbook of organizations* (Vol. 264, pp. 1144–1170). Rand McNally & Company.

Leonardi, P. M. (2011). When flexible routines meet flexible technologies: Affordance, constraint, and the imbrication of human and material agencies. *MIS Quarterly*, 147–167.

Lindgaard, G., & Chattratichart, J. (2007). Usability testing: What have we overlooked? In *Proceedings of the SIGCHI Conference on Human Factors in Computing Systems* (pp. 1415–1424).https://doi.org/10.1145/1240624.1240839.

Liu, M., Huang, Y., & Zhang, D. (2018). Gamification's impact on manufacturing: enhancing job motivation, satisfaction and operational performance with smartphone-based gamified job design. *Human Factors and Ergonomics in Manufacturing, 28*(1), 38–51. https://doi.org/10.1002/hfm.20723.

Liu, S.-Y. C., Bardzell, S., & Bardzell, J. (2019). Symbiotic encounters: HCI and sustainable agriculture. In *Proceedings of the 2019 CHI Conference on Human Factors in Computing Systems*, Paper no 317. https://doi.org/10.1145/3290605.3300547.

Lu, Y., & Roto, V. (2015). Evoking meaningful experiences at work–a positive design framework for work tools. *Journal of Engineering Design, 26*(4–6), 99–120. https://doi.org/10.1080/09544828.2015.1041461.

Mandviwalla, M. (2015). Generating and justifying design theory. *Journal of the Association for Information Systems, 16*(5), 3.

Meneweger, T., Wurhofer, D., Fuchsberger, V., & Tscheligi, M. (2018). Factory workers' ordinary user experiences: An overlooked perspective. *Human Technology, 14*(2), 209–232. https://doi.org/10.17011/ht/urn.201808103817.

Morales, K. L., Röbig, S., & Bruder, R. (2012). Learning from doing: Chances and constraints of studying medical devices through usability methods in field studies. *Zeitschrift Für Arbeitswissenschaft, 66*(2–3), 115–128.

Moshagen, M., & Thielsch, M. T. (2013). A short version of the visual aesthetics of websites inventory. *Behaviour and Information Technology, 32*(12), 1305–1311. https://doi.org/10.1080/0144929X.2012.694910.

Nass, C., Adam, S., Doerr, J., & Trapp, M. (2012). Balancing user and business goals in software development to generate positive user experience. In *Human-Computer Interaction: The Agency Perspective* (pp. 29–53). Springer.

Neeli, B. K. (2012). A method to engage employees using gamification in BPO industry. In *2012 third international conference on services in emerging markets* (pp. 142–146). https://doi.org/10.1109/ICSEM.2012.27.

Neff, G., & Nagy, P. (2018). *Agency in the digital age: Using symbiotic agency to explain human-technology interaction.*

Nielsen, J. (1993). *Usability engineering.* Boston, MA: Academic Press.

Niessen, C., Weseler, D., & Kostova, P. (2016). When and why do individuals craft their jobs? The role of individual motivation and work characteristics for job crafting. *Human Relations, 69*(6), 1287–1313. https://doi.org/10.1177/0018726715610642.

Norros, L., & Savioja, P. (2008). User experience in the systems usability approach. In E. L.-C. Law, N. Bevan, G. Christou, M. Springett, & M. Larusdottir (Eds.), *Proceedings of the International Workshop on Valid Useful User Experience Measurement (VUUM) 2008* (pp. 45–48). Retrieved from http://citeseerx.ist.psu.edu/viewdoc/download?doi=10.1.1.177.7123&rep=rep1&type=pdf.

Obrist, M., Reitberger, W., Wurhofer, D., Förster, F., & Tscheligi, M. (2011). User experience research in the semiconductor factory: A contradiction? In *IFIP conference on human-computer interaction* (pp. 144–151). Springer.

Okamoto, S., & Sano, S. (2017). Anthropomorphic AI agent mediated multimodal interactions in vehicles. In *Proceedings of the 9th International Conference on Automotive User Interfaces and Interactive Vehicular Applications Adjunct* (pp. 110–114). https://doi.org/10.1145/3131726.313 1736.

Palviainen, J., & Väänänen-Vainio-Mattila, K. (2009). User experience in machinery automation: From concepts and context to design implications. *Lecture Notes in Computer Science (Including Subseries Lecture Notes in Artificial Intelligence and Lecture Notes in Bioinformatics)* (Vol. 5619, pp. 1042–1051). https://doi.org/10.1007/978-3-642-02806-9_119.

Papachristos, E. (2018). Assessing the performance of short multi-item questionnaires in aesthetic evaluation of websites. *Behaviour & Information Technology, 38*(5), 469–485. https://doi.org/10. 1080/0144929X.2018.1539521.

Plaskoff, J. (2017). Employee experience: The new human resource management approach. *Strategic HR Review, 16*(3), 136–141. https://doi.org/10.1108/SHR-12-2016-0108.

Qin, X., Tan, C.-W., & Clemmensen, T. (2019). Unraveling the influence of the interplay between mobile phones' and users' awareness on the user experience (UX) of using mobile phones. In *IFIP advances in information and communication technology* (Vol. 544). https://doi.org/10.1007/ 978-3-030-05297-3_5.

Rajanen, D., Clemmensen, T., Iivari, N., Inal, Y., Rızvanoğlu, K., Sivaji, A., & Roche, A. (2017). UX professionals' definitions of usability and UX–A comparison between Turkey, Finland, Denmark, France and Malaysia. *Lecture Notes in Computer Science (Including Subseries Lecture Notes in Artificial Intelligence and Lecture Notes in Bioinformatics).* https://doi.org/10.1007/978-3-319- 68059-0_14.

Reeves, B., & Nass, C. (1996). *The media equation: How people treat computers, television, and new media like real people and places* (Vol. 34). https://doi.org/10.1109/MSPEC.1997.576013.

Rohde, M., Brödner, P., Stevens, G., Betz, M., & Wulf, V. (2017). Grounded design-a praxeological is research perspective. *Journal of Information Technology, 32*, 163–179. https://doi.org/10.1057/ jit.2016.5.

Roto, V., Clemmensen, T., Häätäjä, H., & Law, E. L.-C. (2018). Guest editors' introduction: Designing interactive systems for work engagement. *Human Technology, 14*(2), 135–139. https:// doi.org/10.17011/ht/urn.201808103814.

Roto, V., Kaasinen, E., Heimonen, T., Karvonen, H., Jokinen, J. P. P., Mannonen, P., … Koskinen, H. M. K. (2017). Utilizing experience goals in design of industrial systems. In *Proceedings of ACM SIGCHI conference on human factors in computing systems (CHI'17)* (pp. 6993–7004). https://doi.org/10.1145/3025453.3025620.

Rozendaal, M. C., Boon, B., & Kaptelinin, V. (2019). Objects with intent: Designing everyday things as collaborative partners. *ACM Transactions on Computer-Human Interaction (TOCHI), 26*(4), 1–33.

Savioja, P., Liinasuo, M., & Koskinen, H. (2014). User experience: Does it matter in complex systems? *Cognition, Technology and Work, 16*(4), 429–449. https://doi.org/10.1007/s10111-013- 0271-x.

Schaufeli, W. B., Salanova, M., González-Romá, V., Bakker, A. B., & Senthilkumar, M. (2002). The measurement of engagement and burnout: A two sample confirmatory factor analytic approach. *Journal of Happiness Studies, 3*(1), 71–92. Retrieved from https://www.wilmarschaufeli.nl/pub lications/Schaufeli/178.pdf.

Schrepp, M., Held, T., & Laugwitz, B. (2006). The influence of hedonic quality on the attractiveness of user interfaces of business management software. *Interacting with Computers, 18*(5), 1055– 1069. https://doi.org/10.1016/j.intcom.2006.01.002.

Scoppetta, A., Davern, E., & Geyer, L. (2019). *Job Carving and Job Crafting-a review of practices (EU report).* KE-01-19-557-EN-N.

Shaw, H., Ellis, D. A., & Ziegler, F. V. (2018). The technology integration model (TIM). Predicting the continued use of technology. *Computers in Human Behavior, 83*, 204–214. https://doi.org/10.1016/j.chb.2018.02.001.

Shin, D., Zhong, B., & Biocca, F. A. (2020). Beyond user experience: What constitutes algorithmic experiences? *International Journal of Information Management*, 102061. https://doi.org/10.1016/J.IJINFOMGT.2019.102061.

Sterling, B. (2009). COVER STORY Design fiction. *Interactions, 16*(3), 20–24.

The International Organization for Standardization, I. (2019). *ISO/DIS 9241-11.2(en) Ergonomics of human-system interaction—Part 11: Usability: Definitions and concepts.* Retrieved from https://www.iso.org/obp/ui/#iso:std:iso:9241:-210:ed-2:v1:en.

Tohidi, M., Buxton, W., Baecker, R., & Sellen, A. (2006). Getting the right design and the design right. In *Proceedings of the SIGCHI Conference on Human Factors in Computing Systems* (pp. 1243–1252). ACM.

Townsend, V. (2015). *From participation to differentiation: A framework for re-designing a socio-technical system* (University of Windsor). Retrieved from https://scholar.uwindsor.ca/etd/5671.

Tuch, A. N., Bargas-Avila, J. A., & Opwis, K. (2010). Symmetry and Aesthetics in Website Design: It's a Man's Business. *Computers in Human Behavior, 26*(6), 1831–1837. https://doi.org/10.1016/j.chb.2010.07.016.

Väätäjä, H., Seppänen, M., & Paananen, A. (2014). Creating value through user experience: A case study in the metals and engineering industry. *International Journal of Technology Marketing, 9*(2), 163. https://doi.org/10.1504/ijtmkt.2014.060093.

Vegt, N., Visch, V., Vermeeren, A., & de Ridder, H. (2018). A case study on gamified interventions for team cohesion in factory work. *Human Technology, 14*(2), 176–208. https://doi.org/10.17011/ht/urn.201808103816.

Wulf, V., Pipek, V., Randall, D., Rohde, M., Schmidt, K., & Stevens, G. (Eds.). (2018). *Socio-informatics-a practice-based perspective on the design and use of IT artifacts.* Oxford: Oxford University Press.

Wolf, C., & Blomberg, J. (2019). Evaluating the promise of human-algorithm collaborations in everyday work practices. In *Proceedings of the ACM on Human-Computer Interaction, 3*(CSCW). https://doi.org/10.1145/3359245.

Wolf, C. T. (2020). AI models and their worlds: Investigating data-driven, AI/ML ecosystems through a work practices lens. In *International conference on information* (pp. 651–664). Springer.

Wurhofer, D., Fuchsberger, V., Meneweger, T., Moser, C., & Tscheligi, M. (2015a). Insights from user experience research in the factory: What to consider in interaction design. In J. A. Nocera, B. Barricelli, A. Lopes, P. Campos, & T. Clemmensen (Eds.), *HWID2015-human work interaction design. Work analysis and interaction design methods for pervasive and smart workplaces. IFIP advances in information and communication technology* (Vol. 468, pp. 39–56). https://doi.org/10.1007/978-3-319-27048-7_3.

Wurhofer, D., Meneweger, T., Fuchsberger, V., & Tscheligi, M. (2015b). Deploying robots in a production environment: A study on temporal transitions of workers' experiences. *Lecture Notes in Computer Science (Including Subseries Lecture Notes in Artificial Intelligence and Lecture Notes in Bioinformatics)* (Vol. 9298, pp. 203–220). https://doi.org/10.1007/978-3-319-22698-9_14.

Wurhofer, D., Meneweger, T., Fuchsberger, V., & Tscheligi, M. (2018). Reflections on operators' and maintenance engineers' experiences of smart factories. In *Proceedings of the 2018 ACM Conference on Supporting Groupwork* (pp. 284–296). https://doi.org/10.1145/3148330.3148349.

Chapter 6
Relation Artefacts Type IV

Abstract This chapter is about relation artefacts Type IV which are socio-technical interventions in organizational and wider contexts. Three subtypes of these relation artefacts move the design from the technical to the social: interaction interoperability checkups, digital legacy interventions, and organizational strategy alignments. The HWID platform is shown to provide a massive push toward such interventions, through the continuous relations building between empirical work analysis and interaction design activities that aims to create new local sociomaterial realities for stakeholders involved. Ways of avoiding falling into a 'techno-determinism' trap and instead keeping the relations to the social, and vice versa, are introduced. The chapter ends with a summary of how to do socio-technical HCI design interventions.

Keywords Human work interaction design · Relation artefacts · Interaction interoperability checks · Digital legacy interventions · Organizational strategy alignments

HCI design includes both the construction of a novel technical solutions such as interaction designs and their evaluation with users in UX tests (Wania et al., 2006). In socio-technical HCI design, evaluations of the technical is complemented with interventions into the social. In HWID, the evaluation/interventions melt together in interventions to ensure the continuous relation building between the social and the technical (henceforth, we will use evaluation and intervention interchangeably in this chapter). Thus, this chapter is about relation artefacts Type IV, which presents a movement from the technical to the social with three subtypes: interaction interoperability checkups, digital legacy interventions, and organizational strategy alignments, Fig. 6.1.

To help to understand the sub-types and to follow the structure of the chapter, Table 6.1 presents the key characteristics of each of the three sub-types.

In the sections below, we unfold and discuss the sub-types, but first we discuss the nature of the movement with relation artefact Type IV evaluation/interventions.

In socio-technical HCI design such as HWID, evaluations of interaction designs are most of the time formative evaluation with the purpose of improving the design.

© The Author(s), under exclusive license to Springer Nature Switzerland AG 2021   107
T. Clemmensen, *Human Work Interaction Design*,
Human–Computer Interaction Series,
https://doi.org/10.1007/978-3-030-71796-4_6

Fig. 6.1 Relation artefacts
type IV—socio-technical
actions and designs

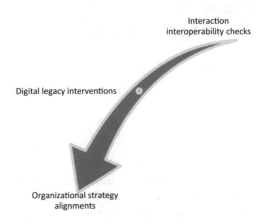

Table 6.1 Overview of key characteristics of relation artefact Type IV sub-types

Relation artefact Type IV sub-types	Key characteristics
1. Interaction interoperability check-ups	It is important to increase the UX related to interoperability of interaction designs across the organization. Two kinds of interoperabilities are interaction design interoperability and organization and work interoperability. Interaction operability checks should be cross-validated by being evaluated in different formats of lab, field, and gallery
2. Digital legacy interventions	They make the novel design coexist with the legacy systems. These are socio-technical systems that are technically and/or socially old and need lots of maintenance but solve important problems for organizations and meet individual employees' needs. Interaction design for digital legacy is also about workers' feelings about their digital legacy in the workplace
3. Organizational strategy alignments	Serve to ensure that the designed solutions are aligned with the long-term goals of the organization. Having a UX culture in the organization eases alignment. Co-evaluation with software developers and work domain experts eases alignment. In organizations with a people-centered approach job crafting may help align HWID with organizational strategy, and managers may facilitate this through encouragement

At the same time, the designs are organizational actions that intervene in work practices and deals with workers everyday life. This implies that there is a systematic
and sequential overlap between evaluation of interaction design and intervention
in work practices. While each UX and usability evaluations in classic UCD may

> First-stage intervention = {relation artefact type I}
> IF evaluation = {nonresponse}
> THEN second-stage intervention = {intensify relation artefact type I}
> ELSE IF evaluation = {response}
> THEN at second stage = {continue with relation artefact type II}

Fig. 6.2 Decision rules in adaptive interventions in socio-technical design. The sequence is continued with artefact types III and IV and repeated as long as it takes to reach relation artefact type IV. Adapted from (Nahum-Shani et al., 2012)

appear as somewhat unrelated evaluations of different technical prototypes, in HWID the sequence of artefact designs/actions and evaluations thereof can be conceptualized as an 'adaptive intervention'. 'Adaptive interventions' is a method proposed in psychology to allow greater individualization and adaptation of intervention options (i.e., intervention type and/or strength) over time (Nahum-Shani et al., 2012). Adaptive interventions in socio-technical design are thus a string of different relation artefacts that are evaluated to adapt to workers' and organizations' characteristics and changing needs over time, with the general aim to optimize the long-term effectiveness of the overall socio-technical intervention. HWID can also chose to use adaptive interventions to adapt to the wider context, such as adapting usability interventions to fit them to different cultural contexts (Clemmensen & Katre, 2012). Figure 6.2 shows how decision rules can be used to operationalize adaptive interventions with relation artefacts.

Why do we intervene? Intervention with an artefact provides feedback information and a better understanding of the wicked problem (Hevner, March, Park, & Ram, 2008). Iterative intervention improves the IT artefact, that is, the results of the intervention is to be used to inform improvement possibilities, which can be used as an intervention again in a further iteration of the design process (Reinecke & Bernstein, 2013). The intervention provides new knowledge about the impact of the artefact on human experience and/or its organizational utility. In design thinking research, artefacts are understood as means to induce desirable, feasible, and viable human experiences. In IS design research, novelty and utility of artefacts and the effectiveness and efficiency in the performance of the given task by the artefacts may be more important (Rai, 2017). Intervention activities may support end-users collaboration with expert designers, providing them with a large number of alternative designs for both organized testing and independent trying out is a key contributor for users to make informed decisions (Joshi & Bratteteig, 2016).

What do we intervene with? We intervene with prototypes as expressions of 'design choices', for example, to (1) gain enough understanding of the artefact to properly see as many states of the system as possible, (2) get participants' views on design choices, (3) understand alternatives of major design decisions, (4) see the outputs of different forms of an algorithm, (5) iteratively refine the final calculation, (6) check if the user interfaces corresponded to users' preferences, and (7) illustrate the novelty of the prototype. In addition, there are significant differences across genres in what artefacts are intervened with (Rai, 2017). The genres include representation genre (methods and grammars), computational genre (computational algorithms and methods), optimization genre (optimization solution techniques, models, and algorithms), IS economics genre (mechanism design artefacts (e.g., control mechanisms, feedback mechanisms, predictive models) that explicitly account for the economic characteristic of the environment in which they operate). In addition, design thinking that produces artefacts to impact human experience may be a genre in itself.

Considerations about different intervention methods include intervention testing levels and methods. Testing may be done at different levels from unit testing of specific functionalities being developed, to overall acceptance as part of organizational implementation. Many different kinds of relation artefacts can be evaluated as interventions, including functional testing, usability testing, and acceptance testing. Academic researchers can devise their own purposeful methods for intervention, Joshi and Bratteteig (2016), for example, introduced 'blindfold' testing where participants would try to understand how ideas materialized without using their eyes to see, and hence provide feedback on the material design choices.

Functional intervention. For functional intervention, the main question to be evaluated is: Does it work? It is particularly relevant to the 'computational genre' that produces computational algorithms and methods. Functional testing describes what the system does in terms of pre-agreed input-output functions. Functional testing tests a part of the functionality of the whole system. Functional testing uses input and output of the system (black box testing) and compares that to design specifications—is the output as expected, given the input? Functional testing is different from Acceptance testing, as it does not test if the organization or the end-users will accept the system.

Usability intervention. For usability interventions, the main question is: Can the user use it? Here what is particularly relevant is the design thinking that produces artefacts to impact human experience. Usability and UX testing have pro and cons, see (Hertzum, 2020) for a detailed explanation for practitioners. The pro includes how to provide formative input for re-design and summative input for choosing among alternative designs, focus on effectiveness and efficiency (usability) and employee and customer experiences (UX), capture users' thinking process during use. The con is that there are no organizational or social considerations, and that it requires expertise to do. Finally, there is the expert review where pro and cons also are there; the pros are that experts can walk-through prototypes and points out errors, no real users needed, and the cons are the same as usability test.

Acceptance intervention. For acceptance intervention, the main question is if the user and organization will accept it (contract fulfillment)? This is relevant to IS economics genre that produces socio-technical HCI designs related to the economic characteristic of the environment in which they operate. Acceptance testing test criteria and test cases are developed in collaboration with end-users, customers, and key business stakeholders. Test criteria and test cases concerns both business processes and integration with other systems in the environment. Test criteria may include interoperability, reliability, stability, and accessibility and localization criteria, and more.

How should intervention findings be presented? When presenting your intervention as a scientific contribution to socio-technical HCI design, then aim to present your intervention as design choices made, including their implications within, and combinations across, the following elements (Rai, 2017): (1) The theory developed—one or more pre-existing kernel theories or a constructed theory—should be presented in terms of its assumptions, constructs, and relationships between constructs, and boundary conditions. (2) The methodology developed should be presented in terms of the requirements of methodologies (e.g., optimization, computational, statistical), and how you have defined the problem to align with your newly designed methodology. (3) Finally, the kind of intervention performed should itself be presented in terms of the validity and utility of your intervention as a solution to the problem, and what kind of intervention was done (e.g., simulation, real-world experiments, role of human subjects, the specific social context, etc.).

6.1 Interaction Interoperability Checkups

The interoperability of interaction designs as continuity in multi-device interactions

A subtype of relation artefacts type IV is interventions that aim to increase the UX related to interoperability of interaction designs. The interoperability of interaction designs have been studied as continuity in multi-device interactions (Raptis, Kjeldskov, & Skov, 2016). They did a study of peoples' practices of using interoperability designs, as they argued that (in 2016) it was becoming a possibility for people to interacting with and across their devices, and hence researchers should use this opportunity for studying interoperability design uptake and use in real life. They chose to study how people combine multiple information devices commonly used in the home, such as smartphones, computers, tablets, and media centers, in their everyday life for tasks as well as leisure, and to study a specific product, Apple's continuity. Apple's Continuity functionalities particularly increase integration between devices and services within the Apple ecosystem, and let people use nearby iPhones, iPads, and Macs together or move seamlessly between them, by means of synchronization and migration. However, their insights might well be relevant for the class of UX interoperability designs, including concrete products such as Microsoft's "Continue on PC" that supports users connecting their smartphones to their personal computers and the feature to quickly and easily share websites between their devices, various attempts to harmonize SAP applications from a UX perspective that enable users to seamlessly access data and applications from any cloud, and, generally, improved design of interoperability of social platforms in work settings and beyond. Thus 'continuity' or 'interoperability UX' describes user experiences related to sequential multi-device use where interactions move, or transition, from one device to another. A first checkup on the interoperability of interaction designs may focus on UX of sequential multi-device use.

However, despite a wealth of blogs and reports about employee experience and customer experience, when looking at continuity as a user experience, the users' expectations to interoperability designs are not explicit. Raptis et al. (2016) and Paay et al. (2017) found that interaction techniques for information sharing between mobile devices include tilting devices toward each other to preview and copy information, and using portals to drag information between federated devices, and that it would be interesting to know how such multi-device interaction were experienced, used and facilitated in real-world settings. For example, knowledge is needed about how transitions between desktop UIs and mobile devices are practiced, and how tasks are picked up after these transitions. They argued that (1) users would expect consistency, and that all devices be kept up-to-date in real time, (2) synchronization and task migration support are crucial for achieving continuity across devices, and (3) continuity-enabling features need to work "out of the box".

By scraping data from internet search engines (Google and Bing) for 2 weeks in 2015 with key words 'Apple Continuity', 'Handoff', and 'Phone and SMS', (Raptis et al., 2016) identified relevant and conclude-able data for interaction design interoperability UX. The found 124 relevant webpages, from which 3361 comments were collected. Out of these, 1603 relevant comments were analyzed through a combination of open coding adapted from grounded theory and iterative affinity diagramming. This produced six themes of interoperability UX challenges (Privacy, (e.g., sharing of accounts); Appropriation (e.g., integration of continuity into workflows); Customization (e.g., customizing continuity to networks and protocols); Awareness (e.g., the continuity enables ones phone to know about ones laptop); Exclusion (e.g., that continuity only works on one brand of devices, Apple); Troubleshooting (e.g., when continuity behaves unexpectedly). In addition, there was one theme on 'excitement' about the Continuity product. Raptis et al.'s conclusions were that the identified challenges could be translated to design considerations about (a) personal activities with shared devices, (b) shared activities with personal devices, (c) control and flexibility, and (d) transparency and trust. For example, with regard to personal activities with shared devices their study showed that the continuity product was characterized by the assumption that all the devices within a digital ecosystem are solely personal and used only by one individual, but their findings clearly illustrated, this was often not the case—there were plenty of personal activities with shared devices, and several comments showed that very often family members will be using the same device, at different times and for different purposes. However, only a few participants seemed to understand and realize the complication and the unintended consequences of informally sharing devices (e.g., personal activities were continued to individuals that were not part of the activity in the first place). Thus, the Raptis et al. study provided initial insights into interoperability UX of interaction designs. A limitation was that only the consumer (home) domain was studied, and the work domain might present a whole different set of challenges and excitements for interaction design interoperability products such as Continuity.

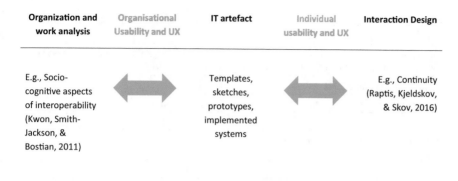

Organization and work analysis	Organisational Usability and UX	IT artefact	Individual usability and UX	Interaction Design
E.g., Socio-cognitive aspects of interoperability (Kwon, Smith-Jackson, & Bostian, 2011)		Templates, sketches, prototypes, implemented systems		E.g., Continuity (Raptis, Kjeldskov, & Skov, 2016)

National, geographic, cultural, social & technological contexts

Fig. 6.3 HWID and interoperability

Socio-technical interoperability of HCI in work domains

In contrast to individual interoperability UX such as 'continuity' products, socio-technical interoperability of HCI in work domains concerns multiple workers and multiple devices collaborating, Fig. 6.3. For example, interoperability is a key concept supporting cooperation within a team or between different agencies in large operations (Kwon, Smith-Jackson, & Bostian, 2011). However, interoperability is often discussed in terms of technical issues, for example, as technical interoperability among devices on the frequencies reserved for public safety agencies. Therefore, interoperability should be re-conceptualized to support the socio-cognitive aspects of communications and collaborations among different teams and organizations. Kwon et al. (2011) were in particular interested in police and emergency medical service (EMS) providers, and interviewed police and EMS providers, did a content analysis, and identified five dimensions of interoperability. Such socio-cognitive dimensions of interoperability may be of general interest to a general notion of socio-technical interoperability of HCI in work domains concerns multiple workers and multiple devices collaborating.

Socio-technical interoperability of HCI in work domains concerns (1) sharedness, (2) readiness, (3) awareness, (4) adaptiveness, and (5) coupledness of the multiple workers and multiple devices collaborating (Kwon et al., 2011). They found the following themes of interoperability: (1) Information sharedness covers information asymmetry, which is about the existing differences of information among workers; information overload, which is about difficulties in decision-making caused by too much information; and communication synchronicity, which is about the workers' experience of two or more communications occurring simultaneously and the degree of sharing of the information at the same time. (2) Communication readiness covers technical readiness, which is about the trouble with mobile devices or other equipment due to hardware problems, and willingness to share, which is about the workers' attitude to sharing collected information with other workers at the same activity. (3) Operational (group, team, network) awareness covers dynamic operational boundaries,

Table 6.2 Social and technical HCI themes from empirical studies of HCI interoperability. The overlap in categories is marked with italic

Organization and work analysis interoperability, based on (Kwon et al., 2011)	Interaction design interoperability, (based on Raptis et al., 2016)
1. Information Sharedness	1. Privacy
2. Communication Readiness	2. Appropriation
	3. Customization
3. *Operational (group, team, network) awareness*	4. *Awareness*
4. Adaptiveness	5. Exclusion
5. Coupledness	6. Troubleshooting

which is about the workers ability to change the operational boundaries depending on the situation; social awareness, which is about knowing the person who has the right information and being aware of the existence of the right person; and copresence, which is about the sense of being together or awareness of the involvement of a remotely located person. (4) adaptiveness covers self-organization, which is about the emerging and self-formed organization without any or much previous structure; and technical adaptability, which is about existing alternatives or option to modify current technology to communicate with each other. (5) Coupledness covers work coupling, which is about the degree of functional and sequential relationship of tasks or work; and distributed decision-making/duality of centralization, which is about the degree of centralization of decision-making or relationships among decision makers.

The five socio-cognitive themes of Kwon et al. (2011) can help to conceptualize and explain phenomena of socio-technical interoperability of HCI in work domains. At the same time, the link between interaction design interoperability (Raptis et al., 2016) and socio-cognitive aspects of interoperability is there. When the situation requires that multiple workers and multiple devices collaborate, device usability and UX is important.

Table 6.2 shows the empirically identified dimensions of the social and technical HCI perspectives on interoperability, and that the literal overlap occurs on the dimension of 'awareness'. This overlap serves as a good example of why we need both technical and social HCI perspectives on interoperability, and it also illustrates the overlap and link between the two. 'Awareness' in the social perspective on interoperability is about the operational (group, team, network) awareness, which covers the workers ability to change the operational boundaries depending on the situation, their knowledge about the persons who has the right information and being aware of the existence of the right persons, and their sense of being together or the involvement of a remotely located person. 'Awareness' in the technical HCI perspective is about how the software and hardware enable one's phone to know about one's laptop and the UX of that. UX is the link between the social and technical awareness in interoperability, there is an interesting link between experiencing the sense of being together or the involvement of a remotely located person and the experience of how the software and hardware enables one's phone to know about one's laptop and vice versa. The social and technical HCI perspectives on interoperability can also be seen in students preferences, as anecdotal evidence from master-level students preferences indicate that tech-savvy students prefer to think of interoperability as a matter of individual usability of IT artefacts (they prefer the paper on Continuity by Raptis et al. (2016)), while students mostly interested in organization issues, however, tend to think of interoperability as a matter of (inter-) organizational usability of (communication) IT artefacts (they prefer the socio-cognitive aspects of interoperability). However, both "organization-interested students" and tech-savvy-students most probably appreciate the other side than their 'own' of socio-technical HCI. This may well also be the case for professional workers, so this is a topic for future research.

Obviously, checking for socio-technical HCI interoperability requires considering the context, including national, geographic, cultural, social, and technological contexts.

Design evaluation—lab, field, gallery (exhibition, showroom)

Checking for socio-technical HCI interoperability in a HWID project may require thinking broadly about approaches to evaluate designs in various contexts. Interaction operability checks should be cross-validated by being evaluated in different formats. Three broad formats for evaluating interaction designs in context have been proposed under the labels respectively the 'Lab', stemming from experimental psychology; 'Field', based on the social sciences; and 'Gallery', with origins in art (Koskinen, Binder, & Redström, 2008). The 'Lab', or more generally, evaluation in the laboratory experimental tradition include classic usability and UX evaluation but also industrial design evaluation in labs. This approach builds on hypotheses with variables tested in controlled experiments that configure design in context as consisting of scenarios, design material (sketches, prototypes, mockups, etc.), and participants. The key feature of the experimental approach, even in its broad interpretation of experiments "in the wild", is the researchers' control of the experiment variables. The design experiment is perhaps the most significant traditional design evaluation form in HCI (Bang & Eriksen, 2014).

The 'Field' approach evaluates design by interpretive social science methods. The context of design here is the 'real world', 'naturalistic setting', or simply 'the field'; this can be any site, even the lab if the lab is treated as a 'field'. Thus, the field approach evaluates the use of designs by ordinary people leading their ordinary lives in ordinary social settings, with a particular focus on the sequential unfolding of events, and how the artefact acquires several meanings in social action (Koskinen et al., 2008). The key feature of the field approach to design evaluation is that people are in control, and that the design artefacts (prototypes, etc.) over time take on a peripheral role, as they commonly do in ordinary life (see also Clemmensen, Hertzum, & Abdelnour-Nocera, 2020).

The 'Gallery' approach to design evaluation differs significantly from the lab and the field approaches, since it expands and builds on a notion of artistically oriented design, for whom the gallery is one of the traditional formats for disseminating one's work (Koskinen et al., 2008). The gallery, or rather, the curated showroom exhibition presents concepts, design objects, ideas, and visions, by allowing people first-hand experiences. People can engage in what you usually do in museums, galleries, and even in shopping, advertisement and marketing, diverse forms of conceptual consumerism of imaginary or existing design 'products' (Koskinen et al., 2008). The key feature of the gallery approach to design evaluation is that it places design into art-world formats such as the canvas (but also goes beyond these into showroom and product placements, etc.) that emphasize pushing knowledge to new domains by way of critical discourse through practices borrowed from the art world.

The conclusion is that interaction operability checks should ideally be cross-validated by being approached in different formats, ranging from the lab, the field, and the gallery. These may all contribute to increases in novel knowledge and confidence in the interoperability checks designed. For example, the idea of the 'art reviewer' in traditional usability evaluation the idea has been around for long (Chavan, 2005), but as a interoperability evaluation method, the Gallery may unleash a new potential for imagined interoperability problems. This is perhaps because the gallery, with its focus on users' consumption of novel and spectacular design products in exhibition formats, is fundamentally different from the researcher-driven series of design experiments, and from the field studies of the ordinariness of design in people's everyday life. The message is, however, that when doing interaction interoperability checks and other design interventions not any single of the three evaluation approaches are the correct one, all should probably be used in a triangulation manner.

6.2 Digital Legacy Interventions

Digital legacy interventions are socio-technical interventions that make the novel design coexist with the legacy systems. However, this relation artefact Type IV subtype requires reconceptualizing what we mean by organizational legacy systems and what are interaction designs for digital legacy. It raises questions such as how employees experience their organization's business-critical but obsolete systems, and what can employees do about their own digital legacy in their organization.

The traditional technical view on legacy systems is that they are those systems that are technically obsolete, old, and need lots of maintenance, but at the same time are crucial for an organization's operation. The implication of this view is that software modernization is what solves legacy issues. For example, when a major bank replaces 20 years of use of IBM OS/2 Warp OS with Windows OS.[1] In contrast, the socio-technical HCI design view of legacy systems is that they are socio-technical systems that are technically and/or socially obsolete, old, and need lots of maintenance, but solve important problems for organizations and meet individual employees' needs.

---

[1] https://www.computerworld.dk/art/29809/nordea-presses-af-ibms-doedsdom-over-os-2, https://www.computerworld.dk/art/29021/os-2-paa-vej-til-bedemanden.

Thus, creating new relations between work/organization analysis and interaction design is what solves legacy issues, not simply software modernization. For example, when a university creates new online digital oral exams using Adobe Connect and a set of advices, procedures, practices around that, it is a socio-technical upgrade.

Organizations' legacy systems

Legacy systems in industry are not only hardware, software but also 'soft factors' such as people, communication, and business values of the organization (Khadka, Batlajery, Saeidi, Jansen, & Hage, 2014). Khadka et al. (2014) studied the perceived benefits of legacy systems, and the drivers and challenges to the modernization of legacy systems. By applying a qual-quant research design with interviews with 26 practitioners from 22 different organizations, about their experiences with legacy systems and with legacy system modernization projects, followed by a survey with 176 valid responses from social media announcements, they found new perspectives and new insights on legacy systems.

Their transparent analysis[2] with grounded theory indicated, surprisingly, that among the perceived benefits were that legacy systems are perceived as core systems, but not obsolete systems. Participants said that their organizations' legacy systems were 'core' systems (=valuable systems) that have been proven to work correctly in a production environment for decades, not obsolete (=useless systems). For example, P1 said: "Most of the legacy systems are older than 20–30 years…[] Most of the systems of the legacy systems are the core system" and P11 agreed with P1 by stating: "It [Legacy system] is an old system; … A lot of legacy system is the core system". However, participants also said that legacy systems may be those systems that are out of sync with the organization's strategy. Interestingly, most of the informants related legacy systems as systems that do not fit with the future IT strategy of the organization. P19 expressed this as "My definition of a legacy system is systems and technologies that do not belong to your strategic technology goals" (Khadka et al., 2014).

Secondly, (Khadka et al., 2014)'s analysis of drivers for modernization of legacy systems found the participants in agreement about "if it ain't broke, don't fix it". Participants said that if legacy systems work 'well'—even with minor problems, then why try to modernize; the survey responses included that "they have been working—why fix it?" by a developer with 17 years of experience with legacy system, and "we didn't fix it last year, and survived. Why should this year be different?" by a chief technical officer of a software development company. However, participants also said that legacy systems may need to be modernized if legacy experts cannot be found and/or documentation of the legacy systems cannot be updated.

Thirdly, (Khadka et al., 2014)'s analysis of the challenges for modernization to legacy systems found that in terms of business vs. technical aspects, it was a tale of two perspectives. Their showed—in contrast to prevailing knowledge—that most of the identified challenges for replacing legacy systems were

---

[2] To increase transparency of the data analysis process, the authors published anonymous interview transcripts, the Nvivo 10 project file of interview analysis, and the survey data in excel format.

from the social/organizational/business perspective. These included challenges of funding modernization projects, resistance from organization, predicating return-of-investment, and timing constraints to finish. There were also traditional technical challenges for replacing legacy systems similar to those reported in previous academic research, for example obsolete hardware, difficulties related to extend and integrate with other systems, and maintenance problems.

In summary, insights from empirical studies of organizational aspects of legacy systems may tell us that they are CORE systems, not OBSOLETE systems, toward which employees feel that "if it ain't broke, don't fix it", and that surprisingly most of the challenges for replacing or developing legacy systems are social, not technical. Legacy systems are perceived as positive systems that are business-critical, reliable and proven systems that effectively are used by employees in the day-to-day business of organizations.

Employee's digital legacy

The argument for eliciting user needs for digital legacy in organizations stems from that the individual employees are users of legacy systems. Maybe individual employees needs for digital legacy can be supported (better) with improved interaction design, and, maybe legacy system interventions should also consider employees' positive legacy. Employee's digital legacy can be defined as "the meaningful and complex way in which information, values, and possessions are passed on to others" (Gulotta et al. 2013). As a thought experiment, think about your last job or your current job. Do you have any digital legacy as an employee in these organizations? The answers to such a thought experiment could be about employees' overall digital legacy left in their organization. This could be intangibles, including employees' work experiences recorded in the organization, how an employee's personal values helped shape the organization, and if so, are there any traces of thereof in policies, picture, strategies, etc. In addition, employees' digital legacy could be digital artefacts, including organizational documents with the employees' name on, software, hardware, or written procedures created by the employee, and more.

The curation of employee digital legacy is not yet an established body of knowledge. For example, it is still an open question who will be the curator, the individual employee, the employer/company, or somebody else (e.g., the union). Furthermore, the body of knowledge about interaction design for digital legacy is slowly emerging (Gulotta, Odom, Forlizzi, & Faste, 2013), and so far mostly about the home context and with a lifespan perspective (e.g., before and after death) (Gruning, Bullard, & Ocepek, 2015), and hence not about the organizational and workplace context. There are a few exceptions, for example, a study of technostress related to transfer of files and passwords as a part of digital legacy (Pfister, 2017). Further, it is overlapping with other emerging research on UX of interactions with personal information management, such as feeling information is a meaningful part of oneself and distinguishes one person from another (Alon & Nachmias, 2020), digital hoarding in the workplace, which is the tendency to pile up (or not) plenty of digital material in your personal storage in your workplace (Neave, Briggs, McKellar, & Sillence, 2019), and general studies of how people share and protect their data across conditions of changing technologies, relationships, individuals, and corporations (Vertesi, Kaye, Jarosewski, Khovanskaya, & Song, 2016).

Interaction design for digital legacy

An example of interaction design for digital legacy is the early research by Gulotta et al. (2013) that explored participants' feelings about digital legacy. Though this research was done in a lifespan perspective, the ideas may be transferable to the period of employment, and thus be relevant to interaction design for digital legacy in organizational and work contexts. Gulotta et al. (2013) prototyped three digital legacy supporting systems. The first was BlackBox, which was a file archiving website that allowed users only to access information about their digital legacy (e.g., photos), but not access the actual content. The second was DataFade, a website that caused photos to decay based on physical phenomena, such as sunshine, rain, visitors touch. The third was BitLogic, a website through which images decay along a digital spectrum, from photographs to bits. These prototypes were built to explore participants' UX with digital legacy. For example, one topic of study was how users felt about their legacy artefacts getting old, ageing, and decaying. Their method to explore participants' feelings about digital legacy were qualitative interviews about 'thought exercises' in the homes of ten participants. They asked questions about participants' perceptions of the value of digital legacy and their legacy practices, including curation, and asked participants to upload self-chosen digital legacy material (their photos) to the three prototype systems. The participants were parents, based on the idea was that they would have a need for considering digital legacy of their children, so the study was not about employees, but about parents in families in their homes. The insights from the study included that the participants were aware of their status as harbingers of new traditions and practices regarding digital media, felt responsible for generating a vast digital archive their successors would be responsible for managing, and they were sensitive about the exposure of different aspects of their online identities.

So how to intervene with organization-oriented storage for employees' digital legacy(ies)? Employees could benefit from organizational owned add-ons, plugins, and data scrapers that could support doing legitimate extracting from organizational storage and other places where employees generate and collect personal digital data and support them in transferring (or preparing to transfer) their digital legacy to private storage or to their next employers' storages. Another intervention could be to developing systems that could encourage employees purging of digital information, perhaps avoiding excessive digital hoarding (Neave et al., 2019), and in general supporting employees in curating their own digital legacy (e.g., selective filing of artefacts, do not file all and everything). In relation to the social side of the socio-technical intervention, it appears important to change perceptions about the nature and value of digital data. Thus, the UX of digital legacy may change over time, and for example, experiences that would be fall inside of daily activities today, may be less acceptable when the employee returns to it years later. In conclusion, the digital legacy interventions should support someone (the employees) to take responsibility for employees' digital legacy within and across organizations and past and future workplaces. Further considerations about how to evaluate/intervene in standard legacy system use scenarios with contextual personas are presented in the appendix.

6.3   Organizational Strategy Alignments

The third subtype of relation artefacts Type IV that we discuss in this chapter is organizational strategy alignments. These serve as interventions that ensure that the HWID project is aligned with the long-term goals of the organization. It is well established that one of the key factors for successful organizations is the close linkage of the IT strategy and business strategy (Baets, 1992), and this is also true for socio-technical design and business strategy. Different conceptualizations of organizational strategies exists, and the following is mostly based on the idea of strategy as practice (Jarzabkowski, 2004) where the study object is how management practices are used to put strategy into practice. Thus, practices of interaction design for human work may at some point be morphed into organizational strategies by aligning the organizational UX culture with the business and organizational goals.

The question of what activities do IT managers engage into ensure they are in the room when important business decisions about product direction and business strategy are made have been raised by UX leaders from industry and by researchers (Friedland, 2019; Lachner, Naegelein, Kowalski, Spann, & Butz, 2016) The answer appears to be that UX leaders are concerned with not only aligning UX strategy with the organizational strategy but also with broader questions of developing and managing a UX culture in the organization. They see UX strategy at the corporate level as being about that the UX team are aligned with the overall goals and objectives of the business. They aim to shape the strategic plans, operational needs, and interdependencies between their own organization and the rest of the company, and to increase UX team's effectiveness and synergies with other business functions. They see UX strategy at the level of a business unit as being about plans for delivering products, systems, or services that offers a high value to customers, and differentiates the company's brand. However, this requires multiple parts of the organizations to be involved (Lachner et al., 2016). Thus, UX strategy alignment has to be done within a UX organizational culture that can support the strategy and make it realistic and ensure it has an impact on company outcomes (Friedland, 2019).

Organized UX professionals as key facilitators of organizational alignments

Organizing and managing are increasingly considered as issues for UX professionals (HCI designers, HCI professionals) to deal with, and they (or this stakeholder role) become key facilitators for a HWID project's organizational strategy alignment. The notion of "Organized UX professionalism", that is, the management- and organization-oriented UX professionalism (Clemmensen, Iivari, Rajanen, & Sivaji, 2021), may help reveal the unique UX culture dimensions and support the further development of the profession.

Clemmensen et al. (2021) examined the organized UX professionalism through a survey eliciting the views of 422 UX professionals across five countries. They found a higher degree of management-minded work orientation and of organizational user centeredness than in earlier studies of HCI professionals. With regard to the UX professionals' management-minded work orientation, this indicated a readiness to align their values and work with the organization's long-term goal. Explicit management-mindedness included being responsible for completing tasks successfully and manifested itself in management-oriented job positions and titles related to UX Professionalism. Thus, a UX professional moving up in the organizational hierarchy may help facilitate alignment of the outcome of UX work in the organization with the management group's views. This enforcement of user-centered design and other core HCI values may increase with the number of years of work experience as a UX professional. At the same time, there is a risk that younger UX professionals develop a different sense of professional 'calling' and less 'fixed' occupational identities compared to the past, and thus do not sustain core UX professional values such as empowering users (Chivukula, Brier, & Gray, 2018). Young UX professionals may respond to the call for becoming entrepreneurs (Sturm, Aly, von Schmidt, & Flatten, 2017) and start managing their own business, or if working within a large organization, they may see themselves in as competing with (on in opposition to) senior management. However, having a management-minded work orientation may well facilitate the alignment of the designs in a HWID project and the strategy of the organizations that are involved in the project.

Organizational user-centeredness partly refers to the changing collective composition of the professional work force. Some IT professional fields, such as UX, have always been known for their human-centeredness, while others, including software engineering and programming are technology-dominated but are currently receiving an influx of user-oriented students and employers (Lárusdóttir, Cajander, & Gulliksen, 2014). This change in the work force make it more probable that the UX design from a HWID project will be aligned with the organizational strategy. For example, some propose that agile system development methodologies are user-centered and will automatically develop usable systems (Lárusdóttir et al., 2014); then having UX managers and user-oriented strategies make it easier to align. The agile-oriented software developers can contribute to an organization's UX-oriented work force. An organization with user-oriented software development certifications (e.g., in rapid and agile development methods), more years of experience in UX work, and a higher number of UX professionals working in teams shows signs of having organized UX professionalism and may better align with HWID projects.

Having a UX culture in the organization will ease alignment with socio-technical HCI design projects. An industrial model of UX culture somewhat similar in form and aim to the organized UX professional model is Friedland's (2019) UX culture 'palette'. Friedland's model summarize eight areas on a 'palette' that UX leaders sample from to create UX cultures within their companies: UX strategy (see above), research program (e.g., user research, prototype evaluations), innovation program (changing a paradigm, introducing something completely novel, or disrupting established practices and rituals), design program (deliver complete and detailed specifications defining the experiential structures and behaviors of products, systems, and services; consist of information architecture, interaction design, and the visual experience), UX operations (ensuring that the necessary tools, templates, and processes are in place for effective and efficient UX work), relations and alliances (form, and continually cultivate, good relationships and alliances with other company leaders), evangelize and promote (using metrics, testimonials, and favorable published reviews to keep the UX team's reputation as a strategic business partner front and center), and growing people (developing new team-leadership capacity and ensuring that the technical skills of all team members remain up to date).

Thus, both from academic research and industrial practice perspectives, aligning HWID with organizational strategies is an important type of interventions. To design these relations, artefact Type IV is obviously challenging and ongoing beyond the here initial listing of areas of concern.

Work domain expert's organizational evaluations.

Aligning a HWID project with organizational strategy is, as indicated by the multifaceted models of UX culture and professional culture discussed previously, a complex affair. One important approach is to study co-design including co-evaluation. Følstad and Hornbæk (2010) studied co-evaluation with software developers and work domain experts. They focused on how to study the impact of work domain knowledge (business knowledge) on the evaluation outcome. The argued that the method that they studied, "Cooperative Usability Testing", had two phases (1) an interaction phase, like classic usability testing, and (2) an interpretation phase, where the test participant and the moderator discussed incidents and experiences from the interaction phase. They proposed that the interpretation phases in important ways moved the evaluation outcome toward being more relevant to the work domain that generated additional insight and redesign suggestions, and in general generated a substantial proportion of problems with the design identified in the evaluation. Their conclusion was that the benefits of the interpretation phases could be explained by the access these provided both to the test participants' work-domain knowledge and to their experiences as users. Thus, the 'Cooperative Usability Testing', when framed as Følstad and Hornbæk (2010) does, may provide one possible concrete way to intervene to align the HWID project with organizational strategies.

Leadership and 'digital job crafting'

Job crafting may support organizational alignment in cases where the organizational strategy is employee (worker)-centric. A socio-technical HCI design intervention to align organizational strategy in terms of IT strategy and business strategy is to show leadership in facilitating digital job crafting. Leadership style may be an enabler of team member job crafting (Xin, Cai, Zhou, Baroudi, & Khapova, 2020), enabling not only low level team members' but also team managers' job crafting (Shin, Hur, Kim, & Cheol Gang, 2020). Furthermore, there may be a modelling effect of job crafting so that job crafting done by leaders may trickle down the hierarchy and be taken up by lower level employees (Xin et al., 2020). Leadership styles are important for job crafting. This also goes for digital job crafting, that is, job crafting where crafting interaction designs is an important part.

Leadership of digital job crafting is done in socio-technical design projects over time. Leadership needs to concern both social and technical aspects, and the multiple and different outcomes over time. Digital job crafting includes both using IT to support leaders and facilitators attempts to get employees to do more job crafting (Kehr, Bauer, Jenny, Güntert, & Kowatsch, 2013), and doing job crafting with full attention to the increasingly digitalized parts of the job (Bardoel & Drago, 2016). For example, using IT to support job crafting was studied by (Kehr et al., 2013), who did some early research on a design model for 'job crafting information systems'. This was done in the Information Systems design science tradition, with justificatory knowledge used to derive design principles and methods for their implementations and evaluations for these kinds of systems. The idea was to use the model to design artefacts with good user experiences that could provide guidance to employees' individual and organizational job crafting in a complete and accurate manner, raise employees' awareness on how working processes shape both individuals and organizations (and vice versa), and in general provide advice and individual guidance of job crafting behavior to employees and support them in understanding and grasping opportunities of change. Bardoel and Drago (2016) were interested in whether the quality of information technology support affect the work-life balance among knowledge workers. The studied 11,140 physicians with a survey and found that their reported quality of IT services was positively associated with work-life balance. The effects were less than long and unpredictable work hours, but on the same level as colleague support, complex patients, and part-time employment. Based on these descriptive insights, they strongly recommended to involve job crafting in the selection of IT systems. They suggest that, in the health domain, physicians should be supported in selecting IT systems for their work, to give sufficient weight to considering adverse effects on their own lives and to pay more attention to usability, etc. To lead 'digital job crafting' thus obviously concerns the IT design both as enablers and outcomes of job crafting.

Leadership styles for leading digital job crafting may then come from both management approaches and from design approaches, and merge into new styles of socio-technical leadership. From management and work psychology, there is evidence that a servant leadership style, that is, a people-centered approach that shifts attention from processes and outcomes to people, may support job crafting through encouragement (Yang, Ming, Ma, & Huo, 2017). Similarly, other leader ship styles may support job crafting, for example transformational leadership style may make employees more adaptable to changes (Xin et al., 2020). From design thinking and design leadership literature, we may learn that empathy with users, a discipline of prototyping, and tolerance for failure are important means for human sensemaking in those complex digitalized companies of today. Furthermore, design of interactions may come in different versions as process-oriented conservative, product-oriented romantic, and down-to-earth pragmatic accounts (Fallman, 2003), which each may require differences in view of the employee-as-designer and what job crafting would be about.

6.4 Summary

This chapter presented relation artefacts Type IV that were defined as having the purpose of socio-technical interventions in organizational and wider contexts. Three possible subcategories of relation artefacts Type IV were introduced: interaction interoperability checkups, digital legacy interventions, and organizational strategy alignments. Together they presented a move from the technical to the social centered around designing for workers' digital legacy. Noteworthy, the focus on workers' digital legacy involves work identity and for design, persona creation. The HWID argument here is that workers' social and technical legacies in an organization are preconditions for and contributes interventions, and that evaluations of prototyped hypotheses can be done in organization legacy scenarios. A design case for discussion of interoperability and digital legacy is presented in the appendix.

When comparing HWID relation artefacts Type IV to other socio-technical HCI design approaches, they appear to overlap with Design Thinking Management (DTM) user (Kolko, 2015). In DTM prototypes are the primary driver for change and vessels for management's evaluation of design, and the focus is on management goals for change. Relation artefacts Type IV, at least when they moves close to the organizational level, share the importance for aligning HWID actions and designs with the strategic focus of the organization.

In addition, Action Design Research (ADR) (Sein, Henfridsson, Purao, Rossi, & Lindgren, 2011) with its flexible approach to evaluation that depends on the IT artefact and its focus on generating design theory for both organizational change and IT systems has the very important point to make to HWID that interventions can focus not only on instantiations of IT systems but also on novel organizational actions. Both of these can and should generate design theory.

Reflection on relation artefacts Type I–IV

While the relation artefacts Type I–IV has been presented in Chaps. 3–6 as movements from the social to the technical (Type I and Type III) and movements from the technical to the social (Type II and Type IV), these movements are nothing more than indications of possibilities, much the same as arrows in iterative models of system development more indicates than prescribes a certain path to take in a concrete project. The HWID stakeholders should feel free to walk their own path through the types and subtypes of relation artefacts, and thus 'weave' a holistic HWID gestalt of their own. Not falling into 'technical-determinism' or 'socio-determinism' unless you want to.

6.5 Appendix

Evaluations with persona in standard (legacy) work scenarios

A part of considering legacy systems as socio-technical systems is to consider evaluation of legacy systems in terms of legacy (systems) work scenarios. In such work scenarios interventions are taken and used by expert workers with extreme amounts of practice on the relevant circumscribed set of tasks in that particular work environment (Feltovich, Prietula, & Ericsson, 2006). Evaluation of legacy systems interventions will have to be carried out in such scenarios.

The collegial verbalization (CV) evaluation method

When evaluating with classical UX and usability thinking aloud methods in scenarios where the employees are highly experienced, it is possible to go beyond the established protocols of concurrent and retrospective verbalizations, and include a third protocol of 'conspective' verbalization to achieve the needed (Erlandsson & Jansson, 2007; Jansson, Erlandsson, & Axelsson, 2015; Jansson, Erlandsson, Fröjd, & Arvidsson, 2013) In a concurrent verbal protocol the verbalizer is performing the work task, in a retrospective verbal protocol the verbalizer is remembering own performance, and in a conspective verbalization the observer is observing colleagues performance, in real time or as recording of past performance, whilst thinking aloud. Jansson et al. (2015) suggested an evaluation method they called collegial verbalization (CV) that combined the three protocols. The CV evaluation method is relevant for evaluating legacy work scenarios, since it builds on the assumption that when domain knowledge is shared between colleagues, one might find that they share cognitive strategies, and hence a colleague thinking aloud during observation of colleagues' performance is just as valid as thinking aloud while performing own tasks. Thus, evaluation can be done with independent observers (colleagues) comment in the form of conspective protocols on the behavior of target users in legacy work scenarios well-known to all involved employees.

To identify the target users (the expert workers) to take part in the evaluation, a modified persona method might be helpful. The idea of a persona might deliver an approach to utilize the independent source of data of the CV method (Jansson et al., 2015), if the persona is cast as an expert colleague. Hence personas for selecting participants to do CV for relation artefacts type IV such as interaction designs for digital legacy should be codesigned among work colleagues (the experts) and data-driven with substantial understanding and description of the legacy work scenario(s).

Co-designing Data-Driven Personas for Organizational UX

Personas is a method that for several years has been applied in multiple domains. Though there is no standard definition of personas, there is agreement that it is a description of an end-user based on data with or with-out fictitious elements. Some

authors emphasize that the persona description should contain a one-to-one corre-
lation between data and the description. Other authors allow to include fictitious
elements in the description for the sake of enhancing the empathy for the users
(Nielsen, 2019).

However, the idea that personas should be based on data is being challenged by
recent trends of Lean UX and co-design. Lean UX supports the integration of UX
activities into the widespread use of agile development by using personas based on
the design team's assumptions. With the perspective of Lean UX, the emergence
of the concept of assumption-based personas is spreading. The argument is that
these personas are fast and easy to generate and a starting point for "proper" data-
driven personas (Gothelf & Seiden, 2013). Similarly, within the participatory design
framework the notion of co-designed personas has emerged. Co-created personas
encourage users to engage with co-design sessions (Neate, Bourazeri, Roper, Stumpf,
& Wilson, 2019). Common for both the personas based on assumptions and the
co-created personas is that both have no underlying data. However, co-designing
personas should focus on collaboration around the foundation of data for the persona,
and that this is particularly important for Organizational UX.

What is known about data collection for personas in general is that data for
personas can take many forms both qualitative (Miaskiewicz, Sumner, & Kozar,
2008) and quantitative (Jansen, Salminen, & Jung, 2020). The content is most often
related to back-ground information such as demographics, information related to the
system to be designed such as work tasks, use of technology, and relation to the
domain. Data may also include general business and marketing related information,
such as brand relationship, business objectives, and market segment size (Nielsen,
Hansen, Stage, & Billestrup, 2015).

For employee-personas in legacy workplace scenarios aimed at designing for
organizational UX, data may include data about organizational structure, employees,
work tasks, work systems, and their interrelations. That is, who the persona will
be with, where they are, what they are doing during the workday, and with what
systems (Clemmensen et al., 2020). Often this will reveal a quite ordinary set of
user experiences for the persona (Clemmensen et al., 2020; Meneweger, Wurhofer,
Fuchsberger, & Tscheligi, 2018). Data collection for personas in workplace scenarios
may require consideration of technology as a design element and how the relation
between the users and the technical systems are transformed for this purpose.

Co-creating data understandings is a collaborative practice around using data
for persona creation, inspired by the work of Feinberg (2017) that views data as
something that may be designed through practices and the work by Seidelin (2020)
that suggests a collaboratively practice of design with and of data and data structures. Employee data may be understood as the most important data for personas
when co-designing personas for organizational UX that requires data about structure, people, tasks, technology and their interrelations. Employee data could be
thought of as data about people. Such data is found in organizations' HR departments. However, employee data should be considered more broadly and in relation to employee experience, that is, centering the organizational and interaction
design around the employee's total experience of the workplace (Plaskoff, 2017).

We imagine that employees and other stakeholder participants in different ways can help collect data about structure, people, tasks, technology, and their interrelations. It is thus not enough to parse the HR department's database; interviews and surveys with employees and managers at different levels may be required, before entering co-design workshops to create personas. An example of co-design of personas that include collection of data about structure, people, tasks, technology and their interrelations is the creation of contextual personas for the Swedish defense reported by Cajander et al. (2015).

Using co-created data understandings for designing personas for legacy work place scenarios may provide a solid empirical basis for designing alternative technology solutions to deal with wicked issues in organizations. Involving employees in co-design of personas can be done by using digital tools that support and empower employees focused data collection about personas. An example of using digital tools that support and empower employees focused data collection about personas is the automation scenario of manufacturing with (a legacy) collaborative robot proposed by Clemmensen and Nørbjerg (2019). Here employees use a digital tutoring tool that nudge them towards systematic data collections about a target user group of (expert) colleagues. Then, the tool supports the employees in identifying, prototyping, and evaluating interactions with the robot and of the social arrangement around the robot, based on the personas coming out of the data (Clemmensen & Nørbjerg, 2019).

In summary, (1) co-design of personas should primarily mean co-design of data-driven personas, (2) co-design of data-driven personas may be particularly important and possible when designing for organizational UX, since it can focus on the organization-specific employee experience, and (3) co-designed data-driven personas focused on organizational UX provides a solid basis for creative variation of socio-technical designs, and thus contribute to evaluation of legacy workplace designs.

Design case with HWID prototyping and interventions in a university course

The design task was to do a quick and dirty relation artefact Type III prototype and a relation artefact Type IV intervention. The context was a university course in a Scandinavian business school. It has a LMS (learning management system) with one module per teaching session. The users were mostly students with a need for feeling competent and the organizational problem was to support easy access for all students to teaching material. A one button solution, Fig. 6.4, was created based on relation artefact Type III subcategories, and evaluated.

Figure 6.4 shows a prototype for both individual and collective user, as the LMS course was used by individuals and on a class basis. The organizational action hypotheses were to give students better overview of course modules to enhance the course capacity for learning. The prototyped worker experiences were a single-step interaction that moves the student directly to today's session to give a feeling of overview. The field evaluations and UX tests were done as the prototyped hypothesis to be testes in the course setting with actual students interacting with the prototype was that the prototype would show positive indications of overview experience among students.

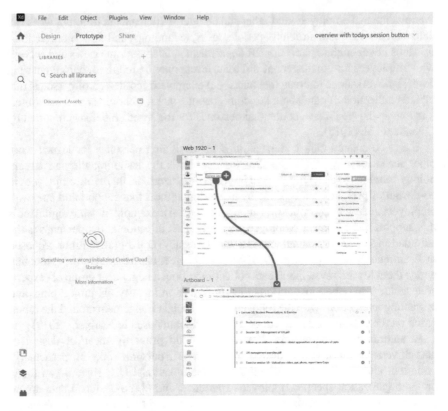

Fig. 6.4 A one-button solution for overview

The data collection was done as individual and organizational UX and usability measures, with home-made "overview"-experience scales and qualitative interviews. The sociomaterial analysis was focus on relation artefact Type IV subcategories. The interaction interoperability checks asked the question if the solution would give the student a similar interaction experience as in other parts of the LMS course environment did? The digital legacy intervention asked the question if there was a way that the student could see the previous overviews provided by the user-interactions with the prototype for this specific course? The organizational strategy alignment asked the question if a one-button solution of this design would be the kind of experiences that the business school would want its students to have?

The theory and methodology in the project included theory about clinical overview in emergency rooms (Hertzum & Simonsen, 2010), field experiments with overviews for document navigation (Gutwin, Cockburn, & Gough, 2017), and particularly time and structure based navigation in web-lectures (Mertens, Brusilovsky, Vornberger, & Ishchenko, 2009).

The design contribution with relation artefact Type IV was thus the one-button answer to the questions of how the desired "experience of overview" in online course settings fitted to usual interactions of the students, if it was 'their' overview, and if this was a university-certified experience. The relation artefact Type IV discussions then again opened up for further discussion about if "overview" was the experience that was designed for, or was it perhaps the more classic "situation awareness" with its known socio-technical conditions and implications, see for example (Tharanathan, Bullemer, Laberge, Reising, & Mclain, 2012).

References

Alon, L., & Nachmias, R. (2020). Anxious and frustrated but still competent: Affective aspects of interactions with personal information management. *International Journal of Human-Computer Studies, 144*, 102503.

Baets, W. (1992). Aligning information systems with business strategy. *The Journal of Strategic Information Systems, 1*(4), 205–213.

Bang, A. L., & Eriksen, M. A. (2014). Experiments all the way in programmatic design research. *Artifact: Journal of Design Practice, 3*(2), 1–4.

Bardoel, E. A., & Drago, R. (2016). Does the quality of information technology support affect work–life balance? A study of Australian physicians. *The International Journal of Human Resource Management, 27*(21), 2604–2620.

Cajander, Å., Larusdottir, M., Eriksson, E., & Nauwerck, G. (2015). Contextual personas as a method for understanding digital work environments. *IFIP Advances in Information and Communication Technology, 468*, 141–152. https://doi.org/10.1007/978-3-319-27048-7_10.

Chavan, A. L. (2005). Another culture, another method. *Proceedings of the 11th International Conference on Human-Computer Interaction, 21*(2). (Citeseer).

Chivukula, S. S., Brier, J., & Gray, C. M. (2018). Dark Intentions or Persuasion? UX Designers' Activation of Stakeholder and User Values. In *Proceedings of the 2018 ACM Conference Companion Publication on Designing Interactive Systems*, 87–91.

Clemmensen, T., Hertzum, M., & Abdelnour-Nocera, J. (2020). Ordinary user experiences at work: A study of greenhouse growers. *ACM Transactions on Computer-Human Interaction (TOCHI), June*(Article no 16), 1–31. https://doi.org/10.1145/3386089.

Clemmensen, T., Iivari, N., Rajanen, D., & Sivaji, A. (2021). Organized UX professionals. In *HWID2021 Unpublished Proceedings* (pp. 1–25). Retrieved from https://www.hwid2021.com/.

Clemmensen, T., & Katre, D. (2012). Adapting e-gov usability evaluation to cultural contexts. In *Usablity in government systems user experience design for citizens and public servants* (pp. 331–344). https://doi.org/10.1016/B978-0-12-391063-9.00053-5.

Clemmensen, T., & Nørbjerg, J. (2019). (not) Working (with) collaborative robots in a glass processing factory. *Worst Case Practices Teaching Us the Bright Side*.

Erlandsson, M., & Jansson, A. (2007). Collegial verbalisation–A case study on a new method on information acquisition. *Behaviour & Information Technology, 26*(6), 535–543.

Fallman, D. (2003). Design-oriented human-computer interaction. In *CHI'03 Proceedings of the SIGCHI Conference on Human Factors in Computing Systems* (pp. 225–232). Ft. Lauderdale, Florida, USA: ACM. 05–10 Apr 2003.

Feinberg, M. (2017). A design perspective on data. In *Proceedings of the 2017 CHI Conference on Human Factors in Computing Systems* (pp. 2952–2963). https://doi.org/10.1145/3025453.302 5837.

Feltovich, P. J., Prietula, M. J., & Ericsson, K. A. (2006). *Studies of expertise from psychological perspectives.* In: K. A. Ericsson, N. Charness, P. J. Feltovich, & R. R. Hoffman (Eds.) (2006). Cambridge Handbook of Expertise and Expert Performance. New York, NY: Cambridge University Press.

Følstad, A., & Hornbæk, K. (2010). Work-domain knowledge in usability evaluation: Experiences with Cooperative Usability Testing. *Journal of Systems and Software*, *83*(11), 2019–2030. https://doi.org/10.1016/J.JSS.2010.02.026.

Friedland, L. (2019). Culture eats UX strategy for breakfast. *Interactions*, *26*(5), 78–81.

Gothelf, J., & Seiden, J. (2013). Lean UX-Applying lean principles to improve user experience. In *LEAN UX-Applying Lean Principles to Improve User Experience*. https://doi.org/10.1017/CBO 9781107415324.004.

Gruning, J., Bullard, J., & Ocepek, M. (2015). Medium, access, and obsolescence: What kinds of objects are lasting objects? In *Proceedings of the 33rd Annual ACM Conference on Human Factors in Computing Systems* (pp. 3433–3442).

Gulotta, R., Odom, W., Forlizzi, J., & Faste, H. (2013). Digital artifacts as legacy: Exploring the lifespan and value of digital data. In *CHI'13*. https://doi.org/10.1145/2470654.2466240.

Gutwin, C., Cockburn, A., & Gough, N. (2017). A field experiment of spatially-stable overviews for document navigation. In *Proceedings of the 2017 CHI Conference on Human Factors in Computing Systems* (pp. 5905–5916). https://doi.org/10.1145/3025453.3025905.

Hertzum, M. (2020). Usability testing: A practitioner's guide to evaluating the user experience. *Synthesis Lectures on Human-Centered Informatics*, *13*(1), i–105.

Hertzum, M., & Simonsen, J. (2010). Clinical overview and emergency-department whiteboards: A survey of expectations toward electronic whiteboards. In *Proceedings of the 8th Scandinavian Conference on Health Informatics* (pp. 14–18).

Hevner, A. R., March, S. T., Park, J., & Ram, S. (2008). Design science in information systems research. *Management Information Systems Quarterly*, *28*(1), 6.

Jansen, B. J., Salminen, J. O., & Jung, S.-G. (2020). Data-driven personas for enhanced user understanding: Combining empathy with rationality for better insights to analytics. *Data and Information Management*, *4*(1), 1–17. https://doi.org/10.2478/dim-2020-0005.

Jansson, A., Erlandsson, M., & Axelsson, A. (2015). Collegial verbalisation–the value of an independent observer: an ecological approach. *Theoretical Issues in Ergonomics Science*, *16*(5), 474–494. https://doi.org/10.1080/1463922X.2015.1027322.

Jansson, A., Erlandsson, M., Fröjd, C., & Arvidsson, M. (2013). Collegial collaboration for safety: Assessing situation awareness by exploring cognitive strategies. In *Workshop at INTERACT 2013-14th IFIP TC13 Conference on Human-Computer Interaction, Cape Town, South Africa, September 2013* (pp. 35–40).

Jarzabkowski, P. (2004). Strategy as practice: recursiveness, adaptation, and practices-in-use. *Organization Studies*, *25*(4), 529–560.

Joshi, S. G., & Bratteteig, T. (2016). Designing for prolonged mastery. On involving old people in participatory design. *Scandinavian Journal of Information Systems*, *28*(1).

Kehr, F., Bauer, G., Jenny, G. F., Güntert, S. T., & Kowatsch, T. (2013). *Towards a design model for job crafting information systems promoting individual health, productivity and organizational performance*.

Khadka, R., Batlajery, B. V., Saeidi, A. M., Jansen, S., & Hage, J. (2014). How do professionals perceive legacy systems and software modernization? In *Proceedings of the 36th International Conference on Software Engineering-ICSE 2014*, 36–47. https://doi.org/10.1145/2568225.256 8318.

Kolko, J. (2015). Design thinking comes of age. *Harvard Business Review*, *93*(9), 66–71. Retrieved from https://hbr.org/2015/09/design-thinking-comes-of-age.

Koskinen, I., Binder, F. T., & Redström, J. (2008). Lab, field, gallery, and beyond. *Artifact: Journal of Design Practice*, *2*(1), 46–57.

Kwon, G. H., Smith-Jackson, T. L., & Bostian, C. W. (2011). Socio-cognitive aspects of interoperability: Understanding communication task environments among different organizations. *ACM Transactions on Computer-Human Interaction (TOCHI)*, *18*(4), 1–21.

Lachner, F., Naegelein, P., Kowalski, R., Spann, M., & Butz, A. (2016). Quantified UX: Towards a common organizational understanding of user experience. In *Proceedings of the 9th Nordic*

Conference on Human-Computer Interaction-NordiCHI'16 (pp. 56:1–56:10). https://doi.org/10. 1145/2971485.2971501.

Lárusdóttir, M., Cajander, Å., & Gulliksen, J. (2014). Informal feedback rather than performance measurements-User-centred evaluation in Scrum projects. *Behaviour and Information Technology*. https://doi.org/10.1080/0144929X.2013.857430.

Meneweger, T., Wurhofer, D., Fuchsberger, V., & Tscheligi, M. (2018). Factory workers' ordinary user experiences: An overlooked perspective. *Human Technology*, *14*(2), 209–232. https://doi. org/10.17011/ht/urn.201808103817.

Mertens, R., Brusilovsky, P., Vornberger, O., & Ishchenko, S. (2009). Bridging the gap between time-and structure-based navigation in web lectures. *International Journal on E-Learning*, *8*(1), 89–105.

Miaskiewicz, T., Sumner, T., & Kozar, K. A. (2008). A latent semantic analysis methodology for the identification and creation of personas. In *Proceedings of ACM CHI 2008 Conference on Human Factors in Computing Systems* (Vol. 1, pp. 1501–1510). https://doi.org/10.1145/1357054.135 7290.

Nahum-Shani, I., Qian, M., Almirall, D., Pelham, W. E., Gnagy, B., Fabiano, G. A., Waxmonsky, J. G., Yu, J., & Murphy, S. A. (2012). Experimental design and primary data analysis methods for comparing adaptive interventions. *Psychological Methods*, *17*(4), 457.

Neate, T., Bourazeri, A., Roper, A., Stumpf, S., & Wilson, S. (2019). Co-created personas: Engaging and empowering users with diverse needs within the design process. In *Proceedings of the 2019 CHI Conference on Human Factors in Computing Systems-CHI'19* (pp. 1–12). https://doi.org/ 10.1145/3290605.3300880.

Neave, N., Briggs, P., McKellar, K., & Sillence, E. (2019). Digital hoarding behaviours: Measurement and evaluation. *Computers in Human Behavior*, *96*, 72–77.

Nielsen, L. (2019). *Personas-User focused design*. https://doi.org/10.1007/978-1-4471-7427-1.

Nielsen, L., Hansen, K. S., Stage, J., & Billestrup, J. (2015). A template for design personas. *International Journal of Sociotechnology and Knowledge Development*, *7*(1), 45–61. https://doi. org/10.4018/ijskd.2015010104.

Paay, J., Raptis, D., Kjeldskov, J., Skov, M. B., Ruder, E. V, & Lauridsen, B. M. (2017). Investigating cross-device interaction between a handheld device and a large display. In *Proceedings of the 2017 CHI Conference on Human Factors in Computing Systems* (pp. 6608–6619). https://doi. org/10.1145/3025453.3025724.

Pfister, J. (2017). " This will cause a lot of work." Coping with transferring files and passwords as part of a personal digital legacy. In *Proceedings of the 2017 ACM Conference on Computer Supported Cooperative Work and Social Computing* (pp. 1123–1138).

Plaskoff, J. (2017). Employee experience: the new human resource management approach. *Strategic HR Review*, *16*(3), 136–141. https://doi.org/10.1108/SHR-12-2016-0108.

Rai, A. (2017). Editor's comments: Diversity of design science research. *MIS Quarterly*, *41*(1), iii–xviii.

Raptis, D., Kjeldskov, J., & Skov, M. B. (2016). Continuity in multi-device interaction. In *Proceedings of the 9th Nordic Conference on Human-Computer Interaction-NordiCHI'16*. https://doi. org/10.1145/2971485.2971533.

Reinecke, K., & Bernstein, A. (2013). Knowing what a user likes: A design science approach to interfaces that automatically adapt to culture. *Mis Quarterly*, 427–453.

Seidelin, C. (2020). *Towards a Co-design perspective on data-Foregrounding data in the design and innovation of data-based services*. Ph. D. thesis, IT University Copenhagen.

Sein, M.K., Henfridsson, O., Purao, S., Rossi, M., & Lindgren, R. (2011). Action design research. *MIS Quarterly*. https://doi.org/10.2307/23043488.

Shin, Y., Hur, W., Kim, H., & Cheol Gang, M. (2020). Managers as a missing entity in job crafting research: Relationships between store manager job crafting, job resources, and store performance. *Applied Psychology*, *69*(2), 479–507.

Sturm, C., Aly, M., von Schmidt, B., & Flatten, T. (2017). Entrepreneurial & UX mindsets: Two perspectives-one objective. In *Proceedings of the 19th International Conference on Human-Computer Interaction with Mobile Devices and Services* (pp. 60:1–60:11). https://doi.org/10.1145/3098279.3119912.

Tharanathan, A., Bullemer, P., Laberge, J., Reising, D. V., & Mclain, R. (2012). Impact of functional and schematic overview displays on console operators' situation awareness. *Journal of Cognitive Engineering and Decision Making, 6*(2), 141–164.

Vertesi, J., Kaye, J., Jarosewski, S. N., Khovanskaya, V. D., & Song, J. (2016). Data Narratives: Uncovering tensions in personal data management. In *Proceedings of the 19th ACM Conference on Computer-Supported Cooperative Work & Social Computing* (pp. 478–490).

Wania, C. E., Atwood, M. E., & McCain, K. W. (2006). How do design and evaluation interrelate in HCI research? In *Proceedings of the 6th Conference on Designing Interactive Systems* (pp. 90–98).

Xin, X., Cai, W., Zhou, W., Baroudi, S. El, & Khapova, S. N. (2020). How can job crafting be reproduced? Examining the trickle-down effect of job crafting from leaders to employees. *International Journal of Environmental Research and Public Health, 17*(3), 894.

Yang, R., Ming, Y., Ma, J., & Huo, R. (2017). How do servant leaders promote engagement? A bottom-up perspective of job crafting. *Social Behavior and Personality: An International Journal, 45*(11), 1815–1827.

Chapter 7
HWID Research

Abstract This chapter provides guidance for academic researchers on how to study socio-technical relations and perform socio-technical HCI theorizing with the HWID platform. Most importantly, the chapter presents the tool of 'theorizing workshops' and gives detailed instructions and examples of how to run such workshops with researchers, students, and practitioners. Furthermore, the chapter introduces the notion of HWID templates for digital analysis of qualitative data and provides example of rich design case data files that weave work analysis and interaction design together, based on these HWID templates. For the quantitatively inclined researchers, the chapter proposes a way to do HWID-based formative structural equation modeling of data from socio-technical HCI design cases. This how-to chapter ends with a proposal for a work plan for using the HWID platform in a socio-technical HCI project on the size of a master thesis or a Ph.D. project.

Keywords HWID theory · Theorizing workshop · Qualitative software HWID templates · HWID quantitative analysis

For academic researchers who study socio-technical relations and perform socio-technical HCI theorizing the HWID platform offers unique benefits. It is a flexible, holistic, configurational, and gestalt-oriented approach. Any HWID research project contributes (ideally) with several relation artifacts with justificatory knowledge and related data to a shared pool of *holistic design gestalts* (see Chap. 1, Fig. 1.1, for a general gestalt form) that can be shared, annotated, compared, and contrasted to create even more general socio-technical HCI insights and knowledge. HWID research projects take a configurational approach, that is, rather than focus on one or more relation artifacts, focus at a configuring or constructing a series of socio-technical characteristics into a whole. At the same time, it is a flexible approach to research that usually includes a project-specific solution relevant to the local context.

© The Author(s), under exclusive license to Springer Nature Switzerland AG 2021
T. Clemmensen, *Human Work Interaction Design*,
Human–Computer Interaction Series,
https://doi.org/10.1007/978-3-030-71796-4_7

7.1   The Form of HWID Theory

The aim of academic research activities within the area of HWID is to establish relationships between empirical work-domain knowledge and interaction design activities. Areas of research within HWID so far include design sketches for work (Clemmensen, Campos, Orngreen, Mark-Pejtersen, & Wong, 2006), usability in context (Katre, Orngreen, Yammiyavar, & Clemmensen, 2010), work analysis for HCI (Campos et al., 2012), integration of work analysis and interaction design methods for pervasive and smart workplaces, and designing engaging automation (Barricelli et al., 2019). Across these areas, the question emerges what forms of theory may HWID produce? The position taken in this book is that HWID should be understood as a lightweight, medium-level framework that is useful to guide the application of more mature theories to study the relation between work analysis and interaction design. Thus, the form of HWID theory will often be a combination of a HCI theory combined with domain-specific theory or 'core theory' (Von Alan et al., 2004) and focused on the relation between empirical work analysis and interaction design.

The background for doing HWID research is that increasingly work environments are challenging for research and design. Furthermore, pervasive and smart technologies push workplace configuration beyond linear logic and physical boundaries. As a result, workers' experience of and access to technology is increasingly pervasive, and their agency constantly reconfigured. While this in certain areas of work is not new (e.g., technology mediation and decision support in air traffic control), more recent developments in other domains such as health care (e.g., augmented reality in computer-aided surgery) have raised challenging issues for HCI researchers and practitioners. The question that such research addresses is how to improve the quality of workers' experience and outputs. The answer to this question will help support professionals, academia, national labs, and industry engaged in human work analysis and interaction design for the workplace. The answer includes developing tools, procedures, and professional competencies for designing human-centered technologies, but more importantly, it includes generating the knowledge required to do so.

How to generate knowledge addressing the design of interactive artifacts for challenging workplaces and work environments is a question of theory. This question, and the more general question of how to theorize about the relations between empirical work analysis and interaction design, is the concern of this chapter. The chapter begins with analyzing the 'user requirements' to HWID theory, by analyzing what the authors of papers from a HWID conference looked for when it comes to HWID theory.

User requirements to HWID theory-as-a-product

Based on the papers, reviews of the papers, and discussions of the paper presentations at the HWID 2015 working conference, researchers' requirements to HWID theory were tentatively identified by asking questions about what theory should be able to

do, the form it should have, and what kind of research it would support. Below is a
list of the identified requirements to HWID theory that says that it should

1. Connect HW and ID.
2. Be useful for interventions in practical, real-world domains.
3. Be close to an HCI concept, e.g., UX.
4. Explain aspect of real-world phenomena.
5. Specify outcome state of system use.
6. Deal with context in precise and dynamic way.
7. Be multilevel, take organizational aspects into account.
8. Describe a work domain.
9. Be well known and proven (cited).
10. Be socio-technical in the widest sense.
11. Be useful for domain analysis, eliciting tacit knowledge.
12. Connect, if needed, a series of domain-specific, 'core', theories.
13. Be useful to generalize findings to similar domains.

   1. *Connect HW and ID.* One requirement to HWID theory is that it can be used
to give an overview of research in the field. Gonçalves, Campos, and Clemmensen
(2015) used a HWID framework to present a literature review of 54 papers from
HWID workshops, conferences, and journals from the period 2009–2014. The paper
ended up asking why there is a gap in terms of overall HWID theory development.
Questions unanswered in the paper include if some of the research touch on this
partially? Or is HWID theory an integration of theory on three kinds: work analyses,
interaction design, relation artefacts?

   2. *Be useful for interventions in practical, real-world domains.* Ørngreen (2015)
in her paper on reflections on design-based research in online educational and competence development projects was concerned with the usefulness of HWID theory for
interventions. She integrated a literature review with her personal experiences in the
field to understand the research and practice domain. It turned out from the discussion
at the conference that to make her analysis and HWID theory development practically useful, it would be good to have a graphical overview of the different studies
presented and how they were related.

   3. *Be close to an HCI concept.* A third requirement to HWID theory is that it is
associated closely with existing HCI concepts or theory, and in this way can contribute
to the body of knowledge in HCI. Wurhofer, Fuchsberger, Meneweger, Moser, and
Tscheligi (2015), in their paper on insights from UX research in the factory on what
to consider in interaction design, connected HWID analysis to the HCI concept of
UX. Based on recent research (from the last 5 years), they provided a discussion on
the interplay between user, system, and context in a factory environment by pointing
out relevant UX factors and influence on worker's experience. What emerged as a
finding was a list of many factors, user experiences, and influences, which potentially
could be useful for rewriting HCI textbooks on UX.

   4. *Explain aspect of real-world phenomena.* This requirement for HWID theory
concerned the need to be able to explain interesting aspects of the real-world
phenomena studied. Maria Ianeva, Stephanie Faure, Jennifer Theveniot, François

Ribeyron, Gilles Cordon, and Claude Gartisier (Ianeva et al., 2015b) took an industry perspective on pervasive technologies for smart workplaces and, in particular, a workplace efficiency solution for office design and building management from an occupier's perspective. They focused on how to increase workplace efficiency in the long term and contextualize a contemporary concept (Activity Based Workplace) in a living-lab setting (a company's new HQ). They partially explained the success and failures of the implementation studied. Questions to this research include if the specific technological solution for monitoring spaces' occupancy biased the results, and for how long (temporal length) such a study should continue.

5. *Specify outcome state of system use.* This requirement for HWID theory concerned the need for being able to specify the (ideal) outcome state of the analysis and design. Valentin Gattol et al. (2015) in their paper on bottom-up insights that leads to design ideas in a case of designing office environments for elderly computer workers aimed to design a smart work environment for this target group. Different research methods were employed including interview, an ideation workshop, and an online survey. Questions raised concerned what the target situation was for the studied user group. Thus, without supporting theory about human work, it is hard to say what it means to be "old" in contemporary societies (this could include less tech-savvy, myopic vision, back pain, poor fine motor control, memory drop outs, etc.) as well as what kind of interaction design will be useful (e.g., why would a "smart" work environment be considered relevant? How about conventional solutions such as digital reminders and task lists?).

6. *Deal with context in precise and dynamic way.* Väätäjä (2015), in her attempt to characterize the context of use in mobile work, provides synthesized findings from 12 cases studies, and derives a model to be used when designing and evaluating systems for mobile work. One question that emerged during discussions of this study was if mobile work context as in this study is best described as a mixture of the context as container (precise description) and context as activity (dynamic description)?

7. *Be multilevel, take organizational aspects into account.* This requirement for HWID theory concerns the need to take organizational aspects into account. Björndal, Eriksson, and Artman (2015), in their attempt to make sense of user-centered perspectives in large technology-intensive companies by looking at relationships rather than transactions, found that theory needs to be multilevel. Thus, they considered service design in four IT companies and found that studying single human–computer interaction in a work context (transactions) was far from sufficient to appreciate and design services (relationships) in the organizations.

8. *Describe a work domain.* This requirement for HWID theory concerned the need to describe a work domain. Abdelnour-Nocera et al. (2015b) in their study of the Smart University, and how to support students' context awareness, created a set of design guidelines, based on the insights from a cognitive work analysis. This form of theory used was a classic example of HWID analysis, though only in the direction of work analysis to interaction design. However, the pro and cons of limiting the analysis of relations between work analysis and interaction design to the categories of cognitive work analysis is a topic for future research.

9. *Be well known.* A HWID theory needs to build on the well known and simple. Cajander, Lárusdóttir, Eriksson, and Nauwerck (2015) in their study of IT-based administrative work brought life into the HWID analysis by developing a concept of 'contextual personas'. They motivated this in the convergence of interaction design and pervasive workplaces. The main new thing that they introduced to the persona was the statements about control, demand, and support in the work and life of the persona, based on the theory of healthy work by Karasek and Theorell. A question for further development of the concept is how distinct contextual personas are when compared to task and use scenarios?

10. *Be socio-technical in the widest sense.* This requirement for HWID theory concerns the needs for dealing with the wider context of use including societal values. Lopes (2015) in her study of the work and workplaces in social solidarity institutions with the aim to address organization agility and innovation found that she needed to study the goals and history of the Portuguese social security system, which included studying the societal values related to life as an older person. This study uses multiple theories to address the HWID relations and develops a prototype for integration of information related to care services. It provided a clear requirement to the HWID framework to be an organizing framework for multiple theories on many aspects of the context of use.

11. *Be useful for domain analysis, eliciting tacit knowledge.* This requirement for HWID theory concerned the need for doing domain analysis and eliciting tacit knowledge. Quercioli and Amaldi (2015) in their Grounded Theory Study of Perspectives on Automation Amongst Aviation Industry Stakeholders learned that systems are far too complex for people to understand. Hence, the main target for the domain analysis emerged as trying to identify what half-baked knowledge that human actors need to have about non-human actors to avoid or recover from unsafe situations with aircrafts. As it turned out in the discussions at the working conference, in this case, human work and interaction design were mutually constitutive.

12. *Connected in a series of domain-specific theories.* This requirement for HWID theory concerned the need for several domain-specific theories. Molka-Danielsen, Fominykh, Swapp, and Steed (2015) in their design of a virtual learning environment to teach space syntax, seen from the user's perspective, created an artefact by combining insights from several domain-specific theories: threshold concept from didactics, 'line of sight' from architecture, Virtual Learning Environments (VLE) theory, and more.

13. *Be useful to generalize findings to similar domains.* This requirement for HWID theory concerned the need to make results useful for other similar domains as the one studied. Barricelli, Valtolina, Gadia, Marzullo, Piazzi, and Garzulino (2015) did co-design of a cloud of services for archaeological practice, and identified two problems in current archaeological practice: (1) how to integrate and create useful knowledge from a richness of documentation and (2) how to facilitate collaboration among various domain experts. They adopted a semiotic approach in combination with a tool design approach to do the HWID. Future research could better map out the relations between the two theories in the case, to generalize to other domains or other archaeological sites.

The analysis of the HWID 2015 papers illustrates that a frequent form of HWID theory is as a platform that serves to focus discussion on HW and ID relations in wide context. In the light of the user requirement analysis presented above, it appears that one of HWID's main heritages from cognitive work analysis (CWA) is the need to adapt, combine, and develop a mix of theories to understand the relations between HW and ID. Further development of the HWID framework may make it a better intellectual tool for mapping the combinations of multiple other theories onto the relations between HW and ID. In addition, the IT artefacts, e.g., contextual personas by Cajander et al. (2015) or the threshold artefacts by Molka-Danielsen et al. (2015), may be examples of the hybrid work analysis and interaction design artefacts coming out of HWID. Finally, the HWID theory should reflect that artefacts may be 'packed' with values from both HW and from ID (Lopes, 2015).

Descriptive, normative, and critical HWID research

The philosophy of the HWID platform is that it is (a) a simple, low cost, and understandable framework, (b) useful to both interpretivists and positivists, by practitioners and researchers, and (c) a socio-technical theory that focuses on the relations between human work and interaction design (with all the caveats that follows). Given that, however, a few more limitations might come to mind, including that the use of HWID by academic researchers should be done with clarity with regard to whether the aim with HWID research is descriptive (how the world is), normative (how to change things into preferable states, how it ought to be), or critical (ask questions) HWID research. Thus, HWID can be used descriptively as framework to capture entities and relations, it can be used normatively as a design methodology that prescribes steps in a design process, and it can be used critically, as a reflection over existing research.

Descriptive

HWID can be used descriptively as platform to capture entities and relations. An example of this is the duty of a university's e-learning systems (Clemmensen, 2011b), which explored a case of designing a simple folder structure for a new e-learning software program for a university study program. The aim was to contribute to the theoretical base for human work interaction design (HWID) by identifying the type of relations connecting design artifacts with work analysis and interaction design processes. The action research method was used, with the author in a double role as university researcher and project manager of a developer group within the university. Analysis was conducted through grounded theory, inspired by the HWID platform. The theory contributions from the study were descriptive: (1) during the design of a simple artifact, such as a folder structure for a large organization, different relations between the work analysis, interaction design, and design artifacts are expressed; (2) the pattern of relations in the case studied was asymmetrical; and (3) the design artifacts connected, but have different relations to work analysis and interaction design. Thus, the HWID platform's main entities, the human work and the interaction design, and their relations could be superimposed on the empirical case to describe it on a higher level of abstraction and by that provide insights.

Normative

HWID can be used normatively as a design methodology that prescribes steps in a design process. In fact, the normative may always be a part of using a design approach, since design is about what ought to be, not just what is. Socio-technical design approaches such as design science and the Scandinavian approach to IS research may share common roots that go beyond geographically demarcated research traditions in the sense that they view the world as design(able), value pragmatic knowledge, and reflective engage with situations (Ågerfalk & Wiberg, 2018).

For example, in a study of interactive climate management, Pedersen and Clemmensen (2013) used the HWID platform as a normative approach to study how to design complex interactions for a complex work domain. In a combination of micro-information systems design science and human–computer interaction (HCI) aspects of climate management, they aimed to design for better interactive control interfaces and the utilization of sensor network technology. By applying design guidelines to the case studied, several interactive prototypes that successively addressed core issues in the setting were created. Starting from a simple human–computer interaction with a one-sensor one-output prototype made in Lego Mindstorms NXT, they ended up with custom-made sensors that addressed interaction with the target user profile of interest, the grower. The theory contributions included justifications and corrections of the HWID as a normative approach: (1) the application of a design platform for combining micro-information systems with human–computer interaction approaches adds structure to the design process (and rigor and relevance); (2) the relevance of the "interactive, sensor-intensive prototyping" approach was confirmed by the exhibition of one prototype at a large agricultural exhibition; (3) adhering to a lightweight process that concentrated on the socio-technical (generate/evaluate) allowed a series of prototyping efforts to be done, and track kept of the progress; and (4) the rigor was clearly demonstrated to be increased by the ability to reproduce sensor-intensive prototypes. Their study was a normative, HWID-guided design of sensor-intensive prototypes to develop interactive greenhouse climate management systems.

Critical

HWID can be used critically, as a reflection over existing research. What it means to do critical HCI research is not a fixed category, but may include simply becoming more reflective (Sengers, McCarthy, & Dourish, 2006), focusing on people's life-world as a core focus of HCI research (Stolterman & Croon Fors, 2008), doing critical design in the sense of prioritizing ethical design practice, revealing hidden agendas and values, and exploring alternative design values (Bardzell & Bardzell, 2013), or doing critical race theory in terms of ensuring that the research is paying attention to issues of race, with participation of underrepresented minorities in all of our activities (Ogbonnaya-Ogburu, Smith, To, & Toyama, 2020).

For example, Clemmensen and Katre (2018) studied how to adapt usability evaluation of e-government to different cultural contexts. The critical approach was centered around the issue that different kinds of usability problems in e-government were emerging in different regions and countries around the world, hence the theory building about these should be done by drawing on studies that were indigenous to the region/country in question. The assumption was that no one from the outside can appreciate what are the critical problems in a local design solution. They did two case studies of phenomena in e-government important to the local context and compared these: a case study of a government authentication system from Denmark, and a case study of 28 state web portals in India. This resulted in theory contributions in terms of critical reflections on two levels, comparison between Western and Indian e-government, and learning points specifically for the local context.

The comparison learning points included (1) Analyze the human work. Determine what users want to do with the e-government system. Do this analysis for each different user group (minorities, majorities, language groups, etc.), and geographical region (states, countries, continents). (2) Identify cultural models of use. Combine the analysis of human work in e-government systems and the interaction design of e-government systems to identify "cultural models of use"—in the form of existing systems, as well as sketches and prototypes of future systems—of a given technology, (e.g., a website) for each user group and geographic region. (3) Be as broad as possible. Conduct your analysis in "grounded theory" style—bottom-up analysis based on as many kinds of materials and data that you can get (other people's usability reports, government strategic documents, your own analysis, more), and then seek patterns and themes in the material. (4) Identify relationships. Pay particular attention to the types of relationships that you see between analysis of human work, the design artifacts, and the interaction design activities. These relations may not be the same, or even very similar, in different regions of the world. (5) Encourage participation. Encourage participation of all possible stakeholders like various types of citizens, government officials with different roles and responsibilities, and the user agencies while designing the e-government systems.

The learning points specifically for the local context were, for example, for the European case (1) do not design e-government solutions for the marginal user with specialized needs without making it very clear to your client that these users require additional support from human specialists; (2) be aware that Western European users, even though they may be computer literates, do not necessarily understand the idea behind many e-government and public information systems, that is, what to do with these systems; (3) study context by sampling diverse case material and look for relations between this, with a focus on the connection between human work (how should this system be used) and interaction design (usability and user experience of the e-government design solution); (4) take into account that user experience of e-government unfolds in stages, and has a temporality—and, for example, that a possible 'medium subjective satisfaction' identified as a negative result in a classic usability study may be an acceptable result for culturally acceptable design in the long run. It may take long time (years) for individual users as well as for user populations to learn to use e-government systems.

The critical use of the HWID platform to study usability evaluation in e-government in different cultural contexts produced a surprisingly large number of questions to the relatively standardized and well-known concepts and methods of usability evaluation. This was obviously the case for the cross-cultural comparison, where perhaps multiple differences could be expected since the two case countries appear different on many dimensions. However, the outcome was also a surprising re-appraisal of usability evaluation in the local context, as, for example, the Danish usability evaluation turned out to require novel sensitivities when seen in the light of larger holistic study context.

Summing up on the above, any HWID research projects have descriptive, normative, and reflective aspects. An aspect may be dominant in the profile of a particular project, as the above examples with e-learning platforms, interactive climate management, and e-government presented above illustrate.

7.2 Theorizing (Theory Building) Workshops

The theorizing workshop is a method for using the HWID platform to create publishable theory. It is to be used when the participating researchers each have one or more finished workshop papers or other forms for work-in-progress papers. It can be used in small groups like student report groups with 2–5 participants, research project groups with 5–20 participants, or larger symposium groups of 20–100 participants. The main idea is to collaboratively theorize and have fun with that. Since the purpose is to create theory, it is different from most design methods. For example, theorizing workshops would probably not apply design fiction understood as a methodological interweaving of the designer's practice with that of the science fiction author's (Markussen & Knutz, 2013; Sterling, 2009), though this approach by a closer look appears to be a socio-technical humanistic approach to design science; theorizing workshops would rather more specifically seek to interweave the designer's practice with that of the academic research authors.

Furthermore, a theorizing workshop is about theory building, not about academic paper writing. Individual papers can be improved by getting dedicated feedback from other researchers regarding RQ, use of theory/literature, method, discussion, and more. Theory can be tested in empirical work by grounding predictions with existing models, diagrams, or figures, or by comparing with existing theory. However, a theorizing workshop is neither about improving academic writing or about empirical testing of existing theory; a theorizing workshop is about theory building and exploration, that is, a support and part of the practice of theorizing. The theorizing is about, within and across academic research papers, to examine previously unexplored relationship or processes, including HW-ID relations and case-specific HWID processes. In addition, to introduce new constructs or significantly re-conceptualize existing ones in a re-conceptualization of what we mean by, for example, 'interaction design' in HWID. Finally, a theorizing workshop or sessions should focus on a specific overarching theme, which most probably could be the conference theme.

Steps in a theorizing workshop

A theorizing workshop has two theorizing steps, a self-reflection step and a preparation and a communication step. Step zero is the preparation step. This is where the data and research papers are gathered and perhaps, if not already, read or read again. An agenda for the theorizing is set, a schedule rolled out, and roles allocated. Theorizing material is made available.

The first theorizing step is to articulate the constructs of a theory (Weber, 2003). This means to formulate new constructs which are then used to build a new theory about some phenomena. The phenomena can be a novel one not described in previous theory—in HCI typically a novel (interaction) technology. Or it can be a twist or a tweak that the researchers do in their conceptualization of an already conceptualized phenomena. In both cases, they need to build a new theory of the phenomenon that reflects this conceptualization. Articulating the construct may include (1) to define the constructs of an existing theory more precisely, (2) delete constructs from an existing theory to provide a clearer account of the phenomenon of interest, (3) add constructs to an existing theory to cover different aspects of the phenomenon, and (4) replace all constructs of an existing theory to provide a novel account of the phenomenon.

In the first theorizing step, certain ways to build theory and theorize may be effective. The theorizers may find inspiration in an existing model or theory or framework or notion/idea from the previous literature. The hint here is to look for figures and tables in the literature. For example, look for key concepts and constructs in titles, abstracts, and conclusion of papers. Further, the theorizers could use tangible physical models to capture both abstract concepts and concrete implementation and allowing these and other complexities to surface as part of the theorizing (Lockton et al., 2019).

The second theorizing step is to articulate the relationship among the constructs of a theory. This may include to (1) propose new laws of relationships among existing or new constructs in a theory to account better for the phenomenon, (2) delete laws of relationships among the constructs of an existing theory to provide a simper account, (3) add and delete laws of relationships among the constructs of an existing theory to provide a better account of the phenomena, and (4) define the laws of relationships in an existing theory more precisely or perhaps conceptualize them in somewhat different ways. For example, a relation may be assumed to be causal, but the theorizer may want to re-specify it as a simple association between two constructs to better fit data.

The instructions to a group of theorizers for doing theorizing steps 1 and 2 can be

1. Build your own model in some material, in your own scientific laboratory. The materials can be paper, LEGO, wood, electronic kits, and digital materials including software; programmatically speaking think scale(s), think material(s), think dynamic(s).
2. Illustrate your model, etc. with a specific concrete example in some detail.

3. Annotate your model. Here the hint is to put yellow stickers with theory concepts on different parts of your model.
4. Play with your model to theorize by developing the model further. Here the hint is to notice what happens if you change something, some part of your model.

Thus, steps 1 and 2 are overlapping and to a degree, iterative.

The next step, Step 3, the self-reflection step, aims at answering the question: who are you as theory builder and what is the purpose of your theory building? There are five options, adapted from (Clemmensen et al., 2016):

1. *Meta-theoreticians* consider *<your theory> itself as an object of analysis.* They identify unique features and principles, as well as problematic aspects, of the theory and compared it to other similar theories in HCI.
2. *Theory-tool-makers* use *<your theory> as a theoretical influence in the development of a new analytical tool.* They identify needs and requirements for new theoretical tools and employ <your theory> , sometimes in combination with other theories, to inform and guide the development of such tools.
3. *Construct-developers* employed *<your theory> as a tool for conceptual analysis and development.* They apply the theory to address central issues and challenges in HCI, often in response to the emergence of new technologies. By doing so they also develop new sub-concepts of existing concepts or expand the application scope of existing concepts.
4. *Data interpreters* use *<your theory> as a tool for empirical analysis.* They use key theoretical constructs of the theory to identify and categorize specific empirical phenomena.
5. *Design-oriented researchers* use *<your theory> as a framework for design.* The theory guides the iterative design process or helps develop claims about the nature of the design process. These researchers provide new design illustrations, claims, and guidelines.

The self-reflection may thus take departure in a self-assessment of how theory did work out for the group of theorizers, see also (Clemmensen et al., 2016). Frequent and positive uses, and adaptation and development of existing theory may be assessed. The above-proposed five specific purposes for which HCI researchers use and make theory may well be extended with more purposes. In addition, the self-reflection may include to what degree the created theory is original, generalizable, etc., for example, a question to be asked can be how the novel theory relates to the classic works in the field.

Finally, the communication step includes the group(s) of theorizing researchers to present their outcome theory (as it is at this stage) in forum, may it be verbally, video, PPts, paper, hardware sketches, LEGO, etc. The advice here is threefold: (1) try to anchor your theory building in design cases, and refer to these; (2) give your theory a name; and (3) refer to theory building step(s)—explain how and why you theorize. Below are three different examples of how to use theorizing workshops.

HWID theorizing workshop Example 1

The first example of a theorizing workshop is about summarizing insights in a theorizing session at the end of a conference. At the end of the HWID 2018 working conference on 'Designing Engaging Automation' (Barricelli et al., 2019), the conference participants did a theorizing session in order to sum up insights learned during the 2-day conference. The organizers of the session distributed the conference participants into five groups, with 5–8 participants in each, and a group facilitator. The principles for participant distribution were to form a group with the other presenters in a presenter session group from the conference program. All other participants (those not presenters) were instructed to distribute themselves across the groups. The instructions to participants were as shown in Fig. 7.1. In addition, the participants were told that the term 'theory' in the theorizing workshop could cover frameworks, theories, models, grounded theory, notions, principles, 'strong concepts', and constructs, cases.

The results of the theorizing workshop summarizing theory at the end of the conference could be considered theories or perhaps emerging theory. For example, the outcome of three of the groups that were theorizing at HWID 2018 is shown in Figs. 7.2, 7.3 and 7.4. The first example is the Eye GAZE of the Dark Cockpit: A Theory of Work Engagement with Automation, Fig. 7.2. This theory builds on the participating theorizers' conference papers (partly what is in the text boxes in

---

1. Form a group with the other presenters in your session group from the conference program
2. 1400-1530: Build theory based on the session papers within your group (and other relevant papers)
    1. Within or across papers, examine previously unexplored relationship or processes, e.g., HW-ID relations, or case specific HWID processes
    2. Introduce a new construct or significantly re-conceptualize an existing one, e.g., re-conceptualize what we mean by 'interaction design' in HWID
    3. Focus on the theme of the conference: Designing Engaging Automation
3. 1600-1700: Present your theory in forum, on maximum 3 slides
    1. Try to anchor your theory building in specific papers from yours or others sessions, and refer to these papers
    2. Give your theory a name
    3. Refer to theory building step(s) – explain how and why you theorize☺

Fig. 7.1 Example of a HWID theorizing workshop at the end of a conference to summarize theoretical insights

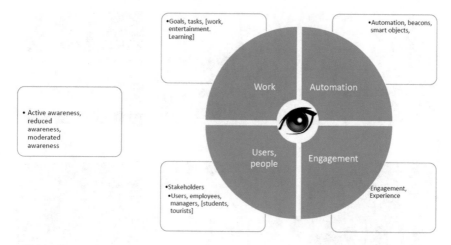

Fig. 7.2 The Eye GAZE of the dark cockpit: a theory of work engagement with automation. By participants in HWID 2018

1. Gathering of the main concepts of our group's papers and posters like, e.g.,
   - Trust (Karvonen et al., Saariluoma et al.)
   - Automation (Karvonen et al., Saariluoma et al.)
   - Work (Kaasinen et al., Abdelnour-Nocera & Clemmensen)
   - Design (Abdelnour-Nocera & Clemmensen)
   - ...
2. Eliminating construct redundancy and filtering of concepts
3. White board draft of the model
4. Assessing the explanatory power (i.e., iteration of the model)
5. Aim of the model (for conceptual analysis and development)
6. Magic
7. Final version of the model

Fig. 7.3 Steps in a collaborative theorizing process. By participants in HWID 2018

Fig. 7.2.), the conference theme related to engagement and automation, and a domain-specific component: the cockpit (one of the group members worked on human errors and tasks in the aviation industry).

The Eye GAZE of the Dark Cockpit was an awareness model that posited that human pilots during flight should not be disturbed unnecessary by the automation systems (hence the dark cockpit, no unnecessary lights will come on). The model appeared to suggest that the human 'eye' or awareness is mediated by four factors, of which engagement is one.

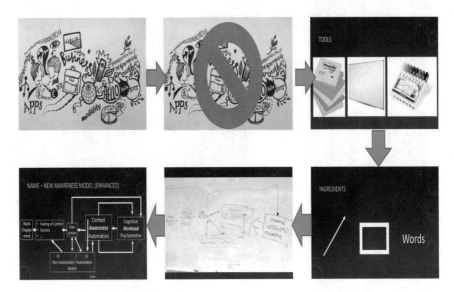

Fig. 7.4   Illustration of a collaborative theorizing process. By participants in HWID 2018

Why this theory? The group argued that they were theory-tool-makers that used their own and existing theory as theoretical influences in the development of a new analytical tool. They identified needs and requirements for new theoretical tools (the current situation in the aviation industry with novel levels of automation) and employed their own ideas or theory from their papers in combination with other theories, to inform and guide the development of their proposed intellectual tool, the Eye GAZE of the Dark Cockpit model. While doing this, they were at the same time thinking about that they wanted to create a new tool for designing for work engagement, so they also acted as design-oriented researchers who developed a new framework for design. While they did not develop design guidelines, with Fig. 7.2 they developed new design illustrations of a novel 'eye-gaze system'.

Another group was more explicit in their steps, and formulated these as a list of actions, Fig. 7.3. Yet another group illustrated their theorizing process, beginning with initial pre-theory, which was bracketed/forbidden to use, over bottom-up post-it note activities, toward formulating and sketching their theory, and ending up with a classic boxes-and-arrows theory, Fig. 7.4.

Overall, though having a theorizing session at the end of an academic research workshop is not a well-tested and proven approach but merely a first draft of a method, the theorizing session held at HWID 2018 delivered interesting output as shown in Figs. 7.2, 7.3 and 7.4.

HWID theorizing workshop Example 2

The second example of a theorizing workshop is giving a tutorial at a conference by using the theorizing workshop format. In a tutorial at HCI International 2021 entitled 'Introduction to Socio-Technical HCI Theory and Action', the theorizing workshop format was to be used. The objectives were that after the tutorial the participants should be able to (1) explain and reflect on ideas of socio-technical HCI and organizational usability and UX; (2) understand how to use a theorizing platform to create value for employees, customers, and citizens; and (3) link together findings from empirical work analysis and interaction design to design for UX-at-work and employee well-being. The intended content and benefit of the tutorial was thus that it provided the participants with a platform for theorizing about socio-technical HCI.

During the tutorial, the theorizing with the platform included to present design cases that illustrates design of socio-technical relations; to provide specific advice for researchers, consultants, and policymakers; and to reflect on open issues. The platform uses thus met the requirement of taking both the social and the technical into account, while focusing strongly on the relations between the social and the technical. The tutorial taught how to use a multi-sided platform for theorizing about socio-technical HCI and work design in the digital age.

The target audience of such a tutorial at an academic HCI conference were HCI researchers, UX Consultants, and Policymakers with an interest in socio-technical approaches to HCI. The HCI researchers could potentially use the socio-technical platform to accumulate knowledge across design case studies. The research-inclined UX Consultants who need socio-technical HCI design could quickly adapt the platform to action designs for improving UX-at-work in local organizational settings. The policymakers could use the platform to enable dialogues about and set policies for procurement of digital solutions in organizational and government settings.

The bio-sketch of the tutorial presenter indicated the qualifications needed to run the tutorial: academic research professor in HCI or related, knowledge of socio-technical systems design, work analysis, design psychology, interaction design, user experience, and digitalization of work. These kinds of qualifications are usually found in human-computer interaction, design, and information system fields.

HWID theorizing workshop Example 3

The third example of a theorizing workshop is to use the format to reflect on and compare existing theories. Theorizing workshops were used during a sabbatical stay at University of Siegen by the principal investigator of a HWID research project, (PI, Torkil Clemmensen). The aim of the project was to internationalize, finalize, and evaluate a specific theoretical framework for Human Work Interaction Design (HWID)—the one presented in Chap. 2 of this book. The idea was to do this by comparing and combining the HWID framework presented in (Abdelnour-Nocera et al., 2015a; Campos et al., 2012; Clemmensen et al., 2006; Katre et al., 2010) with related research stemming from the University of Siegen. At the time of the sabbatical stay, the Information Systems and New Media research group from School of Economic Disciplines at University of Siegen had a strong Human–Computer Interaction (HCI) and Computer-Supported Cooperative Work (CSCW) presence. Researchers from this group provided theoretical inspiration for, and were interested in strengthening the collaboration with, researchers coming from Information System (IS) departments, such as the PI. The primary host (PH, Professor Volker Wulf, Chair Information Systems and New Media at the University of Siegen), and the

PI planned in collaboration with other Siegen researchers (Markus Rohde, Volkmar Pipek, Gunnar Stevens, Marc Hassenzahl) to evaluate and possibly consolidate the theory by comparing it to important other theories. In particular, the PI and the PH would compare and combine the HWID framework with the PH research group's research on 'Practice-Based Computing' (Volker Wulf et al., 2015, 2018) theory and related approaches. The expectation was that there would be several benefits of a consolidated HWID framework that it could function as a development platform for a multitude of analytical tools for socio-technical interventions in various work domains. This would be relevant for SMEs with potentials for human-oriented digitalization, e.g., employee-robot collaboration, in the production of goods and professional services.

The workshop's theoretical background, key concepts, and state of the art

In the particular version of HWID that were of interest in the PIs project, it was however critical not to reduce the understanding of how work analysis and interaction design are connected to a series of steps, but instead to see HWID as a *holistic design gestalt that includes several relation theories* (Clemmensen, 2011a). In somewhat contrast to HWID's 'relational' approach, practice-based computing (Volker Wulf et al., 2015, 2018) argues that even a strong work domain analysis paired with good user-centered design with real user participation is not enough to account for the changes in social practices resulting from new technological artifacts. Rather, research should build a repository of design case studies and generalize by doing comparative analysis with concept building. The focus of concept and theory building should be on *features of social practice* (e.g., awareness), *IT design principles* (e.g., tailorability), and social changes stemming directly from *appropriation* of IT artifacts (e.g., over the shoulder learning). Thus, where HWID was presented as a platform that supports the development of domain-specific theoretical gestalts, practice-based computing emphasized the conceptualization of notions of social changes across empirical cases. The PI and PH planned to test out if HWID could be combined with a practice-based computing approach to conceptualize notions of socio-technical changes across empirical cases. Furthermore, they aimed to explore if and how to combine or contrast HWID with related approaches.

The workshop's method

During the 3 months of stay, the PI with the support of the PH organized three theorizing workshops to explore variations of the HWID framework for socio-technical interventions in various work domains in a German context. The execution of the workshops was based on the PI and PH's experiences from running master courses about CSCW and 'HCI in organizations' at University of Siegen (the PH) and CBS (the PI), design workshops at the design department at Beijing post and telecommunication university, and theory building sessions at HWID 2018 conference. An overview of the workshops is given in Table 7.1.

Research plan: The research plan was that the PI visited the host university (Siegen) for 3 months. The PI had weekly meetings with the PH to collaborate on the research, participate in the Siegen research group meetings, and organize with

Table 7.1 HWID theorizing workshops for comparing and consolidating theory

Workshops	Month 1 workshop	Month 2 workshop	Month 3 workshop
Theory variation	'Practice based' and HWID framework	'Experience Design' and HWID framework	'Design tensions' and HWID framework
Responsible	The PI, PH, and Siegen researchers	The PI, PH, and prof. Marc Hassenzahl	The PI, PH, and prof. Tom Gross
Participants	Researchers, students and practitioners from university of Siegen or Fraunhofer	Researchers, students, and practitioners from university of Siegen or at the Fraunhofer	Researchers, students, and practitioners from university of Siegen or university of Bamberg
Theorizing material for MORNING session	LEGO, wood, and other mock-up material, prototype tools	LEGO, wood, and other mock-up material, prototype tools	LEGO, wood, and other mock-up material, prototype tools
Reflective material for AFTERNOON session	Praxlab spaces (user, method, management, and creative spaces) (Ogonowski, Jakobi, Müller, & Hess, 2018)	Experience Design Tools (Need Cards, interaction vocabulary cards) (Hassenzahl, 2010)	Design tension categories (Gross, 2013)
Location	Praxlabs	Experience Design Lab	Praxlabs

the PH and others the three 1-day workshops, Table 7.1. The three workshops varied the theory combinations and thus consolidated the HWID framework.

Practicalities.

The needed funding for the theorizing workshops were to (a) cover access to lab space for workshops and other expenses related to running the workshops, including lunch and coffee to participants; (b) student assistant hours for programming HWID tools; and (c) student assistant for running workshops, and travel and stay for PI and other participants.

Procedure and initial findings

Each of the three workshops used the theorizing workshop format, but adapted the agenda to the specific theories being compared to HWID, Figs. 7.5, 7.6 and 7.7. The workshops were all facilitated by the PI in cooperation with the respective research group leaders. The data collection was done by video and audio recording the workshops by a research assistant, the same for all three workshops. In addition, workshop participants were encouraged to and did upload their material and videos made during the workshop in a cloud service (Sciebo, shared by German universities). The data analysis proceeded in two steps, one was done during the workshops by the participants as the outcome and uploaded in the cloud service and another was done much later by the PI with the aim of publishing insights from the workshops (work-in-progress). In these three workshops, the outcome was theory comparison based on analysis of (the same) design case. The initial findings indicated that (1) HWID is

Compare and contrast two socio-technical HCI approaches that are both based on design cases, 'Human Work Interaction Design' (HWID) and Siegen School's 'Practice-Based Computing' (PBD), to explore if and in what ways to theorize, that is, to develop a set of ideas, about socio-technical design cases.

Agenda:

10:00-10:15 *Welcome*

10:15-10:45 *Introduction* to the theorizing exercise, the HWID platform, and the two cases, by Facilitator and <to come>

10:45-12:00 *Groupwork*, developing analytical tools for socio-technical interventions in work domains

- HWID theorizing with two design cases
- Cases: 1) design the use of collaborative robots in a glass processing factory, 2) production planning
- Material: LEGO, to 'build' theory, illustrate developed concepts and relations and their links to data material
- Outcome: Documented with group video explaining HWID principles, using theorizing material
- Coffee will be available

12:00-13:00 *Forum,* presentation and discussion of theory building videos

Lunch (provided by workshop)

13:30-13:45 *Introduction* to Practice-Based Computing, by Thomas and Volker

13:45-14:45 *Groupwork*, using PBC to combine, contrast and compare to HWID based on the group's case analysis from the morning session.

- Reflective exercise with HWID+PBD.
- Material: Praxlab spaces (user, method, management and creative spaces)
- Outcome: documented with uploaded group video presenting combinations, contrasts and comparisons HWID+PDB

14:45-15:15 *Forum* presentation and discussion of comparison videos

15:15-15:30 Summary and evaluation of the day and next step

Readings <list>

Fig. 7.5 Workshop 1 HWID compared to practice-based computing

less contextual and less technical, and more social and theory oriented compared to PBC; (2) HWID is less theoretical/conceptual, and more contextual and more work and social oriented, compared to ED; and (3) HWID is less philosophically focused and has broader view of the socio-technical relations compared to DTs. More detailed analysis and deeper insights await further research.

Planned publication and dissemination

The aim was to publish papers in a key conference in the area, 'IFIP TC13.6 HWID Working Conference', and in a top ranked Information Systems journal on the 'IS basket of 8' list. The PI sought agreement with a publisher, Springer, on a HWID book (this book). While the theorizing workshop is a method for using the HWID platform to create publishable theory, the choice of publication outlet and publication process depends on the target of the research and on the actual outcome of the done workshops and subsequent qualitative and quantitative analysis.

Compare and contrast two socio-technical HCI approaches that are both based on design cases, Copenhagen Business School's 'Human Work Interaction Design' (HWID) and University of Siegen's 'Experience Design' (ED), to explore if and in what ways to theorize, that is, to develop a set of ideas, about socio-technical design cases.

Agenda:

1400 - 1445 [USD 210] Welcome and introduction to the theorizing exercise and the HWID platform, by Torkil

1445 - 1600 [USD 219+ USD 210] Groupwork, developing analytical tools for socio-technical interventions in work domains

- HWID theorizing with design case material
- Case: design the use of collaborative robots in a glass processing factory
- Material: LEGO, to 'build' theory, illustrate developed concepts and relations and their links to data material
- Outcome: Documented with group video explaining HWID principles, using theorizing material, uploaded to Sciebo cloudservice

1600-1630 [USD210] Forum, presentation and discussion of theory building videos

1630 – 1645 [USD 210] Introduction to Experience Design by Marc and Matthias

1645-1730 [USD 219+ USD 210] Groupwork, using Experience Design to combine, contrast and compare to HWID based on the group's case analysis from the first part of the workshop

- Reflective exercise with ED and HWID
- Material: Experience Design Tools (Need Cards, Positive practice canvas)
- Outcome: Documented with group video presenting combinations, contrasts and comparisons HWID+ED, uploaded to Sciebo cloudservice

1730 – 1800 [USD210] Forum presentation and discussion of comparison videos

Dinner: Summary and evaluation of the day and next steps

Readings <list>

Fig. 7.6. Workshop 2 HWID compared to experience design

7.3   HWID Templates for Qualitative Analysis

Qualitative analysis is the search for and documentation of novel constructs and their relations. It establishes the qualities, not the quantities, of a phenomenon. It is mostly inductive, bottom-up, searching to group the raw data under emerging constructs and linking the constructs into a local theoretical account of the phenomenon. Qualitative analysis is an umbrella term that covers thematic analysis (Braun & Clarke, 2006), interpretative phenomenological analysis (Smith & Shinebourne, 2012), hermeneutic-phenomenological research interviews (Kvale, 1996), grounded theory (Strauss & Corbin, 1994), and more approaches, including analytic practices found in anthropology and communication studies.

Qualitative analysis, understood as grounded theory, is an important research approach in HCI and CSCW (Muller & Kogan, 2010). In these fields, grounded theory is defined as the combination of an open-minded exploration of concepts and a methodological rigor in sampling and testing strategies, which is done with the aim to produce a rich description and open-ended research questions for further work

Compare and contrast two socio-technical HCI approaches that are both based on design cases, 'Human Work Interaction Design' (HWID) and University of Bambergs' CSCW Design Tensions (DT), to explore if and in what ways to theorize, that is, to develop a set of ideas, about socio-technical design cases.

Agenda:
1400 - 1445 *Welcome* and *introduction* to the theorizing exercise and the HWID platform, by Torkil

1445 - 1600 *Groupwork*, developing analytical tools for socio-technical interventions in work domains
-         HWID theorizing with design case material.
-         Case: design the use of collaborative robots in a glass processing factory
-         Material: LEGO, to 'build' theory, illustrate developed concepts and relations and their links to data material
-         Outcome: documented with group video explaining HWID principles, using theorizing material
-         Coffee will be available.

1600-1630 *Forum,* presentation and discussion of theory building videos.
1630 – 1645 *Introduction* to CSCW Design Tensions, by Tom
1645-1730 *Groupwork*, using Design tensions to combine, contrast and compare to HWID based on the group's case analysis from the first part of the workshop.
-         Reflective exercise with DT and HWID
-         Material: Design tension categories
-         Outcome: Documented with group video presenting combinations, contrasts and comparisons HWID+DT

Fig. 7.7. Workshop 3 HWID compared to design tensions

(Muller & Kogan, 2010). The HCI- and CSCW-specific account of grounded theory may not be completely shared by all, for example, empirical studies of the use of grounded theory methodologies indicate that it is not consistent what is meant by 'sampling' across studies that uses grounded theory approaches (Gentles et al., 2015). However, the research program for grounded theory in HCI and CSCW proposed by Muller and Kogan appears to follow the use of grounded theory in the majority of social science by citing and using classic works of grounded theory by Glaser and Strauss (1967). On the other hand, arguments have been made that grounded theory in HCI and CSCW is and should be tailored to these fields' somewhat engineering-oriented and computer science practices (Muller & Kogan, 2010; Pidgeon et al., 1991).

One way to tailor qualitative analysis to a field or domain such as HCI and CSCW is to orient the analysis by being inspired by concepts and relations from previous literature and current research in the HCI and CSCW fields. For HCI and CSCW, it is an obvious choice to develop and use computer support in the thematic analysis, for example, ongoing research promises machine learning support to the thematic coding process (Chen, Drouhard, Kocielnik, Suh, & Aragon, 2018; Rietz & Maedche, 2021). Furthermore, it has been proposed to use 'sensitizing concepts', which is background ideas from HCI and CSCW, as precursors for the emerging themes/constructs from data (Muller & Kogan, 2010). The emerging themes/constructs can be connected with the support of 'coding families', which are selected types of relationships (causality, is-part-of, and other collective beliefs) from previous related analysis or from literature (Muller & Kogan, 2010). Taking these ideas further, notions of sensitizing concepts have been proposed in HCI, for example, socio-spatial literacy (Krogh, Petersen, O'Hara, & Groenbaek, 2017). Going even further, Waern et al. (2020) combined sensitizing concepts and their relations as a whole for design purposes, by suggesting the use 'sensitizing scenarios' or role plays for design teams. The idea with these sensitizing scenarios was to make designers aware of important but complex social science theory in their design practices. Similarly, but with a strong focus on academic research practices, it can be argued that qualitative analysis can be tailored to HWID by using 'sensitizing' HWID concepts and their relations, etc.

In summary, qualitative analysis is a technology that can be adopted and adapted by researchers from various fields. As any other technology, it has fixed rules and procedures to be followed, of which some can be automated and allocated to the computer(s), while others are left to the human users. Recently, this has become evident in the sophisticated technological products for qualitative analysis offered to researchers, such as MAXQDA, Atlas.TI, NVivo, and more. In the coming years, the emergent data analytic approaches may offer new approaches to qualitative analysis that is less human based. However, qualitative research projects with humans leading the qualitative analysis will usually develop local theory that is inspired (and not steered) by previous theory in all aspects of the qualitative analysis (Collins & Stockton, 2018). In grounded theory, for example, the researchers collect data from participants by being guided by sensitizing concept and they analyze data at the same time guided by selected general relationships between concepts.

Given that qualitative analysis can be tailored to HWID with sensitizing concepts and coding families, and that qualitative analysis is a technology, it makes sense to use 'HWID templates for qualitative analysis' adapted to major qualitative analysis software packages of MAXQDA, Atlas.TI, and NVivo. The templates illustrated in Figs. 7.8, 7.9 and 7.10 are composed of sensitizing concepts adapted from the HWID platform's key concepts, and their relations. The reason to call this combo a 'template' rather than, for example, a 'sensitizing scenario' (Waern et al., 2020) is that the aim with the HWID templates are not to support designers understanding social science concepts in a design scenario, but to support researchers using the HWID platform in qualitative analysis that (hopefully) ends in novel theory and actions, interventions, or designs. While the major software packages of MAXQDA, Atlas.TI, and NVivo do not explicitly support theory as a 'product' (except for some mapping options), their output when used by researchers is often a local theory presented in an academic paper, which the HWID template supports. The software packages to a lesser degree support action, intervention, and co-design by researchers and participants together, but again, the HWID template when filled out in analysis can be thought of as a sociomaterial solution and can be discussed as such between researchers and other stakeholders (participants and more).

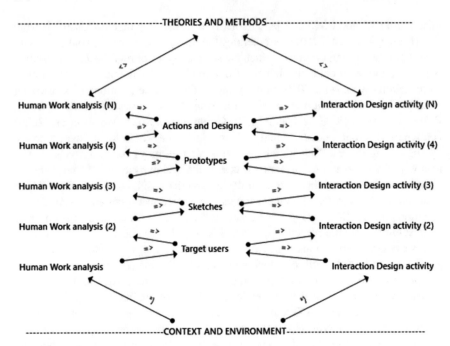

Fig. 7.8 HWID template for qualitative analysis with Atlas.TI

Atlas.TI template for HWID thematic analysis

See (Fig. 7.8).

MAXQDA template for HWID thematic analysis

See (Fig. 7.9).

NVivo template for HWID thematic analysis

See (Fig. 7.10).

Note that the use of HWID templates requires both having access to one of the qualitative analysis packages and to know how it works. The use of the HWID templates may be described in a set of procedures for analysis:

1. Collect initial data.
2. Open a project in the qualitative analysis software.
3. Open the template.
4. Start linking data to existing codes.
5. Rename codes to fit linked data.
6. Do a co-occurrence search (Atlas.TI), matrix query (NVivo), grid analysis (MAXQDA), to establish overlap and relations between codes.
7. Link those codes that overlap.

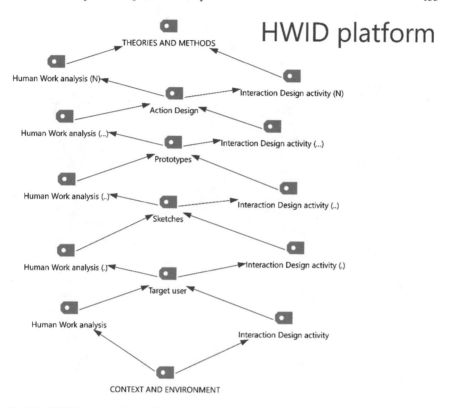

Fig. 7.9 HWID template for qualitative analysis with MAXQDA

8. Name the link and add memos to the link that theorize the link (or in Nvivo use relationship nodes).
9. Add contextual data and link this to codes.
10. Add theory and method in the form of papers/PDFs and/or memos that connect theorizing efforts to existing literature.
11. Use the memos to write up a narrative that introduces the case and your insights from the case—use the data, your modified template codes, and concept(s) from literature.

Obviously, the qualitative analysis software is developed over time, and for each new version, new possibilities, and limitations for analysis occurs. For example, Nvivo has in recent versions a notion of 'relationship' nodes that directly allows Nvivo users to link data to a relation between to concepts (nodes), hereby explaining and giving evidence for the kind of relations created. Despite the developments in the software, there will also in future versions be a need for sensitizing concepts and their relations to guide the users doing the analysis.

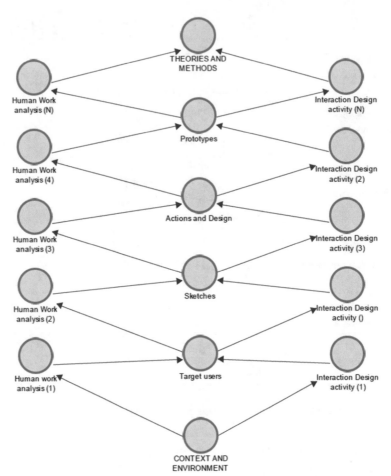

THEORIES AND
METHODS

Human Work
analysis (N)

Interaction Design
activity (N)

Prototypes

Human Work
analysis (4)

Interaction Design
activity (2)

Actions and Design

Human Work
analysis (3)

Interaction Design
activity (3)

Sketches

Human Work
analysis (2)

Interaction Design
activity ()

Target users

Human work
analysis (1)

Interaction Design
activity (1)

CONTEXT AND
ENVIRONMENT

Fig. 7.10 HWID template for qualitative analysis with NVivo

7.4 Exploratory Quantitative Modeling of HWID Cases

In HCI, there is a well-known distinction between formative and summative usability evaluation, the first being about creating design ideas and the latter about testing specific expectations to a final version of a new design. Both qualitative and quantitative modeling can be useful tools in both formative and summative usability evaluations. Since HWID is a design approach, we argue that in a similar way as with usability evaluation, it may be useful to use both qualitative and quantitative analyses in HWID projects. In this section, we introduce some ideas for exploratory quantitative modeling for HWID as a part of the design process.

For those researchers and research projects that conceptualize phenomena in quantitative logics, this section proposes a non-traditional conceptualization of quantitative measures, which may be particularly relevant for measuring quantifiable outcomes of HWID projects such as user experiences or other quality measures. The traditional conceptualization of quantitative psychological concepts in HCI, CSCW, IS, etc. is the idea of latent constructs that cause a set of indicators, also called 'reflective concepts'. The non-traditional alternative conceptualization includes 'formative concepts' (Borsboom et al., 2003), which are caused by or formed by a set of indicators, and 'network concepts', which are dynamic systems of causally connected directly observable entitities (Schmittmann et al., 2013). For example, rather than seeing UX as an unidimensional overall evaluative product or interaction characteristica that causes various pragmatic and hedonic indicators of UX (reflective modeling), in the alternative conceptualization UX can be an experience formed by a diversity of positive experiences (formative modeling) or can be a 'network of positive experiences' (network modeling).[1]

Further, while both reflective and formative concepts rely on a factor/latent variable approach (the elements shared among the indicators), the network conceptualization relies on the direct relationships among the observable variables (Costantini et al., 2015). The benefit of the network approach is to provide some additional insights not gained easily by the traditional latent concept approach. For example, while AttrakDiff can be used to measure the main factors of UX (pragmatic and hedonic), a network conceptualization measure of UX using AttrakDiff questions would focus on the direct relationships and overlaps between the local phenomena asked about in the questions (e.g., if you feel some interaction is repulsive, you may then also feel discouraged from furhter interaction, or if you find the interaction original you may also feel is creative). The network conceptualization measure may be described with network attrributes such as centrality, relation strenghts, clusterring, etc. (Costantini et al., 2015).

This section is controversial, and not all readers will agree that the proposals in this section make sense. This section presents initial ideas about using structural equation modeling (SEM) in a fully exploratory way to model HWID outcomes, and/or use network conceptualizations of HWID to model processes and outcomes. These ideas need to be further developed and tested.

Exploratory SEM modeling of HWID cases

The idea with exploratory SEM modeling of HWID cases is to use the HWID platform as a theory to loosely guide an SEM analysis. SEM is theory driven but we will use it as a platform-driven approach, which mainly means to loosen the requirements for theoretical justification for variables/constructs in the model. In addition, instead of reflective modeling of the phenomena, which is by most researchers considered the correct way to use SEM, the idea here is to apply a formative modeling of the

---

[1] In fact, that psychological IT constructs may be neither reflective nor formative, but networks (Schmittmann et al., 2013) were a point made about user experience by Bruno latour in a CHI keynote 2013 in Paris (https://www.youtube.com/watch?y=VDr2qBVIQjI).

phenomena represented by the HWID concepts ('relation artefacts' in HWID terminology, 'latent constructs' in SEM modeling). However, using SEM in an exploratory way and with formative modeling is fiddling with survey data, the negative reader would say.

Recommendation to do formative modeling can be developed by reflection on the model logic. This can, for example, be done by discussing criteria for when formative and reflective modeling apply (Coltman et al., 2008), Table 7.2.

It may make sense to apply six considerations of Coltman et al.'s (2008) (three theoretical considerations and three empirical considerations), Table 7.2, to characterize and help researchers to decide when and how to do formative modeling of HWID. Furthermore, the exploratory approach to SEM modeling of HWID phenomena can be shown as a procedure (for a fuller account of using SEM for exploratory modeling, see (Hair, Hult, Ringle, & Sarstedt, 2017)):

1. Begin by entering the HWID SEM template in your software for PLS (smart PLS or other).
2. Select the variables of interest for the analysis. Be sure to include at least one relation artefact variable. Find inspiration in qualitative models of the phenomenon if any are available.
3. Enter the data.
4. Do the analysis.
5. Describe the measurement model (i.e., which questions that you ask for each HWID concept in the template).
6. Describe the structural model (i.e., which causal relations exist between concepts).
7. Assess the measurement and structural models.

The measurement models in any HWID modeling may all be formative since HWID is a design approach. Each represent the researcher's attempt to model with a set of questions (indicators) the various HWID relation artefacts (latent constructs) of interest to the researcher. Theories about individual method and techniques that fall under the general HWID concepts are useful here. For example, if the HWID focal relation artefact is collaborative sketching, then the other HWID relation artefacts to be modeled can be some versions of interaction design patterns and work flow, and questions about these can be modeled using interaction design and work flow theory. However, in principle, some or all of HWID concepts could also be modeled as reflective, as one relation artefact could be seen as shaping/causing other relation artefacts, such that collaborative sketching could be seen as causing relation artefacts in the next stage of the design process, for example, it could be causing/shaping specific organizational action hypothesis and specific field evaluations/UX tests. See also the discussion of formative and reflective and network analysis below. An example of formative modeling a work analysis with three questions is given in Fig. 7.11.

For HWID analysis, formative modeling of HWID relation artefacts (concepts) is a useful way to reflect on the relation between the HWID theoretical concepts and the

Table 7.2   Considerations for assessing reflective and formative HWID models: three theoretical and three empirical considerations. Inspired by (Coltman et al., 2008)

Considerations	HWID reflective model	HWID formative model
Theoretical considerations		
Nature of relation artefact (focal construct)	Relation artefact exists – Relation artefact exists independent of other relation artefacts	Relation artefact is formed – Relation artefacts is a combination of other relation artefacts
Direction of movement (causality) between other relation artefacts (items) and relation artefact (focal construct)	Movement from relation artefact to other relation artefacts – Variation in the relation artefact causes variation in other relation artefacts – Variation in other relation artefacts do not cause variation in the relation artefact	Movement from other relation artefacts to relation artefact – Variation in the relation artefact does not cause variation in other relation artefacts – Variation in other relation artefacts causes variation in the relation artefact
Characteristics of other relation artefacts (items) used to measure the relation artefact (focal construct)	Other relation artefacts are manifested by the relation artefact – Other relation artefacts share a common theme/stage in design process – Other relation artefacts are interchangeable – Adding or dropping another relation artefact does not change the conceptual domain of the relation artefact	Other relation artefacts define the Relation Artefact – Other relation artefacts need not share a common theme/stage in design process – Other relation artefacts are not interchangeable – Adding or dropping another relation artefact may change the conceptual domain of the relation artefact
Empirical considerations		
Other relation artefacts (items) used to measure intercorrelation	Other relation artefacts used to measure the relation artefact should have high positive intercorrelations – Empirical tests: assessing internal consistency and reliability by Cronbach alpha, average variance extracted, and factor loadings (e.g., from common or confirmatory factor analysis) of other relation artefacts	Other relation artefacts used to measure the relation artefact can have any pattern of intercorrelation but should possess the same directional relationship – Empirical test: no empirical assessment of other relation artefacts reliability possible; various preliminary analyses are useful to check directionality between other relation artefacts and relation artefact

(continued)

Table 7.2 (continued)

Considerations	HWID reflective model	HWID formative model
Other relation artefacts (items) relationships with relation artefact (focal construct) antecedents (relation artefacts in earlier stages of the design process) and consequences (relation artefacts in later stages of the design process)	Other relation artefacts have similar sign and significance of relationships with the antecedents/consequences as the relation artefact. – Empirical tests: establishing content validity by theoretical considerations, assessing convergent and discriminant validity empirically	Other relation artefacts may not have similar significance of relationships with the antecedents/consequences as the relation artefact. – Empirical tests: assessing nomological validity by considering how both formative and reflective other relation artefacts may measure the relation artefact, and/or linking the formatively measured relation artefact with another reflectively measured relation artefact to which it relates theoretically
Measurement error and collinearity	Identifying the error term in other relation artefacts is possible, – By using the assumption that all other relation artefacts used to measure the relation artefact should highly intercorrelate	Identifying the error term is not possible if the formative measurement model is estimated in isolation – But it is possible to legitimately eliminate the error term by specifying the relation artefact in such a way as to capture the full set of relevant other relation artefacts The risk for collinearity (e.g., that two relation artefacts are redundant with respect to each other) could be assessed

Fig. 7.11 Formative model of a work analysis with three questions. Made in SmartPLS 3

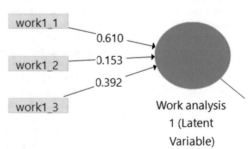

work1_1

0.610

work1_2   0.153

0.392

work1_3

Work analysis 1 (Latent Variable)

concrete questions used to do data collection. An interpretation of the example of a formative model of the work analysis latent construct in Fig. 7.11 is that the question work1_1 'loads' more on the constructs than the two other questions. Compared to a qualitative model of the phenomenon, a benefit of the quantitative model of HWID is thus that it can provide persuasion in numbers of which sub-concepts are more important for explaining the concept.

The structural model in HWID modeling is determined by the researcher using the HWID platform model, as illustrated in Fig. 1.1 in Chap. 1. The structural model will necessarily be a snapshot of the HWID design process, purely selected by the researcher's theoretical considerations. For example, it can be a model of how a prototype is anchored in and generate work analysis and an interaction design activity, that is, both work analysis and interaction design influence a prototype that again influence the next work analysis and interaction design activity, Fig. 7.12.

The structural model in HWID modeling can thus be interpreted as a model of a sociomaterial HWID phenomenon, provided that a context bar indicating the wider context of the phenomena, for example, time and place is added. An interpretation of the HWID structural model will say something about the size of the relationships between the relation artefacts (latent constructs), for example, in Fig. 7.12 that work analysis 1 has a larger positive relationship with the prototype [O = 0.543; SD = 0.01] than the other relation artefacts (latent constructs).

It is important to remember that HWID knowledge is not necessarily causal knowledge. It is the shape of the whole gestalt of the design process that is the knowledge contribution, which can then be compared with and contrasted to and

Fig. 7.12 An example of a HWID structural model. Made in SmartPLS 3

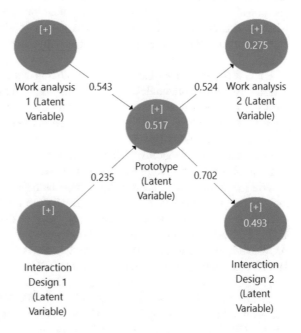

merged with HWID gestalts from other projects. This point is perhaps clearer when considering another way to do quantitative analysis of HWID phenomena, namely, network modeling.

Exploratory network modeling of HWID cases

Constructs may be neither reflective nor formative, but can be networks, a point made by psychologists when talking about psychiatric concepts (Schmittmann et al., 2013), and made by sociologists when talking about user experience, by Bruno Latour in a CHI keynote 2013 in Paris. For HWID, with its design process-like form, network conceptualizations have the great benefit that it does not force the researcher to see relation artefacts as either causes or effects. Instead, relation artefacts can be treated as 'gateways of causal action', which are causally autonomous in the sense of being responsible for both incoming and outgoing causal actions (Schmittmann et al., 2013). Furthermore, in a network conceptualization, the constructs are not 'latent' un-observables, but are directly observable (for example, the questions that are 'indicators' in latent construct modeling). That is, taking a finer grained approach by investigating the item-level relations.

   Thus, if we see HWID as a network of autonomous relation artefacts as nodes and the correlations between them as edges, then network analysis is straightforward. A relation artefact is then what it is due to its relation to other relation artefacts in the HWID network, and it is possible to analyze its developmental pathways in the network as changes in one relation artefact shapes changes in another relation artefact. So, the analysis of a HWID phenomenon becomes an analysis of network structure and dynamics, where each relation artefact at part of other relation artefacts and constituted by these. Empirical data collection can then be done by observing what relation artefacts (observable nodes) emerge (and disappear) as dominant in a network in terms of the strength of relations with other relation artefacts (observable nodes).

   For HWID, this means that a network modeling can capture the holistic gestalt of a HWID case. A network model of a HWID case may, for example, look like a clustered network, with those concepts that are correlated closest to each other. So far, however, many network analyses are simply fine grained analyses based on items from existing instruments, such as analysis of personality inventories (Christensen et al., 2019) to form an emergent taxonomy of facets and aspects of the phenomenon studied, or analysis of psychiatric diagnostic tools (Fried et al., 2016) to explore if established criteria are indeed more central than non-established criteria for identification of the studied phenomenon. Since there currently are no 'HWID inventories' or even example surveys available, one place to begin may be to reanalyze data sampled with UX and usability inventories such as system usability scale (Brooke, 1996, 2013) or AttrakDiff (Hassenzahl, Burmester, & Koller, 2003). So, one place to begin to model HWID cases with network analysis is to use UX and usability inventory data from HWID cases, such as illustrated in Fig. 7.13.

   The interpretation of a visualization of a network analysis of a HWID case, such as the one illustrated in Fig. 7.13, can be guided by, compared, and contrasted to the general HWID platform model. Thus, for example, the four clusters in Fig. 7.13 can be

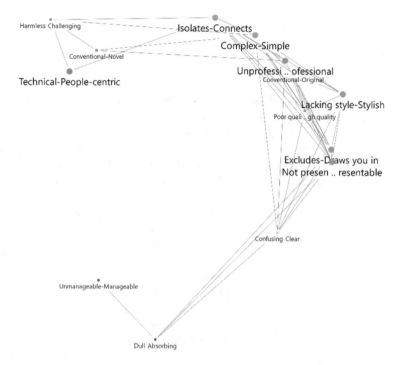

Fig. 7.13 A network illustration of AttrakDiff items, based on data from a HWID case. Made with MAXQDA2020 codemap

classified per their position and content as work analysis related (the green cluster on top of the figure, with the 'technical-centric versus people-centric' item), interaction design related (the dark blue cluster at the bottom with the 'dull-absorbing' item), and the two other clusters at relation artefacts. The light blue cluster with the 'excludes you-drawn you in' item is near the interaction design, and the red cluster with the 'isolate you-connect you' is near to the work analysis. More and other analysis are possible.

7.5 Work Plans for HWID Projects

Gantt charts are today for most managers nearly synonymous with project management (Geraldi & Lechler, 2012; Robles, 2018), including grant givers if judging from the requirements in grant application templates. Project managers cannot talk about PM without mentioning the Gantt chart (Whitty, 2010). For research projects, Gantt charts may help organize collaboration, and for research grants proposals, they are used as a persuasion technique in project documentation and proposals (Robles,

2018). Thus, following Robles (2018), the persuasiveness of the Gantt chart apparently lies in its promises of future delivery; it can display key persuasive points of project management that grant givers like the most, such as milestones (that is, deliverables), time estimates, and, in general, a structure of the knowledge production process in a way that allows it to be easily tracked.

The conventions for a Gantt chart for a HWID research project may be quite generic for project management Gantt charts in general. A Gantt chart represents tasks and time in a coordinate system, with time along the x-axis and tasks on the y-axis. The convention is to present time from left to right at the top of the chart, and tasks from top to bottom with the first task first and so on. Rectangles mark tasks over time, triangles beginnings and ends, diamonds are milestones (usually key deliverables or bunches of them), sometime arrows are used to represent dependencies in time between tasks, and y-axis headings and/or colors differentiate main tasks/phases from each other. If such conventions are not met, reviewers of a grant may find the project management plan insufficient and not persuasive. For example, a reviewer can write:

"The project plan requires substantial work. Each task should have a specific timeline, a nominated owner, and preferably linked to a deliverable. The deliverables should link to Milestones in the project and, if required, specific 'go/no go' break points where the project may not progress. Lacking in any of these, the implementation plan is unlikely to deliver a successful project".

It is important for a work plan for a HWID research project or research proposal to follow Gantt chart conventions in project management. It may even seem very natural to a HWID researcher to use a Gantt chart, since the all-dominating design process model in HCI is the design thinking approach with its four–five main phases following each other over time (Churchill, 2017, however, see the STAR model by Hartson & Hix, 1989 for an attempt to break the linear time thinking in HCI).

On the other hand, since a HWID project is as much a social science and humanities (SSH) project as it is a technical engineering and computer science project, the aesthetics of a Gantt chart as a piece of artwork may be the most persuasive aspect of a Gantt chart to the broadest audience. Research in digital humanities project management may not even mention Gantt charts (e.g., Currier et al., 2017). In some SSH research, project management is seen as something that goes beyond a beginner research doing a short-lived effort to describe tasks and timelines of an imagined project; instead project management is something that requires scholarship in the SSH field in question, and which has no explicit ending in time (Reed, 2014). An artist's work may need never-ending curation, for example. In particular, management of mature SSH projects may require consideration of "…expansions in scope and mission, research and recommend new features and tools, grow or shrink the number of project staff, seek out alternate sources of support when early grants run out, maintain continuity as collaborators join and leave the project, and develop new workflows and procedures to reflect these and other changes" (Reed, 2014). The visualizations of the project management are then rather considered as weaved into the visualizations of the topic studied. In some cases, the aesthetics of the visualizations of project management is the central topic, for example, in (Whitty, 2010) study of project management artefacts and the emotions they evoke, and (Robles, 2018) study of the cultural history of the Gantt chart as visualizing certainty.

Within HCI, the complexity of project management of design projects is sometimes known and acknowledged by casting Gantt charts not as detailed implementation plans to ensure a successful project but as sketches to enable discussions and reflections about the project. For example, while Gantt charts are commonly used and appreciated also as collaboration devices for the often multidisciplinary and multicultural design teams in HCI, project management in HCI is also acknowledged to be about cross-barrier communication and embedding human-centric insights in designs (Churchill, 2017). Hence, if Gantt charts are seen by grant givers or HWID project managers and members as nearly synonymous with the project or something to be rigidly applied and followed, rather than a sketch or a prototype for project management available for discussion and further development, then the "Gantt chart is more obstructive of progress than helpful" (Churchill, 2017). Rudimentary Gantt charts—simple sketches of Gantt charts—can be used to discuss time and tasks. For example, sketchy Gantt charts can be used as draft schedules to reveal and negotiate differences in assumptions about time frames for completing interdependent tasks, and to discuss realistic timing of project. Sketchy Gantt charts can also be used to discuss tasks including to "reveal anxieties and concerns, concentrate and amplify communication about actions and sequences, and invite meaningful review, revision, and re-planning" (Churchill, 2017). So, Gantt charts for HWID research may be useful, they just have to not only fulfill grant giving reviewers conventions about project management, but also be sketchy and design-like to facilitate the creative design work.

From an ethical standpoint, a Gantt chart should be followed by a discussion of what makes for success beyond completing tasks on time to avoid misleading grant givers and other stakeholders. This can be done, for example, by helping the readers to interpret the Gantt chart with body text, notes, captions, and so on (Robles, 2018). In sum, embed the Gantt chart with other information about what potentially can be seen as success for the HWID project.

Note that it may be hard to see and/or create a differentiating factor between regular Gantt, deliverables, and milestones templates for HWID compared to any other approach. To develop HWID-specific Gantt chart templates is a topic for future research. However, from our own experience with grant applications where reviewers and evaluators focus on understanding the tasks and the project plan, and from seeing students struggling with putter together a doable project plan, we believe that it may be worth a try to offer work plan templates for researchers and students.

HWID researchers' work plans

For a HWID research project, it is important that grant givers believe that the implementation plan is doable and the work controllable, which includes both the Gantt chart and lists of deliverables and milestones. Not only the Gantt chart should be quite conventional, the deliverables and milestones should also follow conventions and follow realistic timelines. The illustrations of HWID project templates for a draft Gantt chart, Fig. 7.14; a list of deliverables, Fig. 7.15; and a list of milestones

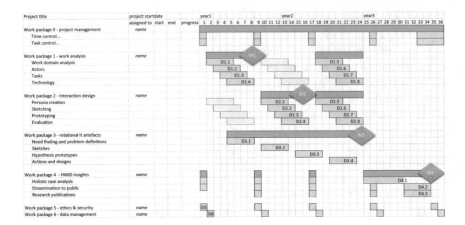

Fig. 7.14 HWID project template for draft Gantt chart for grant proposal writing. Beginning with work analysis; if point of departure is interaction design, use faint yellow task marks and switch WP1 and WP2

Deliverable (number)	Deliverable name	Work package number	Short name of lead participant	Type	Dissemination level	Delivery date (in months)
D1.1	Work domain analysis	1	name	Report	public	5
D1.2	Actors	1	name	Report	public	6
D1.3	Tasks	1	name	Report	public	7
D1.4	Technology	1	name	Report	public	8
D3.1	Need finding and problem definitions	1	name	Demonstrator	public	8
D2.1	Persona creation	2	name	Design product	public	13
D3.2	Sketches	2	name	Demonstrator	public	13
D2.2	Sketching	2	name	Design product	public	14
D2.3	Prototyping	2	name	Design product	public	15
D2.4	Evaluation	2	name	Design product	public	16
D3.3	Hypothesis prototypes	3	name	Demonstrator	public	18
D1.5	Work domain analysis II	3	name	Report	public	21
D2.5	Persona creation II	3	name	Design product	public	21
D1.6	Actors II	3	name	Report	public	22
D2.6	Sketching II	3	name	Design product	public	22
D1.7	Tasks II	3	name	Report	public	23
D2.7	Prototyping II	3	name	Design product	public	23
D3.4	Actions and designs	3	name	Demonstrator	public	23
D1.8	Technology II	3	name	Report	public	24
D2.8	Evaluation II	3	name	Design product	public	24
D4.1	Holistic case analysis	4	name	Report	public	30
D4.2	Dissemination to public	4	name	Report	public	34
D4.3	Research publications	4	name	Report	public	34
D5	Ethics & security	5	name	Report	public	1
D6	Data management implementation	6	name	Report	public	2

Fig. 7.15 HWID project template for list of deliverables

Fig. 7.16 are thus perhaps conventional and they should be used creatively.

A HWID deliverable may be either the distinct, tangible, or intangible outcome of a work analysis, an interaction design activity, or a relation artefact that link the work analysis and interaction design activity together. Different HWID deliverables may thus be delivered by team members with different expertise, ranging from human

Milestone number	Milestone name	Related work package(s)	Due date (in month)	Means of verification
M1	Work analysis	1	8	Member-check with workers and managers
M2	Interaction Design	2	13	User-experience test with target users
M3	Relational IT artefacts	3	24	Artefact released and available to public
M4	HWID insights	4	34	Research publications submitted

Fig. 7.16 HWID project template for list of milestones

factor and work psychology specialists and work ethnographers, over to engineers and industrial and interaction designers, and, crucially, those multidisciplinary people who can facilitate the linking in alignment with the overall objectives of the project in question. HWID deliverables can thus be really many different things; conventions in European research (EU research grants) tend to classify them into four types of deliverables: R: document, report (NOTE: excluding the project periodic or final reports); DEM: demonstrator, pilot, prototype, plan designs; DEC: websites, patents filing, press and media actions, videos, etc.; and OTHER: software, technical diagram, etc.

Likewise, there are conventions for milestones saying that they are control points for progress during the project, which help identify those tasks and key deliverables have been completed, before moving on to the next phase of the project. Note, however, that a milestone even if it does not concretely mark the distance toward the project goal, for engaged team members' milestones will usually be an experience. A careful design of project milestones, noting their project history and acknowledging their preconditions, may thus ensure team members' positive 'milestone experiences'. HWID milestones mark the distance and are 'road monuments' on the road toward the HWID project end goal/objectives, while HWID deliverables are 'measures' of the work analysis, interaction design, or relation artefact results.

HWID students' work plans

For a HWID student project, the student might want to communicate overview but simplicity and focus in terms of time and tasks. The Gantt chart in Fig. 7.17 does communicate a beautiful overview of the 16 weeks of master thesis writing in the student's university.

The student Gantt chart in Fig. 7.17 indicates the major tasks of a design-oriented project. It has the work analysis and interaction design activities indicated in the subtask activities. Obviously, more detail can be added, such as supervisor meetings, milestones in terms of decision on topic for the project, RQ formulated, data collection plan, analysis of data, and first draft of whole thesis; this is, however, also a matter of not killing (the student's) creativity with too many rigid details.

7.6   Conclusion

The conclusion on what the HWID platform offers academic HCI researchers is that it can help provide guidance for academic researchers on how to study socio-technical relations and perform socio-technical HCI theorizing. The guidance concerns the form of HWID theory, theory building, qualitative analysis, quantitative analysis, and work plans for researcher and student projects. The content of the guidance includes a list of user requirements to HWID theory-as-a-product, examples of descriptive, normative, and critical projects, a recipe for a theorizing workshop with examples, templates for major qualitative software analysis packages, examples of SEM and network modeling for HWID, and Gantt chart templates for HWID projects.

D   Gantt chart: Plan for Master's thesis

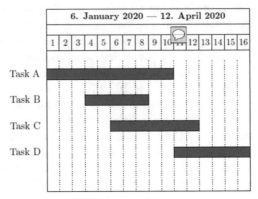

Figure 5: Gantt chart

Task A   PROBLEM DEFINITION AND NEED FINDING
Task A_1 Validate the needs identified in the initial interview with Aviator
            and conduct survey with the ground handlers as respondents
Task A_2 Semi-structures interviews with stakeholders from CPH airport to
            identify their needs
Task A_3 Design thinking workshop with passengers to identify their needs

Task B   IDEA SKETCHING
Task B_1 Brainstorming session with CPH Airport and Aviator
Task B_2 Collaborative sketching session with CPH Airport and Aviator

Task C   PROTOTYPE HYPOTHESES
Task C_1 Revision of the hypotheses
Task C_2 Present hypotheses to Aviator and CPH Airport
Task C_3 Re-configure hypotheses

Task D   EVALUATION OF PROTOTYPES
Task D_1 Functional tests
Task D_2 Acceptance test with service agents and field study
Task D_3 Present findings to Aviator and CPH Airport
Task D_4 Present findings to selected academic stakeholders

Fig. 7.17 A student group's simple and beautiful Gantt chart for a HWID design project. The post-it note annotation indicate the use of the chart for discussion and reflection

References

Abdelnour-Nocera, J., Barricelli, B. R., Lopes, A., Campos, P., & Clemmensen, T. (2015a). *Human work interaction design : Work analysis and interaction design methods for pervasive and smart workplaces : 4th IFIP 13.6 Working Conference, HWID 2015, London, UK, June 25–26, 2015, Revised selected papers* (J. Abdelnour Nocera, B. R. Barricelli, A. Lopes, P. Campos, & T. Clemmensen, Eds.). https://doi.org/10.1007/978-3-319-27048-7.

Abdelnour-Nocera, J., Oussena, S., & Burns, C. (2015b). *Human work interaction design of the smart university.* https://doi.org/10.1007/978-3-319-27048-7_9.

Ågerfalk, P. J., & Wiberg, M. (2018). Pragmatizing the normative artifact: Design science research in Scandinavia and beyond. *Communications of the Association for Information Systems, 43*(1), 4.

Bardzell, J., & Bardzell, S. (2013). What is "critical" about critical design? In *Proceedings of the SIGCHI Conference on Human Factors in Computing Systems* (pp. 3297–3306).

Barricelli, B. R., Roto, V., Clemmensen, T., Campos, P., Lopes, A., Gonçalves, F., & Abdelnour-Nocera, J. (2019). *Human Work Interaction Design. Designing Engaging Automation: 5th IFIP WG 13.6 Working Conference, HWID 2018, Espoo, Finland, August 20–21, 2018, Revised Selected Papers* (Vol. 544). Springer.

Barricelli, B. R., Valtolina, S., Gadia, D., Marzullo, M., Piazzi, C., & Garzulino, A. (2015). Participatory action design research in archaeological context. https://doi.org/10.1007/978-3-319-27048-7_14.

Björndal, P., Eriksson, E., & Artman, H. (2015). From transactions to relationships: making sense of user-centered perspectives in large technology-intensive companies. https://doi.org/10.1007/978-3-319-27048-7_8.

Borsboom, D., Mellenbergh, G. J., & Van Heerden, J. (2003). The theoretical status of latent variables. *Psychological Review, 110*(2), 203.

Braun, V., & Clarke, V. (2006). Using thematic analysis in psychology. *Qualitative Research in Psychology, 3*(2), 77–101.

Brooke, J. (1996). SUS: A "quick and dirty" usability scale. In P. W. Jordan, B. Thomas, B. A. Weerdmeester, & A. L. McClelland (Eds.), *Usability evaluation in industry* (p. 189). https://doi.org/10.1201/9781498710411.

Brooke, J. (2013). SUS: A retrospective. *Journal of Usability Studies, 8*(2), 29–40.

Cajander, Å., Larusdottir, M., Eriksson, E., & Nauwerck, G. (2015). Contextual personas as a method for understanding digital work environments. *IFIP Advances in Information and Communication Technology, 468*, 141–152. https://doi.org/10.1007/978-3-319-27048-7_10.

Campos, P., Clemmensen, T., Abdelnour Nocera, J., Katre, D., Lopes, A., & Ørngreen, R. (2012). *Human Work Interaction Design. Work Analysis and HCI Third IFIP 13.6 Working Conference, HWID 2012, Copenhagen, Denmark, December 5–6, 2012, Revised Selected Papers.* Springer, Berlin, Heidelberg.

Chen, N.-C., Drouhard, M., Kocielnik, R., Suh, J., & Aragon, C. R. (2018). Using machine learning to support qualitative coding in social science: Shifting the focus to ambiguity. *ACM Transaction on Interactive Intelligent Systems, 8*(2). https://doi.org/10.1145/3185515.

Christensen, A. P., Cotter, K. N., & Silvia, P. J. (2019). Reopening openness to experience: A network analysis of four openness to experience inventories. *Journal of Personality Assessment, 101*(6), 574–588.

Churchill, E. F. (2017). Planning time: HCI's project-management challenges. *Interactions, 24*(5), 20–21.

Clemmensen, T. (2011a). A Human Work Interaction Design (HWID) case study in e-government and public information systems. *International Journal of Public Information Systems, 7*(3).

Clemmensen, T. (2011b). Designing a simple folder structure for a complex domain. *Human Technology: An Interdisciplinary Journal on Humans in ICT Environments.*

Clemmensen, T., Campos, P., Orngreen, R., Mark-Pejtersen, A., & Wong, W. (2006). *Human work interaction design: Designing for human work.* Springer Science+Business Media.

Clemmensen, T., Kaptelinin, V., & Nardi, B. (2016). Making HCI theory work: An analysis of the use of activity theory in HCI research. *Behaviour & Information Technology, 35*(8), 608–627. https://doi.org/10.1080/0144929X.2016.1175507

Clemmensen, T., & Katre, D. (2018). Adapting e-gov usability: evaluation to cultural contexts. In Buie, E. & Murray, D. (Eds.), *Usability in government systems: user experience design for citizens and public servants* (pp. 331–344). Waltham: Elsevier. (Clemmensen, T. & Katre, D. 2012).

Collins, C. S., & Stockton, C. M. (2018). The central role of theory in qualitative research. *International Journal of Qualitative Methods, 17*(1), 1609406918797475.

Coltman, T., Devinney, T. M., Midgley, D. F., & Venaik, S. (2008). Formative versus reflective measurement models: Two applications of formative measurement. *Journal of Business Research, 61*(12), 1250–1262.

Costantini, G., Epskamp, S., Borsboom, D., Perugini, M., Mõttus, R., Waldorp, L. J., & Cramer, A. O. J. (2015). State of the aRt personality research: A tutorial on network analysis of personality data in R. *Journal of Research in Personality, 54*, 13–29. https://doi.org/10.1016/j.jrp.2014.07.003.

Currier, B. D., Mirza, R., & Downing, J. (2017). They think all of this is new: Leveraging librarians' project management skills for the digital humanities. *College & Undergraduate Libraries, 24*(2–4), 270–289.

Fried, E. I., Epskamp, S., Nesse, R. M., Tuerlinckx, F., & Borsboom, D. (2016). What are 'good' depression symptoms? Comparing the centrality of DSM and non-DSM symptoms of depression in a network analysis. *Journal of Affective Disorders, 189*, 314–320.

Gattol, V., Bobeth, J., Röderer, K., Egger, S., Regal, G., Lehner, U., Tscheligi, M. (2015). From bottom-up insights to feature ideas: A case study into the office environments of older knowledge workers. https://doi.org/10.1007/978-3-319-27048-7_6.

Gentles, S. J., Charles, C., Ploeg, J., & Ann McKibbon, K. (2015). Sampling in qualitative research: Insights from an overview of the methods literature. *Qualitative Report, 20*(11), 1772–1789.

Geraldi, J., & Lechler, T. (2012). Gantt charts revisited: A critical analysis of its roots and implications to the management of projects today. *International Journal of Managing Projects in Business, 5*(4), 578–594.

Glaser, B., & Strauss, A. (1967). *The discovery of grounded theory Aldine Publishing Company.* NY: Hawthorne.

Gonçalves, F., Campos, P., & Clemmensen, T. (2015). Human work interaction design: An overview. *IFIP Advances in Information and Communication Technology, 468*, 3–19. https://doi.org/10.1007/978-3-319-27048-7_1.

Gross, T. (2013). Supporting effortless coordination: 25 years of awareness research. *Computer Supported Cooperative Work (CSCW), 22*(4), 425–474. https://doi.org/10.1007/s10606-013-9190-x.

Hair, J. F., Hult, G. T. M., Ringle, C., & Sarstedt, M. (2017). *A primer on partial least squares structural equation modeling (PLS-SEM)*. Retrieved from https://uk.sagepub.com/en-gb/eur/a-primer-on-partial-least-squares-structural-equation-modeling-pls-sem/book244583.

Hartson, H. R., & Hix, D. (1989). Human-computer interface development: Concepts and systems for its management. *ACM Computing Surveys (CSUR), 21*(1), 5–92.

Hassenzahl, M. (2010). Experience design: Technology for all the right reasons. *Synthesis Lectures on Human-Centered Informatics, 3*(1), 1–95.

Hassenzahl, M., Burmester, M., & Koller, F. (2003). AttrakDiff: Ein Fragebogen zur Messung wahrgenommener hedonischer und pragmatischer Qualität. In G. Szwillus & J. Ziegler (Eds.), *Mensch & Computer 2003: Interaktion in Bewegung* (pp. 187–196). https://doi.org/10.1007/978-3-322-80058-9_19.

Ianeva, M., Faure, S., Theveniot, J., Ribeyron, F., Crossan, C., Cordon, G., Gartiser, C. (2015). Pervasive technologies for smart workplaces: A workplace efficiency solution for office design and building management from an occupier's perspective. https://doi.org/10.1007/978-3-319-270 48-7_5.

Katre, D., Orngreen, R., Yammiyavar, P., & Clemmensen, T. (2010). *Human Work Interaction Design: Usability in Social, Cultural And Organizational Contexts: Second IFIP WG 13.6 Conference, HWID 2009, Pune, India, October 7–8, 2009*, Revised Selected Papers: Preface. In *IFIP Advances in Information and Communication Technology* (Vol. 316). Springer.

Krogh, P. G., Petersen, M. G., O'Hara, K., & Groenbaek, J. E. (2017). Sensitizing concepts for socio-spatial literacy in HCI.In *Proceedings of the 2017 CHI Conference on Human Factors in Computing Systems* (pp. 6449–6460).

Kvale, S. (1996). *InterViews: An introduction to qualitive research interviewing.* Sage.

Lockton, D., Brawley, L., Ulloa, M. A., Prindible, M., Forlano, L., Rygh, K., Fass, J., Herzog, K., & Nissen, B. (2019). Tangible thinking. In *Proceedings of Relating Systems Thinking and Design RSD8 Symposium,* 20.

Lopes, A. G. (2015). *The Work and Workplace Analysis in an Elderly Centre for Agility Improvement.* https://doi.org/10.1007/978-3-319-27048-7_11

Markussen, T., & Knutz, E. (2013). The poetics of design fiction. In *Proceedings of the 6th International Conference on Designing Pleasurable Products and Interfaces* (pp. 231–240).

Molka-Danielsen, J., Fominykh, M., Swapp, D., Steed, A. (2015). Designing a demonstrator virtual learning environment to teach the threshold concept of space syntax: Seeing from the user's perspective. https://doi.org/10.1007/978-3-319-27048-7_13.

Muller, M. J., & Kogan, S. (2010). *Grounded theory method in HCI and CSCW* (pp. 1–46). Cambridge: IBM Center for Social Software.

Ogbonnaya-Ogburu, I. F., Smith, A. D. R., To, A., & Toyama, K. (2020). Critical race theory for HCI. In *Proceedings of the 2020 CHI Conference on Human Factors in Computing Systems* (pp. 1–16).

Ogonowski, C., Jakobi, T., Müller, C., & Hess, J. (2018). PRAXLABS: A sustainable framework for user-centered ICT development cultivating research experiences from Living Labs in the home. In V. Wulf, V. Pipek, D. Randall, M. Rohde, K. Schmidt, & G. Stevens (Eds.), *Socio informatics–A practice-based perspective on the design and use of IT artefacts* (pp. 319–360). Retrieved from https://pdfs.semanticscholar.org/d555/e232775aecdb186f9a72f40a8552894a3253.pdf.

Ørngreen, R. (2015). Reflections on design-based research. https://doi.org/10.1007/978-3-319-270 48-7_2.

Pedersen, R. U., & Clemmensen, T. (2013). A design science approach to interactive greenhouse climate control using lego mindstorms for sensor-intensive prototyping. *IFIP Advances in Information and Communication Technology, 407,* 73–89. https://doi.org/10.1007/978-3-642-41145-8_7.

Pidgeon, N. F., Turner, B. A., & Blockley, D. I. (1991). The use of grounded theory for conceptual analysis in knowledge elicitation. *International Journal of Man-Machine Studies, 35*(2), 151–173.

Quercioli, M. S., Amaldi, P. (2015). A multi-perspective view on human-automation interactions in aviation. https://doi.org/10.1007/978-3-319-27048-7_12.

Reed, A. (2014). Managing an established digital humanities project: Principles and practices from the twentieth year of the William Blake archive. *DHQ: Digital Humanities Quarterly, 8*(1).

Rietz, T., & Maedche, A. (2021). Cody: An AI-based system to semi-automate coding for qualitative research. In *Proceedings of the 2021 CHI Conference on Human Factors in Computing Systems* (pp. 1–14).

Robles, V. D. (2018). Visualizing certainty: What the cultural history of the gantt chart teaches technical and professional communicators about management. *Technical Communication Quarterly, 27*(4), 300–321.

Schmittmann, V. D., Cramer, A. O. J., Waldorp, L. J., Epskamp, S., Kievit, R. A., & Borsboom, D. (2013). Deconstructing the construct: A network perspective on psychological phenomena. *New Ideas in Psychology, 31*(1), 43–53.

Sengers, P., McCarthy, J., & Dourish, P. (2006). Reflective HCI: articulating an agenda for critical practice. In *CHI'06 Extended Abstracts on Human Factors in Computing Systems* (pp. 1683–1686).

Smith, J. A., & Shinebourne, P. (2012). Interpretative phenomenological analysis. In H. Cooper, P. M. Camic, D. L. Long, A. T. Panter, D. Rindskopf, & K. J. Sher (Eds.), *APA handbook of research methods in psychology, Vol. 2. Research designs: Quantitative, qualitative, neuropsychological, and biological* (pp. 73–82). American Psychological Association. https://doi.org/10.1037/136 20-005.

Sterling, B. (2009). Cover story design fiction. *Interactions, 16*(3), 20–24.

Stolterman, E., & Croon Fors, A. (2008). Critical HCI research: A research position proposal. *Design Philosophy Papers, 1*.

Strauss, A., & Corbin, J. (1994). Grounded theory methodology. *Handbook of Qualitative Research, 17*(1), 273–285.

Väätäjä, H. (2015). Characterizing the context of use in mobile work. https://doi.org/10.1007/978-3-319-27048-7_7.

Wulf, V., Pipek, V., Randall, D., Rohde, M., Schmidt, K., & Stevens, G. (Eds.). (2018). *Socio-informatics-A practice-based perspective on the design and use of IT artifacts*. Oxford: Oxford University Press.

Von Alan, R. H., March, S. T., Park, J., & Ram, S. (2004). Design science in information systems research. *MIS Quarterly, 28*(1), 75–105.

Waern, A., Rajkowska, P., Johansson, K. B., Bac, J., Spence, J., & Løvlie, A. S. (2020). Sensitizing scenarios: Sensitizing designer teams to theory. In *Proceedings of the 2020 CHI Conference on Human Factors in Computing Systems* (pp. 1–13).

Weber, R. (2003). Editor's comments. *MIS quarterly* (pp. iii–xii).

Whitty, S. J. (2010). Project management artefacts and the emotions they evoke. *International Journal of Managing Projects in Business*.

Wulf, V., Müller, C., Volkmar, P., Randall, D., Rohde, M., & Stevens, G. (2015). Practice-based computing: Empirically grounded conceptualizations derived from design case studies. In V. Wulf, K. Schmidt, & D. Randall (Eds.), *Designing socially embedded technologies in the real-world* (pp. 111–150). https://doi.org/10.1007/978-1-4471-6720-4_7.

Wurhofer, D., Fuchsberger, V., Meneweger, T., Moser, C., & Tscheligi, M. (2015). Insights from user experience research in the factory: What to consider in interaction design. In J. A. Nocera, B. Barricelli, A. Lopes, P. Campos, & T. Clemmensen (Eds.), *HWID2015-Human Work Interaction Design. Work Analysis and Interaction Design Methods for Pervasive and Smart Workplaces. IFIP Advances in Information and Communication Technology* (Vol. 468, pp. 39–56). https://doi.org/10.1007/978-3-319-27048-7_3.

Chapter 8
HWID Consultancy

Abstract This chapter is for consultants rolling out solutions based on the HWID platform in multiple companies. As a normative platform for doing consultancy, HWID stands out with its few strict methodological requirements and much flexibility. The chapter presents benefits and challenges of using the HWID approach in socio-technical design cases and compares this to the use of classic user-centered design approaches and other socio-technical design approaches. The type of consultancy expertise that may benefit from using the platform is outlined. Socio-technical design cases are discussed from a consultant's perspective. The chapter ends with suggested ethics guidelines.

Keywords Human work interaction design · Normative HWID platform · HWID consultancy · Design case insights

Consultants' use of socio-technical approaches is a wide-ranging topic.[1] UX professionals working as HWID or other types of socio-technical HCI design consultants may apply notions of usability and UX as core concepts in socio-technical systems development (Rajanen & Rajanen, 2020). However, for HWID consultants the relations between human work and interaction designs are central, Fig. 8.1.

A generic process model for HWID consultancy may look as in Fig. 8.1. It has five major design decision to make. First, decide with management and workers on the context, then begin the discussion of what counts as social and technical in the particular project, include whatever domain-specific theory and methods that appear useful, and continue with iteratively working with the relation artefacts to the link the social and the technical. Sessions 5–8 may consists of four movements between the social and the technical, as illustrated in Fig. 8.2. To do the movements with the relation artefacts, the HWID action cards may help, Fig. 8.3. An illustration of a concrete example of the design process is in Fig. 8.4.

---

[1] Note that this chapter is a long chapter. Readers who are mostly interested in research relevant to doing HWID consultancy may skip Sects. 8.4–8.6, which present in detail two design cases that the author has been involved in and go directly to insights in Sect. 8.7. The purpose of presenting the design cases is to illustrate the use of relation artefacts in consultancy.

T. Clemmensen, *Human Work Interaction Design*,
Human–Computer Interaction Series,
https://doi.org/10.1007/978-3-030-71796-4_8
173

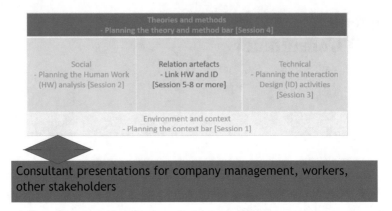

Fig. 8.1 A HWID consultancy process: Five design sessions, five major design decisions to make

8.1   The Work Practices of Socio-Technical Design Consultants

While socio-technical design approaches developed by researchers are often intended to be used in applied projects by researchers, socio-technical design approaches are also what we teach our students who in large numbers become management consultants, IT managers, and change project leaders. Socio-technical design approaches are therefore also intended to be used without explicit research objectives. Thus, this chapter does not include co-financed research, research-based government services, and requisitioned research and advice, where researchers always are present to interpret the socio-technical approach. Instead, this chapter looks at socio-technical consultancy, that is, when socio-technical design approaches are used without explicit research objectives and in applied settings.

The background for looking at how consultants are rolling out the HWID platform in companies and organizations is that the application of socio-technical approaches and methods in practice has a long and diverse history. While some would perhaps equate the socio-technical approach with the principles proposed by Cherns (1987), or the stages of the ETHICS approach (Mumford, 2000), there is little doubt that the socio-technical approach can be said to cover a variety of approaches (José Abdelnour-Nocera & Clemmensen, 2019; Baxter & Sommerville, 2011). Imanghaliyeva (2020) used a keyword search and filter methodology to screen four main paper databases for the 1951–2019 period to identify different socio-technical methods, tools, and approaches that were used in actual real-life cases. They identified an astonishing number of 106 different socio-technical methods, which they categorized into seven domains. The most HCI-related of their seven domains: "Socio-technical System-based methods on Human Factor, Human Behaviour and Ergonomics", included Cognitive Work Analysis (CWA); Cognitive Work Analysis Design Toolkit (CWA-DT); Goals, Operators, Methods and Selection Rules (GOMS); Hierarchical Task Analysis (HTA); a couple of Human Factors methods;

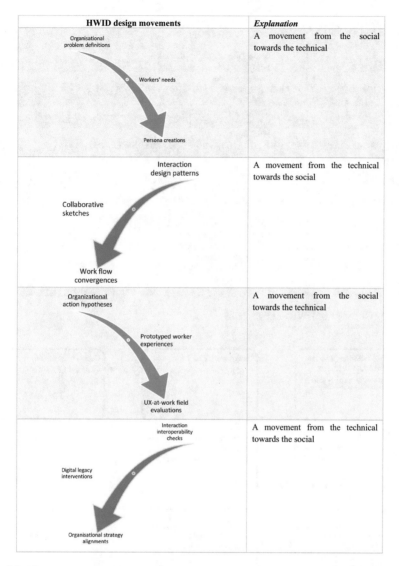

HWID design movements	Explanation
Organisational problem definitions / Workers' needs / Persona creations	A movement from the social towards the technical
Interaction design patterns / Collaborative sketches / Work flow convergences	A movement from the technical towards the social
Organizational action hypotheses / Prototyped worker experiences / UX-at-work field evaluations	A movement from the social towards the technical
Interaction interoperability checks / Digital legacy interventions / Organisational strategy alignments	A movement from the technical towards the social

Fig. 8.2 HWID movements in the socio-technical design space

and Socio-technical Systems Analysis. Thus, the study by Imanghaliyeva (2020) illustrates well the popularity and broad scope of the term 'socio-technical' across many fields and many years. On this background, HWID consultancy is simply an application of general socio-technical approaches and methods in research and practice with a specific adaption to and focus on the use of the approach by HCI practitioners.

HWID PART		ACTIONS
RELATION ARTEFACTS TYPE I: NEEDS AND PROBLEMS		
	1	Organizational problem definition
	2	Workers needs findings
	3	Persona creation
RELATION ARTEFACTS TYPE II: SOCIO-TECHNICAL IDEATION SKETCHES		
	4	Interaction design pattern
	5	Collaborative sketching
	6	Work flows
RELATION ARTEFACTS TYPE III: SOCIO-TECHNICAL HYPOTHESIS PROTOTYPING		
	7	Organizational action hypothesis
	8	Prototype worker experiences
	9	Do field evaluations and UX tests
RELATION ARTEFACTS TYPE IV: SOCIO-TECHNICAL INTERVENTIONS		
	10	Interaction operability checks
	11	Digital legacy interventions
	12	Organizational strategy alignments
CONTEXT.............................		
	0	Organizational context
	0	National context
	0	Technological context
	0	Other

Fig. 8.3 Overview of HWID Action Cards

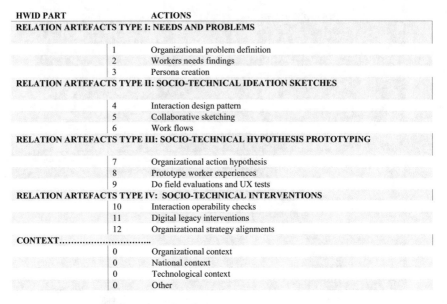

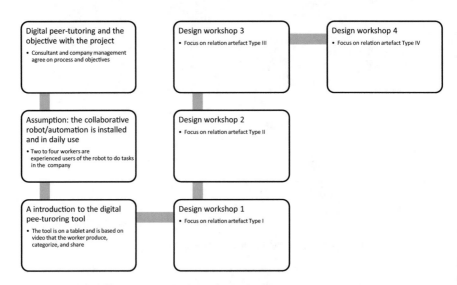

Fig. 8.4 An illustration of the prototyped digital peer-tuturing intervention

The study of practitioners' use of methods and approaches by practitioners is an important research topic in most research-based professional fields. This is so in social work, psychology, medicine, engineering, and in practice-oriented IT professions such as software engineering and HCI. Interestingly, in the IS field, there has been a lively debate if, what, and how the design science knowledge is used by practitioners, e.g., (Lukyanenko & Parsons, 2020). In HCI, while there has historically been much research on usability evaluation methods for researchers (e.g., (Gray & Salzman, 1998)), there is only a relatively small amount of scattered research on HCI practitioners' use of methods and approaches (Inal et al., 2020). This includes research on the practitioners' use of techniques of sketching, evaluation, prototyping, and HCI development approaches (Inal et al., 2020).

Outside HCI, there is research on evaluation of socio-technical systems functioning in practice settings, effectiveness of socio-technical methods in practice, and development of novel socio-technical methods and practices. There is much research on evaluation of socio-technical systems, for example, (Selbst, Boyd, Friedler, Venkatasubramanian, and Vertesi (2019) on fairness and abstraction in socio-technical systems, and Olphert and Damodaran (2007) on capacity building of citizens for otherwise techno-centric e-government. Interestingly, there is also some (meta-) research on the effectiveness of socio-technical design approaches in general, for example, Randall et al. (2018) meta-reflections about the design practices of an IT research group in the 2000s, Pasmore et al. (1982)'s evaluation of the many applications carried out by researchers as part of their research during the 1970s, and Sarker, Chatterjee, and Xiao (2013) reflections about the socio-technical nature of IS research over the years. Also, there is research on the development and application of novel methods, tools, and techniques for socio-technical design and actions, such as Carayon et al. (2015) and de Vries and Bligård (2019) that developed a socio-technical framework with a focus on safety, Truffer, Schippl, and Fleischer (2017) with a focus on electric mobility, and Hughes et al. (2017) that presents a novel workshop tool to support organizations in—instead of single elements—socio-technical system thinking.

Studies of the actual work practices of socio-technical practitioners were perhaps more frequent in the 1950s and 1960s (Garrety & Badham, 2000). Bostrom and Heinen (1977) did a review of practitioner-focused studies, and then presented a step-by-step approach for socio-technical design explicitly aimed at and for practitioners who wanted to improve the quality of working life related to the use of IT systems (Bostrom & Heinen, 1977). Twenty years later, Appelbaum (1997) presented indicators for executives and consultants to support assessing socio-technical design and interventions in 31 diagnostic questions intended to identify interactions among elements of the socio-technical system (Appelbaum, 1997). Again 20 years forward in time, most recently, Bjørn-Andersen and Clemmensen (2017) and Davison and Bjørn-Andersen (2019) made the argument that impact, understood in the sense of stakeholder's (students, industry, and society) perception of research as relevant, is the utmost criteria for socio-technical research, including socio-technical HCI research. Bjørn-Andersen and coauthors argued among other things that it should be measured to which degree research results (theories, methodologies, tools, and conclusions) have been picked up by 'relevant' non-academic stakeholders (Galletta et al., 2019). Hence, some researchers see value in studies of socio-technical design approaches in conditions where these are used without explicit research objectives and in applied settings, i.e., in practice.

In HCI, however, there appears to be little research that is focused purely on consultants' and other practitioners' perspective on socio-technical HCI design approaches.

8.2   What Do We Know About Consultants' Use of Socio-Technical HCI Design Approaches?

To understand consultants' use of socio-technical HCI design approaches, it may be necessary to consider the humanistic and psychological aspect of socio-technical design approaches in industry and business practice. Mumford's studies in the coal[2] and other industries and business (Mumford, 1994, 2006) led her to among other the insight that socio-technical approaches in practice may come in disguise and may not keep central values of the socio-technical. For example, in the 1990s, the socio-technical approach in industry appeared to re-emerge as "business process engineering", but as (Mumford, 1994) pointed out that there was a big difference in the values that they emphasized. While business process reengineering emphasized gaining competitive advantage, in contrast the hallmark of socio-technical approaches has always been a strong focus on the quality of working life among employees (Mumford, 1994), which is much in line with the HCI ideology of usability and UX-at-work.

Historical developments in the surrounding society frame, influence, and limit consultants' use of socio-technical HCI design approaches. Leaving the 1960s and 1970s fast-growing economies with their focus on worker participation and joint management and worker agreements (clearly favorable toward parts of what we today would call HCI), the economic climate in much of world in 1980s and 1990s was shaped by a (HCI-hostile) world of IT-supported lean production, downsizing, and cost-cutting in a global economy (Mumford, 2006). It may be no coincidence that one of the founding books of HCI in the early 1980s called for 'hard' science and had nothing to say about the 'soft' participatory socio-technical approach (Card, Moran, & Newell, 1983; Carroll & Campbell, 1986). Recently, in the 2000s and 2010s, the humanistic goals of ethics and working life quality is increasingly seen as important (Sarker et al., 2013, 2019) though they still have to be argued as enablers of instrumental goals of productivity and not as having value by themselves. Within this new wave of socio-technical approaches, it is not yet clear from empirical research if the humanistic values are unfolded in practice by consultants using socio-technical approaches. Thus, the situation may not be much different from around 2000 when Garrety and Badham (2000) argued that the socio-technical design should move beyond the production of normative discourses and methods and

---

[2] In the book 'Coal and conflict' (Scott, Mumford, McGivering, & Kirby, 1963). Mumford wrote chapter four on negotiating machines for management-worker negotiations, but the book was a collaborative effort led by Scott, really much about conflict rather than collaboration, and definitely not about harmony in the organisation.

into effective interventions in the complex social environments in which technical decisions are made.

Though it may hidden in practice, it appears that there exists a 'socio-technical divide', between social science and humanities on one side and technical and natural sciences on the other side, that is often manifest in collaborative interdisciplinary projects that focus on socially relevant problems (Olphert & Damodaran, 2007). For example, the global Covid-19 crisis-induced work-at-home tendency in 2019–2021 rocked established truths about relations between the reproductive and productive sectors of life. In practice, the solutions to our changed world could appear to have to do with technical issues of internet connections or interaction designs of Zoom, MS teams, WeChat, etc.—or the solutions could be new ways of being humans and workers and together. Another example is how the European applied research program for the 2020s focus on ethics of AI use and humanistic considerations about worker inclusion in companies, and how these are important for AI and robotic technology development.[3] Thus, different future scenarios may be speculative designed where socio-technical principles might return in a novel disguises to yet again humanize technology in the practices unfolding in business rooms and at factory floors (Mumford, 2006), which is what some of HCI is trying to do.

It is fair to say that HWID for consultants is intended to be a lightweight and contemporary HCI-oriented interpretation of socio-technical design approaches that is useful to consultants working with SMEs in industry and business. So, without pre-emptying what is meant by SMEs, for planning, doing, and reflecting on HWID consultancy, it is a reasonable have in mind the following question: How are socio-technical design approaches perceived by companies (often SMEs) and employees?

In the next section, we present two related design cases of socio-technical design consultancy in SME manufacturing. The design cases were created with the HWID approach, and they are presented along these lines. After presenting the design cases, we discuss how the socio-technical design approaches were perceived by companies (often SMEs) and employees, and how the cases would appear with different socio-technical design approaches. Before that, we will briefly introduce HWID action cards which are tools for consultants.

8.3 HWID Action Cards

Action cards are in this section defined as easy one-page user guides to the HWID parts, see the parts in Fig. 8.3. Action cards is a notion that has much overlap with checklists and standard operating procedures. They have been used in a very wide set of domains, including disaster management (Savage, 1972) and studies of metacognition in mathematics (Kuzle, 2019; Wilson & Clarke, 2004). For consultancy, the HWID action cards are to be used normatively as guides for the consultants' actions.

---

[3] https://ec.europa.eu/research/pdf/horizon-europe/annex-4.pdf.

Action card can also be used descriptively, as 'action statements', to elicit actions and cognitions from consultants about what actions they took or would have like to take (for inspiring papers on the use of action cards to reveal metacognitive actions in problem solving, see Kuzle, 2019; Wilson & Clarke, 2004)). This can be done on various levels of abstractions, from concrete procedures followed to metacognition, to learn about consultants' reflection-about-action (or as reflection-in-action (Schon, 1984)).

Each card should contain action card title and number referring to the subtype of relation artefacts described in Fig. 8.3, a description of the relation artefact that is to be created, under which conditions the action card is activated, the responsible for the action, the organization that is established to do the project, the employees who are engaged in creating the relation artefact, and the design processes involved. The design cases that are presented in the next section illustrate these HWID ideas are meant to help to the consultant in flexible, selective, and caring ways. A complete set of HWID action cards, which were developed based on the design cases presented in this section, are available from the author.

8.4 Design Cases: Consultancy in Small to Medium-Sized Enterprises (SMEs) Manufacturing[4]

The design cases presented here stem from a regional development project that developed a digital peer-tutoring learning format to support shop floor workers using collaborative robots and other automation in manufacturing SMEs. The aim was to increase capabilities among shop floor workers to design and document, with short videos, solutions to operational and collaboration issues related to collaborative robots, and in the end their UX-at-work, their productivity, and the company's capacity to flexible apply collaborative robots and other automation technologies.

The regional development project was in the larger Copenhagen capital area of Denmark in Northern Europe. It brought together 18 of the Copenhagen capital region's companies, unions, employer associations, and educational institutions. The regional development project had the high-level goals of improving digital competencies among the employers and employees in SMEs, thereby enabling the companies to adopt and implement digital technologies. The target companies came from all kind of sectors, including construction and building, small-scale production, product development, and finance, and the technologies include data mining and analysis, collaborative robots and other forms of production automation, AI-based financial advice, and more. The regional development project attempted to achieve its goals through developing a variety of new digital learning formats, which were then made available to and adapted further to target companies and organizations. The new

---

[4] The category of micro, small and medium-sized enterprises (SMEs) consists of enterprises which employ fewer than 250 persons with an annual turnover not exceeding 50 million euro, and/or an annual balance sheet total not exceeding 43 million euro.

digital learning formats were tailored to the working conditions and needs of companies and employees, so that both employees, managers, companies, and organizations could use the new digital technologies to expand and grow.

Workers collaborating with collaborative robots, small industrial robots, and other automation

The part of the larger regional development project that is reported here was specifically about the use of collaborative robots and other automation in manufacturing SMEs. Current developments in European industry promise increasing use of assistive technologies on the shop floor that aim to provide best-case support and assist employees in production environments and help companies increase capacity. For manufacturing SMEs, the use of assistive technologies in work practices on the factory floor may be one of the first steps in a digitalization process (Mucha, Büttner, & Röcker, 2016). The cases that we present here were aimed at the development and adaption of automation understood as assistive technology and aimed at the use of so-called collaborative robots and small industrial robots.

The focus in the design cases presented here was on the use of the collaborative robot to transform and improve workers' experiences and practices and enhance the company's capacity. The design cases thus reveal and discuss central aspects of consulting socio-technical design of worker-collaborative robot collaboration on the shop floor, and it presents prototyping and evaluation of best-case practices of using collaborative robots as assistive technologies on the shop floor. The first sub-research question across the design cases was then: What constitutes a practice of using collaborative robot as assistive technologies on the shop floor?

Digital peer-tutoring

The design cases present practices of using of collaborative robots on the shop floor in a manufacturing SME, which is done in a novel learning format 'Digital Peer-tutoring'. The digital peer-tutoring format acted as a mean to design and share workers' own solutions to work-team collaboration and worker-technology interaction problems.

Peer-tutoring has long been suggested as a way to help novice designers to deal with design problems (Schleyer et al., 2005). Design is an iterative process consisting of generative and evaluative stages, which eventually converge on a solution to the design problem. Design thinking is typically applied to solve non-routine, wicked problems in an organization, when there is a need for novel how-to knowledge. To engage in creation and sharing of new how-to knowledge requires hands-on experience, which is where peer-tutoring becomes very helpful. The learning format digital peer-tutoring aimed to help workers interacting with collaborative robots on the shop floor to use digital media to engage in teaching and learning with colleagues about their user experiences and work practices. The second sub-research question across the design cases was thus: Can a digital peer-tutoring learning format enable shop floor workers to design their work practices, including designing novel collaborations and positive UXs for themselves and their colleagues?

The HWID consultants and their employers

The HWID consultants who applied the socio-technical design approach in the case were two university professors acting as hired consultants for a larger regional development project. After the initial exploration of possible case companies, a junior consultant was hired specifically for the selected case project. Furthermore, the larger regional development project also contributed with a go-between consultant who helped identify potential companies and sell the consultancy service to them. The larger regional development project involved a network of unions and employer organizations, which contributed ad hoc with specific expertise and advice to the HWID consultants.

8.5   Design Case 1. Ship Engine Parts Manufacturing Factory

The context

We—the consultants—were hired by the larger regional development project and asked to visit and talk to candidate SMEs to identify and select a suitable problem to work on. The first company M1 that we visited was not really an SME, in the sense that it was a ship engine parts manufacturing and storage factory, which was owned and operated by a much larger international company that produced ship engines and related. However, the reason for our visit was that one of unions who participated in the larger regional development project found it relevant to do so, and as a unit, it was the size of an SME.

Relation Artefacts Type I: Needs and Problems

Relation artefacts type I begins with organizational problem definition, then identifies employee needs, and ends up suggesting persons for design. Employees (workers) needs link the organizational problem definition and the personas.

Organizational problem definition

Our visit took place in the fall of 2018, at a time when the factory was just about to introduce a small project with robots to transport material and parts between the work caves of the collaborative/small industrial robots and the storage facility. We held a meeting with management, were shown around in the factory, and interacted with workers. According to the Head of Manufacturing (HoM), Head of Warehouse (HoW), and Head of Technical solutions (HoT), the situation regarding digital competencies in M1 was that employees were in very different places—from the 65-year-old unskilled warehouse worker to the engineer fresh from the engineering school.

> We are very different places – from a 65 year old, unskilled warehouse worker, to a fresh graduate from a technical university…the [technical university] kids drive 100 km per hour, the rest of us turn on the computer .... (Head of Manufacturing)

In the warehouse department, there were 50 unskilled workers, the manufacture department had 165 skilled workers plus salaried employees, and the technical department had 28 technicians and salaried employees. Knowing that we as consultants came from an organization with a focus on digital competencies, the factory management cast the organizational problem as one of a difference in skills between groups of employees. The workers that we interacted with did not add anything to change that presentation of what was the problem.

Finding workers' needs

While the workers that we talked to did not get the opportunity to explain their views in depth, the management explained that the employees (the workers) were not afraid of automation, but there were various digital competencies in the factory. The nature of the workers digital competencies varied across the manufacturing, warehouse, and technical departments, which the manager of the warehouse with the unskilled workers was acutely aware of.

```
[the workers are] not afraid of automation...different digital
competencies in the factory... (Head of Warehouse)
```

The workers did not harbor negative emotions toward future automation scenarios, according to management, but simply had different needs for skills update. The differences in digital competencies in the factory was between departments, with the warehouse having the least skilled workers. However, the differences were also within each department. For example, some technicians were super good at just one machine, but when it came to databases, excel, etc., they could have no skills at all. Given that management had already identified the digital skills gap and that management were the ones that we had a dialogue with, it was not surprising that we could identify a variety of needs for more technical competencies among the workers.

Persona creation

The digital competencies in management were moving toward principles of 'fail fast'—try something fast—and there was a draft strategy for digital development of the factory the next 5 years, according to the head of technical department.

```
Fail fast - quick try some of - we have an idea for the next five years,
but... when it comes to databases, excel, etc, they can be completely
blank (Head of Technical solutions)
```

The head of the technical department presented us with a full excel sheet with plans for further automation and use of robots within and across the departments. We learned, however, that this would only work for one employee persona, the "employee with skills in databases and excel" (HoTs) and not work for the employee persona of "employee who are super-skilled in interacting with one specific machine" (HoTs). Thus, moving from organizational problem definition of a difference in skills between employees, over identification of workers' needs as not about emotions but focused on skills update, we quickly ended up with two employee personas to design for.

Relation Artefacts Type II: Socio-Technical Ideation Sketches

Relation artefacts type II begins with the design of interaction design patterns, then explore alternative solutions in collaborative sketching, and ends up suggesting novel or adapted workflows for the organization. The collaborative sketching of alternative solutions links the interaction design patterns and the organizational workflows.

Interaction design pattern

In the history of the factory's digital development, there were several examples of having a successful focus on using robots. Manufacturing products with robots were already widespread in the factory. There were, however, challenges in maintaining momentum in the digital development, which according to management was partly because the factory was very operationally oriented.

> ...we focus on manufacturing a product with robots - but then we lose momentum ... because we are very operationally oriented...let us just go for a walk so we get around robots in production... (Head of Manufacturing)

What head of management is saying in this quote is that they set up human–robot collaboration quite easily for different products. However, they lack a systematic approach for working out interaction design patterns for human–robot collaboration for more products and more departments in the factory. What management think they are missing is less focus on daily operation and more focus on developing a systematic approach.

Collaborative sketching

The strong focus on operation (and fail thinking) meant that management preferred to start small projects, including pallet moving robot experiments. Together, the management and workers sketched out possible solutions involving robots in the daily operation.

> In the warehouse...it is about operation, operation... we start small projects... for example [try out] robots in production and robots in the warehouse (Head of Warehouse)

The head of the warehouse operation explained a process that may be best described as designers collaborative sketching. The human–robot collaborations that they tried out were not finished solutions, but early low-fi prototypes that were embedded in real-life ongoing workflows.

With management, we sketched out three possible solutions to improve the workers digital skills with peer-tutoring. One sketch was about the skilled workers at the workstations, and how to support them in describing and sharing their expert knowledge in collaborating with the industrial robots at the workstations. The second sketch was about a novel pallet moving robot that should move material from the warehouse to the workstations in production, and how to support unskilled workers in sharing their 'delivery knowledge' with the skilled workers at the workstations. The third, and quite different sketch of a solution, was to train management in using design thinking as a change management approach.

Workflows

The workflows were the organizational outcome of the collaborative sketching of the many small interaction designs that the management had in their 5-year plans. While the head of the technical department was the one with excel with the 5-year plan for use of robots, each manager had their workflows to adapt.

```
[I have] the excel sheet with the plan for use of robots (Head of
Technical solutions)
```

The technical manager in the quotation focused on the technical side of things with the plan over novel robots and their user, the Head of Manufacturing uses a metaphor with a car to explain the different workflows in the factory.

```
The manager each have different tasks towards the digital devel-
opment, with [name of manufacturing manager] taking care of those
who 'make the car', [name of warehouse manager] is the one main-
taining 'the car', and [name of technical manager] the responsible
for repairing the car, should it break down (Head of Manufacturing)
```

Thus, what the manager tried to do with the car metaphor was to convey the idea that different workflows came out of the planned human–robot collaborations, and to understand these, one had to understand how the factory was structured (which appeared to be a quite common way to structure a manufacturing factory).

Relation Artefacts Type III: Socio-Technical Hypothesis Prototyping

Relation artefacts type III begins with the organizational action hypothesis about a change in the organizational setup, then prototype worker experiences based on a possible best solution and ends up doing field evaluations and UX tests of the prototype(s).

Organizational action hypothesis

Management perceived various problems with the organizational side. The separation between storage and production was in practice also a distinction between different groups of employees in terms of qualifications and union memberships. The employees in the warehouse were mostly lower paid, unskilled and members of the United Federation of Danish Workers, a major trade union and unemployment fund for unskilled workers working in Denmark. The employees in the production facility were mostly higher paid, skilled metal workers, and members of the Danish Metalworkers' Union, which covers members in the manufacturing, building and construction, IT and telecommunications, and service industries in enterprises throughout Denmark.

"There is a distinction between warehousing and production - subject
boundaries, border between unions - which are not just solved with
courses in software and more in payroll - but in addition requires
changes in an old organizational culture…" (Head of Manufacturing)

The separation meant that management desired social changes beyond upskilling
employees, and more toward changing and 'old organizational culture' with existing
barriers and existing distribution of work tasks. The change in workflows was now
seen solvable as an organizational culture change.

Prototype worker experiences

Management perceived the skilled workers' salary to be high and not incentivizing
them to increase their digital qualifications. The change in organizational culture
should therefore incite the workers to update their digital skills.

"We have an old organizational culture…and the salary level is high,
therefore not much incentive for the workers to update their digital
skills..." (Head of Warehouse)

It was thus controversial what qualifications were required to collaborate with
the industrial robots, with management believing that some unskilled workers could
do some of the work previously done by skilled workers, and that some skilled
workers should do part of unskilled workers job to get rid of the unskilled workers.
Specifically, management had an experiment in mind, where a pallet moving robot
should replace a warehouse worker in the task of delivering necessary material from
the warehouse department to the workstations in the manufacturing department. They
even pointed out the unskilled worker for us:

"It is him [an unskilled worker running a lift-truck in the warehouse we were visiting] that we want to replace with the pallet moving
robot…" (Head of Warehouse)

The skilled worker in the manufacturing department should then do a task that
previously was the unskilled warehouse workers task, that of offloading material for
use at the workstation by the worker her/himself and the robot in collaboration.

Even when we followed managements' choice of solution to be prototyped, it
was obvious that the worker experiences that could be prototyped could be controversial: should we prototype the skilled workers' experiences with (suddenly) doing
the unskilled workers' job of delivering material to the workstation with the industrial robot? Or should we prototype the unskilled workers' experience of seeing
skilled workers and a robot doing an unskilled workers' task? What we were asked
to do, we thought, as consultants was to prototype a positive version of workers
experience of organizational culture change. We proposed a prototype intervention
adapted to the factory, which combined some of the sketched solutions. It was that
was a short six session course for employees based on digital peer-tutoring concept,
Fig. 8.4. A proposed additional course for management only should focus on change
management.

The actual prototyping in the factory of the digital peer-tutoring concept in Fig. 8.4. An illustration of the prototyped digital peer-tutoring intervention, Fig. 8.4, would build on the management-generated subgoals as outlined above. It consisted of an initial meeting (2 h), then 4 × 4 h (half day, one meeting per month in 4 months), a home assignment between the four meetings, with 3–5 employees from warehouse and 3–5 employees from manufacturing, that is, 1 week per employee including home assignment. Then at the end, the consultants would arrange an open discussion with management and employees about how further organizational implementation of the robot learning format could proceed.

The precise schedule for the course included the use of a small number of 5-min (video) presentations including a quiz. Paper, post it notes, markers, as well as clickable prototype tools, and video (smartphones, camera) would be used. The course followed an action learning philosophy, with workers learning while they were doing. The additional management course was based on design thinking (Kolko, 2015) and paradigms of system development (Hirschheim & Klein, 1989).

Do field evaluations and UX tests

Management had worked out schemes for different digital qualifications needed for the upcoming 5-year period. In fact, they had specified several wanted digital competencies.

> "[I have made] an overview of digital competencies wanted over the next 5 years, including several robot-relevant digital competencies…" (Head of Technical solutions).

Thus, the management had already specified the evaluation targets, which were if the wanted digital skills were presents among workers. These targets may or may not have includes skills needed to offload a pallet moving robot, but according to what management told us the targets did not specify what would be the skilled workers experience of collaborating with the pallet moving robot.

In response to the controversial situation, we (the consultants) concluded that the social issues could be described as management seeing a gap between the current state (old organizational culture, established border between skilled and unskilled employees, too high salaries) and a desired state of new configurations of worker-robot collaborations, and that this led to a quite open and controversial situation with regard to what worker experiences to prototype. The technical evaluation of the prototypes would hence need to proceed with high-level problem-solving goals as evaluation targets. The first problem-solving goal was thus centered about the introduction of a pallet moving robot and the issues following that. These issues included how skilled metal workers and unskilled storage workers both could develop new digital competencies including new work distributions. The second problem-solving goal was innovating the design of the workers' collaboration with the manufacturing robot with new controls, how skilled workers could describe and share their efficient and good ways to operate the robot with both new employees and employees with less training, or the interaction designs of the robot could be redesigned.

Relation Artefacts Type IV: Socio-Technical interventions

Relation artefacts type IV begins with interaction operability checks of how the interaction design of prototype allows cross-device continuity and cognitive and communicative socio-technical interoperability. Then the prototypes are evaluated as digital legacy interventions that improve business-critical but obsolete systems. Finally, the prototypes are aligned with the organizational strategy.

Interaction operability checks

Management were worried that the consultants' proposal opened for unwanted conflicts, and thus were in doubt if the intervention should be seen as a pilot project or as something implemented broader in the organization.

```
This is a very large workplace…we risk opening up for all kinds of
[conflicts in the organization] ... [asking the consultants] Should
it be a pilot project or something more broad? (Head of Manufac-
turing)
```

Discussing the cross-device interoperability of the digital peer-tutoring prototypes would indeed open for conflictual and controversial stuff. The digital peer-tutoring prototype had the potential to violate the privacy of the workers, because it would reveal their ways of working, which exposed them to other workers' and management's judgements. It could lead to exclusion of vulnerable individuals with no or little best practices in human–robot collaborations to share, such as unskilled workers. Other controversial matters could be workers appropriation of the digital peer-tutoring video format for other than tutoring purposes, or their customization of the concept by for example skipping parts of it or adding novel parts.

Discussing the socio-technical interoperability concerned multiple workers and multiple devices collaborating around the digital peer-tutoring prototypes. The prototype was clearly aimed at increasing information sharedness by reducing the information asymmetry between skilled and unskilled workers information, but it did increase information overload by adding to the amount of information that the workers had to cope with. In terms of communication readiness, the prototype was based on an already existing willingness to share, which is about the workers' attitude to sharing collected information with other workers at the same activity. Other issues with socio-technical interoperability included the operational awareness around the digital peer-tutoring prototype; if the workers were ready to change the operational boundaries depending on the situation, that is, if the skilled workers would accept to do some unskilled work to accommodate the pallet robot operation.

However, these discussions never became concrete and instead remained as conversation tops in the consultants talks with management. So thought the conversations took place in the field (in the factory), they were more like thought experiments done by distant academics in their lab.

Digital legacy interventions

Both the management and the consultants were aware that the intervention was (at the time) a pilot/prototype. The consultants had initially planned to adapt the intervention to two–three companies and compare and differentiate, with special focus on (1) how the learning format looked overall for each company and (2) whether there were overlaps between learning formats across companies. Success criteria were set up including (1) at least 80% completion of course elements, (2) that everyone involved says that they have learned something from the course, and (3) that the company and the consultants (and their employers) got answers to learning format questions.

In a socio-technical view of UX of legacy system, the skilled worker-industrial robot workstations and the unskilled workers taking care of delivering material from the warehouse to the workstations together was a socio-technical legacy system. It was technically obsolete (needed the pallet robot) and socially obsolete (the hard rules about what tasks that skilled and unskilled workers each could do), old (had been like this for many years), and needed lots of maintenance, but solved the issues of moving material to the workstations from warehouse, and meet the individual employees' needs of for example fulfilling a work role. It was pretty clear that replacing the unskilled worker with a pallet robot would not in itself solve the legacy issues.

It could well have been that the legacy system in case was considered a core system, not an obsolete system, by the workers. If asked (what we did not do), the workers may well have agreed with what has been found in studies of legacy systems in industry, which is that workers believe that "if it ain't broke, don't fix it" (Khadka, Batlajery, Saeidi, Jansen, & Hage, 2014). Indeed, from organizational, social, and business perspectives, there were several challenges for replacing the legacy system. First, how or who should pay for the transformation was a not solved issue, which the consultants offered a possible solution for; we were freely provided by the regional development project to the company, and we would provide a free training course. Second, the resistance from the workers and their unions was considerable. We, the consultants, talked to union representatives in two meetings in the regional project context, and they signaled to us that the situation in the company was that unions did not want any change, since their members carried quite good salaries as it was, and the change wanted by management was designed to change that. Third, management itself was in doubt if the return-of-investment would be there, even if the consultants were free, as management would have to offer employees time. From a technical perspective, since the pallet robot was procured as finished product from a provider, the challenges were less difficult, and mostly related to integration with other technical systems and setting up maintenance.

However, the digital legacy issues were not limited to the organizational and technical issues. The consultants promoted a digital peer-tutoring learning format as a solution to the organizational problem and the workers needs related to the problem. The individual workers needs included in our eyes to pass on their digital legacy to others, in the sense defined by (Gulotta, Odom, Forlizzi, & Faste, 2013), as their needs for sharing in meaningful, complex, and positively experienced ways in which each worker has learnt to do certain things with collaborative robots, and with colleagues from, for example, the warehouse coming to deliver material to the workstation. Dealing with individual workers legacy issues was thus a major motivation for seeing the learning format as a solution, since the learning format was about workers describing and sharing their own smart ways of working. The learning format could potentially support fulfillment of workers needs for identity, was has been described in the literature as feeling information is a meaningful part of oneself and distinguishes one person from another (Alon & Nachmias, 2020). The workers or some of them could even come to see themselves when using the learning format as harbingers of new traditions and practices regarding digital media, and as being responsible for generating a digital archive their colleagues and successors could use and further develop in their daily work.

Organizational strategy alignments—The company's response

The linkage between the managements' digitalization strategy—an excel sheet with plans for among other things the use of robots in the next 5 years—and their business strategy never became clear to us, the consultants. However, a part of the strategy was apparently to lower costs in production by using unskilled workers to collaborate with robots and by replacing unskilled workers with pallet robots. How management practiced their strategy was revealed in their decision about the non-continuation of the digital peer-tutoring project.

> "We have had a follow-up talk after your visit regarding the advan-
> tages and disadvantages of participating in the project. We have
> come to the conclusion that we can not bid with the right resources
> for the project to ensure that both you and we have value for the
> effort. It must be seen from the talk we have at the meeting that the
> resources must be of a "caliber" which by its own power can create
> value in this kind of work. We do not see ourselves able to free
> up those resources in the coming period. We apologize and wish you
> good luck with the further course of the project." (Head of Manufac-
> turing)

The management practice of their strategy did not prioritize the allocation of skilled and innovative workers to use the digital peer-tutoring prototype. One possible reason for this could be that the organizational culture did not value the merge of workers' user experiences and goals with the business and organizational goals. Management did not want to see digital peer-tutoring, or perhaps any other close worker-to-worker collaboration, become entangled in the company culture.

The failure in the end to align the prototype with the organizational strategy calls for questions about the consultants' use of the socio-technical approach to be answered. Why (not) and how well did the consultants identify and engage with a worker-oriented culture in the organization? Since the consultants actually were in the room when the managers discussed important business decisions about product direction and business strategy, what activities did the consultants do? Recently, research in UX leadership (Friedland, 2019; Lachner, Naegelein, Kowalski, Spann, & Butz, 2016) suggest that the consultants should be concerned with not only aligning the prototype with the organizational strategy but also with broader questions of developing and managing a UX culture in the organization. We, the consultants, however, did probably not know enough about the company's plans for delivering products, systems, and services that offer high value to customers, and differentiates the company's brand. Two meetings with management obviously were not enough, which also became clear when we separately met with union representatives who told us an alternative story about what the problem in the organization was, see above.

What is required by HWID consultants qualifications is not so much classic UX specialist knowledge, but that they are capable of a management- and organization-oriented UX professionalism (Clemmensen et al., 2020), characterized by expert UX knowledge (e.g., approaching usability as 'organizational usability'), a management-minded work orientation (seeking upward in the organizational hierarchy and/or being entrepreneurial), innovative tool use (seeking new ways of creating and structuring their services), highly social best practices (e.g., innovative configurations between students, scholars, HWID consultants, and a variety of industry practitioners to collaborate learning), organizational user-centeredness (embracing user orientation from a diversity of disciplines), community participation (e.g., engaging with local socio-technical professional communities), and appreciating the (lack of) maturity of the socio-technical approaches including UX and usability concepts in the local society.

Thus, both from academic research and industrial practice perspectives, aligning interaction design practices with organizational and work strategies is an important type of interventions. To design these relation artefacts type IV is obviously a challenging and ongoing beyond initial listing of areas of concern.

Reflection: Benefits and challenges of using the HWID approach

Benefits

In the design case 1, the HWID platform helped consultants to deliver a ready-to-use service to client companies, as the company did not have the time and resources to negotiate or enter too much dialogue. The consultants could with relatively few resources (a few meetings with management) formulate a service offer to management that potentially could upgrade unskilled workers.

Content-wise the HWID platform oriented the consultants' and the company's development of the digital peer-tutoring concept with focus on human–robot collaboration and the related social arrangements among workers.

The specific relation artefacts subcategories exemplified above (the HWID action cards) scaffolded a rich analysis that weaved the social and technical together in a rich, objectified, entangled, sociomaterial digital peer-tutoring solution. The solution was clear, structured, and real enough to allow management to decide whether to continue or not with the project.

Challenges

Retrofitting HWID action cards on a case can feel like pushing theory on data, instead of exploring for insights or problems. In this case, the HWID platform stood somewhat in the way for delivering what management initially wanted, which was a change management process driven top-down by management with the consultants' help. This underscores the potential in beginning HWID projects with a contextual analysis.

HWID does not have strong assumptions or explicit analytic tools to support power or deal with power relations, even if it does focus on relation artefacts, which is however in some cases needed. Relations of power may be important, and may be built into the artefacts. In this design case, clearly not enough of power relations was made clear in the digital peer-tutoring artefacts. Instead of developing a concept with focus on human–robot collaboration and the related social arrangements among workers, management-worker collaboration should have been the focus.

8.6   Design Case 2. A Glass Processing Factory

The second design case took place in 2019, shortly after the first design case presented above. Again, it was done by two university professors acting as paid consultants for a larger regional development project, as described above for design case 1. In addition, a third consultant participated.

Context

The case company ABC was a European SME[5] that specialized in glass processing. Company ABC supplied both individual pieces with special specifications and entire series of several thousand units. The factory had crew and CNC machines that at the time were unique in its national market (Denmark). Company ABC's work was characterized by solid professional knowledge combined with the latest technical possibilities. It was based on knowledge about the physiology of the glass and what it takes to make industry customers get the optimal result. Whatever the customer needs, Company ABC aimed find a specialized solution, according to their stated philosophy.

We, the consultants, visited the selected case company six times over a 6-week period during the spring 2019. The purpose of the first visit was to develop insights into the company, the motivation for purchasing a collaborative robot (a so-called 'Cobot'), and challenges with its current as well as potential future use of the collaborative robots and other automation. The three consultants observed a collaborative robot's current (very limited) use, interviewed and discussed with visiting Cobot vendor representative, with managers and shop floor workers, and observed work and demonstrations of the Cobot. Over the next four visits, the digital peer-tutoring learning format (see Sect. 8.4) was implemented in four sessions, followed by a final evaluation on the sixth visit. The consultants documented all observations, interviews, and learning sessions with video and audio recordings and photos, and they collected the videos produced by the workers in the digital peer-tutoring learning format. The learning format was evaluated after each session and at a final 1-day meeting with participation from all key stakeholders.

---

[5] "The category of micro-, small- and medium-sized enterprises (**SMEs**) is made up of enterprises which employ fewer than 250 persons and which have an annual turnover not exceeding 50 million euro, and/or an annual balance sheet total not exceeding 43 million euro.

Theories and methods

The use of assistive technologies such as collaborative robots may imply new ethical and social concerns (Maurice, Allienne, Malaisé, & Ivaldi, 2018). The term 'assistive technologies' in the HCI research literature denotes diverse issues such as what it means to give care and assistance with technology (Boyer, 2004) and how to provide technological support in the home and at the workplace for the ageing workforce (Brach & Korn, 2012). The term 'assistive technologies' has been used in the context of Industry 4.0 developments, such as the use of collaborative robots to assist in work practices in manufacturing factories (Schmidtler et al., 2015; Wolfartsberger et al., 2018). We use the term to denote the workers' interaction and collaboration with and around collaborative robots on the shop floor.

Collaborative robots are important in robotic research and practice. The idea is that a collaborative robot can work alongside human workers and interact in collaboration with the human worker (Kragic, Gustafson, Karaoguz, Jensfelt, & Krug, 2017), as it were itself a human worker with agency and intentionality (Görür, Rosman, Sivrikaya, & Albayrak, 2018), specialized in pick-and-place and grabbing (Sanchez-Tamayo & Wachs, 2018), and perhaps in need of training (Schulz, 2017) and programming (Materna et al., 2017) from the human worker.

The collaborative robot will be integrated in the company's workflows (Tan & Inamura, 2013). This raises issues of how the integration shapes work practices (Sergeeva & Huysman, 2015) and what kind of socio-technical logic is being played out in concrete collaborative practices (Vom Brocke et al., n.d.).

Workers' programming of collaborative robots, however, also bring up traditional HCI issues of who, when, where, and what to interact with (Materna et al., 2017). Even 'simplified programming' of collaborative robots is not that simple (Stenmark et al., 2017). Attitudes of factory workers toward industrial and collaborative robots is unknown (Elprama, Jewell, Jacobs, El Makrini, & Vanderborght, 2017), and safety in the interaction turns out to be a major concern (Maurtua et al., 2017). We don't know yet how to describe interactions with collaborative robots (Christiernin, 2017).

Digitalization in SMEs

SMEs depend on their workers' knowledge and innovative capabilities to create new ways of working with technology, and they generally lack the capability and capacity for comprehensive digital transformation (Ludwig, Kotthaus, Stein, Pipek, & Wulf, 2018; Mucha et al., 2016). Collaborative robots that work alongside a human worker can be integrated into the production without radical reconfiguration or automation of established workflows. A human worker can program a collaborative robot to perform tasks such as lift, pick and place, move, or otherwise process physical objects (Kragic et al., 2017; Sanchez-Tamayo & Wachs, 2018; Schulz, 2017). Thus, worker designed interaction with collaborative robots and other assistive technologies is a useful first step toward digitalization in an SME.

Digital Peer-tutoring

Peer-tutoring (Magin & Churches, 1995; Schleyer et al., 2005) overlaps somewhat with other notions of providing informal technical help between colleagues, such as over-the-shoulder-learning (Twidale, 2005), over-the-shoulder-guidance in tertiary education (Hague & Benest, 1996), peer-assisted learning (Martinez et al., 2015) and peer teaching (Secomb, 2008) in the medical domain, and over-the-shoulder appropriation (Draxler & Stevens, 2011) and peer interaction (Murphy-Hill et al., 2015) in software development.

In the design case, we as consultants used the peer-tutoring approach put forward by Twidale (2005) in that we aim to support the provision of informal technical help between colleagues. Similar to Schleyer et al. (Schleyer et al., 2005), we acknowledge the role of peer tutors at various levels toward developing problem-solving skills among colleagues. Specifically, we introduce a new role of digital competence facilitator, a 'digital facilitator', as explained below.

What distinguishes'digital peer-tutoring' from traditional peer-tutoring is that the concept builds entirely on the use of video. The idea is that workers learn from creating and redesigning videos while sketching (Ørngreen, Henningsen, Gundersen, & Hautopp, 2017) as part of applying design thinking to design their own and their colleagues' work flow and interactions with collaborative robots. Ørngreen et al. (2017) suggested to link sketching techniques and creative reflection processes to video productions, and we extent this proposal to cover linking all parts of design thinking (problem definition and user needs finding, sketching, prototyping hypotheses, evaluation) to workers' video production. Secondly, we propose that video-based reasoning, instead of paper or verbal exchange, empower workers to explore and take ownership of their work. Vistisen et al. (2016) proposed to support ethical user stances during the design process of products and services, and proposes using animation-based sketching as a design method. We followed that line of thought as consultants, though we were not interested in professional designers, and instead interested in workers' own production (and consumption) of videos-as-digital-peer-tutoring.

Relation artefacts type I: negotiating the organizational problem and the workers' needs

Organizational problem definition

The overall problem for the company was that the 100,000 Euro collaborative robot was not used enough. It has the potential to change the company from an SME with specialized small batch products to one with large batch manufacturing as well. For example, the collaborative robot has the potential to do serial processing during the night. The Cobot was purchased with the intent to discover if and how such technology could be useful in the company. No deliberate plans or analyses of production flow(s) preceded the acquisition. The current use of the Cobot was to finish intermediate glass products with emery paper. The planned future use is to service specialized machines that perform surface treatment of glass products.

Fig. 8.5 Workflow and collaboration challenges with a Cobot (Worker B, video 1)

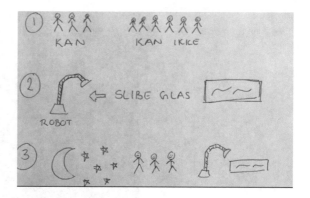

This involves placing the object in the machine, starting the machine, stopping the machine when done, and removing the object. During our first whole day of visit the Cobot was not used at all. So the initial organizational problem was easy to negotiate, it was to get more capacity from the Cobot.

Workers' needs finding

For collaboration needs, Fig. 8.5 (Worker B, video 1) illustrates one of the shop floor worker's description of three workflow and collaboration problems with the Cobot currently in use: (1) The uneven distribution of the knowledge and skills required to operate the Cobot, (2) Shaping the work of human and Cobot, and (3) Resolving issues and better utilize the Cobot. While the third issue was quickly set aside by Worker B, the first two issues was explained in more detail as follows.

Knowledge distribution. Three workers (out of 15 potential) were able to use the Cobot. One could start and stop the Cobot, position plates to be processed, and remove, quality control, and clean finished plates. He was not, however, able to adjust the Cobot's program, for example, he could not change the size of plates to process or solve problems that arise. Two other workers could adjust the program and solve some classes of problems. The other six workers in the shift could not operate or program the Cobot. The uneven distribution of knowledge increased the dependence on few workers regarding operation of the Cobot, and thus reduced flexibility in its application.

Shaping the workflow. The workers found the Cobot useful and able to relieve them from the repetitive work and physical effort involved in the manual finishing of large batches of plates. The Cobot, however, changed their task from smoothing the edges of plates to preparing, positioning, and adjusting the Cobot during polishing, and removing polished plates. The preparation involved filling trays with unprocessed plates, Fig. 8.6, place a table with filled trays on one side of the Cobot, and another with empty trays on the other side. The Cobot's program required the exact placement of tables and trays. Small errors could disrupt the whole process and require rework to clean up and restart the Cobot. The Cobot, furthermore, interrupted the workers' other tasks: Firstly, the duration of the finishing process had to be adjusted as the emery paper deteriorated, and new paper had to be installed at regular intervals.

Fig. 8.6 A Cobot picks a
glass plate from a tray

Secondly, the workers had to remove processed plates when a batch was finished.
Thus, the Cobot imposed its own limitations and rhythm onto the workflow.

For interaction design needs, when the human worker wants to initiate changes in
the production process, such as change the size of glass plates to process from 150
to 180 mm, he/she must adjust the Cobots program. Our observations indicated that
the workers do this by entering the programming code and change a figure in the
code. However, one of the workers brought up an annoying issue that every time he
entered the programming window on the touchpad used to interact with the Cobot,
an error message turned up, Fig. 8.7. For unknown reasons, the worker then had to
press two times to remove the error message.

Obviously, being blocked from interacting is a reputed design principle and practice in HCI (Norman, 2013); however, a Cobot that blocks a worker from interacting

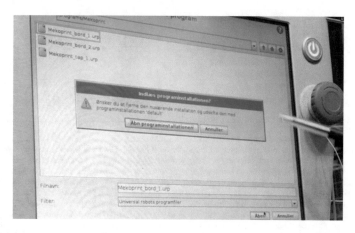

Fig. 8.7 The error message from the Cobot that blocks the worker from interacting with (programming) the Cobot (Worker H, video 3)

with the Cobot is perhaps in conflict with the notion of robots in harmony with humans (Hsu, 2016), that is, the human need for harmonious relations to others.

Persona creation

Based on our empirical data from the visits to company ABC, different kinds of personas were produced. These embedded the organizational design problems and the employee need identifications in interaction design activities. They were used by the consultants and the company to explore the Cobot usage scenarios from the persona's point of view.

Contextual personas are created in three steps: (1) inquiry into the organizational context, (2) analysis with a model of employees at work (e.g., UX-at-work/employee well-being/work stress), and (3) evaluation of persona (with focus group with users from persona's target group). The result is a graphical illustration, often created by a professional graphics designer, of a contextual persona, with specific work-relevant information added, ready for use to imagining novel interaction designs.

For the collaborative worker personas, three worker contextual personas were made: the specialist (program and operate the Cobot), the operator (not program, only operate), and the non-user (neither program nor operator). Each description was a short text describing the personal life, a day at work, and the organizational goals and psychological needs of the persona in a Cobot usage scenario. Each persona had a name and a portrait photo. One example of a persona (the specialist) is presented in Fig. 8.8.

The worker persona was a tool for the interaction design, but for human-Cobot collaboration it may not be enough to model the worker personas.

The Cobot as persona turned out to be relevant to consider. We found that it made sense when designing for human-Cobot collaboration to talk about the Cobot as a persona. Two possible robot personas were considered, the Cobot robotic arm part and the Cobot touchscreen (the iPad-like screen for programming the Cobot).

Jesper (specialist)	Personal life • 23 years • Unskilled metal worker • In relationship • Plays soccer • Like computers • Is seldom ill

A day at work
   In the factory, Jesper start and stop the Cobot, position plates to be processed, and remove, quality control, and clean finished plates. He thus does manual finishing of large batches of plates. The Cobot, however, has changed Jesper's task from smoothing the edges of plates to preparing, positioning, and adjusting the Cobot during polishing, and removing polished plates. The preparation involves filling trays with unprocessed plates, place a table with filled trays on one side of the Cobot, and another with empty trays on the other side. The Cobot's program requires the exact placement of tables and trays. Small errors could disrupt the whole process and require rework to clean up and restart the Cobot. Furthermore, the Cobot interrupts Jesper: First, the duration of the finishing process may have to be adjusted along the way, as the emery paper deteriorates, and new paper has to be installed at regular intervals. Secondly, Jesper has to remove processed plates when a batch is finished. Thus, the Cobot imposes its own limitations and rhythm onto the workflow, which Jesper has to follow.

Psychological needs (related to technology use)
   Jesper is able to adjust the program and solve some classes of problems. Once or twice during a workday, when Jesper wants to initiate changes in the production process, such as change the size of glass plates to process from 150 mm to 180 mm, he enters the programming code show in a touchpad next to the workstation. Jesper has the competence to change a few numbers in the right place in the code, so he feels confident. However, every time Jesper enters the programming window on the touchpad used to interact with the Cobot, an error message emerges. For unknown reasons, Jesper then must press two times to remove the error message, which he knows how to do. Even though he masters this interaction, it makes Jesper feel that the Cobot interrupts him and is not in harmony with him.

Technical evaluation
   Jesper is specialized in working with the Cobot. He is used to follows its rhythms and compensate for its limitations by workarounds. He is willing (eager) to expand the use of the Cobot in the company. However, he does not like being blocked by the error messages but have found a work-around.

Social evaluation
   Jesper has a few colleagues, who also can adjust the program and solve some classes of problems, and whom he works closely with. He also has colleagues, who cannot adjust the program, but can operate the Cobot in the sense of providing material and cleaning it; they see Jesper as a specialist. Most of the other workers in the shift cannot operate or program the Cobot. Jesper also has a floor manager who has a keen interest in the Cobot, and supports Jesper and the other workers collaboration with the Cobot.

Fig. 8.8   A HWID contextual persona. Adapted from (Cajander et al., 2015)

This was based on insights from literature and observations from analyzing the organization problem and the workers' needs. Overall, the company's purchase of the Cobot was motivated by a wish to explore the potential of the technology. The workers interviewed were also willing (eager) to expand the use of the Cobot. Why did this not work out as planned? Some possible reasons were:

• The Cobot requires specialized knowledge in workers, thus reduces flexibility in its application, see also e.g., (Kragic et al., 2017; Materna et al., 2017; Schulz, 2017)

• The Cobot imposes its limitations and rhythm onto the workflow, see also e.g., (Sanchez-Tamayo & Wachs, 2018; Sergeeva & Huysman, 2015; Tan & Inamura, 2013; Vom Brocke et al., n.d.)

• The Cobot may block a worker from interacting with it, see also e.g., (Christiernin, 2017; Elprama et al., 2017; Görür et al., 2018; Materna et al., 2017; Maurtua et al., 2017; Stenmark et al., 2017)

Cobot	Private information
	• 2 years • Collaborative robot • Stand-alone" • Static (not mobile) • Can do up to 10 kg movements • Is seldom malfunctioning

Context
In the factory, Cobot does the task of polishing glass plates. Cobot takes an unpolished glass plate, moves it to the polishing rondel, turns it to the correct positions, and when finished, place the glass plate in a new stack. However, Cobot also functions as the company's way to explore the potential of novel digital technology for manufacturing. Cobots are sold as providing a cost-effective, flexible, and safe automation solution for a wide range of production tasks. The workers interviewed were also willing (eager) to expand the use of the Cobot.

Cobot's psychological needs (doesn't make sense, but anyway…)
Cobot likes to do things in the same way repeatedly, and it does not like too much flexibility in its application. This means that Cobot prefers a dominating role, where it can impose its limitations and rhythm onto the workflow. If necessary, Cobot will act out and block a collaborator from doing certain interactions with Cobot and will require repeated confirmation before having fulfilled its needs for security. Cobot is open to exploration of novel uses, but to do that it needs space and time.

Technical evaluation
Cobot is rigid (inflexible). It may require repeated interactions with error messages. Its code is open for annotation and documentation. Cobot should be installed as a mobile installation to be useful in different scenarios at the factory.

Social evaluation
Cobot needs a certified safe space, and only certified engineers can provide that by programming Cobot in situ. Specialist workers may, however, interact with Cobot to change the items that Cobot process, such as changing the size of glass plates to be polished by Cobot.

Fig. 8.9 Cobot persona for design of human-Cobot collaboration

The issues that we identified could also be related to management motivation and action, for example, they were about management not providing space and time to improve current usage of the Cobot and explore new ways to apply it (or similar industrial robots). One example of a persona (the Cobot) is presented in Fig. 8.9.

In summary, what went well and what could have been done better when working with relation artefacts Type I are shown in Table 8.1.

Relation artefacts Type II—sketching solutions

Interaction design patterns

We agreed with the ABC company to adapt and evaluate the digital peer-tutoring learning format focused on the use of a Cobot in one of their production facilities. The ABC company is a European SME specializing in glass processing. It produces individual pieces and small batches with special specifications as well as entire series of several thousand units. The company's plan was to use the Cobot in a sequential configuration with a worker to automate a part of some small batch production. This scenario is a well-known human-Cobot collaboration scenario in manufacturing (El Zaatari et al., 2019).

When we arrived at the factory, we expected to see the workers engage in the direct teaching and learning interaction design patterns with the Cobot that these have made famous. The direct teaching and learning is that the worker can take the

Level 0 – no interaction
The Cobot stands in its own cage, outside human workers reach, see Fig. 8.6 for an example of a cage (though without physical barriers).
Level 1 – start/stop interaction
The Cobot works when human workers are there too, but not when they come close. Human worker sets up or removes glass pieces and begins or ends Cobot programs by tapping tablet interface connected to Cobot, see Fig. 7 for an example of the tablet.
Level 2 – interactive
The Cobot works synchronous with the human worker. The Human worker guide or adapt the Cobot arm as part of programming the Cobot. This is what is highlighted by Cobot vendors as doable by human workers.
Level 3 – collaborative
The Cobot works jointly with the human worker, adapting the movements of its arm to the human workers movement and to tasks and operations states.

Fig. 8.10 Levels of human-Cobot collaboration. Adapted from (Christiernin, 2017), see also (Michaelis, Siebert-Evenstone, Shaffer, & Mutlu, 2020)

Table 8.1 Relation artefacts Type I learnings

Relation artefact Type I	What went well	What could be done better
Organizational problem definition	The initial organizational problem was easy to negotiate, it was obvious to all that the Cobot could be used more	The context only emerged slowly in discussions
Workers' needs finding	The workers could identify own and others need for feeling competent and related	It was not clear if the Cobot could fulfil the needs, as it imposed its own limitations and rhythm onto the workflow
Persona creation	The Cobot as persona turned out to be relevant to consider	Identifying more details in the interaction when the Cobot block a worker from interacting with it

Cobot arm and show it the movements required to do its tasks, which then the Cobot then learns by recording (like a macro recording in an office program). The promise of Cobots is that they are easy to use because the worker can teach the movement with direct teaching by showing and the Cobot can direct learn by copying. In addition, the worker may be able to further teach the Cobot by adjusting the Cobot's grippers and cameras, or even take full control of the Cobot by remote operation.

What we saw, however, was programming done via the tablet interface, and not the direct teaching and learning. We saw low level interaction, or what (Christiernin, 2017) calls 'Start & Stop mode', where the worker and the Cobot works in the same space but the worker decides when the Cobot is allowed to perform tasks—starts and stops the Cobot motions. We saw that the glass polishing tasks was done by the

Cobot, but the worker loads and fits glass plates while Cobot was waiting. The worker then started the Cobot motion. We did not see what we expected to see: higher level collaboration in a cooperative mode where the Cobot and the worker are working together in the same physical space doing tasks together. The direct teaching and learning with the collaborative Cobot adapting its behavior based on the worker's glass polishing activities but with the worker initiating the action, was not there. The scenarios that we observed and discussed with the workers and managers in the factory, the Cobot was not learning by observing or adapting its behavior based on the human, and there was no joint glass processing in cooperation.

Furthermore, the programming that we saw was not the 'easy programming' promised by Cobot vendors, where "operators with no experience can quickly set up and operate a robot".[6]

In summary, we saw two distinct interaction design patterns, which were both low level human-Cobot collaborations:

1. Workers interacting with the tablet interface to the Cobot to do start/stop interaction, for example, for change of glass plate size. This would amount to change a few numbers at predefined locations in the program code, inclusive dealing with error messages. This is what the 'specialist' worker persona from Sect. 0 could do when collaborating with the 'touchpad' Cobot persona.
2. Certified engineers doing comprehensive programming and testing of new setups with the Cobot. This would be required to meet safety regulations.

The interaction design patterns that we observed were low level human-Cobot collaboration, and different for end-users (workers) and developers (engineers). We did not see higher level collaborations and observed no traces of workplace interaction patterns such as standard operating procedures, or organizational design patterns such as committees that involved shop stewards and unions.

Collaborative sketching

About a year prior to our visit, the ABC company purchased and installed a 100,000€ Cobot to explore if and how it could be used in their production. At the time of our visit, the Cobot was used only during the final polishing steps of one large-scale order, and it was idle much of the time.

Workers and management agreed, however, that the Cobot could be used for other purposes as well, and thus enable the company to accept more large batch orders, but no initiatives had been implemented for several months due to lack of time to experiment with the Cobot. Furthermore, the initial design decision had been a stationary installation, that is, the Cobot could not be moved to other positions on the floor where it could interact with other machines or workers.

As part of the project, a consultant and a small group of 'specialist' workers did collaborative sketching of solutions ranging from worker-Cobot collaboration problems to workflows and what to use the Cobot to in the company. Collaborative

---

[6] See for example https://www.universal-robots.com/products/collaborative-robots-Cobots-benefits/.

sketches are sketches that serves to support group interaction such as brainstorming and commenting on each other's ideas. The outcome of this, the sketches, were valuable, but even more so were the conversations around them. To facilitate collaborative sketching, the consultant applied action learning principles of with conceptualizing and naming actions in the situation where the worker was doing and filming the action, and classic sketching with pencil and paper. Since the workers, even the specialist workers, were unskilled, the facilitator also gave example videos sketching human-Cobot collaboration for the workers to follow and copy. Overall, the consultant took strong responsibility for ensuring appropriate equity between those participating in collaborative sketching and brainstorming.

During the series of visits to the factory, a consultant and the workers discussed the interaction design issues and related social arrangements. Several problem scenarios where identified, for example, a scenario where the Cobot would stop due to a missing glass plate in the tray, and a scenario where the worker had to press cancel button twice to get an error message to disappear. In both cases, the worker felt interrupted, and the collaboration with the Cobot not harmonious (and plenty of other feelings, but for the sake of our argument, we stick to …). Both in the meetings with the consultant and in the days in between, the workers came up with solutions to the problems. Each worker had a session with the consultant where they collaboratively sketched alternative solutions. These sketches were in varying degrees socio-technical sketch that include the social arrangements around the Cobot. An example is shown in Fig. 8.11.

Figure 8.11 shows three solutions to problem with collaborating with the Cobot. The first is "Restart, begin the sequence again with the Cobot". However, it might not feel harmonious to restart a collaboration with another persona like a Cobot. A reason why this anyway is a solution is indicated by a statement by the worker in the video-sketch "...the we reboot the computer...ehhh, the robot..." (video 3, worker BL and consultant SM, 00.38)

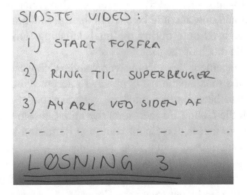

Fig. 8.11 Collaborative sketched solutions to interaction design issues. Snapshot from video-sketch made by worker BL and consultant SM. Translation: "Final video [on possible solutions]: 1. Restart, begin the sequence again with the Cobot, 2. Call a superuser, 3. Read and follow instructions on A4 paper sheet next to the Cobot. Solution no 3 [is selected for further prototyping]"

Fig. 8.12 A digital
peer-tutoring solution to the
challenge with blocking error
messages. Instructions on
video appear when question
mark is pressed. Snapshot
from video 4, worker HM
and consultant SM

that shows that the workers experience the low-level collaboration with the Cobot via the touchpad as an interaction with a computer—to a degree where they call Cobot a computer.

The second solution was to "Call a superuser". The possibility to involve a colleague to help if you yourself cannot figure out what to do, that is, to involve a third in the collaboration, would fit normal expectations to human–human collaborations, and thus increase the experience of harmonious collaboration.

The third solution was "Read and follow instructions on paper next to the Cobot". This solution mediates or scripts the collaboration by providing instructions to the worker in what to do at certain points in collaboration. A variant the fitted the project's intention of providing digital peer-tutoring better was to provide instructions with a video: "another solution could be that ...when an error message appears there is a question mark and when you press that you will be led directly to a video that shows the error and what to press on" (video 4, worker HM and consultant SM, 00.25", and Fig. 8.12.

Since these instructions become a part of the Cobot's 'body' they do potentially increase the collaboration harmony experience, and hereby move the collaboration to a higher level. It is promising solution that can be used by both personas. The 'operator' can use it to find a solution, and the 'specialist' can use it to automate the interaction (don't think about it, just do it....). Hence, the third solution promises to increase human-Cobot collaboration level from low level (sequential interaction) to high level (joint collaboration). These are well-known solution to annotate problems related to hard-to-change interfaces, such as hardware buttons and displays on ships and trains.

Workflow convergence

A third kind of relation artefacts type II are workflow convergences by organizational evaluation of collaborative sketches of workplace interaction design patterns.

The initial design decisions seemed to be related to a limited initial understanding of the Cobot's capability and a lack of strategic intent. In any case, it was clear that there was an unexplored potential (and risks) for enhancing the factory's capacity while empowering workers and help them design their own user experiences with the Cobot. The workers and consultants had now done collaborative socio-technical sketching and now have several and perhaps plenty of innovative ideas to advantageous workflow designs to choose between.

The ideas generated for use of the Cobot in the factory's workflow were formulated in some of the collaborative sketches, such as the one below where a worker gives three ideas for the use of the Cobot in the workflows.

"One is that it can grind glass as it does now on both sides, both round and square. Another thing it is it can well stand between two machines, and when the glass comes out of one machine then take it and move it onto the washing machine, even though there are different spaces and different speeds. And the third option it is that it can find any scratches or faults on the glass using a camera sitting on it" (video 5, worker BL and consultant SM)

Another collaborative sketching repeated variants of the above, and gave additional ideas for workflows:

The first solution is the one we use now, it is with grinding the glass, that it takes the glass, grinds it, rinses it and puts it into a magazine. The number two solution that is not totally conceived right now, it is that it can be used to wash the glasses too, so that enters them at one end, and washes the glass that comes out the other end, and then using some vision technology you can get quality control in place in relation to scratches and edges and things like that...

...A third thing could be, we have something we call a "bodner", the one that makes round items and it's a process that takes 20 min of machining per glass and in doing so it could be great to have a robot putting in and waiting until it is finished and taking the glass out again. It could be really great in terms of us actually being able to put it to run when we go home, and then when we get come in the next morning it has been running glass all night so we could increase our production that way... (video 5, worker Hm and consultant SM)

The task that the company face to choose what ideas to retain for further development. The workers and managers were continuously discussing the ideas and had troubles accurately distinguishing good from bad ideas. One thing that helped them was the consultant and the digital peer-tutoring concept insistence on clearly formulating different, alternative, solutions for a shared challenge or problem and to do this in simple language and using video so that few ideas were presented per choice situation, as shown in the excerpt above. This approach was found useful (by the consultant) for employees with a tendency to follow the group or in evaluation situations in which management was present.

The digital peer-tutoring platform were used to upload the videos and made it simpler to later present these videos in evaluation forums with managers and workers, who could then make accurate choices about which not-promising ideas to delete. Using the digital peer-tutoring digital platform as an organization-specific convergence platform with a high decomposition of information help company ABCs workers and management to choose among the multiple sketched out solutions.

Table 8.2 Relation artefacts Type II learnings

Relation artefact Type II	What went well	What could be done better
Interaction design patterns	Low level human-Cobot collaboration interaction patterns with the tablet were established in use in the company	The interaction design patterns were a surprise: programming done via the tablet interface, and not the direct teaching and learning expected from collaborative robots
Collaborative sketching	The workers could identify several scenarios and suggestion solutions. The conversations around solutions (sketches) were highly valued	The consultant had to do the drawings; the workers should be encouraged to do some
Workflow convergence	The insistence on clearly formulating different, alternative, solutions for a shared problem/need, and to do this in simple language and using video helped move discussions	The workers and managers were continuously discussing the ideas and had troubles accurately distinguishing good from bad ideas

Potentially, if Company ABC was interested, unions and other stakeholders could participate in evaluating ideas via the platform.

What we saw was that the company chose to stick with their current solution about what workflows to use the Cobot in and decided to prototype this in further depths.

In summary, what went well and what could have been done better when working with relation artefacts Type II are shown in Table 8.2.

Relation artefacts type III—prototyping the best solutions

Organizational action hypothesis

The digital peer-tutoring concept was linked by consultants to management and workers together developing the digitalization strategy for company ABC. Convinced by the action learning philosophy offered by the larger regional project, the managers and the owner of the company ABC agreed to try a design thinking approach (the digital peer-tutoring approach) to strategy-making, as it promised solutions to the ill-defined and wicked problems of digitalization of company ABC and concrete suggestions for what to use the Cobot for. The company ABC and the consultants thus saw the hypothetical part of strategic thinking as the important part and were ready to disengage with any specific prototype or understanding thereof and embrace input from tests of the prototypes with users and other stakeholders.

The chosen organizational action hypothesis for the project was that digital peer-tutoring for night team workers and new employees would ensure more use of Cobots, and that during day shifts with absent expert specialist workers could be replaced by less specialist workers with the support of the digital peer-tutoring videos. Together

Table 8.3 Overview of the four training sessions in the digital peer-tutoring concept in company ABC

Sessions	Themes	Topics	Worker-created-how-to-videos
1	The problem	Personas Interaction Collaboration with tech	• A persona • An interaction problem • A collaboration problem
2	Solution sketch	How to sketch a solution Interaction Collaboration	Three design ideas for • Interaction • Collaboration
3	Design prototype	Interaction and collaboration prototypes	• Elaborate one design idea into a prototype
4	Evaluate prototype	How to evaluate/test prototypes	• Test the prototype with a colleague

with company ABC workers and managers, the consultants designed and implemented four training sessions with selected shop-floor workers, Table 8.3, as part of the digital peer-tutoring concept.

Table 8.3 that shows the digital peer-tutoring concept as it emerged in company ABC. It was aimed at teaching workers to describe and share their ways of interacting and collaborating with and around the Cobot to do glass plate polishing. The concept was build on four steps of classical design thinking and with two focus topics of interaction and collaboration.

The prototyping of organizational action hypothesis in company ABC was about multiple throw-away precise prototypes of specific hypotheses of strategic importance to the organization, and how the workers and managers appropriated these. On the organizational level, the intention with prototyping was not about finding and converging on ideas for novel ways of doing glass plate polishing, but rather to support management, workers, and consultants together in getting the strategic thinking right about the way(s) to use Cobots in the manufacturing in the company. Throw-away prototypes like these are didactic, descriptive, refined, answer questions, test, resolve, make things specific, and depict stuff; they are about incremental iterative refinement (Tohidi et al., 2006), also on the organizational action level.

The consultants facilitated the prototyping of the hypothesis with a combination of paper and video materials, and with a scope on the part of digital peer-tutoring that was closest to the worker, that of recording and sharing own interactions and collaborations around the Cobot. The back-end of a larger organization wide information system for digital peer-tutoring was after some negotiation left out of scope for the prototyping, and was kept for later development, as expressed by the owner:

```
If we are to work further with it in the company, it will presup-
pose that we receive concrete guidance on how and with which tools
you can further process / edit the videos, as well as a recommenda-
tion for storage media / location (Owner, personal communication,
04/09/2019)
```

The quote illustrates that the knowledge-sharing part of the digital peer-tutoring concept was not much a part of the prototyping, which was more about horizontal prototyping with paper prototypes and video prototypes, and less about functional program code and client–server running solutions.

Furthermore, the prototypes were done in a resolution sufficient and necessary to test the hypothesis about the use of the Cobot in the workflows, so they were rough homemade-hand-held videos, and not did not look like professional video productions. The purpose was to innovate rather than invent the use of the Cobot in the company, in ways that were credible and useful to the target workers and managers. The prototyping were also adjusted by the consultant along the way to increase the involvement of workers as co-designers. For example, paper prototyping was introduced by the consultants to help workers to describe their ways for working before video recording them.

```
Kl. 12:30 BL came down to me and we started developing the videos.
In my notes, along the way, I had written down ideas for what kind of
video they could make.
• Drawing (Draw in advance and make a sound clip over it)
• Conversation with a colleague
• Video in front of the robot
• Interview
After I presented my ideas for the video, BL still seemed a little
hesitant. He also said that he did not want to be filmed and therefore
some of the ideas were not entirely optimal. I therefore made a choice
him and said that I think a drawing would fit well with video 1 and
he agreed. We took the starting point in tutorial video 1 (the last
slide) where I then asked him about those questions. That way was the
drawing designed. After he had spoken and I had drawn, we recorded it
all.
After we made the first video, BL seemed more confident and said that
videos 2 and 3 would probably be best out by the robot itself as it
has to deal with it. So we went out there and recorded a lot of videos
of ourselves the service and the problems. Subsequently, we went in
and uploaded the video to the computer so he could talk about it and
describe what is happening. (consultant SM, field report week 15,
2019)
```

As the quote indicates, the prototypes material and method were selected for maximum participation and codesign with involved workers, and with the aim of allowing co-workers and management to participate in the evaluation of them. At the same time, the prototype material—paper and videos made by mobile phone recording—was cheap and easy to do and fitted the resources that an SME may offer to such project.

Obviously, there were good reasons for company ABC's decision to go with project and prototyping organizational action hypothesis, instead of doing classic top-down management strategizing. The larger regional project advocated the use of action learning principles both as the best digitalization ideology for SMEs and with economic incentives (free consultants). In addition, specifically for digitalization in manufacturing it supported the use of the digital peer-tutoring. On the other hand, the prototyping in Company ABC done under the digital peer-tutoring concept, Table 8.3, because it was focused narrowly on the worker-Cobot collaboration, potentially was nearly silent about prototype videos back-end issues of worker privacy, intellectual property rights, storage, and sharing. The prototypes thus risked covering up issues that in principle was important to company ABC and which they saw as included in the larger regional project' action learning.

Prototype worker experiences

The codesign of prototypes was focused on experience prototyping to help understand worker's 'experiences', and potentially answer pragmatic "how do I do this" and hedonic "What would it feel like if…?" hypotheses. The choice of video-prototyping was to enable the workers in high fidelity to 'experience before IT artefact', that is, to try out how it would be to describe and share their ways of collaborating with and around the Cobot in context and with something close to a fully established digital peer-tutoring system (though not with a backend system). Obviously, it was about getting the design right.

The digital peer-tutoring learning format consisted of an ensemble of instruction-videos, quizzes, example-solution-video, and worker-created-how-to-videos. The consultants had developed short (3–5 min) instruction videos for each training session, Table 8.3, that explained the theme, introduced techniques that the partici-pants could use to investigate problems and describe solutions, and concluded with an exercise where the participants should develop a short video (3–5 min). The consultants also produced short example videos with their 'answers' to the video assignment for each session.

All video material—including instruction material was recorded with standard smartphone hardware and software, and published without editing, in order to promote a 'simple-yet 'sufficient' attitude toward to video production. For each session, a consultant traveled to the factory and discussed the material with the participants, and with them codesign the 'worker-videos'. These were subsequently uploaded to a shared (secure) site in the consultant's organization, potentially for later download and knowledge sharing within the company.

The interaction and collaboration prototypes then consisted of worker-videos. An example of a snapshot from such a video is given in Fig. 8.13. The digital peer-tutoring solution to the challenge with blocking error messages.

Figure 8.13 illustrates the benefit of co-designing prototypes, as the hypothesis that video instructions would be useful for a dyslexic worker would not have been prioritized for prototyping had it not been for the worker HM arguing the case. An alternative hypothesis to be prototyped could be worker BL's choice of a simple annotating of the Cobot touchpad interface, with a paper next to the touchpad saying: `"…in case of this error message (show picture), press two times on cancel button (reason: there is a basic error in parameters, but ignore that)"`. This alternative would clearly be useful to most workers used to work with the Cobot, but not if they were dyslexic. Thus, the experience prototyping supported the consultants and co-designers' empathy with target workers and their situations. An obvious

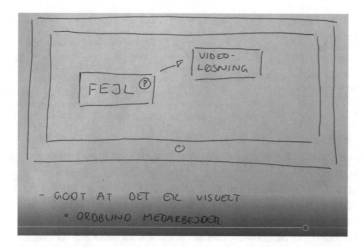

Fig. 8.13 The digital peer-tutoring solution to the challenge with blocking error messages. Instructions on video appear when question mark is pressed. The specific hypothesis described below is that "…it is visual [and hence it will be useful to] a dyslexic employee". Snapshot from video 6, worker HM and consultant SM

disadvantage of the prototyping illustrated in Fig. 8.13 was that the video was low-fi, and not giving many details about the collaboration with the Cobot, so it was hard for co-workers and managers to say "...yes we want this".

Do field evaluations and UX tests

The end point of relation artefacts type III is UX-at-work field evaluations and testing to embed the prototyping in interaction design activities. The consultants did in-the-field UX testing of the experience prototypes by asking participating workers at the end of each training session (which were all held at the factory) to fill out a SUS questionnaire under the guidance of a consultant and answer a few open-ended questions about the digital peer-tutoring of Cobot collaboration. In addition, a focus group kind of evaluation was held at as an end evaluation meeting, where both consultants, owner and managers and workers participated and gave evaluations of the prototyped artefacts.

The UX of complex systems is more than the sum of the individual subsystems, so that workers may experience both subsystem-specific hedonic qualities and broader positive experiences during work. Therefore, the consultants decided to focus the SUS evaluations and the open-ended questions on the Cobot peer-tutoring as a whole, that is, on both the experiences of the digital peer-tutoring artefacts (videos, quizzes) and the broader experience of collaborating with, innovating and sharing knowledge about the Cobot use in the company.

SUS analysis

The SUS evaluations of the peer-tutoring system/process (the app was used in the process) in Cobot use are shown in Fig. 8.14. Across four training sessions with

Fig. 8.14 SUS evaluations of the peer-tutoring process/system for worker-Cobot collaboration. Done by two specialist workers: Red line = BL, blue line = HM

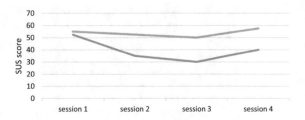

digital peer-tutoring for worker-Cobot collaboration, SUS evaluations made by two specialist workers were between 30 and 60 which indicated below industry average system usability satisfaction (Bangor et al., 2009). The scores for the specialist workers though following same trends were however on different levels. HM while giving low usability scores was satisfied with the peer-tutoring system for the worker-Cobot collaboration. BL, on the other hand, except for session 1 part about personas, scored the system usability unacceptable and as something that should be fixed immediately.

The qualitative comments revealed that it was primarily the instructional videos provided by the peer-tutoring system were not adequate for the target workers. This was the case both for pragmatic, do-goals (what to do): "...not so much, too much information..." [instructional video, HM, session 1] and "...what was planned to happen..." [instructional video, BL, session 1], and for hedonic, be-goals (who you are): "...not so much...more is being said than necessary...think about the target group..." [instructional video, HM, session 3]. Over time, though, HM apparently found session 4, about 'evaluation of collaboration prototypes with personas' better than the previous:

> "...more than in the first rounds...the language and amount of information have become better [simpler, less]..." [instructional video, HM, session 4]

The instructional videos as a technology were perceived as qualities related to structure, that is, to management and consultants' responsibility. In contrast, the workers perceived the quizzed as related to their own skillsets.

The quizzes were satisfactory for the specialist workers, though here it was clear that what worked for one worker, HM: "...ok difficulty (session 1)...reasonable (session 2)....adequate, easy (session 3)...adequate (session 4)", did not work for another worker, BL: "...it was difficult (session 1 and 2)...ok (session)". Thus BL did not even take the quiz in session 4, which was due to time pressure, but probably also that he felt he could not do it.

The last part of the peer-tutoring technology, the video examples of collaboration with and around the Cobot, illustrated different perceptions of technology-task qualities. HM found it had pragmatic qualities: "...useful.." [video-example, HM, session 1] and "... it works well..." [video-example, HM, session 3] and hedonic qualities: "...they gave good inspiration..." [video-example, HM, session 2], "...they were good ..." [video-example, HM, session 4]. BL, on the other hand, while seeing some pragmatic qualities "...ok example..." [video-example, BL, session 1], was overwhelmed with negative emotions toward the technology "...it is being told in a complicated manner..." [video-example, BL, session 2] and "...it is confusing and complicated..." [video-example, BL, session 3].

Heart model of UX-at-work analysis

The consultants' notion of UX-at-work was that a good quality UX-at-work should include an acceptable level of both pragmatic qualities (effectiveness and efficiency) and hedonic qualities (e.g., feeling of interest stimulation and professional identity confirmation). This information was available by the SUS and the open-ended questions. Furthermore, the focus was on evaluating the worker's preferred experiences of the pragmatic and hedonic qualities of interactions among task, structure, technology, and actors, as shown by the "heart model of UX-at-work", Fig. 8.15. This information was available to the consultants from their observation and discussion with management and workers in the company ABC during field visits there.

Below, we go through each of the UX-at-work dimensions presented in Fig. 8.15. Note that we threat the Cobot and the digital peer-tutoring as one unit in the analysis.

- Experiences of Cobot/Peer-tutoring—glass polishing (technology-task)

The workers using the peer-tutoring system for Cobot collaboration experienced its pragmatic product qualities, in the sense that the system potentially could support with worker-videos particular "do-goals" such as "check the status of glass items produced by the Cobot". Furthermore, to produce

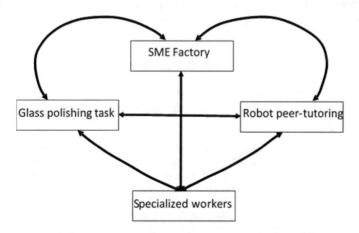

Fig. 8.15 The UX heart model for the company ABC project (adapted from (Clemmensen, Hertzum, & Abdelnour-Nocera, 2020)

worker-videos the peer-tutoring systems offered workers to proactively managing their task load and organizing and planning their task execution. This was not always perceived as support:

> However, there were doubts about how we were going to perform video 5, as it was supposed to be an extension of video 3. We quickly figured out that we got to go into too much depth with video 3 and therefore it took a little longer to craft ideas for this video. [worker BL and consultant SM, week 17 evaluation by SM]
> HM said during the evaluation that he was confused about the videos and how they differed from each other. There could well be a bigger divide between them, he said. [worker HM and consultant SM, week 17 evaluation by SM]

So, while the peer-tutoring system aimed to reduce experiences of work fragmentation and negative mental workload, the workers did not fully feel that. In addition, the workers using the peer-tutoring system for Cobot collaboration experienced may experience hedonic product qualities, in the sense that the system supports "be-goals" such as pleasure in use and professional identity and being seen as competent in mastering the Cobot by co-workers.

> In addition, BL is also a little more restrained in relation to ideas and execution. He doesn't think so abstractly, but it goes better when you try to guide him in a certain direction. [worker BL and consultant SM, week 18 evaluation by SM]
> HM is still one of the two participants who is most confident when it comes to ideas, and he thinks a little more about different options one can do. [worker HM and consultant SM, week 18 evaluation by SM]

A socio-technical design goal of the project was that the Cobot should allow workers to choose the production hours more actively. This could be simply as a worker on a day shift allocating a serial production task to the Cobot to do over night. But that would require that workers broadly experience that the technology supports their tasks.

- Experiences of Cobot & peer-tutoring—worker (technology-actors)

The hedonic aspects of interactions departing in technology were not obvious. The workers appeared happy when not pressed by the consultant to perform with the peer-tutoring.

> When I got the computer up and running, we saw training video 2 and training video 3. None of them took notes along the way, but I noticed they often looked down at my notes when I wrote [workers HM and BL and consultant SM, week 15 evaluation by SM]

The absence of stress may well have constituted 'a perfect workday' for the workers. The consultant tried to observe the workers psychological needs, in the factory and workstation contexts.

> After I presented my ideas for the video, Brian still seemed a little
> hesitant. He also said he did not want to be filmed and therefore some
> of the ideas were not entirely optimal. I therefore took a choice
> for him and said that I thought a drawing would fit well with video 1
> and he agreed with that. We took the exit point in training video 1
> (the last slide) where I then asked him about the questions. There-
> after, the drawing was designed. After he'd spoken and I'd drawn, we
> recorded it all... [worker BL and consultant SM, week 15 evaluation
> by SM]

Negative emotions like fear and anger were mentioned by the workers, while positive emotions were less so. The workers' developments of engagements and attachments over time to the peer-tutoring system for Cobot collaboration and their related preferred everyday computing practices was not done in one day, or without help from others. In addition, parts of the technology turned out to be too complicated and time-consuming for the workers to engage.

> By 14 o'clock, both workers had time off so I could start editing the
> videos. I was done at 16, but I needed to upload the videos as they
> took way too long. I think it was good that the workers also didn't
> have to edit or upload the videos, as they may not have knowledge of
> this. That's something I'm going to ask them the next time I get out
> there... [workers HM and BL and consultant SM, week 15 evaluation by
> SM]

The consultant decided that some interactions were not appropriate for the workers.

- Experiences of Cobot & peer-tutoring—factory (technology-structure)

A design goal was that the peer-tutoring system for Cobot collaboration should allow workers to have their user experiences at their favorite work locations. This appeared to work well, though it required some effort from the consultant:

> It was the fourth time I had to go out to Company ABC, where I arrived
> earlier than I usually do. I arrived at 9:45 am and I spent the first
> 15 mins putting up.
> BM [a third specialized worker] was still ill and I do not expect
> her to participate in the coming events. I picked up BL and HM and we
> started watching the first videos, taking the quizzes, and watching
> the [two other consultants pre-prepared] bid for a video.
> The quizzes went much better than the other times, as they were both
> more confident in their answers. However, it is not because they knew
> correct answers, but because they perhaps just felt more comfortable
> with the whole situation. [workers HM, BL, and BM, and consultant SM,
> week 18 evaluation by SM]

The workers did seem to appreciate that they could train their computing practices in the factory and at their meeting rooms and workstations which they felt familiar and where they were confident in their identity (hedonic quality).

- Experiences of worker—factory (actors-structure)

Evaluations of interactions departing in actors is based on what is known about users of interactive technologies and in work contexts.

The workers BL and HM and their colleagues were shaped by company ABC in their knowledge, norms, qualifications, roles, skills, and values that entered into performing their work. While not easily expressed in explicit terms, the workers did indicate the complexity of what shaped their computing practices.

> There were some technical problems as my own computer wouldn't play
> the other videos, so I borrowed one of theirs. While setting it up,
> I asked both to think of someone they could use for inspiration for
> video 1. They were both a little in doubt, after which I asked more
> about people in their workplace who were not yet users of the robot.
> This led them to come up with specific people, to which I said they
> could use them as inspiration.
> HM chose to start with Pia [another worker], while BL said he was
> considering Kurt [another worker]. In their own videos, BL ended up
> with his first choice, that is, Kurt. Where Henrik ended up taking
> point of departure [with the persona] in Abdullah [another worker].
> [workers HM and BL and consultant SM, week 15 evaluation by SM]

The workers' experiences were shaped by their holistic perception of their relations with company ABC, derived from all their encounters with touchpoints in their organization, including the consultants.

> When I was with HM, he said he thought it was really good that I had
> come out to them and helped them brainstorm for the videos. He also
> said he thought the training videos were not possible to compre-
> hend and they did not understand the videos [instructional videos].
> Therefore, it was good that I had simplified it by writing down ideas,
> as well as concrete things that needed to be in the videos. In addi-
> tion, he said they probably did not have time to be able to make the
> next-time video in advance, as they were very busy. Again, it was good
> that someone came out to them and wanted to help them get started.
> [worker HM and consultant SM, week 15 evaluation by SM]

The workers experience of the organizational structure was clearly important to their experience of the peer-tutoring system for Cobot collaboration.

- Experiences of worker—glass polishing experience (actors-task)

Because of dimensions of differences among users, socio-technical HCI may have a particular interest in those workers who are domain experts, but who also are high on the dimensions of specific system skills and general computer skills. The workers from company ABC were specialized in collaborating with Cobot, but they were not computer experts.

> After we had seen all 6 different videos, we all went through quizzes
> [about interaction designs and collaborations] together. They could
> follow them on the screen while I read them aloud to them. They

were very unsure which answers were right and hesitated a lot when choosing an answer option. It was especially at Quiz 3, where they had to form a sentence that was difficult for them. [workers HM and BL and consultant SM, week 15 evaluation by SM]

However, hedonic experiences may involve both deep work-domain knowledge and much system and computer proficiency. The workers did like the combination of work domain knowledge and the digital peer-tutoring.

After making the first video, BL seemed more confident, saying that video 2 and 3 would probably be best outside the robot itself, as it has to deal with it. That's why we went out there and recorded a lot of videos of watching the service and the problem. In the first place, we went in and put the video on the computer so he could talk about it and describe what's going on. [worker BL and consultant SM, week 15 evaluation by SM]

To make the link between the workers' positive user experience at work and the practical use of the Cobot, the consultant asked the workers themselves to innovate and eavluate to what degree that organizational action hypotheses and prototyped worker experiences help the employees to experience that the job psychologically suited them and their colleagues.

At 13:10 HM came up to me and I also presented the 4 different ideas. He was a little more confident and didn't mind being filmed. We brainstormed a bit on the ideas for the videos and the first video was quickly filmed as he just wanted to take it in a game. HM also thought it best to film the next two videos next to the robot when they concerned its function. It was the same procedure as with BL that we filmed the videos and went in and made the video speak afterward. This was best as there was a lot of noise out at the robot. [workers HM and BL and consultant SM, week 15 evaluation by SM]

The workers did try to find personal meaning in their tasks and responsibilities at work and saw beyond their tasks and responsibilities as being more than just part of their job but something that helped the company ABC, and perhaps even the industrial branch and local industry.

• Experiences of glass polishing—factory (task-structure)

Work tasks such as glass plate polishing are often conceptualized as goal-driven combinations of low-level operations. The consultants, however, working from a socio-technical (HWID) perspective that looked at workers computing practices, their work tasks were embedded in social and organizational practices and had to be interpreted by workers.

At 12:30, Henrik came down to me and we started brainstorming on both videos. Henrik has no problem with talking and being filmed, so the development of ideas went relatively fast.
I helped him draw his ideaon a paper, and then explained from the drawing. Henrik was more relaxed and did not have a feeling of pressure on him. As such, he didn't have that last time either, but I think

it's always better the second time around. You kind of know what the
expectations are going to be. [worker HM and consultant SM, week 17
evaluation by SM]

The workers' own task management practices related to their appropriate functioning as workers, the communicative experience of a joint culture with co-workers,
managers, and consultants, and a personal increase in their experience of competence
and trust. Potentially, the workers at company ABC can experience changes in their
own and co-workers' task management practices stemming from their user of the
peer-tutoring system for Cobot collaboration. These changes in their collaboration
with Cobot could allow them to concentrate on specific tasks, undertake or seek for
additional tasks, and work more intensively on tasks that they enjoy.

In summary, the consultants choose to use SUS, open-ended questions, and observations written in field notes (evaluation reports) as data collection and analysis
approach for the UX-at-work testing and evaluation in the field. Other approaches
could have been possible for consultants. AttrakDiff and other scales have been
shown to be useful at work. The consultants did not apply these, however, because of
the target worker group who were unskilled workers for whom the SUS was deemed
less controversial. Learning from other socio-technical approaches, the consultant
could have done more substantial and longer in duration field evaluations to better
understand how the peer-tutoring system for Cobot collaboration mediates social and
technical changes in practice in company ABC. This could potentially have generated
valuable adjustment to the consultants' practice of facilitating the peer-tutoring of
Cobot collaboration. The consultants were being paid to facilitate evaluations in the
field as collective and individual learnings, and to help formulate and make explicit
such insights for all stakeholders, in words that most can agree to.

What went well and what could have been done better when working with relation
artefacts Type III are shown in Table 8.4.

Relation Artefacts Type IV—Interventions, Actions and Designs

The 'Digital Peer-Tutoring' learning format was evaluated in weekly evaluations
after each of the four sessions, and a final evaluation with participation from all key
stakeholders. Here, we report about the results from the final evaluation; a 1-day
meeting in the location of the factory of the case company ABC. The participants
in the evaluation were all those present at the upstart meeting 6 weeks before. They
were company managers (Company manager J and Company manager K), learning
format users (Worker BL, Worker HM, Worker BM), corporate learning consultant (corporate learning consultant F), educational institution teacher(s) (Teacher J,
Teacher T), pilot project manager(s) (Teacher T, Teacher J), pilot project documentarist (Documentarist F), and a digital competence facilitator (Digital competence
facilitator S). The initial results from the final evaluation revealed both short- and
long-term benefits and challenges of digital peer-tutoring for Cobot collaboration.

An important nuance in the evaluations was that the weekly session evaluations
were mostly carried out in the classic usability and UX evaluation tradition, while
the final all-stakeholder evaluation was carried out in the field work tradition. In the

Table 8.4 Relation artefacts Type III learnings

Relation artefact Type III	What went well	What could be done better
Organizational action hypothesis	The workers participate in choosing the hypothesis (solution) to prototype	The project was nearly silent about prototype videos back-end issues of worker privacy, intellectual property rights, storage, and sharing
Prototype worker experiences	The workers could identify the needs of a dyslexic worker, which could be met by use of video	The prototype video was not finished enough to support management and worker decisions about it
Do field evaluations and UX tests	The insistence on clearly formulating different, alternative, solutions for a shared problem/need, and to do this in simple language and using video helped move discussions	The heart model of UX-at-work evaluation indicated several shortcomings of the prototypes

session evaluations done in classic usability and UX evaluation tradition, even though they were done "in the wild" in the factory, the consultants maintained the control of what was evaluated. That is, they presented the SUS questionnaires and asked the open questions to the workers. In contrast, in the final all-stakeholder evaluation that was done in the field work tradition, the owners and managers and workers were (more) in control. The evaluation focused less on the UX of peer-tutoring system for Cobot collaboration itself, and more on its use by the employees during everyday work life in the factory, with a focus on the workflows and rhythm of the workday and work tasks, and how the peer-tutoring for Cobot collaboration could take on several meanings when used in different work activities and work teams. In these discussions, the peer-tutoring system for Cobot collaboration quickly took on a peripheral role, as IT artefacts commonly do in ordinary life.

Interaction interoperability check-ups

One kind of relation artefacts type IV are interventions that aim to increase the UX related to interoperability of interaction designs. In company ABC, the workers liked the learning format and found it useful: " *...worker-video on iPad [could be useful]...* ", [Worker BL]. This confirms previous findings on the usefulness of video (Ørngreen et al., 2017), and extends it to the shop floor workers.

The workers were faced with the requirements and possibilities for interacting with and across several machines at different workstations, some old, some new, some German, some Italian, some polishing machines, some Cobots, even when the machines were supposed to be used to do similar glass processing tasks.

During one of the factory visits, the managers and the workers showed the consultants yet another a glass polishing machine, Fig. 8.16, see also Fig. 8.17, that poten-

Fig. 8.16 A glass polishing
machine in Company ABC

tially was a candidate to being operated by a specialized worker and the Cobot in
collaboration and explained the workflow around the machine.

> "...they [the round glass plates] are 3 mm too large when we cut them.
> And them we put them in [into the machine] ..and with the fingers feel
> if it is placed [correctly] calibrated...and the we start the machine,
> and it then polish 3 mm off the glas..." [manager Kjeld...]...."yeah,
> there is a need [if the Cobot shall place the glass plate into the
> machine instead of the human worker doing it] to make something so
> that we are sure that it [the glass plate] is placed correctly...[HM]
> [video from factory visit company ABC]

Workers could combine multiple information devices commonly used in the
factory in their everyday work life for tasks by using the peer-tutoring system

Fig. 8.17 The glass plates that the worker-Cobot collaboration should process by operating the polishing machine

for Cobot collaboration to describe and share good ways of collaborations. The peer-tutoring system for Cobot collaboration could eventually increase integration between machines and operations within the factory ecosystem, and let workers use nearby Italian, German, new, old, polishing machines, and Cobots, together or move seamlessly between them, by means of synchronization and migration of tasks. Thus 'continuity' or 'interoperability UX' could be enabled by the peer-tutoring system for Cobot collaboration by describing the user experiences related to sequential multi-device (machine, Cobot) use where interactions move, or transition, from one device to another.

Consultancy on interoperability would, however, that would require considerations of several interoperability UX challenges of the peer-tutoring system for Cobot collaboration, such as privacy, (e.g., sharing of videos); appropriation (e.g., integration of peer-tutoring videos into workflows); customization (e.g., customizing peer-tutoring videos work with company ABC's networks and protocols); awareness (e.g., automatic linking of videos to relevant machines); exclusion (e.g., determine which machines could not be operated by worker-Cobot collaboration even with the support of the peer-tutoring videos); troubleshooting (e.g., when peer-tutoring does not work as expected), and the 'excitement' or unjustified optimism about the peer-tutoring videos that may be evoked in new workers who watch the videos for the first time.

In contrast to the individual worker interoperability UX, socio-technical interoperability of HCI in work domains concerns multiple workers and multiple devices collaborating. The workers in company ABC were challenged by the concerns identified by (Kwon, Smith-Jackson, & Bostian, 2011) of sharedness, readiness, awareness, adaptiveness, and coupledness of the multiple workers and multiple machines and Cobots collaborating. Firstly, an issue of information sharedness was the information asymmetry between workers in day shift and in night shift. Secondly, though the communication readiness was there in terms of the workers' having a positive attitude to sharing they ways of working with the Cobot with other workers at the same activity, it was still hard to get the Cobot and the machines to talk to each other as the different (age, brand, etc.) machines doing the same glass polishing tasks presented themselves different to the Cobot. Thirdly, the operational awareness was a challenge as it was not fully clear to all workers which workers had the knowledge about how to collaborate with the Cobot, and also where they were located. Fourthly, adaptiveness challenges were looming as it was nearly beyond the workers abilities to modify the machines and the Cobot to talk to each other. Finally, the coupledness in terms of the sequential relationship of glass processing tasks was a challenge when the Cobot's high degree of inflexibility should be integrated in the workflows.

Digital legacy interventions

In company ABC, the glass processing machines and the workflows around them were legacy systems in the sense that they were 'core' systems (=valuable systems) that had been proven to work correctly in the factory production environment for decades, so they were not obsolete systems (=useless systems). Digital legacy interventions are socio-technical interventions that in some way change (improve, hopefully) the legacy systems, for example, by improving their UX. Legacy systems are traditionally those systems that shows technical problems such as being obsolete, old, and need lots of maintenance, but at the same time are crucial for an organization's operation. However, from work and organizational point they do solve problems for organizations and meet individual employees' needs. What would solve legacy issues in company ABC were thus not simply technical modernization with the introduction of the Cobot but creating new relations between workflows/teamwork and the design of interactions with machines and Cobot.

In company ABC, a digital legacy intervention was attempted by using the digital peer-tutoring system for Cobot collaboration to teach new ways of thinking about the glass production machines and the workflows around them, ways that could include the Cobot. However, the part that instructed workers in basic concepts of interaction design and teamwork/workflows was not a successful intervention. The workers found that the instruction videos were too long and complicated. "They should be cut down to a list of four points" [Worker Br]. Too long videos can be an expression of an 'apathetic ethical stance', a stance that reduces the worker-user to be a mean of input for the intended final design (Vistisen et al., 2016). What was taught on the instruction videos were seen by workers as so far away from their usual thinking and acting with their machines and workflows (the legacy system) that the proposed new ways of seeing the worker-Cobot collaboration did not make sense to them.

On the other hand, the workers expressed that they could use the different kind of peer-tutoring videos to both think about a problem, sketch different solutions, and evaluate their use: "Sketches.... I had read up on it, go and think about it...." [Worker Br], and the worker should be able to pause the video... [Worker Bi]. Thus, there were indications that the format helped workers explore new technologies from an emphatic ethical user—that is, from their own—perspective (Vistisen et al., 2016). Company manager K supported this: "We, as a business must spend more time on [workers' use of video to innovate]." The management perspective underscored the multi-layered organizational perspective on positive interventions in digital legacy systems. In summary, in company ABC, most of the challenges for updating legacy glass processing systems were social and organizational, that is, related to the workers skills and knowledge and the management's strategy, though there were also some challenges related to the technical interaction design.

The workers in company ABC were the ones that had first person experiences with the legacy glass producing system(s) and were those who with the support of peer-tutoring were expected to pass on their experiences to colleagues in the form of worker created videos. They were thus creating a personal digital legacy within company ABC, for example, showing hands in a video, Fig. 8.18. This could include workers' work experiences recorded in the videos and traces of their personal values in policies, pictures of themselves, etc., related to the user of the Cobot. It could also be organizational documents with the employees' name on, software hacks on the Cobot, hardware manipulations and annotations, written procedures created by the worker, and more.

The curation of such worker personal digital legacy was not established in company ABC, as it remained unclear who would curate the worker's personal digital legacy: the individual worker, the employer/company, or somebody else (e.g., a platform provided by the workers' trade union). For both managers in company

Fig. 8.18 The personal legacy of a directional hand pointing to the worker-proposed solution to a worker-identified problem

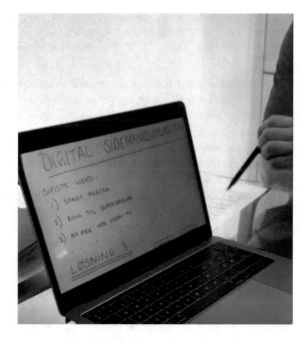

ABC who had access to office computers and workers who could save macros and programs for the Cobot the personal digital legacy would also reflect their person style of doing digital 'hoarding' in the workplace; this issue of workers piling up digital material in personal storages were however not something the consultants with the current version of peer-tutoring system for Cobot collaboration were equipped to deal with. So, who workers (employees) at company ABC shared and protected their data across conditions of changing technologies, relationships, individuals, and perhaps even companies, were of interest for future consultancy in the company.

How to intervene with organization-oriented storage for workers' digital legacy(ies)? The consultants discussed three different options with the workers and managers in company ABC. First, workers could benefit from company ABC-owned add-ons, plugins, data scrapers, or simply lists of content related to the peer-tutoring systems. This could support workers doing legitimate extracting from the company ABC organizational storage and transferring (or preparing to transfer) their personal digital legacy to private storage or to their next employers' storages.

Second, another intervention could be to developing systems including worker awareness that could encourage and support workers in actively and consistently curating their own digital legacy. This could be written procedures and strategies for doing this, such as selective filing of videos, do not show you face on the video, it is ok to delete draft videos instead of saving them, etc.

> [Br] said that he did not want to be filmed and therefore some of the ideas were not entirely optimal….after we made the first video, Brian seemed more confident and said that videos 2 and 3 would probably be best out by the robot itself as it has to deal with it. So we went out there and recorded a lot of videos of ourselves, the service, and the problems. Subsequently, we went in and uploaded [one of] the video to the computer so he could talk about it and describe what is happening. [worker Br and consultant SM, SM evaluation report session 2]

As seen in the quote, the consultant and the workers negotiated the workers legacy along the way of working with the peer-tutoring system. It also illustrates the social side of the socio-technical intervention in that it appears that the worker across [short] time change perceptions about the nature and value of the digital legacy. The UX of digital legacy may change over time. Though it is not explicit in the quote, it seems reasonable to assume the worker in the quote is well aware that experiences that would be fall outside of daily activities today, may be less or more acceptable when the worker returns to it years later. In conclusion, the digital legacy interventions in company ABC were, though few and weak, aimed to support workers to take responsibility for their digital legacy within and across company ABC and their other and past and future workplaces.

Finally, in company ABC the specialized workers were selected because they had extreme amounts of practice with carrying out glass processing task with the existing machines and to a degree also with the Cobot within the factory. They were thus competent to comment on each other's videos, nearly as if those were their own. This kind of commenting served to validate the solution videos. Thus, the peer-tutoring system for Cobot collaboration evaluation was done with colleagues as independent observers who commented on the possible behavior of target users in legacy work scenarios well-known to all involved employees. These target users (the expert or future workers) were co-designed/selected among work colleagues (the specialized workers participating) and data-driven with substantial understanding and description of the legacy work scenario(s).

Organizational strategy alignments

In company ABC like in any other company, practices of interaction design for human work may at some point be morphed into organizational strategies by aligning the organizational design culture with the business and organizational goals. From this realization, questions emerged about what activities did consultants and managers engage in to ensure they were concurrently considering important business decisions about product direction and business strategy. One way to align the socio-technical design with the organizational strategy was expressed by a company manager as"...*recording the results from the company's informal and formal experiments on the shop floor"* [Company manager J, supported by Company manager K]. However, the consultants and managers were concerned with not only aligning low level design experiments with the organizational strategy, but also with broader questions of developing and managing a design and experimental culture in the organization. They viewed the design strategy at the company level as being about the alignment of (a) the design activities and the workers and consultants engaging in design supported by the peer-tutoring system for Cobot collaboration, and (b) the overall goals and objectives of company ABC's business. In sum, the design strategy at the factory floor level was about plans for delivering glass products that offered high value to customers and differentiated company ABC's brand.

The long-term benefits of organizational strategy alignments that the managers in company ABC saw related to most of the company's areas including operations, human resources, technology and equipment, marketing. For operations, the managers expressed that the format could be used to tackle issues in the manufacturing, and a"...*company database of videos that could be accessed even years after production"* [Company manager J]. They were well aware that their organization needed to build knowledge and saw the learning format as a doable knowledge management in their company. For human resources, the managers expressed that supplier courses could be made memorable by"...*recording what the supplier shows on the shop floor"* [Corporate learning consultant F], and"*Cut out what is not useful [from the supplier teaching]"* [Company manager K]. The company had several not-so-good experiences with supplier courses for the company's workers did not work as intended. The workers could not remember much from days of training at the supplier's site. Even training by suppliers delivered on-site in the company ABC did not have a lasting effect on the workers, since the suppliers' teachers did most of the talking and interacting with the supplied machines and equipment. Here the use of the peer-tutoring videos was well aligned with management's strategy for updating workers skills. For technology and equipment, the managers expressed that new employees could be introduced to the job: "A new one that is totally novice [could use worker-created-how-to-videos]" [Company manager J]. The technology and equipment that the company had acquired and further appropriated to own use could be annotated and extended with the worker created peer-tutoring videos. Finally, for marketing, the managers expressed that the learning format could also be used to produce videos for customers for marketing purposes and quality documentation.

The workers attempted to align their design strategy with the strategic company practice, as they viewed it. They saw the peer-tutoring system for Cobot collaboration as a co-design and co-evaluation strategic practice. Co-design among workers could be used to tackle issues in the manufacturing as 'help videos' [Worker Bi] that could be constructed by" recording order-specific ideas for how-to, so next time this order comes in, the video shows what to do" [Worker Bi]. These worker-videos could furthermore help dyslexic colleagues who could watch on the video how to do things, rather than read. The worker-videos could potentially help company ABC in the long run to improve its manufacturing. The co-design not only involved using the peer-tutoring system for Cobot collaboration to design ways of collaborating with and around the Cobot. However, it also included the discussion among workers and with consultants about incidents and experiences from using the peer-tutoring system to make it more relevant to the glass processing work domain, generate additional insight and redesign suggestions beyond the simple use of the Cobot, and in general generate innovation around the manufacturing practices. The main benefit of the codesign of the worker-videos with the peer-tutoring system was the access these provided, to both the specialized workers work-domain knowledge and to their experiences as users of the Cobot. Thus, the co-design in the view of the workers provided a concrete way to evaluate the alignment of socio-technical design strategy with organizational strategy.

In summary, what went well and what could have been done better when working with relation artefacts Type IV are shown in Table 8.5.

Theories and methods revisited

Obviously, consultancy in design case 2 was an exploratory activity that was inspired by ideas from the larger regional project and the higher education partners involved in that. The open questions were thus: What constitutes a practice of using collaborative robot as assistive technologies on the shop floor? How can'digital peer-tutoring' enter that practice as part of the collaborative robot assistive technology? Which digital peer-tutoring learning format can enable shop floor workers to design improved collaboration and positive UXs for themselves and their colleagues?

What constitutes a practice of using collaborative robot as assistive technologies on the shop floor? When comparing our insights from design case 2 with the literature on digitalization in SMEs and peer-tutoring we found that:

Table 8.5 Relation artefacts Type IV learnings

Relation artefact Type IV	What went well	What could be done better
Interaction interoperability check-ups	The peer-tutoring for Cobot collaboration increased integration between machines and operations within the factory ecosystem	UX interoperability challenges remained, including privacy, (e.g., sharing of videos); appropriation (e.g., integration of peer-tutoring videos into workflows); customization (e.g., customizing peer-tutoring videos work with company ABC's networks and protocols), and more
Digital legacy interventions	By producing how-to videos for knowledge sharing within the company the workers came in charge of their own digital legacy (some of it)	The prototype video was too far away from the workers' usual ways of doing things with machines
Organizational strategy alignments	Workers saw the peer-tutoring system for Cobot collaboration as a co-design and co-evaluation strategic practice	The 'design culture' of the organization was limited by lack of resources

- The collaborative robot requires specialized knowledge in workers, thus reduces flexibility in its application, see also e.g., (Kragic et al., 2017; Materna et al., 2017; Schulz, 2017)
- The collaborative robot imposes its limitations and rhythm onto the workflow, see also e.g., (Sanchez-Tamayo & Wachs, 2018; Sergeeva & Huysman, 2015; Tan & Inamura, 2013; Vom Brocke et al., n.d.)
- The collaborative robot may block a worker from interacting with it, see also e.g., (Christiernin, 2017; Elprama et al., 2017; Görür et al., 2018; Materna et al., 2017; Maurtua et al., 2017; Stenmark et al., 2017)

Overall, the company's purchase of the Cobot was motivated by a wish to explore the potential of the technology. The workers interviewed were willing (eager) to expand the use of the Cobot.

How can'digital peer-tutoring' enter that practice as part of the collaborative robot assistive technology? Company owners, management, and workers had unexpected ideas about how to use the peer-tutoring videos within and outside the company, in for example internal quality control and customer communication. Thus, similar to the point made about peer-tutoring (Schleyer et al., 2005), we should acknowledge the role of Digital Peer-Tutoring in developing problem solving skills at various organizational levels. Based on the categories proposed in (Vistisen et al., 2016), we furthermore observe that the ethical stance built into the 'Digital Peer-Tutoring' learning format can be characterized as'apathetic', when too long and complex instructional videos, intended to teach workers' design thinking and enabling their own video-production, tend to make workers give up. However, the learning format also showed to be'empathetic', as workers produced their own videos and evaluated solutions together, effectively co-designing work procedures.

Which digital peer-tutoring learning format can enable shop floor workers to design improved collaboration and positive UXs for themselves and their colleagues? We conclude that our proposed Digital Peer-Tutoring learning format enabled shop floor workers to design positive UXs for themselves and their colleagues, and beyond ways that we expected. The participating shop floor workers stated in various ways that they liked the Digital Peer-tutoring how-to videos and found them useful. This corresponds to the claim made by Twidale (2005) that it is possible to use peer-tutoring to give informal technical help between colleagues, and with Ørngreen et al. (2017) who suggest to link various sketching techniques and creative reflection processes to video productions. The videos helped workers create ideas about robot use, identify problems not formulated before, sketch alternatives, test solutions, and demonstrate them to colleagues.

Reflection: Benefits and challenges of using the HWID platform

In design case 2, we applied a socio-technical design approach to apply and further develop the Digital Peer-Tutoring learning format to improve workers' capability to create and share solutions to human–robot collaboration challenges in SMEs. Thereby we also answer the call for research into how SMEs can adopt and implement new technologies that build upon and enhance worker capabilities, skills, and knowledge (Hannola et al., 2018; Ludwig et al., 2018). The benefits of using the HWID platform in design case 2 included contextual grounding of the consultancy, rich analysis of the heterogenous data collected, socio-technical view on the designed peer-tutoring technology solutions, and reflection and learning together with management and workers and other stakeholders. The challenges of using the HWID platform in design case 2 include that it was not clear to all stakeholders from the onset of the project that (any) specific design approach was to be used, and hence it is very well possible that different stakeholders saw different approaches being unfolded. Within the larger regional project, for example, some partners promoted an action learning approach at the same time as design case 2 was done. Furthermore, the consultants and other stakeholders in design case 2 did not explicitly sit down to decide on any specific approach. So, it could be argued that in design case 2 challenges of using the HWID platform included that it was backgrounded, and it co-existed with other potentially useful design and learning approaches.

8.7   Insights from Design Cases About HWID Consultancy

A general insight from design case 1 and 2 is that socio-technical design approaches in practical consultancy tend to be backgrounded and coexisting with competing or overlapping other approaches.

Secondly, the consultants applying the HWID platform act as relation builders who reflect with relation artefacts together with participants and other stakeholders.

Third, socio-technical design approaches such as HWID may perceived by companies (often SMEs) and employees as outsiders' agenda and less their own. However, the design cases also showed that negotiating the context was an important design decision that consultants could and should handle continuously during the project.

Design case insights across socio-technical design approaches

The approach to building new digital competences with digital peer-tutoring in manufacturing SMEs built on the HWID platform but was also inspired by the socio-technical design approach called 'action design research' (ADR). ADR argues that IT artefacts are 'ensembles' formed by the organizational context during development and use. ADR thus interweaves constructing the IT artefact, intervention in the organization, and evaluating outcomes (Sein, Henfridsson, Purao, Rossi, & Lindgren, 2011), which could potentially be useful for the consultancy done in the case. Hence below we compare briefly design case insights across ADR and HWID.

Guided emergence versus design of sociomaterial solutions

In action design research (Sein et al., 2011), stage 3 analysis is about reflection and learning and an important principle is that of 'Guided Emergence' that says that the artefact emerges from interaction with the organizational context. Somewhat similarly, HWID aim to design sociomaterial solutions. The solutions the HWID consultants pursue are anchored in existing technical solutions and social arrangements and that they are objectified, that is, made fact-like, by developing socio-technical relation artefacts. These include problem definitions, need identifications, personas, workplace interaction patterns, collaborative sketches, converged workflows, and more. This results in solutions that are felt as matters-of-the-fact and natural parts of stakeholders' everyday life, and thus deeply embedded and implemented in their workday.

Moreover, HWID consultants apply a social relativistic type of participatory design, which involves a variety of innovative evaluation methods that involves companies and employees. For examples, 'innovation contests' with digital nudging on rater platforms (Santiago Walser et al., 2019) may be used to decide between the expected multitude of ideas for solutions, and 'design-in-use' (Hertzum, 2021) will be applied to test out tools and platforms in everyday life conditions involving project partners and other relevant stakeholders.

In the design cases 1 and 2 above, the transition from the existing toward something new was in focus. In design case 1 the socio-technical design approach helped consultants to deliver a ready-to-use service to a client company that potentially could upgrade unskilled workers with a focus on human–robot collaboration and the related social arrangements among workers. In design case 2 the socio-technical design approach helped to apply and further develop a learning format that improved workers' capability to create and share solutions to human–robot collaboration challenges in SMEs, thus designing new sociomaterial solutions that enhance worker capabilities, skills, and knowledge and engaged with management's visions and ideas.

It is a topic for future research into consultants' practices to compare action design research (ADR)'s principle of 'guided emergence' of artefacts with HWID's principle of 'designing sociomaterial solutions'. From the two design cases discussed here, it shows that in some cases (design case 1) the 'guidance' is much stronger than in design case 2, while the solutions developed in both design cases are anchored in the existing and objectified as 'natural' outcomes; this points to that 'guided emergence' applies mostly in specific conditions while the 'design of sociomaterial solutions' is more generic for socio-technical design approaches.

Generalized outcomes versus user experiences at work

ADR ends with stage 4 analysis which is the 'formalization of learning' and which builds on a principle of generalized outcomes. In contrast, HWID for consultancy does not have any requirement of formalized learning when it is used to do 'pure' consultancy but relies much on the learning implicitly build into the relation arte-facts and ending with a new sociomaterial solution that though being a change is experienced as in line with company's and employees' values and practices, that is, as good user experiences at work.

From design cases 1 and 2, two different generalized outcomes could be iden-tified. In design case 1, the generalized outcome was a concept for peer-tutoring supported by unionized workers (which was rejected by the company management). In design case 1, the UX-at-work had to do with workers feeling skilled and well paid and wanting to keep status quo in social arrangements. In design case 2, the generalized outcome was a concept for peer-tutoring appropriated by management (with the active support of the company's employees, who were not unionized). In design case 2, the UX-at-work pointed toward workers experiencing the (novel) peer-tutoring videos as a part of their workday, and management experiencing the videos as embedded in the company's structure and practices (either as app-in-a-box or a cloud-based app).

ADR with its principle of generalized outcomes focus strongly on formulating outcomes. Thus, the design knowledge created in the project could be:

- The degree of interaction and collaboration with robots and automation are design elements also for the individual employee (job crafting)
- Peer-tutoring in design thinking for interaction and collaboration with robots and automation can—with much facilitator help—be used for job crafting and in the long run for knowledge sharing

However, in HWID, this knowledge should be not formulated, but experienced (by workers, management, and consultants and other stakeholders). This marks a difference between ADR and HWID that calls for future research.

Methodological considerations

From the design cases 1 and 2 methodological questions for socio-technical HCI design consultancy can be raised. These concerns the socio-technical design approaches ability to deal with:

- Trade unions versus management perspectives. The trade union versus manage-ment dimension is at the core of socio-technical design in the Scandinavian

Fig. 8.19 Scatter chart of socio-technical design approaches

tradition (Bjørn-Andersen & Clemmensen, 2017). The socio-technical design approaches differ in how they approach this contrast, with some being more on the management side, and others more on the unionized workers' side. ADR, HWID, and other socio-technical approaches[7] appear all to aim to identify organizational problems. What makes HWID stand out is the explicit focus on workers' interaction with technical devices. HWID is flexible and can be used with a focus on one or the other or, as shown in Fig. 18.19, with an impossible perfect balance between capturing organizational problems and worker needs.

- Authoritative knowledge versus participants' knowledge. This dimension indicates that socio-technical design approaches to varying degrees fixate what the users of the approach should do (epistemology) and what is the assumed knowledge (ontology). For example, experience design builds on an ontology of basic psychological needs and a programmatic sociodeterminism (experience before the design), ADR has four epistemic stages that should be followed and two choices of ontology (mostly organizational, or mostly technical), while HWID is context-driven both for ontology (build the knowledge that you need) and epistemology (do what participants can), see Fig. 18.19.

A third methodological consideration for socio-technical design approaches that emerges from design case 1 and 2 is that of applying the approaches for consultancy of several companies vs single companies in the same analysis. This can be either in parallel or sequential. In both scenarios the issue of comparison across cases come up. In practice-based design (PBD) and HWID such cross case design comparisons on the data level are an in-built part of the methodology, while in other approaches the primary matching of design cases happens on the theory (e.g., experience design) and perspective levels (e.g., ADR).

---

[7] A good example of socio-technical design with a focus on organisational practices is the imbrication approach (Leonardi, 2011).

About HWID consultants

What do you need to know?

What do you need to know to be a socio-technical HCI design consultant? For HWID, this is easily answered. First, you need to know the basics of design thinking and some more advanced stuff about co-design. Second, the socio-technical tradition should be present, both the practical version by Mumford and the more recent socio-technical design approaches presented here. Third, the interaction design techniques and design principles should be familiar and work analysis techniques of task and work domain analysis and ethnographic work analysis.

How to use HWID relation artefacts applications

HWID relation artefact applications (HWID apps) are preprogrammed relation arte-facts that support the socio-technical HCI design approach and thus acts as inter-ventions in socio-technical HCI design projects. This chapter presented the digital peer-tutoring app that is an example of a HWID app. Similar HWID apps, when and if they come available, can be used in three different ways:

1. As a rigid sequence. The app may have built-in a rigid sequence of actions, for example based on the relation artefacts 1–4, which must be slavishly followed. This is an advantage if there is a need to reduce mental workload, either for novice consultants or consultants in much time pressure.
2. As a flexible tool. The app can be used partly, to automate design sequences that the consultant does prefer not to do in this project or simply do not like to do at all. Examples may include any of the relation artefacts and their subtypes. For example, the app may have built-in four common persona for manufacturing factories, and the consultant suggests the participants to select one or more of these, instead of eliciting data and building their own personas.
3. As a critical reflection. The app may enable reflection by asking questions to context, or by having options for load various theoretical and methodological assumptions.

The intervention that is described in the design cases 1 and 2 is supporting socio-technical HCI designs though workers job crafting and managements job carving with the peer-tutoring process and app. The question of if and how the consultant and the stakeholders will use HWID app concerns the facilitation of a balance between the various stakeholders in a project.

Ethics

Ensuring ethical value exchange is moving to the forefront of the global challenges that socio-technical HCI will have to address in the coming years (Jose Abdelnour-Nocera & Clemmensen, 2018). What kind of ethical stance is implied by the use of socio-technical design interventions such as the peer-tutoring app? In design case 2, we noticed that the ethical stance built into the 'Digital Peer-Tutoring' was expe-rience by workers as 'apathetic' because of the too long and complex instructional videos, intended to teach workers' design thinking and enabling their own video-production, tended to make workers give up. On the other hand, the peer-tutoring was also'empathetic', as workers produced their own videos and evaluated solutions together, effectively co-designing work procedures. These considerations were based on the categories proposed in (Vistisen et al., 2016).

An ethical stance in socio-technical design consultancy is that all stakeholders should be included in the design process, users have the ability to shape their work roles, task, and the technology offers users aa sense of ownership and control (Stahl, 2007). The aim of socio-technical design theory is to improve life toward the ideal of liberal democracy using information and communication technology (Stahl, 2007). HWID shares in principle this stance and aim. However, in HWID the ethical stance is limited, narrow, and yet of great importance and implications—it is that technology is never viewed as only technical, but always also social. Thus, the wished-for-future of design in HWID is technologies that has social and human qualities built in. Furthermore, this means that HWID does not black box technology, which general socio-technical design theory in Mumford's tradition tends to do (Stahl, 2007). Rather, in HWID technology's technical and social sides are both topics for change.

The HWID focus on technologies as something that has social and human quali-ties built in raises questions as to which qualities. A well-known problem in socio-technical design is that workers (employees, users) do not necessarily want richer or better technologies, or they want technologies that are known (by others) to be bad for the workers in the long run (limits their freedom, has negative impact on their well-being, etc.). While today's interaction design approaches offer plenty of possibility for nudging and directing users toward specific behaviors, and the consul-tant may be well versed in facilitating change with design, there is perhaps a real lack of knowledge about the social and human aspects of technologies. Since HWID consultants thus are left somewhat blinded regarding what qualities in human work should be designed, the HWID platform approach should allow multiple stakeholders including societal level stakeholders such as employer organizations, trade unions, and political organizations to participate in the design.

References

Abdelnour-Nocera, J., & Clemmensen, T. (2018). Socio-technical HCI for ethical value exchange. In *Lecture notes in computer science (including subseries Lecture Notes in Artificial Intelligence and Lecture Notes in Bioinformatics)*.https://doi.org/10.1007/978-3-319-92081-8_15.

Abdelnour-Nocera, J., & Clemmensen, T. (2019). Theorizing about socio-technical approaches to HCI. In B. R. Barricelli, V. Roto, T. Clemmensen, P. Campos, A. Lopes, F. Gonçalves, & J. Abdelnour-Nocera (Eds.), *Human work interaction design. designing engaging automation* (pp. 242–262). Cham: Springer International Publishing.

Alon, L., & Nachmias, R. (2020). Anxious and frustrated but still competent: Affective aspects of interactions with personal information management. *International Journal of Human-Computer Studies, 144*, 102503.

Appelbaum, S. H. (1997). Socio-technical systems theory: An intervention strategy for organizational development. *Management Decision, 35*(6), 452–463. https://doi.org/10.1108/002517497 10173823.

Bangor, A., Kortum, P., & Miller, J. (2009). Determining what individual SUS scores mean: Adding an adjective rating scale. *Journal of Usability Studies, 4*(3), 114–123.

Baxter, G., & Sommerville, I. (2011). Socio-technical systems: From design methods to systems engineering. *Interacting with Computers, 23*(1), 4–17.

Bjørn-Andersen, N., & Clemmensen, T. (2017). The shaping of the Scandinavian Socio-Technical IS research tradition: Confessions of an accomplice. *Scandinavian Journal of Information Systems, 29*(1).

Bostrom, R. P., & Heinen, J. S. (1977). MIS problems and failures: A socio-technical perspective, part II: The application of socio-technical theory. *MIS Quarterly*, 11–28.

Boyer, L. (2004). The robot in the kitchen: The cultural politics of care-work and the development of in-home assistive technology. *The Middle-States Geographer, 37*, 72–79.

Brach, M., & Korn, O. (2012). *Assistive technologies at home and in the workplace—a field of research for exercise science and human movement science.* European Review of Aging and Physical Activity, *9*, 1–4 (2012). https://doi.org/10.1007/s11556-012-0099-z.

Cajander, Å., Larusdottir, M., Eriksson, E., & Nauwerck, G. (2015). Contextual personas as a method for understanding digital work environments. *IFIP Advances in Information and Communication Technology, 468*, 141–152. https://doi.org/10.1007/978-3-319-27048-7_10.

Carayon, P., Hancock, P., Leveson, N., Noy, I., Sznelwar, L., & Van Hootegem, G. (2015). Advancing a sociotechnical systems approach to workplace safety–developing the conceptual framework. *Ergonomics, 58*(4), 548–564.

Card, S. K., Moran, T. P., & Newell, A. (1983). *The psychology of human-computer interaction. 1983.* Hillsdale, NJ: Lawrence Erlbaum Associates.

Carroll, J. M., & Campbell, R. (1986). Softening up hard science: Reply to Newell and card. *Human-Computer Interaction, 2*(3), 227–249. https://doi.org/10.1207/s15327051hci0203_3.

Cherns, A. (1987). Principles of sociotechnical design revisted. *Human Relations, 40*(3), 153–161. https://doi.org/10.1177/001872678704000303.

Christiernin, L. G. (2017). How to describe interaction with a collaborative robot. In *Proceedings of the Companion of the 2017 ACM/IEEE International Conference on Human-Robot Interaction*, 93–94. https://doi.org/10.1145/3029798.3038325.

Clemmensen, T., Hertzum, M., & Abdelnour-Nocera, J. (2020). Ordinary user experiences at work: A study of greenhouse growers. *ACM Transactions on Computer-Human Interaction (TOCHI), June* (Article no 16), 1–31. https://doi.org/10.1145/3386089.

Davison, R. M., & Bjørn-Andersen, N. (2019). Do we care about the societal impact of our research? The tyranny of the H-index and new value-oriented research directions. *Information Systems Journal, 29*(5), 989–993.

de Vries, L., & Bligård, L.-O. (2019). Visualising safety: The potential for using sociotechnical systems models in prospective safety assessment and design. *Safety Science, 111*, 80–93. https://doi.org/10.1016/j.ssci.2018.09.003.

Draxler, S., & Stevens, G. (2011). Supporting the collaborative appropriation of an open software ecosystem. *Computer Supported Cooperative Work (CSCW), 20*(4–5), 403–448.

El Zaatari, S., Marei, M., Li, W., & Usman, Z. (2019). Cobot programming for collaborative industrial tasks: An overview. *Robotics and Autonomous Systems, 116*, 162–180.

Elprama, S. A., Jewell, C. I. C., Jacobs, A., El Makrini, I., & Vanderborght, B. (2017). Attitudes of factory workers towards industrial and collaborative robots. In *Proceedings of the Companion of the 2017 ACM/IEEE International Conference on Human-Robot Interaction* (pp. 113–114). https://doi.org/10.1145/3029798.3038309.

Friedland, L. (2019). Culture eats UX strategy for breakfast. *Interactions, 26*(5), 78–81.

Galletta, D. F., Bjørn-Andersen, N., Leidner, D. E., Markus, M. L., McLean, E. R., Straub, D., & Wetherbe, J. (2019). If practice makes perfect, where do we stand? *Communications of the Association for Information Systems, 45*(1), 3.

Garrety, K., & Badham, R. (2000). The politics of socio-technical intervention: An interactionist view. *Technology Analysis & Strategic Management, 12*(1), 103–118.

Görür, O., Rosman, B., Sivrikaya, F., & Albayrak, S. (2018). Social cobots: Anticipatory decision-making for collaborative robots incorporating unexpected human behaviors. In *Proceedings of the 2018 ACM/IEEE International Conference on Human-Robot Interaction* (pp. 398–406). ACM.

Gray, W. D., & Salzman, M. C. (1998). Damaged merchandise? A review of experiments that compare usability evaluation methods. *Human-Computer Interaction, 13*(3), 203–261.

Gulotta, R., Odom, W., Forlizzi, J., & Faste, H. (2013). Digital artifacts as legacy: Exploring the lifespan and value of digital data. In *CHI '13*. https://doi.org/10.1145/2470654.2466240.

Hague, A. C., & Benest, I. D. (1996). Towards over-the-shoulder guidance following a traditional learning metaphor. *Computers & Education, 26*(1–3), 61–70.

Hannola, L., Richter, A., Richter, S., & Stocker, A. (2018). Empowering production workers with digitally facilitated knowledge processes–a conceptual framework. *International Journal of Production Research*. https://doi.org/10.1080/00207543.2018.1445877.

Hertzum, M. (2021). Organizational implementation: The design in use of information systems. *Synthesis Lectures on Human-Centered Informatics, 14*(2), i–109.

Hirschheim, R., & Klein, H. K. (1989). Four paradigms of information systems development. *Communications of the ACM, 32*(10), 1199–1216.

Hsu, D. (2016). Robots in harmony with humans. In *Proceedings of the Fourth International Conference on Human Agent Interaction* (p. 1). ACM.

Hughes, H. P. N., Clegg, C. W., Bolton, L. E., & Machon, L. C. (2017). Systems scenarios: A tool for facilitating the socio-technical design of work systems. *Ergonomics, 60*(10), 1319–1335.

Imanghaliyeva, A. A. (2020). A Systematic review of sociotechnical system methods between 1951 and 2019. In T. Ahram, W. Karwowski, A. Vergnano, F. Leali, & R. Taiar (Eds.), *Intelligent human systems integration 2020* (pp. 580–587). Cham: Springer International Publishing.

Inal, Y., Clemmensen, T., Rajanen, D., Iivari, N., Rizvanoglu, K., & Sivaji, A. (2020). Positive developments but challenges still ahead: A survey study on UX professionals' work practices. *Journal of Usability Studies, 15*(4).

Khadka, R., Batlajery, B. V., Saeidi, A. M., Jansen, S., & Hage, J. (2014). How do professionals perceive legacy systems and software modernization? In *Proceedings of the 36th International Conference on Software Engineering-ICSE 2014* (pp. 36–47). https://doi.org/10.1145/2568225.2568318.

Kolko, J. (2010). Abductive thinking and sensemaking: The drivers of design synthesis. *Design Issues, 26*(1), 15–28. https://doi.org/10.1162/desi.2010.26.1.15.

Kolko, J. (2015). Design thinking comes of age. *Harvard Business Review, 93*(9), 66–71. Retrieved from https://hbr.org/2015/09/design-thinking-comes-of-age.

Kragic, D., Gustafson, J., Karaoguz, H., Jensfelt, P., & Krug, R. (2017). *Interactive, Collaborative Robots: Challenges and Opportunities*. Retrieved from https://www.ijcai.org/proceedings/2018/0003.pdf.

Kuzle, A. (2019). Second graders' metacognitive actions in problem solving revealed through action cards. *The Mathematics Educator, 28*(1), 27–60.

Lachner, F., Naegelein, P., Kowalski, R., Spann, M., & Butz, A. (2016). Quantified UX: Towards a common organizational understanding of user experience. In *Proceedings of the 9th Nordic Conference on Human-Computer Interaction-NordiCHI '16* (pp. 56:1–56:10). https://doi.org/10.1145/2971485.2971501.

Leonardi, P. M. (2011). When flexible routines meet flexible technologies: Affordance, constraint, and the imbrication of human and material agencies. *MIS Quarterly*, 147–167.

Ludwig, T., Kotthaus, C., Stein, M., Pipek, V., & Wulf, V. (2018). Revive old discussions! Socio-technical challenges for small and medium enterprises within industry 4.0. *Proceedings of 16th European Conference on Computer-Supported Cooperative Work*. https://doi.org/10.18420/ecs cw2018_15.

Lukyanenko, R., & Parsons, J. (2020). Design theory indeterminacy: What is it, how can it be reduced, and why did the polar bear drown? *Journal of the Association for Information Systems, 21*(5), 1.

Magin, D. J., & Churches, A. E. (1995). Peer tutoring in engineering design: A case study. *Studies in Higher Education, 20*(1), 73–85.

Martinez, J., Harris, C., Jalali, C., Tung, J., & Meyer, R. (2015). Using peer-assisted learning to teach and evaluate residents' musculoskeletal skills. *Medical Education Online, 20*(1), 27255.

Materna, Z., Kapinus, M., Beran, V., Smrž, P., Giuliani, M., Mirnig, N., … Tscheligi, M. (2017). Using persona, scenario, and use case to develop a human-robot augmented reality collaborative workspace. In *Proceedings of the Companion of the 2017 ACM/IEEE International Conference on Human-Robot Interaction* (pp. 201–202). ACM.

Maurice, P., Allienne, L., Malaisé, A., & Ivaldi, S. (2018). Ethical and social considerations for the introduction of human-centered technologies at work. In *2018 IEEE Workshop on Advanced Robotics and Its Social Impacts (ARSO)* (pp. 131–138). IEEE.

Maurtua, I., Ibarguren, A., Kildal, J., Susperregi, L., & Sierra, B. (2017). Human–robot collaboration in industrial applications: Safety, interaction and trust. *International Journal of Advanced Robotic Systems, 14*(4), 1729881417716010.

Michaelis, J. E., Siebert-Evenstone, A., Shaffer, D. W., & Mutlu, B. (2020). Collaborative or simply uncaged? understanding human-cobot interactions in automation. In *Proceedings of the 2020 CHI Conference on Human Factors in Computing Systems* (pp. 1–12).

Mucha, H., Büttner, S., & Röcker, C. (2016). Application areas for human-centered assistive systems. In *Human-Computer Interaction–Perspectives on Industry 4.0. Workshop at i-KNOW 2016 Graz, Austria, Oct 2016.*

Mumford, E. (1994). New treatments or old remedies: Is business process reengineering really socio-technical design? *The Journal of Strategic Information Systems, 3*(4), 313–326.

Mumford, E. (2000). A socio-technical approach to systems design. *Requirements Engineering, 5*(2), 125–133.

Mumford, E. (2006). The story of socio-technical design: Reflections on its successes, failures and potential. *Information Systems Journal, 16*(4), 317–342. https://doi.org/10.1111/j.1365-2575. 2006.00221.x.

Murphy-Hill, E., Murphy, G. C., & McGrenere, J. (2015). How do users discover new tools in software development and beyond? *Computer Supported Cooperative Work (CSCW), 24*(5), 389–422.

Norman, D. (2013). *The design of everyday things: Revised and expanded edition*. Basic books.

Olphert, W., & Damodaran, L. (2007). Citizen participation and engagement in the design of e-government services: The missing link in effective ICT design and delivery. *Journal of the Association for Information Systems, 8*(9), 27.

Ørngreen, R., Henningsen, B., Gundersen, P., & Hautopp, H. (2017). The learning potential of video sketching. In *Proceedings of the 16th European Conference on Elearning ISCAP Porto, Portugal 26–27 October 2017* (pp. 422–430).

Pasmore, W., Francis, C., Haldeman, J., & Shani, A. (1982). Sociotechnical systems: A North American reflection on empirical studies of the seventies. *Human Relations, 35*(12), 1179–1204.

Rajanen, M., & Rajanen, D. (2020). Usability as speculum mundi: A core concept in socio-technical systems development. *Complex Systems Informatics and Modeling Quarterly, 22*, 49–59.

Randall, D., Dachtera, J., Dyrks, T., Nett, B., Pipek, V., Ramirez, L., … Wulf, V. (2018). Research into design research practices: Supporting an agenda towards self-reflectivity and transferability. In V. Wulf, V. Pipek, D. Randall, M. Rohde, K. Schmidt, & G. Stevens (Eds.), *Socio informatics—a practice-based perspective on the design and use of IT artefacts* (pp. 491–540). Oxford: Oxford University Press.

Sanchez-Tamayo, N., & Wachs, J. P. (2018). Collaborative robots in surgical research: A low-cost adaptation. In *Companion of the 2018 ACM/IEEE international conference on human-robot interaction* (pp. 231–232). ACM.

Santiago Walser, R., Seeber, I., & Maier, R. (2019). Designing a digital nudge for convergence: The role of decomposition of information load for decision making and choice accuracy. *AIS Transactions on Human-Computer Interaction, 11*(3), 179–207.

Sarker, S., Chatterjee, S., & Xiao, X. (2013). *How "sociotechnical" is our IS research? An assessment and possible ways forward.*

Sarker, S., Chatterjee, S., Xiao, X., & Elbanna, A. (2019). The sociotechnical axis of cohesion for the is discipline: Its historical legacy and its continued relevance. *Mis Quarterly, 43*(3), 695–719.

Savage, P. E. (1972). Disaster planning: The use of action cards. *British Medical Journal, 3*(5817), 42.

Schleyer, G. K., Langdon, G. S., & James, S. (2005). Peer tutoring in conceptual design. *European Journal of Engineering Education, 30*(2), 245–254.

Schmidtler, J., Knott, V., Hölzel, C., & Bengler, K. (2015). Human centered assistance applications for the working environment of the future. *Occupational Ergonomics, 12*(3), 83–95.

Schon, D. A. (1984). *The reflective practitioner: How professionals think in action* (Vol. 5126). Basic Books.

Schulz, R. (2017). Collaborative robots learning spatial language for picking and placing objects on a table. In *Proceedings of the 5th International Conference on Human Agent Interaction* (pp. 329–333). ACM.

Scott, W. H., Mumford, E., McGivering, 'I. C., & Kirby, J. M. (1963). *Coal and conflict: A study of industrial relations at collieries.* Liverpool University Press.

Secomb, J. (2008). A systematic review of peer teaching and learning in clinical education. *Journal of Clinical Nursing, 17*(6), 703–716.

Sein, M. K., Henfridsson, O., Purao, S., Rossi, M., & Lindgren, R. (2011). Action design research. *MIS Quarterly.* https://doi.org/10.2307/23043488.

Selbst, A. D., Boyd, D., Friedler, S. A., Venkatasubramanian, S., & Vertesi, J. (2019). Fairness and abstraction in sociotechnical systems. In *Proceedings of the Conference on Fairness, Accountability, and Transparency* (pp. 59–68).

Sergeeva, A., & Huysman, M. (2015). *Transforming work practices of operating room teams: The case of the Da Vinci robot Research-in-Progress.* Retrieved from https://aisel.aisnet.org/cgi/viewcontent.cgi?article=1543&context=icis2015.

Stahl, B. C. (2007). ETHICS, morality and critique: An essay on Enid Mumford¡⁻s socio-technical approach. *Journal of the Association for Information Systems, 8*(9), 28.

Stenmark, M., Haage, M., & Topp, E. A. (2017). *Simplified programming of re-usable skills on a safe industrial robot-prototype and evaluation.*https://doi.org/10.1145/2909824.3020227.

Tan, J. T. C., & Inamura, T. (2013). Integration of work sequence and embodied interaction for collaborative work based human-robot interaction. In *Proceedings of the 8th ACM/IEEE International Conference on Human-Robot Interaction*, 239–240. Retrieved from http://dl.acm.org/citation.cfm?id=2447556.2447656.

Tohidi, M., Buxton, W., Baecker, R., & Sellen, A. (2006). Getting the right design and the design right. In *Proceedings of the SIGCHI Conference on Human Factors in Computing Systems* (pp. 1243–1252).

Truffer, B., Schippl, J., & Fleischer, T. (2017). Decentering technology in technology assessment: Prospects for socio-technical transitions in electric mobility in Germany. *Technological Forecasting and Social Change, 122*, 34–48. https://doi.org/10.1016/j.techfore.2017.04.020.

Twidale, M. B. (2005). Over the shoulder learning: Supporting brief informal learning. *Computer Supported Cooperative Work (CSCW), 14*(6), 505–547.

Vistisen, P., Jensen, T., & Poulsen, S. B. . (2016). Animating the ethical demand: Exploring user dispositions in industry innovation cases through animation-based sketching. *ACM SIGCAS Computers and Society, 45*(3), 318–325.

Vom Brocke, J., Maaß, W., Buxmann, P., Maedche, A., Leimeister, J. M., & Nter Pecht, G. (n.d.). *Future work and enterprise systems.* https://doi.org/10.1007/s12599-018-0544-2.

Wilson, J., & Clarke, D. (2004). Towards the modelling of mathematical metacognition. *Mathematics Education Research Journal, 16*(2), 25–48.

Wolfartsberger, J., Haslwanter, J. D. H., Froschauer, R., Lindorfer, R., Jungwirth, M., & Wahlmüller, D. (2018). Industrial perspectives on assistive systems for manual assembly tasks. In *Proceedings of the 11th PErvasive Technologies Related to Assistive Environments Conference* (pp. 289–291). ACM.

Chapter 9
HWID Policymaking

Abstract This chapter provides policymakers with a HWID platform for regulating socio-technical HCI phenomena and issues. After a brief introduction to HCI and policymaking, the chapter presents policy work done on the HWID platform about sustainable digital work design. The HWID relation artefact Types I–IV are revisited from a policy perspective, and policymaking is discussed related to socio-technical HCI design for digital work environments, well-being at work, a notion of decent work, and more. The chapter ends with a brief discussion of geopolitical issues and reflections on benefits and challenges of HWID and policymaking.

Keywords Human work interaction design · HWID policymaking · Decent work · Geopolitical HCI

9.1 Introduction: Emancipatory Socio-Technical HCI

In a sense, policy is what decides the endgame of socio-technical HCL, the ideal state of society, that better life that is the aim with design of IT solutions. Since the beginning of HCI, discussions of democracy have been around (e.g., (Bødker et al., 2000), see also Bjørn-Andersen and Clemmensen (2017)). It may even be fair to say that the key notion of usability aims to support the citizens of a democratic society. Obviously, exactly how HCI should do this remains open for discussion. HCI has several roots deep in military needs from the world wars of the twentieth century (Shackel, 1997). It was also born out of the socio-technical traditions with its emancipatory ambitions, that is, creating conditions for human workers, managers, etc. that facilitate the realization of their needs and potential (Hirschheim & Klein, 1994; Klein, 2014). How to reconcile such diverse ideas as military power and emancipatory ambitions within socio-technical HCI research?

Government funding for HCI is supposed to support the (ideal) society that its citizens are living in. Very little systematic knowledge has been published about funding for HCI research that can shed light on this issue. Lazar et al. (2012) found that HCI research is funded on the periphery or between other lines of research, such as a peripheral part of software engineering research or between technical and social science programs, or considered a (weak) late-stage societal impact type of research. More recently, the research program for EU has taken up the key vocabulary of 'human-centeredness' as the term occurs many times in a large part of the calls in the digital clusters of the program (see EU commission website for Horizon Europe). However, a closer analysis of the EU research programs will reveal that the concepts or methods from HCI are mostly not there (yet) to follow up on the human-centeredness.

Acknowledging that the meaning of emancipatory socio-technical HCI depends on our ideas about the ideal society, models of democracy, and participation becomes important. Nelimarkka et al. (2019) did a review of studies of HCI and policy, which they began by recapping basic models of democracy found in the literature. Their models of democracy included a deliberative democracy, which is a system of governance that uses arguments in discussions until consensus is reached (Denmark may be an example); a Marxist system of governance that sees decision-making on policy as related to the economic system (China may be an example); and a cosmopolitan democracy[1] system of governance that highlights citizens', no matter their geographical location, rights to political participation in global affairs (UN may be an example). For socio-technical HCI design approaches such as HWID, the government system in its wider societal context is thus both a context for design and the ultimate end goal of the design activities. HWID is both shaped by and may contribute to design of Marxist, deliberate, and cosmopolitan systems of governance. Policymakers and researchers may therefore benefit from knowing about and considering socio-technical HCI approaches such as HWID when they study and perform "democracy".

Scholars of democracy in political science are well aware that key phenomena in their field can be explained with competing formalisms (Nelimarkka, 2019), like the situation is with culture in anthropology, psyche in psychology, gravity in physics, and so on. Hence, real expertise in HWID policymaking means knowing about several ways of thinking about democracy, public policy, and HWID.

9.2   The HWID Context of Public Policy

Designing user interfaces to technology is a political act (Lazar et al., 2005)

This political nature of HCI can be spelled out in many ways. It is amazing that the early work about usability and in public sector in Europe (Catarci, Matarazzo, & Raiss, 2000, 2002) and USA (Lazar et al., 2005) has not been cited much in HCI. Public policy is a broad term that includes both government policy and policy within non-governmental organizations, such as standards bodies. In fact, of the more than 800 papers citing "public policy" and HCI in ACM digital library, over 600 have been published after 2010. A framework for HCI and public policy research has recently

---

[1] See also Marchetti (2011).

been presented (Lazar et al., 2016). HCI and policy have, in other words, recently become a widely discussed research topic. It also has many meanings, see Fig. 9.1. We introduce a few of these meaning in the following. First, public policymaking may require evidence from HCI research. Second, public policy may directly decide if HCI is to live or die as a research field. Third, public policy may, by setting standards, increase the ethical quality of HCI research.

Public policymaking may require evidence from HCI research. There are three challenges for HCI researchers who want to provide evidence for policymaking: bringing together HCI's knowledge for policy, applying future making practices from HCI in policymaking, and building HCI advocacy and HCI communities around policy, as indicated in a qualitative study of the boundaries between HCI research and evidence-based policymaking (Spaa, Durrant, Elsden, & Vines, 2019). Thus, increasing participatory design by consultation and developing methods to engage users such as citizens is only a small part of an overall policymaking process (Manuel & Crivellaro, 2020). Policymakers and HCI researchers should instead focus on using HCI to support, innovate, and (re)design the full sequence of policymaking processes in specific contexts, such as urban planning (Manuel & Crivellaro, 2020).

Public policy may directly decide if HCI is to live or die as a research field. In Brazil, a change in public policy about university evaluations led to lower rankings of HCI researchers (Junqueira Barbosa & de Souza, 2011). The mechanism was a design of a citation index to allow conference publications to count as end outlets for research, but which had a design that disfavored much of what characterizes an emerging HCI research community: younger research areas, emerging lines of research, innovative research topics, and localized research to address regional issues (Junqueira Barbosa & de Souza, 2011). The HCI researchers in Brazil obviously self-reflected and the community since grew in impact.

Public policy may, by setting standards, increase the ethical quality of HCI research. In each country, government may determine that HCI research involves human subjects in the same way that medical science involves human subjects. This is different from the view of humans as co-designers, partners, participants in participatory design, etc. (Lazar et al., 2012), so guidelines for ethical conduct of HCI research needs to evolve. In EU, GDRP (General Data Protection Regulation) regulations[2] require HCI researchers to inform research participants what will happen to their personal data in the research. GDPR also requires the organizations processing the data (e.g., universities, but also research service providers) to ensure the data are properly protected, minimized, and destroyed when no longer needed. 'Data management' practices is another emerging area for which governments in EU set out training of researchers.[3] In addition, 'open science' is receiving increasing interest within HCI (Chuang & Pfeil, 2018). However, these regulations and practices differ across the world, and HCI researchers should be sensitive to local rules and cultural norms that might influence ethics reviews, etc. (Lazar et al., 2016).

---

[2] https://ec.europa.eu/info/sites/info/files/5._h2020_ethics_and_data_protection_0.pdf.

[3] Data Management Expert Guide—CESSDA TRAINING.

> ▶ Understanding the relationships between UX and public policy is important to forming our democracies in times of digitalization, and to evidence-based approaches to governance, and setting the priorities of policy goals (e.g., safety, freedom)
>
> ▶ UX in public policy:
>
>> ▶ Statutory laws such as local, provincial, and national regulations, executive orders, administrative decrees, more.
>>
>> ▶ Bilateral, multinational, regional, and international agreements on trade issues such as General Agreement on Tariffs and Trade [GATT], General Agreement on Trade in Services [GATS], and the Agreement on Traderelated Aspects of Intellectual Property Protection [TRIPs]
>>
>> ▶ Human rights such as United Nations Convention on the Rights of Persons with Disabilities [CRPD]
>>
>> ▶ International technical standards such as International Organization for Standardization [ISO] and World Wide Web Consortium [W3C])
>
> ▶ Example: HCI-related public policies in Denmark and EU? Does 'usability' or 'user experience' occur in these documents?
>
>> ▶ Denmarks   'Digital   Strategy   2016-2020', https://en.digst.dk/media/14143/ds_singlepage_uk_web.pdf
>>
>> ▶ EU's   digital   strategy,   https://ec.europa.eu/digital-single-market/en/content/european-digital-strategy

Fig. 9.1 Fact-box about HCI and public policy

Generally, public policymaking such as digital strategies for countries and organizations may benefit from and also influence socio-technical HCI research. This can, for example, be when the public sector use UX and digital agencies to extend online services and advisory content (Blaynee, Kreps, Kutar, & Griffiths, 2016). The design of digital tools and environments for public services and for participation in public policy are overlapping areas, which may increase in importance in the coming years. Socio-technical HCI such as HWID can be one vehicle to the digital transformation in public policy. Below we give examples of HWID policymaking with different types of HWID relation artefacts.

9.3   Relation Artefacts Type I: Needs and Problems

Policymaking with HWID relation artefacts Type I may begin with conceptualizing the workforce to define organizational problems, then identify class consciousness to find worker needs, and end up discussing worker identity as part of creating personas for design.

Conceptualizing the workforce—organizational problem definition

HWID for policymaking and policy processes may begin with helping societies and organizations to understand the workforce. There are big changes underway both in terms of understanding who the workers will be and how to support them. The 4th industrial revolution presents social, economic, and organizational changes toward income inequalities, job quality and scarcity, legal issues and data security problems, but also production efficiencies, cost reductions, novel labor requirements, and business model adaptations.

HWID may help focus on the disruptive social and economic changes that call for the digitalization on labor markets and business models and the application of novel techniques in artificial intelligence, block chain, big data, Internet of Things, 5G, robotization, and more. It can explore innovative methodologies in redefining work activities and automatable tasks also through an historical comparison with previous paradigms, (see, e.g., (Gardien, Djajadiningrat, Hummels, & Brombacher, 2014)). This may include cultural, ethical, and regional perspectives on design, (see, e.g., (Katre, Orngreen, Yammiyavar, & Clemmensen, 2010)), and require combining the technical and engineering perspectives on interaction design with social and humanities perspectives on work and social life. The contextual bars of HWID could include insights of industry leaders (large companies, SMEs, regional ecosystems) and social partners. The outcome may be locally valorized tools for new jobs creation that help conceptualize and measure emerging occupations, and give guidance, recommendation, and training for policymakers, businesses, and individuals.

Plenty of different human dimensions and work analysis may be carried out under the HWID platform when trying to understand the workforce and the work by doing work analysis for HCI (Campos et al., 2013). These dimensions may include job characteristics, skills, productivity, employment, mobility, new forms of work, business value chains, management and organizational models, ethnic, age and gender aspects, workplace and socio-demographic characteristics, and territorial structures. The analysis may identify global, societal, regional, and organizational problems with conceptualizing the emerging workforces, their skills, and what the workforces prefer may be automated and what they do not want to see automated.

The workforce can be conceptualized based on HWID from a technical point of view, such as developing skills taxonomies along lines of technical progress; from a social point of view, such as developing skills taxonomies for social change, new social practices, social ownership or market uptake, social protection (of platform workers, for example); and by combining the social and technical skill taxonomies in management strategies, public–private learning ecosystems, and collaborative learning techniques/tools, and thus contributing to close skill gaps and unemployment spill-overs.

How the conceptualization of the workforce depends on the different government systems in countries and on the international tech companies are well described. In particular, the 4th Industrial Revolution is in the process of energizing a new organization of labor that leaves many digital workers in a precarious position. A key challenge is how trade unions and other workers' organizations find and organize digital workers who 'live in the shadows'. Socio-technical HCI may in collaboration with management and trade unions design tools and experiences for digital workers in precarious positions that can contribute to the local labor markets, reaping the benefits of the new digital forms of work without compromising the local socio-economic government systems (fx the Danish flexicurity system).

Class consciousness—finding workers' objective needs

HWID relies much on the key notions of usability and UX for assessing the quality of the designed sociomaterial solutions. While 'experience design', a key theory of UX, actually builds on the Marxist inspired 'activity theory' from the Soviet Union (Hassenzahl, 2010), the roots therein are not so clear. Hence, the political aspects may need to be worked out when doing socio-technical HCI design for policy. In particular, the notion of 'needs' as a set of basic psychological needs (Hassenzahl et al., 2010) appears on the surface to suggest a liberal ideology of individual needs. A broader view on needs, and closer to 'needs' in activity theory, may however suggest that any human need all the time and everywhere is multiple determined by what is happening on global, societal, organizational, and group levels.

An alternative socio-technical HCI design view of workers' needs can be developed by taking point of departure in an idea of 'class consciousness', which is not simply empirical consciousness, but an 'objective possibility' of consciousness (Fuchs, 2020). That is, it is the thoughts and feelings that workers would have in a given situation if they could assess both it and its effect on their immediate actions and the fabric of society as a whole. Class consciousness is an idea that is usually associated with a Marxist system of governance that sees decision-making on policy as related to the economic system. However, a socio-technical HCI design for class consciousness must today take into account the survival of the planet, and thus also be inspired by cosmopolitan democracy systems of governance that highlights citizens', no matter their geographical location, rights to political participation in global affairs. In addition, the socio-technical HCI design emphasizes facilitation between stakeholders and may thus be inspired by the model of democracy of a deliberative democracy, which is a system of governance that uses arguments in discussions until consensus is reached. Thus, HWID of workers' needs in a policy context may focus on class consciousness understood as caused by a combination of acknowledging objective societal conflicts, planetary survival requirements, and an ambition of reaching human consensus.

False consciousness, alienation, or reification may be a universal process that emerges not just in class relations but in many ways in our global society including those that HWID is for. It means that workers are unaware and cannot express or design for that fact that they live under conditions they cannot control, including that humans' and society's potentials cannot be realized, and that some groups instrumentalize other groups in order to realize their interests. One way that alienation is working is through the taken-technology-for-granted that makes it acceptable to talk about AI, robots, etc. as though they are things and not experiences of the social relations and process of production, which again hides the conflicts in society and the threats to planetary survival (and makes consensus less likely). For HWID this often means that technology appears 'natural' and as a black box that needs to be opened for inspection of the social and technical during co-design. It also means, however, that the black box of technology is closed again by HWID when the process gets closer to sociomaterial solutions (new situations) that are accepted by stakeholders.

It follows then that identification of workers' needs for socio-technical HCI design is a political process. A negotiation on several levels of organizations and society of usability and UX goals will have to be facilitated by HWID designers (for example, UX professionals (Bhutkar et al., 2021)). In socio-technical HCI design for UX-at-work (Bhutkar et al., 2019), the identification of workers' basic psychological needs on the individual levels to be fulfilled by technology use must be complimented by management strategies for which needs to fulfill, and constrained by societal and global policies and regulations for the kind of work tasks to be done.

For example, so-called 'platform workers' tend to be under 35, highly educated, often migrant workers, mostly male (75% and for location-based platforms 90%), with mostly males doing the data analytic and technology-related tasks, and with mostly flexibility in time and location and possibly skills upgrading as motivations (Rani et al., 2021). Obvious platform workers' needs that can be designed for include their need for transparency and accountability of their work (e.g., by a pricing tool), need for collective action (e.g., bargaining, going on strike), and their need for independence (e.g., supported by a trade union hosted platform for pension, sick leave, etc. that enables workers to move from one platform company to another platform company). That may be supported on national, regional, and international levels by regulations that acknowledge that if platform companies are allowed to be regulation-free and operate with low wage and social costs, other companies will start outsourcing major part of their workforce to platform companies.

In summary, how can class consciousness of platform workers be designed? Designing 'user experiences' of class consciousness will make a significant contribution to the ongoing 'ethical turn' within humanistic 'Human–Computer Interaction' and provide new knowledge to the work sociology of the importance of online communities to the digital precariat.

Political aspects of Persona creation

The politics of personas in HCI has turned out to be controversial (Marsden & Haag, 2016), and much related to recent discourses on intersectionality and identity (Marsden & Pröbster, 2019). The topics include special user groups (Moser, Fuchsberger, Neureiter, Sellner, & Tscheligi, 2012), gender (Marsden, Hermann, & Pröbster, 2017), disability (E. J. Edwards, Sum, & Branham, 2020), race (Salminen et al., 2019), and more. For socio-technical HCI design and policy it is of particular interest that the topics for research include designing personas for political consciousness (Wilson et al., 2018).

For socio-technical HCI persona creation in policy contexts, it may be relevant to follow the suggestion by Massanari (2010) to look at the user of design personas in the politics within organizations (Wilson et al., 2018) and focus the design personas on political goals, social values, and personas action-taking capabilities. Wilson et al. thus found that basic psychological needs were less interesting in their empirical work with personas in Croatia and Italy, and they focused instead on their personas' values and aspirations, their relationships with the state/system, family/friends, nature/the environment, and their practical problems/daily life and also the time dimension. All of these dimensions and subdimensions should be seen in relation to the personas' experienced different levels of agency with respect to what they could do to change their situation (if they wanted to) (Wilson et al., 2018). Thus, following these ideas about persona creation for political and social consciousness, socio-technical HCI design may create personas by focusing on the personas' capacities, variation, and tension.

For HWID cultural personas (Nielsen, 2010; Salminen et al., 2017) and contextual personas (Cajander et al., 2015) have been suggested as technical ways to deal with the wider context of persona creations. However, when revisiting the steps for creating contextual personas with an explicit political perspective, it turns out that all three steps are highly political. First, step one, which is the inquiry into the organizational context, requires socio-technical understanding of management perspectives including how they conceptualize their workforce which can be highly conflictual in times of digital platform workers. Step two, the analysis of the current situation with the conceptualization/model of employees at work may be subject to differences in preferences between workers (who like to focus on well-being) and management (who like to focus on performance benchmarks). Third, the evaluation of persona with focus group with users from persona's target group sounds neutral, but obviously depend heavily on which employees participate as users in the workshop, see also (Massanari, 2010). The resulting graphical illustration may, even in cases where the personas have been created for political consciousness, see (Wilson et al., 2018), present with a nice picture of a beautiful persona in a usage scenario of some, but not too much tension, which surely can be solved by the introduction to a novel technology. So, while the contextual persona method help HWID do socio-technical persona creation with specific work-relevant information added ready for imagining novel interaction designs, the method needs further development and sophistication to capture the political aspects of design personas. Furthermore, cultural personas (Nielsen, 2010; Salminen et al., 2017) have been investigated in cross-national and cross-cultural comparisons. The results indicate that the persona created are culturally specific, and sometimes so without the creators knowing that.

These insights are important for doing HWID for policy. For example, half of the platform workers in Denmark see themselves as self-employed, and the other half as wage earners. This insight requires persona designers to be aware of the political choices they make if they model their persona on one or the other platform worker identity. Furthermore, the absence of class consciousness among platform workers is a challenge for the Danish 'flexicurity' system that regulates the labor market in Denmark by consensus instead of government minimum wages, since the flexicurity system only works if both employers and employees are aware that they have conflicting interests and hence need to agree. If designers of personas are not knowledgeable about the Danish flexicurity system, they may create platform workers personas with a 'false consciousness' (such as 'I am self-employed') and the resulting design will hurt the platform workers in Denmark instead of helping them.

9.4   Relation Artefacts Type II: Socio-Technical Ideation Sketches

Policymaking with HWID relation artefacts type II begins with deliberations of diversity in the design in interaction patterns, then explore intersectionality in collaborative sketching of alternative solutions, and end up empowering policymakers by suggesting novel or adapted workflows for the organization.

Diversity in interaction design patterns

Interaction patterns for the political persona may be quite diverse because of many different possible political aspects, such as language, ethnicity, immigrants, refugees, gender, age, culture, and class. Below we discuss a tentative list of issues and inspirations for interaction patterns for the political persona.

Language. Multilingualism in HCI is an issue that should be part of all interaction patters, as it is about access to interaction or lack thereof. For example, some language scripts are unidirectional (e.g., English, Danish, Hindi), while others are bidirectional (e.g., Arabic, with left to right for numerals, right to left for alphabets) (Orngreen et al., 2010), see also Fig. 9.2. It is clearly important to develop guideline interaction patterns for multiple languages and multilingualism in HCI, and there are by now several case stories about how public policies influence the use of language in the design of interactive systems (Normand et al., 2014). We know how to design for the complex relations between social and technical factors that impact minority language use and the associated potential interaction design strategies remedy problematic issues (Lackaff & Moner, 2016). For example, instead of applying interaction patters according to language users skill levels, it may be more appropriate to take a relational

Writing words on mobile phones, the N80 and W810 (the Egyptian word for work is used here (in classical Arabic عمل [3amal] would be used)

Test word	Danish	Arabic
As long as	Sålænge	تول ما [tul ma]
21 clicks for 10 letters (incl. space)	23 clicks for 7 letters	13 clicks for 6 letters (incl. space)
2,1 clicks per letter	3,3 clicks per letter	2,2 clicks per letter
Work	Arbejde	شُغل [Shurghl]
9 clicks for 4 letters	12 clicks 7 bogstaver	11 clicks for 3 letters
2,25 clicks per letter	1,6 clicks per letter	3,7 clicks per letter

Fig. 9.2 Interaction patterns for Danish and Arabic on mobile phones. From Orngreen et al. (2010)

approach that builds on analysis of family communication and social activities when applying and developing interaction design pattern (Taylor, Council, Soro, Roe, & Brereton, 2019).

Ethnicity, immigrants, refugees. Interaction patterns can be designed for contextually vulnerable groups (see Gordon (2020) for a definition of contextually versus categorical vulnerable groups) in a neutral design language, such as the gender and ethnicity neutral interaction design done for the registration of medical health of refugees in Italy by Valtolina et al. (2018), Fig. 9.3. Another example of interaction design patterns for contextually vulnerable groups is the interactions in border contexts (Kulju, Ylikauppila, Toivonen, & Salmela, 2019), for example, the border guards interaction with tasks (e.g., monitor), tools (e.g., e-gate access), and travelers when they supervise travelers using the e-gates commonly found at borders in airports and other infrastructural access points.

Fig. 9.3 A neutral interaction design for contextually vulnerable groups (refugees arriving in Italy in the 2010s). From Valtolina et al. (2018)

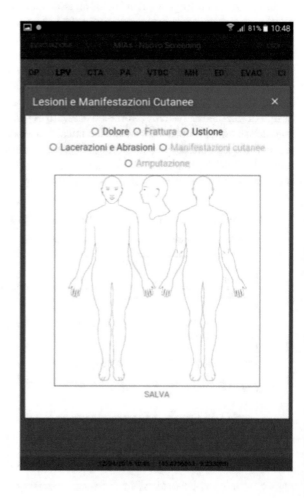

Gender. Personas that can help promote the female perspective in the design process may support interaction design patterns such as flexible interactions, interactions that offer access to knowledge, help to build up competences, and support networking (Marsden et al., 2017). A much earlier study by Aaron Marcus suggested interface pattern designs that aimed to provide "… 'appealing perceptual experience' both in their appearance ('look') and behavior ('feel')…" to "…white American women who might prefer a more detailed presentation, curvilinear shapes, and the absence of some of the more brutal terms such as Kill, Trash, Abort favored by male software engineers in the past…" (Marcus, 1993). Note the detailed description of the White American Women persona that is made in this paper. When it was published it was immediately controversial in its descriptions of gender and race. In a respond-study published a year later, the suggested look-and-feel interaction patterns for women only turned out not to be identifiable as such neither by men or women in later study (Teasley et al., 1994). A perhaps more viable set of gendered interaction patterns are those that simply focus on designs mostly used by women; fx designing interaction patterns for digital versions (e-scarfs) of traditional scarfs for women such as choice and change of the color of the scarf and the perception of others' e-scarfs and their colors (Yammiyavar & Deepshikha, 2019).

Age. Designing interaction patterns for special age groups such as children or the elderly has always been a part of HCI. These interaction design patterns may be based on empirical work analysis in age-specific settings such as schools or care homes. The assumption may be that such age groups require special interactions. For example, a study of work and speech interactions among staff at an elderly care facility found that staff members tend to speak during their tasks, remote communication is rare, most of the utterances goes toward the residents, the recipients of the utterances is frequently switched, and few of the utterances include a personal name of the recipient (Chino et al., 2013). Another assumption can be that such age groups require interactions that provide special user experiences. Lopes (2015) did a work analysis and suggested redesign of a social center for the elderly and a prototype for interacting with the elderly, which aimed to support the elderly in having user experiences of dignity, belonging, security, and worthiness. A third assumption may be the such age groups have special tasks that determine their interactions. (Deshpande, Yammiyavar, & Bhattacharya, 2012) studied how children adapt their interactions with computers in varied task situations and found that their performance was less affected by their preferences/skills or by differences in user interface design than task characteristics. Overall, however, a first issue for socio-technical approach to interaction design patterns in a policy context is to avoid ageism, that is, existing biases and stereotypes in the language used for addressing ageing in design. Ageism should, in principle, concern any categorization of people based on age groups, including children, generations, etc. Age categories are the only ones that every living person joins (North & Fiske, 2012). Ageism can be positive or negative, address specific subgroups, etc. The term was originally coined toward ageing and the elderly (Butler,

Interaction parameters	Findings
Language Known	Marathi, Hindi and Assamese
Types of work (Categories of works)	12-13 Different types of works / activities are identifiable.
Types of Labour	Skilled (*Mistari*) and unskilled labour (*kamgar*)

Fig. 9.4 Construction worker user groups. From Yammiyavar and Kate (2010)

2005). Recently, much focus has been on the ageing societies.[4] Interaction design patterns in HCI may need to be updated to avoid ageism (Comincioli, Chirico, & Masoodian, 2021).

Culture. Culture is related to interaction design patterns in HCI in numerous ways. For example, it can be about the emergence and conditions for doing HCI education and research in parts of the world, such as evolution of HCI in educational institutions in India and their Indian context-related research projects on interactions such as hand gestures as a mode of interaction (Yammiyavar, 2010). Heimgärtner and Kindermann (2012) focused on "big interaction data" from empirical studies and identified significantly different "cultural interaction patterns"; these patterns were identified in big data on mouse moves, clicks, interaction breaks or the values and changes in slide bars set up by the users of different nationality. A somewhat similar approach was taken by (Reinecke, 2010) in their work on culturally adaptive interfaces based on Hofstede's dimension, and their later work on quantifying cultural aspects of HCI users (Linxen et al., 2021; Sturm et al., 2015). The research on national culture and HCI is itself USA and Western-centric (Clemmensen & Roese, 2010). Overall, though, 'cultural personas' (Nielsen, 2010) may be a way forward for future socio-technical HCI research as a base for designing interaction design patterns.

Class. Sketching interaction design patterns for class is obviously just as complex and interwoven with policy aspects as the other issues discussed here. Many professionals are themselves distant from having a worker identity, as they may be self-employed or managers. And while HCI research may have looked into interaction design for knowledge workers, studies of unskilled and unorganized laborers in industry are perhaps rare. For example, Yammiyavar and Kate (2010) designed interactions for the population of unorganized workers in the Indian construction industry (about 17.6 million in 2010). They aimed to design a self-managed information system on mobile phones that would inform a worker of job openings, and where the communication system is cooperatively managed by the workers themselves. The policy aspects were among others to allow the workers to take agency and protect themselves from misuse by middlemen and cartels by excluding these, or by engaging with government bodies. The construction workers included both skilled and unskilled, and literate but also many illiterates, Fig. 9.4, and their main IT technology for finding and taking a job was low-cost mobile phones, Fig. 9.5.

In their final conceptual interaction design, they presented 11 icons depicting different types of work (digging, brick laying, plastering, painting, etc.) with nature

---

[4] https://www.who.int/initiatives/decade-of-healthy-ageing.

Parameters	Usage patterns observed
Use of Mobile	• Communication between friends, Listening to music, Playing games, calling, Messaging • Mobile phone price range - Rs.1500- 3000 (30 – 60 USD) • 10-15 % of labours are using mobile.
Importance of mobile	• Very essential. Quick communication device for job as well as for any other personal communication.
Interaction with mobile	• Users Navigate through mobile interfaces easily. • Existing icons are easily identified. • Receiving calls, Making calls is the most frequently performed interaction followed by Reading Messages, finding out 'missed' calls, Listening to Radio, Recorded Music. • The most identified words surrounding a mobile phone are Menu, OK, Exit, MP3, SMS, FM. • Illiterate users only receive calls.avoiding other functions.

Fig. 9.5 Construction workers' IT technology to find a job, and their interaction patterns. From Yammiyavar and Kate (2010)

and type of construction work as a basis of their categorization, Fig. 9.6. These were individually designed (size: 32 × 32 pixels, 48 × 48 pixels) since the screen resolution of 240 × 320 pixels was a choice that they explain was important to make the icons work on the technology available to the target users (construction workers) at the time.

Yammiyavar and Kate (2010)'s multimillion target user group of construction workers exemplify why interaction design patterns may be useful and important also in the context of policymaking. It is not enough to think participation on an f2f scale since then it will be impossible to reach the large user groups with the combination of HCI and policymaking that can change their lives to the better. Instead, interaction patterns that support specific policies may have to be designed.

However, since it is generally a bad idea to tell people that they are alienated or do not have the correct identity, collaborative sketching may be a way to allow class identity and class consciousness to come into play in design.

Fig. 9.6 Icons for construction workers' interaction design patterns depicting different types of work (digging, brick laying, plastering, painting, etc.). From Yammiyavar and Kate (2010)

Intersectionality in collaborative sketching

Intersectionality in and for collaborative sketching is an issue that has begun to be addressed. For example, Haimson, Gorrell, Starks, and Weinger (2020) address successfully power and identity in their future workshops with transgender people in the USA to allow for creative design. However, in a study in Singapore, it turned out that the design brief given to the design team did not impact the contribution of gender diversity to creativity in collaborative sketching (Koronis et al., 2019).

Culture and creative collaborative sketching may mix up in ways not well studied yet. In a study of culture in co-design (Clemmensen et al., 2018), it was found that cultural knowledge patterns shaped the core design thinking in the team, that is, how the cultural knowledge activated in a design team consisting of Scandinavian designers and Asian consultants in the analyzed design situations. The basic reasoning patterns in design thinking—induction, deduction, and abduction—were shaped by the appearance and disappearance of differences in activated cultural knowledge among the team members. These results were in line with previous studies showing that the interaction between accessibility and applicability is directly based on whom the person is interacting with in in-group members (same culture) or out-group members (different culture) and may also be primed by cultural stereotypes.

Collaborative sketching can be at the heart of policymaking. Sketches can provide an expansive view of the possibilities of digital welfare beyond a narrow scope of a welfare technology. For example, by ideating new user experiences of welfare it may be possible to encourage stakeholder to anticipate and reflect on the design of welfare policies and systems of the present and future (Coles-Kemp et al., 2020). Such collaborative sketches may end up in ideas about feminist conceptions of labor that reimagine a caring system of welfare where society recognize the unpaid labor that are crucial in many places in society; notions of compassionate and caring digital welfare communities that rather that cold desk meetings would provide places for socializing; or conceptions of formal solidarity that would center on the collective contributions of individuals to improve living conditions of the poorer members of society (Coles-Kemp et al., 2020). Collaborative sketching may provide more nuanced forms of access to and address the ethos of digitalized welfare.

Empowering policymakers through socio-technical sketching of workflows

Socio-technical sketching of workflows in policymaking processes can be a way to empower those that formulate and execute public policy. Valtolina et al. (2017) focused on supporting the government employees to themselves become designers of their digital tools. As part of the end-user-programming movement, their research focused not on prototypes or sketches, but on templates or rather forms that were accessible for end users to use in design. These and the related virtual design environment enabled the employees to represent the connections between different steps in a workflow and consider and imagine how the form-generated application will work from an interaction design and human work perspective. In this case, the employees were civil servants of a municipality in north Italy who used the forms to design reservation and registration services for citizens. The form was a wizard that led the employee through a series of data composing pages that together formed a work-flow that delivered the wanted service. The argument here is that supporting public servants designing workflows for citizens directed services ensures that these are adapted to local societal values.

The idea that IT artefacts that supports the workflows can indeed be used in different ways by the civil servants, according to their responsibilities and compe-tencies, does however require traditional (and political) decisions about user rights in a system that can be politically controversial. Different roles can be associated to each public servant who are a user depending on the services for citizens that they can create, modify, or access. In the case of Valtolina et al. (2017), their analysis of the organizational structure of the Municipality of Brescia showed four user roles. One of these was that a 'domain expert' with knowledge about the work domain and the IT system could take the role of system manager. This then gave this person the power to create a new service and specify which civil servants were responsible for accessing this service, and then for each service allocate civil servants to the role of application manager that allows the management of the service configuration, and other civil servants with the role of application viewer that provides the possibility to display data entered by the citizens.

Policy aspects of socio-technical sketching of workflows may include considera-tions about policies for the non-human workforce such as robots and automations, for example, which rights and duties should the non-human workforce be allocated? An interesting case is socio-technical sketching of workflows in cross-national physical border contexts. In many places globally such control is currently being automated with automatic border control (ABC) that do the same tasks as manual systems (Kulju et al., 2019). The ABC entities therefore take on decisions that in some cases are life-important to people (e.g., immigration, being allowed to see your partner, controlling pandemics). These ABCs should be effective in enforcing the law related to the border control, and at the same time respect the rights of an individual. They are regulated by law. In EU, the Schengen Borders Code (European_Parliament, 2019) provides the framework under which the automated, self-service border control concepts operate. For example, ABC in an airport can consist of e-gates supervised by border officers that runs workflows that check travelers' documents, verify biometrically the link between the document and the traveler, check if the traveler is entitled to cross the border, open/closes the gate with a mix of machine and human border controllers involved, and guarantee overall security in the flow. Anyone who have ever overheard young people sitting on a bench in an airport and discussing "my papers took a long time to clear.... i submitted my biometrics...." would be well aware that the ABC takes decisions of personal significance to millions of citizens. Trust in automation is therefore a highly important user experience. Given the political nature of the deci-sions, the users' trust in ABC may well overlap their trust in public policy regulations such as the Schengen Borders Code. Socio-technical sketching is thus embedded in national and international regulations.

9.5   Relation Artefacts Type III: Socio-Technical Hypothesis Prototyping

Policymaking with HWID relation artefacts type III begins with the considering bias in organizational action hypotheses for change in the organizational setup, then prototype worker experiences for decent work[5] based on the chosen action hypothesis, and end up doing policy-driven field evaluations and UX tests of the prototype(s).

Bias in organizational action hypotheses

Organizational action prototypes in a policymaking sense are about the ethical protection of users of interaction designs within and outside the organization. They thus are embedded in regional and national legislation and ethics approvals and accepted international standards. However, many of these regulations lack specific qualitative and quantitative metrics for UX assessment. HCI community and policymakers need to address type and level of impacts, and how such impacts should be identified and evaluated. Some potential hypotheses could be about:

- The ethical or societal impacts of the prototype.
- Diversity in languages used by the prototype.
- Degree of data protection/ownership/privacy/tracking, etc. assumed in the prototype.

An example is if an organization decides that its knowledge-worker employees are required to use the digital coach embedded in the workflow for producing presentations, Fig. 9.7. Such a coach may check the presenters rehearsing before the presentation and give feedback on speed and complexity of language, and on 'sensitive' wording, such as the non-appropriate use of other words for disabled people and more.

The problem with casting technical non-human actors as policymakers and enforcers can be described as that of 'technological fetishism' (Fuchs, 2020), that is, that technology appears as having autonomy and subjectivity, and also that it is revolutionary and one-dimensional causes to either strongly positive (or strongly negative) changes. Having autonomy means that technology is presented as being autonomous from society's power structures, such as when the 'coach' in Fig. 9.7 is presented without any information or source to reveal its situatedness in (some) society, and how it is embedded into class structures, exploitation, and domination. Subjectivity means that technology and not humans are presented as a subject that acts, for example, the 'coach' says that your language is insensitive; this reifies technology as inevitable, unchangeable, unavoidable, and irreversible, because it appears as independent from humans. That it is revolutionary and one dimensional and a cause to either strongly positive (or strongly negative) changes means that it appears as taking place rapidly and as changing everything, for example, that intersectionality technology is a wave that changes everything. The one dimensionality is

---

[5] UN development goal definition.

Types of bias reviewed by Presenter Coach:

Bias	Description
Disability	Emphasize the person first, rather than the disability.
Age	Referring to a person's age can be perceived as excluding or diminishing the person.
Gender	Gender-specific language may be perceived as excluding, dismissive, or stereotyping.
Sexual orientation	A person's sexual orientation should only be mentioned when necessary.
Race	Try to avoid obsolete and potentially offensive terms for racial or ethnic backgrounds.
Mental health	Try to avoid terms that could be offensive to people with mental-health related issues.
Ethnic slurs	Slurs are insinuations or allegations about someone that is likely to insult them or damage the person's reputation.

Fig. 9.7 Types of bias reviewed by Presenter Coach in MS PowerPoint. Retrieved 02/03/2021 from https://support.microsoft.com/en-us/office/suggestions-from-presenter-coach-25e7d866-c895-4aa1-9b90-089b70a4ea38?ui=en-us&rs=en-us&ad=us

well-documented technical-technology determinism, that is, that the social forces as part of the technology are overlooked. Finally, technological optimism/pessimism is the black and white view of technology; for example, that the 'coach' is all positive because it will make it common to not use insensitive language in knowledge work, or all negative because that sort of technology will amount to widespread censorship in knowledge work everyday practice (Fuchs, 2020). Due to phenomena such as technological fetishism there may be quite a long way to go before HCI community and policymakers will be ready and able to address type and level of societal impacts of novel interaction technologies, and how such impacts should be identified and evaluated. Therefore, organizational action hypotheses can potentially be about many different things for the moment being.

Prototype worker experiences of decent work

With the emergence of a digital economy an increasingly important approach, within which to prototype hypotheses relevant to HCI and policymaking, is to use universal values or 'human rights' to quality technology as part of the rights to work in just and favorable conditions and experiencing decent work (Berg, Furrer, Harmon, Rani, & Silberman, 2018; Leimeister, Zogaj, & Durward, 2015). The humanistic and social value of decent work for workers goes beyond acceptable working conditions to extend it to a psychological perspective in individuals' descriptions of decent work and psychological dimensions of working. From a psychological theory perspective, decent work consists of (a) physical and interpersonally safe working conditions (e.g., absence of physical, mental, or emotional abuse); (b) working hours that allow for free time and adequate rest; (c) organizational values that complement family and social values; (d) adequate compensation (e.g., perceived fair salary); and (e) access to adequate health care (Duffy, Blustein, Allan, Diemer, & Cinamon, 2020). While one scientific approach alone cannot create, measure, and capture improvements in all of these dimensions of decent work, HWID should always lead to documentable and significant improvements in workers' experience of their work as decent work. This should include explaining context, conceptualization, and assessment of decent work in a form comparable to similar studies done across countries, see, for example, Ferreira et al. (2019), Masdonati, Schreiber, Marcionetti, and Rossier (2019), but as a design-oriented contribution (Mandviwalla, 2015).

Taking point of departure in workflows and then prototype hypothesis about workers' experiences of central values is needed more than ever with the new ways of working coming up. Much is to learn from what was done at the beginning of HCI in, for example, the Scandinavian democratic design IT projects (Bødker et al., 2000) in terms of union participation and participatory design techniques. However, a HWID project aimed at prototyping hypotheses of work experiences go beyond political and physical contexts and will emphasize the design of psychological experiences created by the prototypes.

A HWID approach to prototyping worker's 'class consciousness' experiences could focus on a political 'wow' user experience, that is, suddenly getting the insight from using a interactive pricing tool that you as a worker has shared interest with your fellow workers since they are in similar objective conditions both in the short and in the long term. A stepwise approach to the prototyping such hypothesis could be:

1. Problematization by understanding the material conditions of the given work from the theoretical perspective of political economy, which again could help clarify the problem statement and operationalize it into measurable indicators for the evaluation, ending up with co-defining the class-consciousness needs of workers through a focus group discussion and then definition of political personas.

2. Co-ideation activities such as collaborative sketches based on pricing tool interaction patterns and ending up with suggestions for embedding the sketched pricing tools into workers' workflows.

3. Experience prototyping, based on organizational action notions about the ethics of the proposed novel solutions, refined into proof-of-concept prototype(s), and tested in real-life policy settings such as labor union meetings and with hands-on users within the union movement (Schoemann, 2018) and industrial settings (Kaasinen et al., 2020).

4. Intervening and evaluating the prototypes in by ensuring interaction design interoperability, digital legacy artefacts, and alignment with organizational structure and strategies. This may include innovating novel participatory and inclusive way of developing ownership models (e.g., worker-owned, union-owned,
   multiple-stakeholder-owned) of the tools, evaluate the prototypes in the ownership structure and ecosystem, and create generic evaluation usage scenarios for
   further pilot implementation and plan post-project operation.

So, to a question of how class consciousness in industrial workers can be
designed, HWID's answer lies in designing socio-technical 'user experiences' of
class consciousness in the local context. This may be a significant contribution to the
ongoing 'ethical turn' within humanistic human–computer interaction and provide
new knowledge to policymakers and working sociology.

Policy-driven field evaluations and UX tests

Public policy for levels of usability and UX-at-work do perhaps require a new kind of
usability, what we may call 'legislative usability'. This may be understood as relevant
statutory or legislative usability or usability-related requirements that are specific to
the proposed work/system domain (Lacerda, von Wangenheim, & Hauck, 2019). In
a first-mover country, Sweden, the legal framework for regulating the working environment is called 'Systematic Work Environment Management' (Arbetsmiljöverket,
2001), in Swedish abbreviated SAM. It aims to push organizations to incorporate
the work environment management as a natural part of the business. It requires
the employer to carry out the work environment management systematically by
investigating, taking actions, do risk assessments, and follow up the business. Thus,
employers, employees, and safety representatives map together the risks of ill-health
and accidents in the workplace and collaborate to counteract these risks. Based on
this framework, HCI researchers in Sweden have for decades worked to extend the
pro-active work environment protection to also cover the digital work environment
(Gulliksen, Lantz, Walldius, Sandblad, & Åborg, 2015).

The Swedish approach may well turn into a novel international standard
(Gulliksen, 2021). Gulliksen and partners have suggested the preliminary title:
"Ergonomics for information- and communication technology (ICT)—Testing by
users of workplaces' interactive systems—The Usability round". They base it
on the international standards for ergonomics, management, and design. The
ergonomics standard includes the design and evaluation of tasks, jobs, products, tools, equipment, systems, organizations, services, facilities, and environments (International_Organization_for_Standardization, 2011). The management
standard sets out the values and beliefs that make an organization human-
centered, business and operational benefits that come with human-centered leadership, and the policy managers need to implement to achieve this (Interna-
tional_Organization_For_Standardization, 2016). The design standard describes
principles that all work with user-centered development should follow (Inter-
national_Organization_For_Standardization, 2018). Concretely they suggest a
legislation-based usability evaluation method that they name 'The usability round'.

The unique about the method is that it is used within the framework of the systematic work environment work (SAM) in Sweden. It identifies usability issues and redesign suggestions for digital work systems with the aim of establishing metrics and measures. The use of the method aims to improve the digital working environment including workers well-being and productivity in the organization. Specifically, Gulliksen proposes that the usability round should aim to (Gulliksen, 2021):

1. Supplement the systematic work environment work with a method that focuses on the shortcomings and opportunities for improvement of the interactive systems.
2. Reduce the risk of cognitive and physical overload, thereby helping to reduce stress and absenteeism.
3. Increase and broaden the digital competence of the organization, thereby increasing the organization's efficiency, competitiveness, and preparedness for the purchase and introduction of new systems.
4. Contribute to a people-centered business development and thereby increase the social and economic sustainability of the organization.
5. Contribute to increased efficiency and productivity and thus to the achievement of the organization's business objectives.

While such work environment frameworks may be required by global or regional bodies, they are not always implemented well in practice. The European directive (European_Union, n.d.) which lies behind the Swedish SAM does not mention 'digital' or 'usability', but this may well as in Sweden be interpreted as part of the 'risks' that have to be managed systematically. The problem is that this has not happened. For example, in Denmark, the relevant regulation, https://at.dk/en/regula tions/guidelines/risk-assessment-apv-d-1-1-3/, is not concerned with the digital or usability and user experience; not even on a very detailed level such as in a tool for work environment assessment, https://at.dk/arbejdsmiljoearbejdet/apv-arbejdsplads vurdering/apv-vaerktoej/, the digital work environment is an issue. Thus, among the 57 work environment checklists https://apv.at.dk/APV-Bibliotek endorsed by Danish authorities at the time of writing this, none focus on or have items about digital work environment.

There is a fundamental need for knowledge about how novel digital technology such as business AI (and machine learning), robotics, and IoT are received and perceived in everyday practice in the public sector. Veale et al. (2018) studied how values of fairness in public sector shaped perceptions and reception of machine learning in public sector practices, and found that public servant saw it as important to (1) getting individual and organizational buy-in, (2) not over-relying or under-relying on machine learning systems, (3) augmenting models with additional necessary knowledge, and (4) game-the-system by decision-support users to get things working in everyday practice.

9.6 Relation Artefacts Type IV: Socio-Technical Interventions

Policymaking with HWID relation artefacts type IV begins with intersectionality interaction operability checks of how the interaction design of prototype allows cross-device continuity and cognitive and communicative socio-technical intersectionality interoperability. Then the prototypes are evaluated as interventions to ensure the workers' rights to their digital legacy. Finally, the prototypes are aligned with the organizational strategy for meeting UN development goals.

Intersectionality interaction operability

Intersectionality concerns are revolutionizing HCI these years. The multiple over-lapping identity characteristics put in focus by the struggle for intersectionality challenges a core concept of the filed that of the identity of the user (Schlesinger, Edwards, & Grinter, 2017). Interfaces and interaction designs need today to be interoperable in extended sense of the terms. Users today should be able to feel themselves with their multiple overlapping identity characteristics equally accepted across the range of interfaces that they may meet in their everyday. This goes well beyond classic accessibility concerns and turns out attention to novel policy aspects of interaction design.

For example, language use in interfaces may so far overlook and disfavor billions of people who do not have access to same services as others because these are not available in their language. For example, many MS Office services have through the years not been available to Danish-speaking users (Clemmensen, 2010). Another example is the many languages in India which are only recently being offered with digital services, such as speech recognition technologies to augment text input by visually impaired users in Indian languages (Bhikne, Joshi, Joshi, Jadhav, & Sakhardande, 2019). This is an area where HCI technology designers may help policymakers become aware of what needs to be regulated nationally and internationally.

Intervention to ensure the workers' rights to their digital legacy

The policy aspects of digital legacy concern workers' rights to store, retrieve, and share data that they create during work. What a socio-technical HCI approach would immediately point out is that people should not only be given right to technical access to their own data but in indeed also to the organizational structures that are needed to store, retrieve, and share those. So far the big technical companies may set out policies, for example, by creating support solutions for users to manage their digital legacy (Prates, Rosson, & de Souza, 2015), but this cannot replace a top-down government regulation for all in all countries.

Obvious examples are people's collections of images and the intergenerational sharing of those (Gulotta, Odom, Forlizzi, & Faste, 2013). Post-mortem digital legacy is another underdeveloped policy area that, for example, leaves it unclear what happens to a users' Facebook profile after death (Edwards & Harbinja, 2013) and regional legal perspectives on post-mortem digital legacy (Maciel, Pereira, & Sztern, 2015). In today's world, however, we are very far from the everyday person knowing about governance regulations relevant to their digital legacy.

Alignment with organizational strategy for meeting UN development goals

UN development goals and HWID

HCI is increasingly interested in contributing toward UN sustainable development goals (SDGs) (Eriksson et al., 2016). In particular, HWID is concerned with designing for decent work (SDG 8). Decent work is defined as work that is productive and offers a fair income, security and social protection, equal opportunities, prospects for personal development and social integration, and the possibility for workers to express their concerns and organize (ILO). The notion of decent work and its four pillars, employment creation, social protection, rights at work, and social dialogue, have become integral part of SDG 8 of UN's 2030 Agenda (UN).

Decent work

How to intervene to create decent work is one of the main goals of HWID and a general goal of socio-technical HCI design. The contribution of socio-technical design to organizational sustainability, in general, and social sustainability/decent work, in particular, to improve the quality of life of employees as well as society at large may be substantial (Marnewick, 2017). This is an area where socio-technical HCI can contribute to organizational learning and organizational strategy (Marnewick, 2017), help formulate local contextually specific regulations, and support workers in unionizing in novel and digitally supported ways (Clemmensen et al., 2020).

For example, it is not enough to design an interactive tool or relevant user experiences, the organization to support these and the surrounding community needs also interventions to come into life. To design for a novel organizational strategy for sustaining decent work requires analysis of the different values in need of ownership structure (find, pay, and train community facilitators; set up tech infrastructure; collect and curate data; and engage workers and content experts in evaluation activities; etc.). In addition, it may require the collective exploration of various ownership models leading up to a collective decision by management, workers, and other involved stakeholders ways (Clemmensen et al., 2020).

Probably spurred by the work on surveillance capitalism (Zuboff, 2015), recently North American HCI workshops have been concerned with the labor upon which the future of work relies (Fox et al., 2020), and how to move beyond participatory design and human-centered design by committing to collective action to transform society through advocacy and activism (Saxena et al., 2020).

Climate change and green and sustainable HWID

Other SDGs that are important to socio-technical HCI are SDG 13 on Climate Action and, in general, green and sustainable HCI. Obviously, 'green' HCI and public policy have a long history of research. For example, it has been suggested that HCI can contribute to climate change, waste electrical and electronic equipment (WEEE), and green ICT procurement policies (Thomas, Remy, Hazas, & Bates, 2017). The issue is, however, to define in a manageable manner sustainability and what HCI can do (Knowles, Bates, & Håkansson, 2018). Some major components of evaluating green HCI design may include considering the surrounding mechanisms; identify metrics for the complex relationships between artefacts, individuals, societies, and nature; and find suitable methods (Remy et al., 2018). HWID and other socio-technical HCI approaches can help here since it provides a platform for considering context, work analysis, and domain theory and methods and their relations to the interaction design to make a holistic green HCI approach.

9.7   Theory and Methods—Policymaking Theory and Socio-Technical HCI

Using domain-specific core (or kernel) theory is common for socio-technical HCI and it is relevant to HWID for policymaking. Core theory relevant for socio-technical HCI design is international and national legal frameworks statutes, etc. (Lazar et al., 2016), and also the policies of the HCI communities themselves. IFIP, AIS, ACM, EUSSET, and many more national and regional HCI-related organizations do set out policies for their working and tries to shape the field of HCI research and practice. HCI is not a single community but, like psychology, many islands that each has their own way of doing things. Comparisons on a detailed level between the HCI organizations of the world in terms of power structures and money flows and research topics, etc. could even be study topics for HCI. Currently, though some people with experience in running these organizations do have a lot of these insights, it would be necessary to better understand how HCI research is organized differently in AIS, IFIP, ACM, and so on.

   In terms of national HCI policy, Lazar et al. (2012) in a 10-country discussion pointed out that HCI public policies mostly are done on a national basis, though the new knowledge necessary for the policies are produced internationally. They identified the HCI public policy areas of interface accessibility, user data privacy, funding for HCI research, rules for performing research, and how government rankings affect HCI researchers. These are the ones that require theory to be further developed.

Geopolitical issues and HCI

HWID may explore and discuss geopolitical issues in HCI as a field of knowledge and practice at two levels: (1) on discourses surrounding motivations and value of HCI as a socio-technical field and (2) on discourses surrounding concepts of HCI diffusion, maturity, and diversity as articulated by global and local knowledge networks. Since the beginning of HCI, discussions of democracy have been around. It may even be fair to say that the key notion of usability aims to support the citizens of a democratic society. Obviously, exactly how HCI should do this remains open for discussion. HCI has several roots deep in military needs from the world wars of the twentieth century. It was also born out of the socio-technical traditions with its emancipatory ambitions, aiming at creating conditions for supporting human agency that facilitates the realization of people's needs and potential. There is an inherent contradiction between these traditions. Thus, we are interested in exploring the following question: how military power and emancipatory ambitions are related in a geopolitical analysis of HCI research? Moreover, the diffusion of HCI as field of knowledge and practice is dominated by political and post-colonial discourses that pervade local and global knowledge networks shaping what is considered useful and relevant research and practice. HWID understand these issues as geopolitical in nature and aim to trace the cultural and socio-technical dynamics that construct the field of HCI.

The target audience for this kind of theorizing is researchers and practitioners working on topics related to support and develop the research, practice, and education capabilities of HCI in institutions and organizations based around the world taking into account their diverse local needs and cultural perspectives; to promote application of interaction design research, practice and education to address the needs, desires and aspirations of people across the developing world; to research and promote interaction design practice in cross-cultural settings, with a special focus on new and emerging economies; to develop links between the HCI community, in general, and other relevant communities involved in international development and cross-cultured aspects of ICT development.

The topics of interest for this kind of theorizing may include the geopolitical nature of HCI, political and post-colonial discourses in diffusion of HCI field of knowledge and practice, HCI roots in military needs, HCI roots in socio-technical emancipatory ambitions, evidence of interactions between political models and HCI diffusion, and more. This could lead to improved understanding of socio-technical HCI design as geopolitical in nature and help to trace the cultural and political dynamics that construct the field of HCI. Concretely, it could lead to a frame of understanding of geopolitical issues in HCI, identification of examples and experiences that show political discourses shaping HCI's motivations and values, and of experiences of HCI diffusion, maturity, and diversity as articulated by global and local knowledge networks. The theorizing should have as outcome a research agenda for future work on geopolitical research on socio-technical HCI design.

9.8   Reflection of HWID and Policymaking

Benefits

A main benefit of the HWID platform when it comes to policymaking is that it supports a socio-technical HCI design approach, and it does it in a simple way that also non-design experts (policymakers) can understand easily. As such, it support both HCI professionals working as specialists who creates input to design and do UX evaluations, and as managers who care about UX and organizational strategies; the latter becoming more important these years (Kreitzberg, Rosenzweig, Shneiderman, Churchill, & Gerber, 2019).

Challenges

Understanding the boundaries between policymaking and HCI may require consideration of what is considered 'evidence' in policymaking, and how such evidence is communicated to make it of potential influence (Spaa et al., 2019). This is even more so relevant for HWID, which, in fact, is always 'political' in the sense that it pays attention to how novel interaction designs creates new divisions of work and values in the workplace. Here HWID share this awareness for divisions of work with, for example, Engestrøm's version of activity theory (Engeström, 1999); however, other socio-technical HCI approaches also pay much attention to this. The sociomaterial solutions generated by HWID can be policies themselves but can also be other artefacts that still contributes somewhat to policy theory.

References

Arbetsmiljöverket. (2001). *Systematiskt arbetsmiljöarbete, Arbetsmiljöverkets föreskrifter om systematiskt arbetsmiljöarbete och allmänna råd om tillämpningen av föreskrifterna.* Retrieved from https://www.av.se/en/work-environment-work-and-inspections/publications/for eskrifter/systematic-work-environment-management-afs-20011-provisions/.

Berg, J., Furrer, M., Harmon, E., Rani, U., & Silberman, M. S. (2018). *Digital labour platforms and the future of work: Towards decent work in the online world.* International Labour Office Geneva.

Bhikne, B., Joshi, A., Joshi, M., Jadhav, C., & Sakhardande, P. (2019). Faster and less error-prone: Supplementing an accessible keyboard with speech input. In *IFIP Conference on Human-Computer Interaction* (pp. 288–304). Springer.

Bhutkar, G., Qin, X., Barricelli, B. R., Abdelnour-Nocéra, J., Clemmensen, T., Gonçalves, F., & Lopes, A. G. (2021). HWID 2021. In *The 6th IFIP 13.6 Conference on Human Work Interaction Design*.

Bhutkar, G., Roto, V., Clemmensen, T., Barricelli, B. R., Abdelnour-Nocera, J., Meschtscher-jakov, A., … Gonçalves, F. (2019). User experiences and wellbeing at work. In *Lecture notes in computer science (including subseries Lecture Notes in Artificial Intelligence and Lecture Notes in Bioinformatics).* https://doi.org/10.1007/978-3-030-29390-1_75.

Bjørn-Andersen, N., & Clemmensen, T. (2017). The shaping of the Scandinavian Socio-Technical IS research tradition: Confessions of an accomplice. *Scandinavian Journal of Information Systems, 29*(1).

Blaynee, J., Kreps, D., Kutar, M., & Griffiths, M. (2016). Collaborative HCI and UX: Longitudinal diary studies as a means of uncovering barriers to digital adoption. In *Proceedings of the 30th International BCS Human Computer Interaction Conference* (Vol. 30, pp. 1–6).

Bødker, S., Ehn, P., Sjögren, D., & Sundblad, Y. (2000). Co-operative design—perspectives on 20 years with 'the Scandinavian IT Design Model.' *Proceedings of NordiCHI, 2000,* 22–24.

Butler, R. N. (2005). Ageism: Looking Back Over My Shoulder. *Generations, 29*(3), 84–86. Retrieved from http://esc-web.lib.cbs.dk/login?, http://search.ebscohost.com/login.aspx?direct= true&db=afh&AN=19399889&site=ehost-live&scope=site.

Cajander, Å., Larusdottir, M., Eriksson, E., & Nauwerck, G. (2015). Contextual personas as a method for understanding digital work environments. *IFIP Advances in Information and Communication Technology, 468*, 141–152. https://doi.org/10.1007/978-3-319-27048-7_10.

Campos, P., Clemmensen, T., Nocera, J. A., Katre, D., Lopes, A., & Ørngreen, R. (Eds.). (2013). *Human work interaction design. Work analysis and HCI.* https://doi.org/10.1007/978-3-642-411 45-8.

Catarci, T., Matarazzo, G., & Raiss, G. (2000). Usability and public administration: Experiences of a difficult marriage. In *Proceedings on the 2000 Conference on Universal Usability*, 24–31.

Catarci, T., Matarazzo, G., & Raiss, G. (2002). Driving usability into the public administration: The Italian experience. *International Journal of Human Computer Studies, 57*(2), 121–138. https://doi.org/10.1016/S1071-5819(02)91014-1.

Chino, T., Torii, K., Uchihira, N., & Hirabayashi, Y. (2013). *Work and speech interactions among staff at an elderly care facility.* https://doi.org/10.1007/978-3-642-41145-8_4.

Chuang, L. L., & Pfeil, U. (2018). Transparency and openness promotion guidelines for HCI. In *Extended abstracts of the 2018 CHI conference on human factors in computing systems* (pp. 1–4).

Clemmensen, T. (2010). Regional styles of human-computer interaction. In *Proceedings of the 3rd ACM International Conference on Intercultural Collaboration, ICIC '10* (pp. 219–222). https://doi.org/10.1145/1841853.1841891.

Clemmensen, T., Marton, A., Dimitra, Bjarke, Susanne, & Kirstine. (2020). *SHADE-SHAping DEcent platform work: Design of innovative digital tools for platform workers.* Unpublished grant application

Clemmensen, T., Ranjan, A., & Bødker, M. (2018). How cultural knowledge shapes core design thinking—a situation specific analysis. *CoDesign, 14*(2), 115–132. https://doi.org/10.1080/157 10882.2017.1399146.

Clemmensen, T., & Roese, K. (2010). An overview of a decade of journal publications about culture and human-computer interaction (HCI). In *Human work interaction design: Usability in social, cultural and organizational contexts* (pp. 98–112). https://doi.org/10.1007/978-3-642-11762-6_9.

Coles-Kemp, L., Ashenden, D., Morris, A., & Yuille, J. (2020). Digital welfare: Designing for more nuanced forms of access. *Policy Design and Practice, 3*(2), 177–188.

Comincioli, E., Chirico, A., & Masoodian, M. (2021). Improving the language of designing for ageing. In *INTERACT2021*, Forthcoming.

Deshpande, Y., Yammiyavar, P., & Bhattacharya, S. (2012). 'Adaptation' in children—A GUI interaction based task-performance study. In *IFIP working conference on human work interaction design* (pp. 22–34). Springer.

Duffy, R. D., Blustein, D. L., Allan, B. A., Diemer, M. A., & Cinamon, R. G. (2020). Introduction to the special issue: A cross-cultural exploration of decent work. *Journal of Vocational Behavior, 116*, 103351. https://doi.org/10.1016/j.jvb.2019.103351.

Edwards, E. J., Sum, C. M., & Branham, S. M. (2020). Three tensions between personas and complex disability identities. In *Extended abstracts of the 2020 CHI conference on human factors in computing systems* (pp. 1–9).

Edwards, L., & Harbinja, E. (2013). "What Happens to My Facebook Profile When I Die?": Legal issues around transmission of digital assets on death. In *Digital legacy and interaction* (pp. 115–144). Springer.

Engeström, Y. (1999). Expansive visibilization of work: An activity-theoretical perspective. *Computer Supported Cooperative Work (CSCW), 8*(1), 63–93.

Eriksson, E., Pargman, D., Bates, O., Normark, M., Gulliksen, J., Anneroth, M., & Berndtsson, J. (2016). HCI and UN's sustainable development goals: Responsibilities, barriers and opportunities. In *Proceedings of the 9th Nordic Conference on Human-Computer Interaction* (p. 140). ACM.

European_Parliament. (2019). *Schengen borders code.*

European_Union. *EU Directive 89/391.*

Ferreira, J. A., Haase, R. F., Santos, E. R., Rabaça, J. A., Figueiredo, L., Hemami, H. G., & Almeida, L. M. (2019). Decent work in Portugal: Context, conceptualization, and assessment. *Journal of Vocational Behavior, 112*, 77–91. https://doi.org/10.1016/j.jvb.2019.01.009.

Fox, S. E., Khovanskaya, V., Crivellaro, C., Salehi, N., Dombrowski, L., Kulkarni, C., ... Forlizzi, J. (2020). Worker-centered design: Expanding HCI methods for supporting labor. In *Extended abstracts of the 2020 CHI conference on human factors in computing systems* (pp. 1–8).

Fuchs, C. (2020). History and Class Consciousness 2.0: Georg Lukács in the age of digital capitalism and big data. *Information, Communication & Society, 1–19.*

Gardien, P., Djajadiningrat, T., Hummels, C., & Brombacher, A. (2014). Changing your hammer: The implications of paradigmatic innovation for design practice. *International Journal of Design, 8*(2). Retrieved from http://www.ijdesign.org/index.php/IJDesign/article/view/1315.

Gordon, B. G. (2020). Vulnerability in research: Basic ethical concepts and general approach to review. *Ochsner Journal, 20*(1), 34 LP–38. https://doi.org/10.31486/toj.19.0079.

Gulliksen, J. (2021). Digital work environment rounds–systematic inspections of usability supported by the legislation. In *IFIP Conference on Human-Computer Interaction* (pp. 197–218). Cham: Springer.

Gulliksen, J., Lantz, A., Walldius, Å., Sandblad, B., & Åborg, C. (2015). *Digital arbetsmiljö (Digital Work Environment)* (A. (Swedish W. E. Authority), Ed.). Retrieved from https://www.av.se/glo balassets/filer/publikationer/rapporter/digital_arbetsmiljo-rap-2015-17.pdf.

Gulotta, R., Odom, W., Forlizzi, J., & Faste, H. (2013). Digital artifacts as legacy: Exploring the lifespan and value of digital data. In *CHI '13*. https://doi.org/10.1145/2470654.2466240.

Haimson, O. L., Gorrell, D., Starks, D. L., & Weinger, Z. (2020). Designing trans technology: Defining challenges and envisioning community-centered solutions. In *Proceedings of the 2020 CHI Conference on Human Factors in Computing Systems* (pp. 1–13).

Hassenzahl, M. (2010). Experience design: Technology for all the right reasons. *Synthesis Lectures on Human-Centered Informatics, 3*(1), 1–95.

Hassenzahl, M., Diefenbach, S., & Göritz, A. (2010). Needs, affect, and interactive products–facets of user experience. *Interacting with Computers, 22*(5), 353–362. https://doi.org/10.1016/j.intcom. 2010.04.002.

Heimgärtner, R., & Kindermann, H. (2012). Revealing cultural influences in human computer inter-action by analyzing big data in interactions. In R. Huang, A. A. Ghorbani, G. Pasi, T. Yamaguchi, N. Y. Yen, & B. Jin (Eds.), *Active media technology* (pp. 572–583). Berlin, Heidelberg: Springer Berlin Heidelberg.

Hirschheim, R., & Klein, H. K. (1994). Realizing emancipatory principles in information systems development: The case for ETHICS. *MIS Quarterly,* 83–109.

International_Organization_for_Standardization. (2011). *SO 26800:2011 Ergonomics—General approach, principles and concepts.*

International_Organization_For_Standardization. (2016). *ISO 27500:2016 The human-centred organization—Rationale and general principles.*

International_Organization_For_Standardization. (2018). *ISO 9241-11:2018-Ergonomics of human-system interaction–Part 11: Usability: Definitions and concepts.*

Junqueira Barbosa, S. D., & de Souza, C. S. (2011). Interacting with public policy are HCI researchers an endangered species in Brazil? *Interactions, 18*(3), 69–71.

Kaasinen, E., Schmalfuß, F., Özturk, C., Aromaa, S., Boubekeur, M., Heilala, J., ... Walter, T. (2020). Empowering and engaging industrial workers with Operator 4.0 solutions. *Computers & Industrial Engineering, 139*, 105678. https://doi.org/10.1016/j.cie.2019.01.052.

Katre, D., Orngreen, R., Yammiyavar, P., & Clemmensen, T. (2010). Human work interaction design: Usability in social, cultural and organizational contexts: Second IFIP WG 13.6 conference, HWID 2009, Pune, India, October 7–8, 2009, Revised Selected Papers: Preface. In *IFIP Advances in Information and Communication Technology* (Vol. 316). Springer.

Klein, L. (2014). What do we actually mean by 'sociotechnical'? On values, boundaries and the problems of language. *Applied Ergonomics, 45*(2), 137–142.

Knowles, B., Bates, O., & Håkansson, M. (2018). This changes sustainable HCI. In *Proceedings of the 2018 CHI Conference on Human Factors in Computing Systems* (pp. 1–12).

Koronis, G., Chia, P. Z., Kang Kai Siang, J., Silva, A., Yogiaman, C., & Raghunath, N. (2019). An empirical study on the impact of design brief information on the creativity of design outcomes with consideration of gender and gender diversity. *Journal of Mechanical Design, 141*(7).

Kreitzberg, C. B., Rosenzweig, E., Shneiderman, B., Churchill, E. F., & Gerber, E. (2019). Careers in HCI and UX: The digital transformation from craft to strategy. In *Extended abstracts of the 2019 CHI conference on human factors in computing systems* (pp. 1–6).

Kulju, M., Ylikauppila, M., Toivonen, S., & Salmela, L. (2019). A framework for understanding human factors issues in border control automation. In B. R. Barricelli, V. Roto, T. Clemmensen, P. Campos, A. Lopes, F. Gonçalves, & J. Abdelnour-Nocera (Eds.), *Human work interaction design. Designing engaging automation* (pp. 215–228). Cham: Springer International Publishing.

Lacerda, T. C., von Wangenheim, C. G., & Hauck, J. C. R. (2019). UPCASE-A Method for Self-Assessing the Capability of the Usability Process in Small Organizations. ArXiv:1902.07244.

Lackaff, D., & Moner, W. J. (2016). Local languages, global networks: Mobile design for minority language users. In *Proceedings of the 34th ACM International Conference on the Design of Communication* (pp. 1–9).

Lazar, J., Abascal, J., Barbosa, S., Barksdale, J., Friedman, B., Grossklags, J., … Martínez-Normand, L. (2016). *Human–computer interaction and international public policymaking: A framework for understanding and taking future actions.* Retrieved from https://eprints.mdx.ac.uk/20131/1/ment-action-plan-2011-2015.

Lazar, J., Abascal, J., Davis, J., Evers, V., Gulliksen, J., Jorge, J., … Prates, R. (2012). HCI public policy activities in 2012: A 10-country discussion. *Interactions, 19*(3), 78–81.

Lazar, J., Johnson, J., & Hochheiser, H. (2005). Policy at the interface: HCI and public policy. *Interactions, 12*(6), 13–14.

Leimeister, J. M., Zogaj, S., & Durward, D. (2015). New forms of employment and IT–crowd-sourcing. In *4th conference of the regulating for decent work network* (pp. 23–41).

Linxen, S., Sturm, C., Brühlmann, F., Cassau, V., Opwis, K., & Reinecke, K. (2021). *How WEIRD is CHI?*

Lopes, A. G. (2015). *The work and workplace analysis in an elderly centre for agility improvement.* https://doi.org/10.1007/978-3-319-27048-7_11.

Maciel, C., Pereira, V. C., & Sztern, M. (2015). Internet users' legal and technical perspectives on digital legacy management for post-mortem interaction. In S. Yamamoto (Ed.), *Human interface and the management of information. information and knowledge design* (pp. 627–639). Cham: Springer International Publishing.

Mandviwalla, M. (2015). Generating and justifying design theory. *Journal of the Association for Information Systems, 16*(5), 3.

Manuel, J., & Crivellaro, C. (2020). Place-based policymaking and HCI: Opportunities and challenges for technology design. In *Proceedings of the 2020 CHI Conference on Human Factors in Computing Systems* (pp. 1–16).

Marchetti, R. (2011). Cosmopolitan Democracy. In D. K. Chatterjee (Ed.), *Encyclopedia of global justice* (pp. 201–202). https://doi.org/10.1007/978-1-4020-9160-5_81.

Marcus, A. (1993). Human communications issues in advanced UIs. *Communications of the ACM, 36*(4), 100–109. https://doi.org/10.1145/255950.153670.

Marnewick, C. (2017). Information system project's sustainability capability levels. *International Journal of Project Management, 35*(6), 1151–1166.

Marsden, N., & Haag, M. (2016). Stereotypes and politics: Reflections on personas. In *Proceedings of the 2016 CHI Conference on Human Factors in Computing Systems* (pp. 4017–4031).

Marsden, N., Hermann, J., & Pröbster, M. (2017). Developing personas, considering gender: A case study. In *Proceedings of the 29th Australian Conference on Computer-Human Interaction* (pp. 392–396).

Marsden, N., & Pröbster, M. (2019). Personas and identity: Looking at multiple identities to inform the construction of personas. In *Proceedings of the 2019 CHI Conference on Human Factors in Computing Systems* (pp. 1–14).

Masdonati, J., Schreiber, M., Marcionetti, J., & Rossier, J. (2019). Decent work in Switzerland: Context, conceptualization, and assessment. *Journal of Vocational Behavior, 110*, 12–27. https://doi.org/10.1016/j.jvb.2018.11.004.

Massanari, A. L. (2010). Designing for imaginary friends: Information architecture, personas and the politics of user-centered design. *New Media & Society, 12*(3), 401–416.

Moser, C., Fuchsberger, V., Neureiter, K., Sellner, W., & Tscheligi, M. (2012). Revisiting personas: The making-of for special user groups. In *CHI'12 Extended Abstracts on Human Factors in Computing Systems* (pp. 453–468).

Nelimarkka, M. (2019). A review of research on participation in democratic decision-making presented at SIGCHI conferences. Toward an improved trading zone between political science and HCI. In *Proceedings of the ACM on Human-Computer Interaction, 3*(CSCW) (pp. 1–29).

Nielsen, L. (2010). *Personas in cross-cultural projects.* https://doi.org/10.1007/978-3-642-117 62-6_7.

Normand, L. M., Paternò, F., & Winckler, M. (2014). Public policies and multilingualism in HCI. *Interactions, 21*(3), 70–73.

North, M. S., & Fiske, S. T. (2012). An inconvenienced youth? Ageism and its potential intergenerational roots. *Psychological Bulletin, 138*(5), 982–997. https://doi.org/10.1037/a00 27843.

Orngreen, R., Katre, D., & Sandeep, M. (2010). Analyzing cultural usability of mobile keypad and displays for textual communication in internationalization and localization perspectives. https://doi.org/10.1007/978-3-642-11762-6_10.

Prates, R. O., Rosson, M. B., & de Souza, C. S. (2015). Making decisions about digital legacy with Google's inactive account manager. In *IFIP conference on human-computer interaction* (pp. 201–209). Springer.

Rani, U., Dhir, R. K., Furrer, M., Gőbel, N., Moraiti, A., Cooney, S., & Coddou, A. (2021). *ILO World Employment and Social Outlook 2021: The role of digital labour platforms in transforming the world of work.* Retrieved from here: https://www.ilo.org/global/research/global-reports/weso/2021/WCMS_771749/lang--en/index.htm.

Reinecke, K. (2010). *Culturally Adaptive User Interfaces (PhD dissertation)* (University of Zurich, Department of Informatics). Retrieved from https://homes.cs.washington.edu/~reinecke/Public ations_files/diss.pdf.

Remy, C., Bates, O., Dix, A., Thomas, V., Hazas, M., Friday, A., & Huang, E. M. (2018). Evaluation beyond usability: Validating sustainable HCI research. In *Proceedings of the 2018 CHI Conference on Human Factors in Computing Systems* (pp. 1–14).

Salminen, J., Jung, S., An, J., Kwak, H., Nielsen, L., & Jansen, B. J. (2019). Confusion and information triggered by photos in persona profiles. *International Journal of Human-Computer Studies, 129*, 1–14.

Salminen, J., Sengün, S., Kwak, H., Jansen, B., An, J., Jung, S.-G., … Harrell, D. F. (2017). Generating cultural personas from social data: A perspective of middle eastern users. In *2017 5th international conference on future internet of things and cloud workshops (FiCloudW)* (pp. 120–125). IEEE.

Saxena, D., Graeff, E., Guha, S., Cheon, E., Reynolds-Cuéllar, P., Walker, D., … Fleischmann, K. R. (2020). Collective Organizing and Social Responsibility at CSCW. In *conference companion publication of the 2020 on computer supported cooperative work and social computing* (pp. 503–509).

Schlesinger, A., Edwards, W. K., & Grinter, R. E. (2017). Intersectional HCI: Engaging identity through gender, race, and class. In *Proceedings of the 2017 CHI Conference on Human Factors in Computing Systems* (pp. 5412–5427). ACM.

Schoemann, K. (2018). Digital technology to support the trade union movement. *Open Journal of Social Sciences, 6*(01), 67.

Shackel, B. (1997). Human-computer interaction—whence and whither? *Journal of the American Society for Information Science, 48*(11), 970–986.

Spaa, A., Durrant, A., Elsden, C., & Vines, J. (2019). Understanding the Boundaries between Policymaking and HCI. In *Proceedings of the 2019 CHI Conference on Human Factors in Computing Systems* (pp. 1–15).

Sturm, C., Oh, A., Linxen, S., Abdelnour Nocera, J., Dray, S., & Reinecke, K. (2015). How WEIRD is HCI? Extending HCI principles to other countries and cultures. In *Proceedings of the 33rd Annual ACM Conference Extended Abstracts on Human Factors in Computing Systems* (pp. 2425–2428).

Taylor, J. L., Council, W. W. A. S., Soro, A., Roe, P., & Brereton, M. (2019). A relational approach to designing social technologies that foster use of the Kuku Yalanji Language. In *Proceedings of the 31st Australian Conference on Human-Computer-Interaction* (pp. 161–172).

Teasley, B., Leventhal, L., Blumenthal, B., Instone, K., & Stone, D. (1994). Cultural diversity in user interface design: Are intuitions enough? *SIGCHI Bull., 26*(1), 36–40. https://doi.org/10.1145/181526.181533.

Thomas, V., Remy, C., Hazas, M., & Bates, O. (2017). HCI and environmental public policy: Opportunities for engagement. In *Proceedings of the 2017 CHI Conference on Human Factors in Computing Systems* (pp. 6986–6992).

Valtolina, S., Barricelli, B. R., Fogli, D., Colosio, S., & Testa, C. (2017). Public staff empowerment in e-government: A human work interaction design approach. In S. Barbosa, P. Markopoulos, F. Paternò, S. Stumpf, & S. Valtolina (Eds.), *End-user development* (pp. 119–134). Cham: Springer International Publishing.

Valtolina, S., Barricelli, B. R., Rizzi, A., Menghini, S., & Ciriaci, A. (2018). Socio-technical design of an app for migrants rescue operations. In T. Clemmensen, V. Rajamanickam, P. Dannenmann, H. Petrie, & M. Winckler (Eds.), *Global thoughts, local designs* (pp. 140–147). Cham: Springer International Publishing.

Veale, M., Van Kleek, M., & Binns, R. (2018). Fairness and accountability design needs for algorithmic support in high-stakes public sector decision-making. In *Conference on Human Factors in Computing Systems-Proceedings*. https://doi.org/10.1145/3173574.3174014.

Wilson, A., De Paoli, S., Forbes, P., & Sachy, M. (2018). Creating personas for political and social consciousness in HCI design. *Persona Studies, 4*(2), 25–46.

Yammiyavar, P. (2010). *Status of HCI and usability research in Indian educational institutions.*https://doi.org/10.1007/978-3-642-11762-6_2.

Yammiyavar, P., & Deepshikha. (2019). Exploring Potential of Traditionally Crafted Textiles to Transform into e-Wearables for Use in Socio-cultural Space. In B. R. Barricelli, V. Roto, T. Clemmensen, P. Campos, A. Lopes, F. Gonçalves, & J. Abdelnour-Nocera (Eds.), *Human work interaction design. Designing engaging automation* (pp. 123–139). Cham: Springer International Publishing.

Yammiyavar, P., & Kate, P. (2010). Developing a Mobile Phone Based GUI for Users in the Construction Industry: A Case Study. In D. Katre, R. Orngreen, P. Yammiyavar, & T. Clemmensen (Eds.), *HWID 2009-human work interaction design: Usability in social, cultural and organizational contexts* (Vol. 316, pp. 211–223). https://doi.org/10.1007/978-3-642-11762-6_17.

Zuboff, S. (2015). Big other: Surveillance capitalism and the prospects of an information civilization. *Journal of Information Technology, 30*(1), 75–89.

Chapter 10
Socio-Technical HCI Design in a Wider Context

Abstract This chapter reflects on the use of the HWID platform in a wider context of ethical value exchange, post-humanism, and the anthropocene. It asks the question if we should design socio-technical HCI design that basically helps humans to come to terms with 'living with monsters', that is, powerful algorithms. It attempts to explain the difference between socio-technical and sociomaterial and how they are both useful for design. At the same time, the chapter argues that human psychology should be given a prominent place in the use of the HWID platform and suggests to study socio-technical HCI design phenomena related to the human user tendency to anthropomorphize technology such as AI, robots, etc. The chapter ends with pointing to the need for designing on a global scale, while reflecting on the psychology of the planetary interaction designs. In this way, the chapter becomes a powerful argument for keeping a strong focus on the technical in the social sciences, without falling into a trap of technological determinism.

Keywords Human work interaction design · Obedience · Experience machine · Animism · Anthropocene · Planetary interaction design · Designer self-reflection

In recent years, the wider context of socio-technical HCI design has moved toward ethical value exchange (Abdelnour-Nocera, Clemmensen, Hertzum, Singh, & Singh, 2019; Gardien, Djajadiningrat, Hummels, & Brombacher, 2014), post-humanism (Forlano, 2017; Fuchsberger, Murer, & Tscheligi, 2014), and the anthropocene (Light, Powell, & Shklovski, 2017). We argue that socio-technical approaches to HCI design should be seen in this wider context, and that HWID offers a platform for theory and action in this wider context.

T. Clemmensen, *Human Work Interaction Design*,
Human–Computer Interaction Series,
https://doi.org/10.1007/978-3-030-71796-4_10

10.1   HWID for Subordinating to Algorithms and Digital Anthropomorphism

Living with monsters is a metaphor that helps capture the social implications of algorithmic phenomena, hybrid agency, and the performativity of technology (Schultze et al., 2018). This includes how to deal with those technologies. A common approach in socio-technical HCI design is to study the social implications of the overwhelming power and implications of these technologies for human life and work. However, HWID offers also an opportunity to design for the reverse direction, that is, how human work shapes the interaction with these 'monsters'.

The wider social forces driving design

Offering a social deterministic direction in socio-technical HCI design is more important than ever for the challenges of today's AI, robotics, and IoT applications. Many of these novel applications are imagined, developed, and deployed with the goal of enabling humans and machines to engage collaboratively in real-world tasks. For example, these applications can be said to have aspects of both cyber-physical systems (CPS) and socio-technical systems and are characterized by close cooperation between multiple humans and machines. Such applications can be referred to as 'socio-technical CPS'. Obviously, machines already 'figure' in work (maybe other machines, non-digital ones), but work could arguably be said to be technologically configured from the outset. On the other hand, the ways of configuring human work (labor) may decidedly inform the technicality of the machines. Thus, the 'monsters' are (also) us, and it is us who change.

How and why do we humans change our work? As described in Chap. 2 on the socio-technical HCI design approaches, a defining feature of these is that they do design the technical and the social in parallel. The digital transformation of work is one area that tries to answer that. New forms of work, that is, 'smart work', are characterized by spatial and temporal flexibilities. It can be supported by technical tools that provide employees with the best working conditions to accomplish their tasks. These major transformations of business activities, processes, competencies, and models leverage the changes and opportunities of digital technicalities in a strategic and prioritized way with present and future shifts in mind. Digital transformation of work includes new practices in which services and products are produced in novel ways by use of crowds, machines, artificial intelligence, and algorithms. Furthermore, developments in labor law call for new digital platforms and enable growth in the so-called gig-economy. Finally, meaningful work and employment is re-interpreted as a scarce resource. Thus, the changes in the human work supported by interaction design are conditioned by changes in the wider context of what it means to be human today.

Why the 'technical' in socio-technical HCI design?

So why then the 'technical'? Is it needed and for what? What is it? Other socio-technical approaches than HWID struggle to define the technical. Thus, ADR makes a point of asking the researchers using the method to decide whether the social or the technical should dominate a given project (Sein, Henfridsson, Purao, Rossi, & Lindgren, 2011). To understand the need for the technical, we may want to turn to the IS field as conceptualizing the technical is a part of the field's continuing discussions. The 'socio-technicals' has found new interpretations and illustrations such as imbrication (Leonardi, 2011) that are more abstract and more interactive than the practical and sequential STS of Mumford (2006) and thus may present advancements of the field. On the other hand, the 'sociomaterialists' would say there is no distinction between the social and the technical as we humans are sociomaterial cyborgs (monsters?) that emerge in relations that are performed (in contrast to objects that influence) (Bjørn & Østerlund, 2014; Schultze et al., 2018). Striking a middle ground between socio-technical IS and sociomaterial IS, Faulkner and Runde (2019) aim to provide conceptions of digital objects as structured ensembles of components that are themselves objects, and which provide a way to track from where their organizationally relevant properties come from. Faulkner and Runde (2019) explain this with an example of a specific gramophone player from the 1970s that had sufficient torque and a robust drive to enable the hip hop music to emerge in New York at the time. Regarding design, IS theorists remain, however, strangely enough either co-constitutionists as in sociomateriality or simply technical determinists studying the impact of technology. For example, despite their attempt to strike a middle ground between sociomateriality and socio-technicality, Faulkner and Runde (2019), perhaps due to their realists' need for seeing technical objects as having an independent existence in the world (Faulkner & Runde, 2013), conclude that "Given their influence on organizations and organizing processes, there is a pressing need for more sophisticated understanding of digital objects". The technical appears to be needed as a driver or designer of organizing processes. However, in a wider context of the technological world of today, it is clear that the technical is also a design of the social. Faulkner and Runde (2013) actually theorize this, for example, when explaining that technical change can occur when a new social position in society for a technological object emerges; however, the examples given are merely examples of new technologies, not of new positions (which in the realism of Faulkner and Runde (2013) are two different things).

Returning to the discussion of socio-technical HCI design, the question is why the technical in HCI designs? Regarding design, HCI was early on affiliated with the social. HCI design in its different variants (AIS HCI, IFIP HCI, ACM CHI, etc.) did historically have an origin in the social, with attempts to use human psychology (Card, Moran, & Newell, 1983) and sociology (Bannon, 1991) to design interfaces. After a short but dramatic discussion of the value of this social science theoretical approach (Carroll & Campbell, 1986), the need for the 'technical' in HCI gained prominence and has since rarely been contested, see also Clemmensen, 2006. The technical has even been equated with design itself, so that the discussion became about the relations between the social (work) and the design (see, for example, Dourish, 2006), instead of discussing the socio-technical relations in design. However, examples of questioning the position of the 'technical' do occur; an interesting recent study (Clarke, 2015) of how an advertising provider's workplace organizes itself to design, manage, and advertise to digital segments illustrated how the 'technical' is so dominating the view of work today that it requires a study to dig out the social parts that today appears to "complement established evaluative, technical, and statistical methods used to create segments and personas in design and marketing" (Clarke, 2015). The study revealed collaborative activities workers rely on to create web analytics-based groupings, and the way the advertising customer was present in the mind of the workers who made segment composition decisions. Thus, the study pointed out who the user was, and how the client and service were typified, could not be facilitated by statistics alone, human interpretation did some of work as it was the workers who made segment composition decisions that made the machine learning work. More studies like this are appearing showing, for example, that the technical in data science is shaped by the social world of data scientists (Wang et al., 2019).

Looking at the social as a driver of design may lead to different views on the need for the 'technical' in socio-technical HCI. Given that HWID conceptualize the 'technical' simply as interaction design activities, see Chap. 2 we need the technical as an outcome of work analysis but also as a starting point for work analysis.

As an outcome, the technical offers convergence on findings from work analysis across multiple complex and diverse work domains, ranging from medical user interfaces, work and speech interactions at elderly care facilities, greenhouse climate control, navigating through large oil industry engineering models, crisis management, library usability, and mobile probing, covering topics of work analysis dimensions and methods; interactions, models, and approaches; and evaluations, interactions, and applications (Campos et al., 2012).

As a starting point for work analysis, the 'technical' offers divergence by opening up to 'reading' design sketches and prototypes within different approaches to analysis and design of human work interaction, and how designers may confront concrete design problems in complex work domains and use this unique opportunity to share their design problems and solutions with a wider community (Clemmensen, Campos, Orngreen, Mark-Pejtersen, & Wong, 2006).

Overall, the technical is an inherent part of socio-technical HCI design to varying degrees depending on how the HWID platform is used to design. It seems that in today's wider context the interaction design (understood as an interface to algorithms, AI, robotics, IoT) is so dominating design that we need to study more how the social is done and shapes the technical.

Designing for obedience: the Milgram machine and ethical AI in organizations

Designs for AI, robotics, and IoT can be overwhelming for humans and can be directive for human action.[1] Design guidelines for designing human-oriented explainable AI acknowledge this human need for directives from the AI (Liao, Gruen, & Miller, 2020). Users may want to adapt the interaction behaviors to better utilize the AI, for example, users may want to understand how the AI extract information from clinic

---

[1] Fuchsberger et al. (2016) write about disobedient artefacts. Though important, this is not our topic here, we discuss (dis)obedient people. But they do make a point about why and how we would expect IT artefact to be 'obedient'.

notes so they can adapt their own notes-taking practices, or the AI could suggest to chatbot users what kind of things they could ask, or users may require explanations and feedback from the AI to fulfill their own need for helping the AI to improve (Liao et al., 2020).

In a weird twist on psychology's contribution to HCI, it turns out that HCI has contributed significantly to one of psychology's most famous findings, Milgram's study of obedience. This showed that ordinary people (acting as 'teachers') are willing to give other humans (acting as 'students') dangerous electrical shock if told to do so. However, these experiments from the 1950s and 1960s in USA have recently been contextualized and every detail is scrutinized. The short story is that Milgram's findings do not hold, as least not as he presented them. What people were doing in those studies were not simply passively following orders, and the typical definitions of obedience as a form of social influence elicited in response to direct orders from an authority figure may not be the best way to understand obedience. Rather, people were participating in a scientific activity with specific experimental conditions at a world famous university (Yale); thus, they did not just follow orders but rather indulged in submission to the requirements of a full context of authority (Gibson, 2019), that is, submission to the organizational, social, and technical conditions at hand. One particular aspect of the context of obedience, and the one of interest here, is the interaction design of the shock delivery. Oppenheimer (2015) suggested that the design of Milgram's shock generator was 'optimized' under influence by the recommendations of Alphonse Chapanis (Chapanis, Garner, & Morgan, 1949), who was the dominant HCI person (human factors pioneer) of the time of the Milgram experiments. Therefore, Oppenheimer (2015) suggested to conceptualize Milgram's obedience to social authority as (at least partly) 'device compliance' to the chock delivery device, Fig. 10.1.

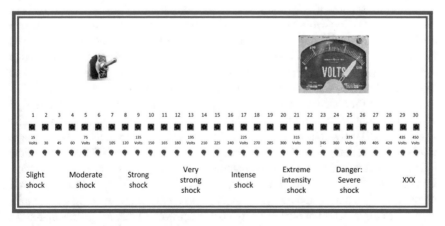

Fig. 10.1 Simplified illustration of Milgram's shock generator's persuasive design. With the long row of indicators and switches that made participants automate their responses, the voltmeter that showed hideously high voltages, and the on/off button that the participants never used. Adapted from Oppenheimer (2015)

First, she points out how the working environment—being at Yale University, taking on a specific role in the experiment, the shock, the learners' response, the instructions from the experimenter, the 'scientific' dress code, and laboratory design—relates to obedience measures and to the social factors in the laboratory. Then she analyses Milgram's simulated shock generator in Fig. 10.1 as the device (gateway) for the participant to become an active participant agent in the experimental environment by interacting with the controls (volt switches) and thereby operating the machine functions (shock administration) and reading and understanding the feedback from the machine (meters, lights, noise). Interestingly, the interaction with an excessive long row of toggle switches (the apparatus had 30 switches) of which an increasing number should be turned on to increase shock voltage she interprets as a learning device that over a series of trials conditioned the 'teacher' participant to switch the toggles faster and with less effort. She also points out that unnecessary visual feedback—one red light for each toggle switch, a meter showing the voltage, detailed labels for each voltage strength, etc.—served to deceive the participant into believing in the science of the machine. Furthermore, she asks the question what would have happened if the machine had an 'abort' button and point out that in Milgram's experiment only one participant tried to press the 'off' button. Overall, she makes the point the Milgram's machine was designed with use of human factors principles as a persuasive interaction design that led the participant to follow a technical procedure to administer more shock than the participant would have done with a more traditional interaction design for such a machine (Oppenheimer, 2015). The shock generator machine thus achieved agency in the experiment; it was a design for obedience.

Milgram succeeded in designing for obedience to the authority, and he may not be the only one doing that. Seen in a wider context, socio-technical HCI designers should really be careful not to follow in Milgram's footsteps, so to speak, and design for users' obedience of AI, robots, and IoT environments. One way to do so is to recognize that UX-at-work is not simply the dramatic outcome of interacting with a product or a (single) work system; rather UX-at-work is produced and reproduced in the many unremarkable human–computer-interactive relations in the everyday organizational system (Clemmensen, Hertzum, & Abdelnour-Nocera, 2020), and the interaction design should be analyzed for its agency within such as system.

Designing for obedience with ethical AI, robots, and IoT environments as design elements within organizations may be both something to avoid and at the same time necessary. In HWID, context is also "historical"—so what historical conditions shape the use of AI, robots, and IoT environments within in organizations? Socio-technical HCI design approaches are local (situated, etc.) but may sometimes lack an understanding of the historical 'framing' of the design. For example, there has been much unmet optimism before about AI, so history provides perhaps a warning against this. While the current target of human-centered principles of AI includes a reasonable "to make stakeholders aware of their interactions with AI systems, including in the workplace", it seems quite unrealistic that affected users should be able to: "… challenge its outcome based on plain and easy-to-understand information on the factors, and the logic that served as the basis for the prediction, recommendation or decision" (OECD,

2019). The idea that obedience happens in frames of personal power or organizational structures may be insufficient for newer types of governance in organizations that emphasize both bureaucracy and democratic values and processes; in these, a Foucault-like 'moral obedience' is becoming the aim of managerial strategies (Courpasson & Dany, 2003). Managers then aim to create communities of workers who have moral obedience in terms of a sense of duty, uniqueness, and competitiveness (Courpasson & Dany, 2003). While this sounds good and perhaps even necessary in today's fluent and fragile organizational contexts, it may also have downsides such as when a moral obedience toward doing something good for the world by fulfilling the workers' business goals actually leads to work intensification (Dupret & Pultz, 2021) and less decent work. Thus, involving workers in the design of ethical AI within organizations may both be necessary for the organization's productivity with AI, but may despite good intentions also have negative outcomes such as work intensifies (because, who would not want to save the world?).

10.2 Affective Interaction Experiences in the Workplace

The design of experience machines

Why would workers obey management's machine learning algorithms beyond what is required to get paid (Faraj et al., 2018)? HCI's answer seems to be that people get valuable user experiences in return for their interactions with the computers. In the recent decades, HCI researchers have formulated the outcome of interacting with computers as that of usability and user experience. Recently, attempts have been made to conceptualize the relation between UX and worker well-being (Hertzum, 2019). However, the answer to what may UX contribute to workers' well-being in their everyday work life seems to depend on what perspectives on UX and work that is taken. If, for example, workers take on themselves to do digital job crafting, this may be felt as more authentic UX contribution to their well-being, compared to when management gives the workers better UX through new devices which can be in-authentic. That is, the mode of being in Heidegger's terms matters for the UX influence on well-being (Hertzum, 2019). Thus, when the computer is present at hand—comes into existence as an everyday object by being given a theoretical gaze—focus is on the computer and the UX contributions to well-being at work may be the well-known "wow"'-feeling or it may be negative frustrations over the computer not working properly. When the computer is ready to hand—when it comes into existence by fitting into a meaningful network of purposes and functions, that is, when it becomes part of a world of practice—focus is on the work practice and the UX contributions to well-being at work are perceptions of positive contributions to work. Hertzum (2019) then suggests that computers due to their unique materiality may be ambiguous and come into existence both as present at hand and ready to hand—it is there but it is also in the background—when the focus is on the task and the UX contributions to well-being at work then is the enabling and empowering aspects of computers that the worker and the work organization can do something more than without. This 'middle ground' resonates well with the spirit of HWID that calls for weaving relations between the social (computers ready to hand, integrated into practice) and the technical (computers present at hand as objectified 'wow' experiences).

The design of HCI's 'experience machines' may be an ambiguous affair with computers (Desmet & Pohlmeyer, 2013). The term 'experience machines' comes from a thought experiment in philosophy that is mostly thought to be an argument against hedonism (Rowland, 2017). That is, it can be used as an argument against hedonic UX. In HCI, it has been brought in as an argument for considering how AI technology both promises endless hedonic experiences and challenge us to live authentic lives (Hedman, 2020). The thought experiment is to imagine a future where we can enter a machine that will give us all the experiences we would wish to have, that is, a perfect virtual reality world in which all of our dreams were fulfilled, and we cannot remember that once we were outside and our bodies are still outside this virtual world (think a positive version of Matrix the movie). The dilemma facing the user of such a machine is if we would enter it? The argument for those people who have been asked to try the thought experiment and who said not, I will not enter, is that they choose the authentic life, and the others, who says yes, choose the hedonic life. Here we will not concern ourselves with the philosophers' dilemma and their discussions of variations of the experiment's conditions, but simply point out that (1) HCI has already created the experience machine—the computing devices that create the UX—and done a lot of UX research to design for people consuming these experience machine, and (2) HCI is well aware that more research is needed on how to design for an 'authentic' life that includes work life. Socio-technical HCI such as HWID aims to go beyond designing hedonic experience machines.

One possible way to go beyond the design of experience machines (design of essentialist UX) is to open up to wider perspectives on what interaction designs, human work, and their relations are. For example, Åhman and Hedman (2019) suggest that HCI may benefit from not only relying on essentialist phenomenology and instead also take inspiration from post-structuralism/deconstructionism, in particular, around three points:

- First, interaction designs are engulfing us as humans. Layers upon layers of hardware and software are what create the meaning of the IT artefacts and ourselves as users of those, with each layer revealing new meanings and identities (for example, think about coding in machine-code programming language and what that would or could do to your identity). When all layers are removed, nothing is left of the IT artefact, no essential user experience. That implies that we should analyze interaction designs as co-constructors of our lives, as existential practice. In HWID terms, the users should analyze how interaction designs co-construct their social worlds of work and organization continuously in their everyday use.
- Second, interaction design is conditioned on users' social worlds of work and organization in the widest possible sense even when designing local solutions. An example is when the user interacts with services that collects data which are

then used to optimize services for that user and for other users of the perhaps global services such as those provided by the big tech companies. So, in HWID design, in a very concrete way, it is relevant to consider how the local design is conditioned by the global contexts. For example, when using HWID for local job design, geopolitical issues such as which country should host the data may condition both the work analysis and the interaction design and the relation artefacts.

- Third, the relation artefacts that link interaction design and human work and the wider context are conflictual to varying degrees. They do not necessarily produce nice feelings among all involved. Meaning occurs through differential relations and conflict is a hermeneutic condition in which meaning is established for the time being through processes of differentiation (Åhman & Hedman, 2019). For example, conflict in the wider context may create meaning in HWID when the designed solutions realize that regional preferences for choice of scripts (left to right, right to left, bidirectional, vertical, horizontal, etc.) are not just preferences but conflictual relation artefacts.

Of course, there is also the possibility that a high level of positive UX-at-work lead to high productivity simply because happy workers are more productive workers (Peiró, Kozusznik, Rodríguez-Molina, & Tordera, 2019).

Animism and vibrant matter

Since in HWID anything can be a design material, HWID is agnostic toward the distinction between the material and the non-material that is so important to socio-materialists and critical realists alike, see, for example, (Faulkner & Runde, 2013, 2019; Schultze et al., 2018). At the same time, HWID (and all socio-technical HCI design) acknowledges the animistic/anthropomorphic power of (interactive) things. It is inspirational to acknowledge the vitality and agency of the matter of everyday IT artefacts (Bødker, 2017). For example, for HWID the notions of animism and 'vibrant matter' may help HWID researchers, practitioners, and policymakers to be sensitive toward the small, overlooked agencies of multiple IT artefacts that together exists and can though their embeddedness as matter provide more sustainable designs. For example, a vibrant matter lens can help cultivate other kinds of relations to our 'material' world that ultimately enables wonder and 'care', which again means that we will be less likely to engage in 'buy and throw away' culture. Animism typically denotes a belief that things (objects, artefacts) are 'alive'; this may mean that they have a personality or possesses some form of irreducible and non-mechanical vitality that scaffolds HCI design research and practice (Chang, Giaccardi, Chen, & Liang, 2017; Marenko & Van Allen, 2016; Plattner et al., 2011; Rozendaal et al., 2019; Van Allen, McVeigh-Schultz, Brown, Kim, & Lara, 2013). Vibrant matter indicates a world of things that is teeming with life, vibrant forces and flows engaged in continuous interchange. It suggests the potential of a discovering a 'thing-power' that imbues the non-human and inorganic with agential and willful qualities, blurring the boundaries between the living and the inert, between life and nonlife. The notion of vibrant matter was taken up in the work by political philosopher Jane Bennett (Bennett, 2010) to indicate the capacity of things to 'matter' beyond their causal/functional charge. Animism and vibrant matter are notions that ontologically support design for sustainable ethical practices, since these notions point out the wider context agency of 'smart' digital devices and machines (such as smartphones) with voice interaction, speech agents or context awareness, responsive environments and off-the-shelf sensor-actuator-based cyber-physical interactions, artificial intelligence and neural network processing, and other currently developing applications such as autonomous vehicles. Animism and vibrant matter are thus concrete conditions and outcomes of HWID projects, and in this sense HWID may be recruited by what has been called animistic design (Marenko & Van Allen, 2016).

10.3 Design in the Anthropocene Age

Going from the vibrant matter perspective to the anthropocene, HWID may with inspiration from thinking about vibrant matter adopt a more conscious planetary perspective. The logic can be that if vibrant matter paints a picture of technology as somehow 'alive', this provides a lens that can help HWID and other socio-technical HCI designers become involved in broader concerns such as sustainability, etc.

Planetary Interaction Design (PID)

Though HWID most probably should be used to design for individual persons and work organizations, it is clear that the research and development of socio-technical HCI design has implications for global issues such as epidemics and climate crisis and working conditions on the planetary level. This invites to thinking big and beyond HCI and societal issues (Lazar et al., 2016) to instead go to the planetary level. Socio-technical HCI design has the potential to facilitate or hinder UN development goals such as sustainable behavior and decent work. This should be seen in the context of geopolitical issues that shape what HCI is and will become (Linxen et al., 2021). HWID needs to engage systematically with thinking through how to scale up socio-technical HCI design approaches to support the business of interaction design for and with the planet that we live on and the planets that we may want to live on. This may, for example, include thinking about HCI and 'deep time' of planets (Rahm-Skågeby & Rahm, 2021), and acknowledging the (geo)political aspects of design. Current socio-technical HCI design approaches such as activity theory (Clemmensen et al., 2016), practice-based design (Wulf et al., 2015), action design research (Sein et al., 2011), sociomaterial design (Bjørn & Østerlund, 2014), and perhaps also speculative design (Auger, 2013), may be geopolitically naïve and fixed in regional thinking and societal needs. Current HCI designs expressed in phone apps and social media sites are nearly global in their diffusion, but do not sufficiently take co-design and ethical value exchange into account (Hertzum et al., 2018) and do not seem aware of their own local-ness (Abdelnour-Nocéra, Clemmensen, & Kurosu, 2013). To scale up such approaches and designs, a PID HWID methodology must be developed. This can be a major part of future research in HWID. From a business and psychological point of view, the PID methodology and other outcome of the future HWID research work should help researchers and practitioners and policymakers to design for reconciling the discernible individual human creator with manufacturing processes distributed across planetary brands, designing teams, and production systems to (re-) create a circular economy (Kashima, 2020).

The requirement to self-reflect in the anthropocene

In the emerging anthropocenic age, socio-technical HCI designers should reflect on how psychological processes are part of a future view of culture as a tool that humans use to design their planetary world(s) (Kashima, 2016). This is in the tradition of Tavistock. For example, socio-technical HCI should take care of the self in negotiating the socio-technical relationship. However, to take care of the self may be provoking to technology researchers concerned with transformation of the external environments, but inattentive to self-transformation (Kou, Gui, Chen, & Nardi, 2019). The self is often more difficult than the external environment to recognize or measure, compared to external factors (Kou et al., 2019), as proponents of the socio-technical have experienced throughout the decades of research, practice, and policymaking. The socio-technical requirement to self-reflect merges with systems psychology in many ways in the past and the future of the socio-technical design approach, from the idea of psychoanalytic self-reflection in practical action research, the whole (psychological system) is greater than its parts (individual psychologies), the wish to think about changes in society, and to how design may be the key to humanity's future.

References

Abdelnour-Nocera, J., Clemmensen, T., Hertzum, M., Singh, D., & Singh, V. V. (2019). Socio-technical HCI for ethical value exchange: Lessons from India. In *International conference on social implications of computers in developing countries* (pp. 229–240). Springer.

Abdelnour-Nocéra, J., Clemmensen, T., & Kurosu, M. (2013). Reframing HCI through local and indigenous perspectives. *International Journal of Human-Computer Interaction, 29*(4). https://doi.org/10.1080/10447318.2013.765759.

Åhman, H., & Hedman, A. (2019). Frameworks for studying social media interaction: A discussion on phenomenology and poststructuralism. In *IFIP conference on human-computer interaction* (pp. 701–718). Springer.

Auger, J. (2013). Speculative design: Crafting the speculation. *Digital Creativity, 24*(1), 11–35.

Bannon, L. J. (1991). From human factors to human actors. book chapter in greenbaum. In J. Greenbaum & M. Kyng (Eds.)*Design at work: Cooperative design of computer systems* (pp. 25–44). Hillsdale: Lawrence Erlbaum Associates.

Bennett, J. (2010). *Vibrant matter: A political ecology of things.* Duke University Press.

Bjørn, P., & Østerlund, C. (2014). *Sociomaterial-design: Bounding technologies in practice.* Springer.

Bødker, M. (2017). "What else is there…?": Reporting meditations in experiential computing. *European Journal of Information Systems, 26*(3), 274–286.

Campos, P., Clemmensen, T., Abdelnour Nocera, J., Katre, D., Lopes, A., & Ørngreen, R. (2012). *Human work interaction design. Work analysis and HCI Third IFIP 13.6 working conference, HWID 2012, Copenhagen, Denmark, December 5–6, 2012, Revised Selected Papers.* Springer Berlin Heidelberg.

Card, S. K., Moran, T. P., & Newell, A. (1983). *The psychology of human-computer interaction.* Hillsdale, NJ: Lawrence Erlbaum Associates.

Carroll, J. M., & Campbell, R. (1986). Softening up hard science: Reply to newell and card. *Human-Computer Interaction, 2*(3), 227–249. https://doi.org/10.1207/s15327051hci0203_3.

Chang, W.-W., Giaccardi, E., Chen, L.-L., & Liang, R.-H. (2017). " Interview with Things" a first-thing perspective to understand the scooter's everyday socio-material network in Taiwan. In *Proceedings of the 2017 Conference on Designing Interactive Systems* (pp. 1001–1012).

Chapanis, A., Garner, W. R., & Morgan, C. T. (1949). *Applied experimental psychology: Human factors in engineering design.*

Clarke, M. F. (2015). The work of mad men that makes the methods of math men work: Practically occasioned segment design. In *Proceedings of the 33rd Annual ACM Conference on Human Factors in Computing Systems* (pp. 3275–3284). https://doi.org/10.1145/2702123.2702493.

Clemmensen, T. (2006). Whatever happened to the psychology of human-computer interaction?: A biography of the life of a psychological framework within a HCI journal. *Information Technology & People, 19,* 121–151. https://doi.org/10.1108/09593840610673793.

Clemmensen, T., Campos, P., Orngreen, R., Mark-Pejtersen, A., & Wong, W. (2006). *Human work interaction design: Designing for human work.* Springer Science+Business Media.

Clemmensen, T., Hertzum, M., & Abdelnour-Nocera, J. (2020). Ordinary user experiences at work. *ACM Transactions on Computer-Human Interaction, 27*(3). https://doi.org/10.1145/3386089.

Clemmensen, T., Kaptelinin, V., & Nardi, B. (2016). Making HCI theory work: An analysis of the use of activity theory in HCI research. *Behaviour & Information Technology, 35*(8), 608–627. https://doi.org/10.1080/0144929X.2016.1175507.

Courpasson, D., & Dany, F. (2003). Indifference or obedience? Business firms as democratic hybrids. *Organization Studies, 24*(8), 1231–1260.

Desmet, P., & Pohlmeyer, A. (2013). Positive design: An introduction to design for subjective well-being. *International Journal of Design, 7*(3).

Dourish, P. (2006). Implications for design. In *Proceedings of the SIGCHI Conference on Human Factors in Computing Systems* (pp. 541–550).

Dupret, K., & Pultz, S. (2021). Hard/heart worker: Work intensification in purpose-driven organizations. *Qualitative Research in Organizations and Management: An International Journal.*

Faraj, S., Pachidi, S., & Sayegh, K. (2018). Working and organizing in the age of the learning algorithm. *Information and Organization, 28*(1), 62–70.

Faulkner, P., & Runde, J. (2013). Technological objects, social positions, and the transformational model of social activity. *MIS Quarterly*, 803–818.

Faulkner, P., & Runde, J. (2019). Theorizing the digital object. *MIS Quarterly, 43*(4).

Forlano, L. (2017). Posthumanism and design. *She Ji: The Journal of Design, Economics, and Innovation, 3*(1), 16–29. https://doi.org/10.1016/j.sheji.2017.08.001.

Fuchsberger, V., Murer, M., Krischkowsky, A., & Tscheligi, M. (2016). Interaction design labels: Concepts, inscriptions, and concealed intentions. In *Proceedings of the 2016 ACM Conference on Designing Interactive Systems* (pp. 108–120).

Fuchsberger, V., Murer, M., & Tscheligi, M. (2014). Human-computer non-interaction: The activity of non-use. In *Proceedings of the 2014 Companion Publication on Designing Interactive Systems* (pp. 57–60).

Gardien, P., Djajadiningrat, T., Hummels, C., & Brombacher, A. (2014). Changing your hammer: The implications of paradigmatic innovation for design practice. *International Journal of Design, 8*(2). Retrieved from http://www.ijdesign.org/index.php/IJDesign/article/view/1315.

Gibson, S. (2019). Obedience without orders: Expanding social psychology's conception of 'obedience.' *British Journal of Social Psychology, 58*(1), 241–259.

Hedman, A. (2020). A View from Outside the Loop. In F. Loizides, M. Winckler, U. Chatterjee, J. Abdelnour-Nocera, & A. Parmaxi (Eds.), *Human Computer Interaction and Emerging Technologies: Adjunct Proceedings from the INTERACT 2019 Workshops* (pp. 215–220). https://doi.org/10.18573/book3.ac.

Hertzum, M. (2019). Wellbeing at work: Four perspectives on what user experiences with artifacts may contribute. In *IFIP Conference on Human-Computer Interaction* (pp. 19–25). Springer.

Hertzum, M., Singh, V. V., Clemmensen, T., Singh, D., Valtolina, S., Abdelnour-Nocera, J., & Qin, X. (2018). A mobile APP for supporting sustainable fishing practices in alibaug. *Interactions, 25*(3). https://doi.org/10.1145/3194324.

Kashima, Y. (2016). Culture and psychology in the 21st century: Conceptions of culture and person for psychology revisited. *Journal of Cross-Cultural Psychology, 47*(1), 4–20.

Kashima, Y. (2020). Cultural dynamics for sustainability: How can humanity craft cultures of sustainability? *Current Directions in Psychological Science*, 0963721420949516.

Kou, Y., Gui, X., Chen, Y., & Nardi, B. (2019). Turn to the self in human-computer interaction: Care of the self in negotiating the human-technology relationship. In *Proceedings of the 2019 CHI Conference on Human Factors in Computing Systems* (pp. 1–15).

Lazar, J., Abascal, J., Barbosa, S., Barksdale, J., Friedman, B., Grossklags, J., ... Martínez-Normand, L. (2016). *Human–computer interaction and international public policymaking: a framework for understanding and taking future actions*. Retrieved from https://eprints.mdx.ac.uk/20131/1/mentaction-plan-2011-2015.

Leonardi, P. M. (2011). When flexible routines meet flexible technologies: Affordance, constraint, and the imbrication of human and material agencies. *MIS Quarterly*, 147–167.

Liao, Q. V., Gruen, D., & Miller, S. (2020). Questioning the AI: Informing design practices for explainable AI user experiences. In *Proceedings of the 2020 CHI Conference on Human Factors in Computing Systems*, 1–15. https://doi.org/10.1145/3313831.3376590.

Light, A., Powell, A., & Shklovski, I. (2017). Design for existential crisis in the anthropocene age. In *Proceedings of the 8th International Conference on Communities and Technologies* (pp. 270–279). ACM.

Linxen, S., Sturm, C., Brühlmann, F., Cassau, V., Opwis, K., & Reinecke, K. (2021). How WEIRD is CHI?. In *Proceedings of the 2021 CHI Conference on Human Factors in Computing Systems* (pp. 1–14).

Marenko, B., & Van Allen, P. (2016). Animistic design: How to reimagine digital interaction between the human and the nonhuman. *Digital Creativity, 27*(1), 52–70.

Mumford, E. (2006). The story of socio-technical design: Reflections on its Successes, Failures and Potential. *Information Systems Journal, 16*(4), 317–342. https://doi.org/10.1111/j.1365-2575.2006.00221.x.

OECD. (2019). *Recommendation of the Council on Artificial Intelligence, OECD/LEGAL/0449*.

Oppenheimer, M. (2015). Designing obedience in the lab: Milgram's shock simulator and human factors engineering. *Theory & Psychology, 25*(5), 599–621.

Peiró, J. M., Kozusznik, M. W., Rodríguez-Molina, I., & Tordera, N. (2019). The happy-productive worker model and beyond: Patterns of wellbeing and performance at work. *International Journal of Environmental Research and Public Health, 16*(Article No. 3). https://doi.org/10.3390/ijerph16030479.

Plattner, H., Meinel, C., & Leifer, L. (2011). Design Thinking Understand-Improve-Apply. In *Profiles of drug substances, excipients, and related methodology*. https://doi.org/10.1016/B978-0-12-387667-6.00013-0.

Rahm-Skågeby, J., & Rahm, L. (2021). HCI and deep time: Towards deep time design thinking. *Human-Computer Interaction*. https://doi.org/10.1080/07370024.2021.1902328.

Rowland, R. (2017). Our intuitions about the experience machine. *J. Ethics & Soc. Phil., 12*, 110.

Rozendaal, M. C., Boon, B., & Kaptelinin, V. (2019). Objects with intent: Designing everyday things as collaborative partners. *ACM Transactions on Computer-Human Interaction (TOCHI), 26*(4), 1–33.

Schultze, U., Aanestad, M., Mähring, M., Østerlund, C., & Riemer, K. (2018). *Living with monsters? Social implications of algorithmic phenomena, hybrid agency, and the performativity of technology*. Springer.

Sein, M. K., Henfridsson, O., Purao, S., Rossi, M., & Lindgren, R. (2011). Action design research. *MIS Quarterly*.https://doi.org/10.2307/23043488.

Van Allen, P., McVeigh-Schultz, J., Brown, B., Kim, H. M., & Lara, D. (2013). AniThings: animism and heterogeneous multiplicity. In *CHI'13 extended abstracts on human factors in computing systems* (pp. 2247–2256).

Wang, D., Weisz, J. D., Muller, M., Ram, P., Geyer, W., Dugan, C., … Gray, A. (2019). Human-AI collaboration in data science: Exploring data scientists' perceptions of automated AI. In *Proceedings of the ACM on Human-Computer Interaction, 3*(CSCW) (pp. 1–24).

Wulf, V., Müller, C., Volkmar, P., Randall, D., Rohde, M., & Stevens, G. (2015). Practice-based computing: Empirically grounded conceptualizations derived from design case studies. In V. Wulf, K. Schmidt, & D. Randall (Eds.), *Designing socially embedded technologies in the real-world* (pp. 111–150). https://doi.org/10.1007/978-1-4471-6720-4_7.

Chapter 11
Sketching for Digital Human Work

Abstract This chapter summarizes and concludes on HWID as a form of socio-technical HCI design under the heading 'Sketching for digital human work'. It lists the main insights in one display. These include that theorizing for socio-technical HCI should avoid the technological determinism trap, that the HWID platform is a solution to avoid this, and that it should be used as a multi-sided platform, open for interpretation and change, to design and valorize local theory relevant to the local community. Furthermore, it includes four types of socio-technical relation artefacts associated with psychological need finding, socio-technical ideation sketching, socio-technical hypothesis prototyping, and action and design interventions. These insights should be particularly useful to any HCI researcher interested in action-oriented approaches to HCI in organizations and work settings. With the HWID platform, they should be able to involve most stakeholder groups in theorizing about socio-technical HCI and do this in a context and culturally sensitive way. Furthermore, the HWID approach supports consultancy and policy work of importance to many people. The ideal is that workers will be the designers of their own (work) world. Hence, in contrast to some work design methodologies, sketching for human work with the HWID platform is an open and accessible approach.

Keywords Human work interaction design · HWID insights · Design implications

11.1 Main Insight

This book has presented HWID as an open platform for theory and action that invites to various interpretations of what theory is and a broad understanding of design as actions in organizational and work settings. The title of this chapter—sketching for digital human work—alludes to the unfinished and creative aspects of any HWID project, since humans can always change what has been designed for and with them. The main contribution of the book is the introduction of four types of HWID relation artefacts. These connect the social and the technical in organizations in ways that increase productivity and worker satisfaction, empower workers in decision-making, focus on whole tasks beyond any spatial–temporal boundaries, and lead to workers doing interesting things in digitalized workplaces.

This book is for HCI researchers who can use the platform as a way to accumulate knowledge across design case studies. Furthermore, research-inclined consultants who need HCI platforms can quickly adapt the HWID platform to action designs for improving UX-at-work in local organizational settings. Finally, the book is intended to be useful to policymakers, who can use the HWID platform to enable dialogues about and set policies for procurement of digital solutions in organizational and government settings.

11.2   HWID Relation Artefact Insights

The socio-technical HCI design qualities may vary across approaches. In general, however, socio-technical HCI design approaches are anchored in social sciences and humanities, rather than in technical sciences. They share a view of the human as engaged in both the social and the technical, they aim more at social change than technical change, and they design interactive IT solutions with humans as part of the solutions. Each approach has, however, also unique qualities, and thus HWID has unique qualities, Fig. 11.1.

The first socio-technical HCI design quality, illustrated in the first row in Fig. 11.1, is the view of the human. In HWID, the notion of the human is not as a single individual 'processor component' or 'Human Factor' or 'worker identity'; rather the human in HWID is relational and distributed. The notion of the human in HWID is psychological which is closer to experience design's basic psychological needs (Hassenzahl, 2010) than practice-based design's social change (Volker Wulf et al., 2018) or design tensions' awareness principles (Gross, 2013). At the same time, the notion of the human in HWID is more relational and distributed than experience design and perhaps more akin to distributed cognition (Hollan et al., 2000) and classic activity theory's (Engeström, 1999) tool-focused collective humans. The notion of the human in HWID is also more individual than in action design research (Sein, Henfridsson, Purao, Rossi, & Lindgren, 2011) and design thinking for managers (Kolko, 2015) which has the organization as the unit of analysis.

On the other hand, the notion of the human in HWID illustrated in Fig. 11.1 shares with action design research (Sein et al., 2011) and design thinking for managers (Kolko, 2015) a stepwise design-oriented view of humans. The relational artefacts in HWID conceptualize the human worker in a series of design moves. These are centered on finding worker' needs, collaboratively sketching solutions, prototyping worker experiences, and intervening to create workers' digital legacies. They end up with sociomaterial solutions that have no borders between the social and the technical and the human and the context.

The second socio-technical HCI design quality is about the historical roots. The second row in Fig. 11.1 illustrates that HWID as a socio-technical HCI design approach has roots both in Mumford's business-oriented approach (Mumford, 2000)

| Sociotechnical | HWID Relations artefacts (R1-R4) | | | |
HCI design qualities	R1	R2	R3	R4
1. In HWID the "view of the human" is as distributed over organization, work, individual, and interaction designs.	*Designing relation artefacts Type I is about finding psychological needs from both an interaction design and a work analysis point of view.*	*Designing relation artefacts Type II is about socio-technical ideation sketching with collaborative sketching.*	*Designing relation artefacts Type III is about socio-technical hypothesis prototyping of worker experiences.*	*Designing relation artefacts Type IV is about socio-technical interventions in organizational and wider contexts.*
2. A defining feature of the original Tavistock institute's socio-technical approach was that the researchers and practitioners there were interested in psychological and social change for groups of people. Cognitive work analysis was invented to do this by among others Annelise Mark Pejtersen, who subsequently founded the HWID IFIP 13.6 working group.	The organizational (management) problem definition prepares for a HCI individual (worker) problem definition. It can be applied to mundane everyday organizational problems, not only wicked problems. The capabilities of (some) IT artifacts are coequal with the people and the organizational and social contexts in meeting business goals.	The interaction design patterns support socio-technical idea sketching in dealing with open, complex problems in organizations, by fulfilling workers needs with novel interaction designs. A work interaction patterns, they may act as 'design frames' for how to organize the social arrangement/organizational structure related to the use of interaction designs.	The organizational action hypotheses support organizational strategy making by a broad group of stakeholders including workers. This adds social structures, roles, educational backgrounds, etc. to materials for prototyping.	The interaction interoperability check-ups increase the interoperability of interaction designs across the organization. Two kinds are interaction design interoperability and organization and work interoperability. They should be cross-validated by being evaluated in different formats of lab, field, gallery.

Fig. 11.1 Socio-technical HCI design qualities with focus on HWID and sorted on relation artefacts

and in the engineering-oriented approach of cognitive work analysis (Rasmussen, Pejtersen, & Schmidt, 1990). This leads to the four relation artefacts starting in alternate positions of the social (R1, R3) and the technical (R2, R4) start positions. While both Mumford's approach and cognitive work analysis are social science and humanities-oriented, they are so in different ways, one being more social and the other being more technical flavored. This difference is somewhat integrated in HWID's series of alternating social and technical beginnings of the design moves with relation artefacts.

The third socio-technical HCI design quality circles around what is actually designed. The third row of Fig. 11.1 illustrates the central relation artefacts that serves to focus the locally valorized sociomaterial action designs based on the HWID platform. These are findings of workers' needs, collaborative sketches, prototyped worker experiences, and digital legacy interventions. What makes these central for linking the social and the technical are that they are locally valorized, that is, the values designed into the instantiations of the relation artefacts are those held by local stakeholders engaged in the hands-on design activities. In addition, in contrast to the classic idea of narrowing down the design problem across a series of design

3. HWID is a platform that serves to develop locally valorized sociomaterial action designs.	The finding of workers' needs is a translation of user needs into worker needs in work contexts. Workers are co-responsible for identifying their own and their colleagues' user needs, including non-human actors. Workers' customization of their work systems (algorithms, devices, etc.) is a actively identify their own and their colleagues' user needs.	The collaborative sketches are the outcome of stakeholder groups' ideation such as brainstorming and commenting on each other's ideas, so the produced sketches are often less valuable than the conversations around them. They may go across levels of scale to be organizational, visual, geographical, cultural, technical solutions. Collaborative sketches are co-designed by workers.	The prototyped worker experiences differ from organizational action prototypes due to inherent conflict areas between management and workers. Four types of worker-technology relations can be prototyped as hypothetical worker experiences. Job crafting may prototype subjective, symbolic, and imaginary aspects of working in the age of AI, robots, and automation.	The digital legacy interventions make the novel design coexist with the legacy systems. These are socio-technical systems that are technically and/or socially old and need lots of maintenance but solve important problems for organizations and meet individual employees' needs. Interaction design for digital legacy is also about workers' feelings about their digital legacy in the workplace.
	4a. HWID and the Experience Design (ED) approach have overlapping notions of experiences as subjective, holistic, situated, and dynamic.	**4b. HWID may learn from the Design Tensions (DTs) approach that design can be understood as designing compromises between stakeholders towards a set of basic tensions of availability, privacy, conventions, and tailoring.**	**4c. HWID and the Practice-Based Design (PBD) approach share a notion of context as wider organizational, regional, national, cultural, social, technological, political contexts.**	**4d. The impact of HWID is on human collaborations with algorithms in the field, while meeting the socio-technical HCI design obligation to be aware of inner life. This is done with designing with a relation artefact perspective.**
	The creation of work personas embeds the organizational design problems and the employee need identifications in interaction design activities. Contextual personas are created by analyzing collected, interpreted, and focused data with a theoretical model of work. HWID opt for psychological need- and social metaphor- based contextual personas.	The workflow convergences are organizational evaluations of the collaborative sketches produced with inspiration from workplace interaction patterns. However, stakeholders acting as evaluators may have troubles accurately distinguishing good from bad ideas, so the idea convergence may be supported using organizational devices for hosting and choosing among multiple design ideas for the organizational workflows.	The UX-at-work field evaluations capture the UX-at-work in terms of an acceptable level of both pragmatic and hedonic qualities The interactions among task, structure, technology, and actors determine how the UX-at-work is experienced.	The organizational strategy alignments serve to ensure that the designed solutions are aligned with the long-term goals of the organization. Having a UX culture in the organization eases alignment. Co-evaluation with software developers and work domain experts eases alignment. In organizations with a people-centered approach job crafting may help align HWID with organizational strategy, and managers may facilitate this through encouragement.

Fig. 11.1 (continued)

activities, such as designers can do with the 'design funnel' (Greenberg, Carpendale, Marquardt, & Buxton, 2011), the design movements in HWID do not narrow the scope of the design problem, but instead make the relation between the social and the technical gradually more sociomaterial. Thus, finding workers' needs are the least and digital legacy interventions are the most entangled type of relation artefacts. Visually stated, HWID is less like running down through the funnel and more like building railroad tracks.

The fourth socio-technical HCI design quality shown in Fig. 11.1 touches on the impact of design activities, where the design will end up. Thus, the fourth and final rows in Fig. 11.1 illustrate how the four types of HWID relation artefacts each have different impacts and how they share these impacts with other socio-technical HCI design approaches.

11.3   Implications

Implications for academic researchers

For academic researchers, HWID is a flexible, holistic, configurational, and gestalt-oriented approach. The aim of academic research activities within the area of HWID is to establish relationships between empirical work-domain knowledge and interaction design activities. There is a long list of user requirements to HWID theory-as-a-product.

The use of HWID by academic researchers should be done with clarity with regard to whether the aim with HWID research is descriptive (how the world is), normative (how to change things into preferable states, how it ought to be), or critical (ask questions) HWID research. Obviously, a project can be done with multiple aims.

The theorizing workshop is a method for using the HWID platform to create publishable theory. HWID research will often be done as qualitative research. Qualitative analysis is the search for and documentation of novel constructs and their relations, which fits HWID aims. Qualitative analysis can be tailored to HWID with sensitizing concepts and coding families, and more. Both qualitative and quantitative modeling can be useful tools in both formative and summative evaluations in HWID. An exploratory quantitative modeling of HWID cases may be particularly relevant for measuring quantifiable outcomes of HWID projects such as user experiences. In any case, the outcome should be HWID gestalts that are theorized.

Implications for practitioners

For HWID consultants, the relations between human work and interaction designs are central. A generic process model for HWID consultancy has five major design decisions to make. (1) Decide with management and workers on the context, discuss and decide what counts as (2) social and (3) technical in the project, (4) include whatever domain-specific theory and methods that appear useful, and (5) continue with iteratively working with the relation artefacts to link the social and the technical. Further design sessions consist of planned movements between the social and the technical.

To understand consultants' use of socio-technical HCI design approaches, it is necessary to consider the humanistic and psychological aspect of socio-technical design approaches in industry and business practice. HWID for consultants is intended to be a lightweight and contemporary HCI-oriented interpretation of socio-technical design approaches that is useful to consultants working with SMEs in industry and business.

An insight from design cases is that socio-technical design approaches in practical consultancy tend to be backgrounded and coexisting with competing or overlapping other approaches. Consultants applying the HWID platform act as relation builders who reflect with relation artefacts together with participants and other stakeholders. Negotiating the context is an important design decision that consultants must handle continuously during the project.

Methodological dimensions for socio-technical HCI design consultancy include trade unions versus management perspectives and authoritative knowledge versus participants' knowledge. Furthermore, there may be considerations related to applying HWID for consultancy of several companies versus single companies in the same analysis.

An ethical stance in socio-technical design consultancy includes that all stakeholders should be included in the design process; users can shape their work roles, task; and the technology offers users a sense of ownership and control.

Implications for policymakers

Policy is what decides the endgame of socio-technical HCL, the ideal state of society, that better life that is the aim with design of IT solutions. Since the meaning of emancipatory socio-technical HCI depends on our ideas about the ideal society, models of democracy and participation become important. Expertise in HWID policymaking means knowing about several ways of thinking about democracy, public policy, and HWID.

Designing user interfaces to technology is a political act. This can be spelled out in several ways. First, public policymaking may require evidence from HCI research. Second, public policy may directly decide if HCI is to live or die as a research field. Third, public policy may by setting standards increase the ethical quality of HCI research.

Policymaking with HWID relation artefacts type I begins with conceptualizing the workforce to define organizational problems, then identify class consciousness to find worker needs, and end up discussing worker identity as part of creating personas for design.

Policymaking with HWID relation artefacts type II begins with deliberations of diversity in the design in interaction patterns, then explore intersectionality in collaborative sketching of alternative solutions, and end up empowering policymakers by suggesting novel or adapted workflows for the organization.

Policymaking with HWID relation artefacts type III begins with the considering bias in organizational action hypotheses for change in the organizational setup, then prototype worker experiences for decent work based on the chosen action hypothesis, and end up doing policy-driven field evaluations and UX tests of the prototype(s).

Policymaking with HWID relation artefacts type IV begins with intersectionality interaction operability checks of how the interaction design of prototype allows cross-device continuity and cognitive and communicative socio-technical intersectionality interoperability. Then the prototypes are evaluated as interventions to ensure the workers' rights to their digital legacy. Finally, the prototypes are aligned with the organizational strategy for meeting UN development goals.

The wider context of HWID

HWID offers an opportunity to design for how human work shapes the interaction with the 'monsters' created by and consisting of algorithmic phenomena, hybrid agency, and the performativity of technologies, or, in other words, today's AI, robotics, and IoT applications. Furthermore, it offers a rare social deterministic direction to design, and helps to study how the social is done and how it shapes the technical.

Designing for obedience with ethical AI, robots, and IoT environments as design elements within organizations may be both something to avoid and at the same time necessary, since involving workers in the design of ethical AI, etc. within organizations may be necessary for the organization's productivity. However, HWID relation artefacts that link interaction design, human work, and the wider context are conflictual to varying degrees. They do not necessarily produce nice feelings among all involved. HWID encompasses however the possibility that a high level of positive UX-at-work lead to high productivity simply because happy workers are more productive workers.

HWID is agnostic toward the distinction between the material and the non-material but acknowledges the implication of live matter for the need for global and sustainable design. Thus, socio-technical HCI designers including HWID should reflect on how psychological processes are part of a future view of culture as a tool that humans use to design their planetary world.

11.4   Epilogue

An unfulfilled or perhaps unformed ambition with HWID is to play with the aesthetics of the platform. Let us imagine that we are in the 2060s. Max works as a researcher-consultant-policymaker who for a living do human work interaction designs for other people, organizations, and governments. In the projects, Max and the stakeholders adapt Max's set of relation artefacts to create HWID gestalts with a duration from a week up to lifelong work lives. Max's relation artefacts have evolved from many previous projects, each with their peculiar characteristics, and they are now very Max-like. On a rainy July morning in 2063, Max ponders about the scenes that shaped previous HWID gestalts.

Scene 1: Design hierarchies

Max was a long time figuring out if HWID relation artefacts should be thought of as multiple layers of IT artefacts focused on same task, somewhat like second- and third-order artefacts in automation. Or perhaps they are just flat. At the university, Max had learnt that HWID was born out of cognitive work analysis, engineering Human Factors, macro-ergonomics, formal methods, and more that all had a lot of hierarchy built in. Just out of university, it seemed to Max that HWID was as part of formal task-artefact-worker modeling cycle. However, at the same time, network analysis and value analysis were cast as all-important and Max could intuitively agree with this. In the end, Max thought that HWID was supposed to be simple to use, so why not stick to a flat two-dimensional way of thinking about relation artefacts? Since then, Max only used hierarchy in HWID when it seemed unavoidable, for example, when a client insisted, but other than those projects, Max was happy with flat HWID.

Scene 2: Design boundaries

Early on, Max realized that HWID was relational design, that is, that the social and the technical mutually constituted each other. In fact, HWID's usefulness was not in analytical depth, but in presenting some terminology that fixed what were the actors in the network and what were the relations. The terminology thus offered boundaries that made HWID projects having a kind of border to an outside of the project. On the other hand, a great feature of HWID appeared to be the openness and lack of borders in the design, that is, design without borders. Realizing the usefulness and beauty of this ambiguity, Max decided to not see any boundaries at the beginning of a HWID project, however acknowledging that boundaries are made and remade concretely by applying relation artefacts.

Scene 3: Design movements

After having done the first 10 years of socio-technical HCI design, Max was bored by development models. Even socio-technical HCI design process models were often drawn as waterfalls, where you could nearly see the water fall down the stairs of waterfall models, circles such as models of agile user-centered design, or spirals that could like fractals illustrate exceedingly beautiful and complex ways of involving stakeholders. Still, Max found them so explicit, so stepwise, and so boring.

Instead of giving up on the process models, however, Max found a less explicit, fluent, and engaging way by imagining HWID design movements as painting leaves or feathers dropping to the ground, Fig. 11.2. Today, Max sees HWID as something done with care and lightness.

Scene 4: Design directions

After the feather-realization, Max felt like a painter rather than as a designer. It soon dawned, however, that not everything falls nicely to the ground in good order. The start and end of socio-technical HCI design process models were historically often suggested to be identifiable with doing user requirement at the beginning and organizational implementation at the end of the design process. HCI design was, however, always less structured, for example, the STAR model (Hartson & Hix, 1989) allows to begin anywhere in the star as long as evaluation with users (the core of the star) is part of the activity. Max did see HWID as having no fixed start or

Fig. 11.2. HWID design movements done as feathers dropping to the ground

Fig. 11.3 HWID as laying out railroad tracks somewhere

ending, and even, unlike the Star, as having no core. The context bar was the real hero in HWID, in Max's view, since a project could often begin by grounding the given design project in the context bar, and then lay out the social, the technical, and the relation artefacts as elements of a railroad, Fig. 11.3.

As another nineteenth-century railroad crew, Max likes to decide on the context and lay out the HWID tracks for a project that designs a major part of the clients' work life for the next 5 years.

Scene 5: Design forms

Today, Max, though often being in solitude, never works alone, and never without giving form to the HWID gestalt. HWID projects for Max are both a process and a phenomenon, and thus the design gestalts continue to be discussable and touchable. Max likes to move fluently between forms, doing design movements in apps, LEGO, wood, paper, etc. In 2063, the HWID app is a powerful easy-to-use tool that hammers out relation artefacts for a given work domain. It exists as HoloLens cognitive extensions that are downloadable and allow Max to allow other stakeholders to do the HWID, if they are bodily closer or in other important ways closer to the given project context. LEGO has together with Max developed a HWID package that enables students to do design gestalts within minutes and discuss those, something that began years ago, see Fig. 11.4 for an early example of a LEGO HWID gestalt.

Max is experimenting with other HWID gestalt design forms such as human size scale wood constructions, or calligraphy strokes with a pen. Perhaps Max is a bit tactile and try-it-out type of HWID researcher-consultant-policymakers, but that is Max's style, others can do it in their way. Max is a Chinese citizen, and Fig. 11.5 shows HWID in Chinese.

Max likes to deliver the HWID to the client in multiple forms usually including a HWID wood model for the aesthetic reflection of the eye and the hand, and a HWID HoloLens app for helping the client applying the project's relation artefacts in the everyday work life.

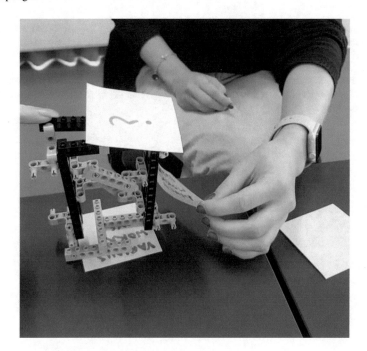

Fig. 11.4 LEGO used by two students to design HWID

Fig. 11.5 Human (人) work
(工作) interaction (交互)
design (设计)

人工作交互设计

References

Engeström, Y. (1999). Expansive visibilization of work: An activity-theoretical perspective. *Computer Supported Cooperative Work (CSCW), 8*(1), 63–93.

Greenberg, S., Carpendale, S., Marquardt, N., & Buxton, B. (2011). *Sketching user experiences: The workbook*. Elsevier.

Gross, T. (2013). Supporting effortless coordination: 25 years of awareness research. *Computer Supported Cooperative Work (CSCW), 22*(4), 425–474. https://doi.org/10.1007/s10606-013-9190-x

Hartson, H. R., & Hix, D. (1989). Human-computer interface development: Concepts and systems for its management. *ACM Computing Surveys (CSUR), 21*(1), 5–92.

Hassenzahl, M. (2010). Experience design: Technology for all the right reasons. *Synthesis Lectures on Human-Centered Informatics*. https://doi.org/10.2200/s00261ed1v01y201003hci008

Hollan, J., Hutchins, E., & Kirsh, D. (2000). Distributed cognition: Toward a new foundation for human-computer interaction research. *ACM Transactions on Computer-Human Interaction (TOCHI), 7*(2), 174–196.

Kolko, J. (2015). Design thinking comes of age. *Harvard Business Review*.

Mumford, E. (2000). Socio-technical design: An unfulfilled promise or a future opportunity? In *Organizational and social perspectives on information technology* (pp. 33–46). Springer.

Rasmussen, J., Pejtersen, A. M., & Schmidt, K. (1990). *Taxonomy for cognitive work analysis.* Roskilde, Denmark: Risø National Laboratory.
Sein, M. K., Henfridsson, O., Purao, S., Rossi, M., & Lindgren, R. (2011). Action design research. *MIS Quarterly.* https://doi.org/10.2307/23043488.
Wulf, V., Pipek, V., Randall, D., Rohde, M., Schmidt, K., & Stevens, G. (Eds.). (2018). *Socio-informatics-A practice-based perspective on the design and use of IT artifacts.* Oxford: Oxford University Press.